# Violence and the
# Mimetic Unconscious

# Violence and the Mimetic Unconscious

## VOLUME 2
## THE AFFECTIVE HYPOTHESIS

**Nidesh Lawtoo**

Michigan State University Press · *East Lansing*

Michigan State University Press
East Lansing, Michigan 48823-5245

This project has received funding from the European Research Council (ERC) under the European
Union's Horizon 2020 research and innovation programme (grant agreement n°716181).

Library of Congress Cataloging-in-Publication Data is available
ISBN 978-1-61186-465-6 (paperback)
ISBN 978-1-60917-742-3 (PDF)
ISBN 978-1-62895-506-4 (ePub)

Cover design by David Drummond, Salamander Design, www.salamanderhill.com.
Cover art is *Color-Trance* by Michaela Lawtoo, www.michaela-lawtoo.eu

Visit Michigan State University Press at *www.msupress.org*

*To Nia*
*home of my* sympatheia

Have you not observed that imitations, if continued from youth far into life, settle down into habits and second nature in the body, the speech, and the thought?
　　—Plato, Book 3 of *Republic*


To witness suffering does one good, to inflict it even more—that is a harsh proposition, but a fundamental one, an old, powerful, human all-too-human proposition.
　　—Nietzsche, *On the Genealogy of Morals*


People get a taste, and they just can't get enough.
　　—Detective Tedeschi, *Vice*

# Contents

# Acknowledgments

Violence is not an abstract subject that can be captured via a totalizing, universal theory; rather, it emerges from specific historical contexts that consciously and often unconsciously inform cultural theory—including mimetic theory. It is thus not indifferent that the genealogical starting point of this Janus-faced study goes back to a visiting appointment I held at Johns Hopkins University from 2013 to 2016. At Hopkins, I had the privilege of working at the legendary Humanities Center that played such a major role in the birth of (French) theory back in 1966—including poststructuralism and mimetic theory. Baltimore also provided the less privileged experience of living in a city plagued by segregation, violence, and racist oppression. Freddie Gray was murdered during my stay; so was a four-year-old African American child in my son's primary school in West Baltimore. If the first context provided the logos to reopen the ancient dossier on the relation between representations of violence and the unconscious, the latter provided the contemporary pathos that urged me to start writing in the first place.

The emergence of a new theory of mimesis, no matter how innovative and original, is only possible thanks to the long chain of thinkers that came before. Inspired by a long-standing genealogical practice that traverses the ages, in the pages that follow I express my gratitude to influential predecessors—from Plato and Aristotle to the present—by quoting their work, furthering embryonic insights, and engaging occasionally in intellectual forms of mimetic agonism that do not lead to violence. On the contrary, they push what I came to call mimetic studies toward new productive and future-oriented directions.

My thanks to the long list of supporters of the *Homo Mimeticus* project expressed in volume 1 of this Janus-faced study equally apply to volume 2. I here echo my thanks to my editor, William (Bill) Johnsen, for seeing with characteristic mimetic insight that these two books "mirror" my first two books on Nietzsche and Conrad—redoubling phantoms and shadows for the digital age. Together they close a cycle of research on mimesis that benefited enormously from Bill's unflagging support as well as from the whole editorial team at Michigan State University Press. I remain forever grateful to the European Research Council (ERC) for generously funding my research from 2016 to 2022, during which time both books were written. The intellectual freedom provided by the ERC was unparalleled and allowed for the problem-oriented, interdisciplinary, high-risk, and exploratory approach that informs this study. I hope the result will prove high gain for new mimetic studies as well.

Sections of volume 2 have appeared in modified form in the following journals and collections. I am grateful they could be reproduced and expanded to form a broader argument.

"Violence and the Mimetic Unconscious (Part Two), The Contagious Hypothesis: Plato, Affect, Mirror Neurons," *Contagion* 26 (2019): 123–60.

"The Mimetic Unconscious: A Mirror for Genealogical Reflections," in *Imitation, Contagion, Suggestion: On Mimesis and Society*, edited by Christian Borch, 37–53. London: Routledge, 2019.

"The Double Meanings of Violence: *Catharsis* and *Mimesis*," in *Violence and Meaning*, edited by Lode Lauwaert, Laura Katherine Smith, and Christian Sternad, 137–65. London: Palgrave MacMillan, 2019.

"The Insurrection Moment: Intoxication, Conspiracy Assault," *Theory & Event* 26.1 (2023): 5–30.

# Prologue

But what right does our age have to give an answer to Plato's great question about the moral influence of art? Even if we had the art—where do we see the influence, any influence in art?

—Nietzsche, *Human, All Too Human*

This is a Janus-faced study about the affective power of violent images that cannot simply be contemplated from a safe visual distance. Instead, they tend to break through the screen of representation, affecting and infecting us in our daily lives—if not consciously, at least unconsciously so. I say "us," rather than "humans" or "them," because a degree of first-person, affective, and perhaps even embodied participation coming from a plurality of—gendered, ethnic, sexual, social, national, etc.—perspectives, is called for to come to terms with the all too human relation between violence and the unconscious. My wager is, in fact, that it is necessary to initially experience the connection with the pathos of violence from an affective proximity in order to better theorize it from a critical distance.

Perhaps, then, to involve you from the outset as an active participant in this diagnostic investigation, let me start by asking you a few questions. If you picked up this book, you are already interested in the relation between violence and the unconscious. But let me start closer to home, by inverting perspectives, and asking you something more personal, maybe too personal, but also more experientially felt. After all, these feelings may have been accentuated by the prolonged period of lockdown caused by the coronavirus pandemic across the world since 2020—a pandemic that, at the moment I write, is still ongoing and is quite likely to return in the near future.

So, here come my questions: Does your unconscious want something that is beyond your reach? Now imagine a place where there are no laws, no rules, no consequences. Imagine it in detail. Relax, immerse yourself in an imaginary scene of your own choice, and give free rein to your most secret fantasies. . . . You would like to travel to exotic locations? Why not rent a luxurious bungalow on a deserted island surrounded by turquoise water? You want money and a rush of excitement? Enact a bank robbery modeled on legendary cinematic classics. You dream of a more active nightlife? Imagine no restrictions and go out clubbing with stunning models dancing to the beat of intoxicating music, from dusk till dawn. Or perhaps you are in the mood for a little adventure, some romance, or maybe even uncensored eroticism? Transgress a few taboos with the same models who respond to intimate embraces with pathos and sex appeal—or anything else you ever dreamed of. And since there are no laws, and thus no consequences, you can go far, very far, to the limit of transgressive experiences where sex turns into violence—and death.

Cut! Rewind. Now replay the scene in slow motion.

Is the pathos triggered by these imaginary fantasies revisited from a critical distance already making you uncomfortable? That is indeed part of the point. But please rest assured. In a superficial sense, there should be no cause for concern. After all, I have just welcomed you to join a fictional, rather than real, scenario—an imaginary scenario that sets the critical, but also affective and conceptual, stage for an ancient yet also modern and, as we shall see, still contemporary riddle on the cathartic and/or contagious effects of representations of violence on the unconscious in the digital age.

### A Fictional Scene

"Welcome to *Vice*!" says Bruce Willis at the opening of a trailer for a science-fiction (sf) film titled *Vice* (2015), directed by Brian A. Miller. With his inimitable sarcastic smile, Willis appears against the very background of the cinematic fantasies I have just echoed at one remove, on the page; the

**FIGURE 1.** Julian Michaels (Bruce Willis) and VICE Resort in *Vice* (dir. Brian Miller, 2015).

film originally projects these fantasies on the digitized screen of your own choice, redoubling the actor's suggestive power to trigger viewers' transgressive imagination.

Elegantly dressed, radiating confidence, success, and a prestige amplified by his status as a cinematic star, Bruce Willis plays the role of a fictional character named Julian Michaels, the CEO of an "adult entertainment" company who welcomes spectators—both within the film and, at one remove, outside the screen—into a futuristic world of leisure, pleasure, sex, and violence. Staring straight into the camera, the actor voluntarily breaks the fourth wall and asks: "Have you ever wanted something that is beyond your reach? Now imagine a place where there are no laws, no rules, no consequences." And by saying so, "he," Bruce Willis, that is, Julian Michaels, invites spectators to join him, if only for a few hours, on his side of the screen to vicariously participate in a futuristic and quite exclusive resort called VICE, which he sells as nothing less than "a utopian paradise where you can have or do *anything* you want." Not only luxurious hotels, robberies, clubbing, and uncensored eroticism, but also physical assault, rape, and murder are fair game in the world of VICE—precisely because it is "just" a game. Or rather, it is a cinematic fiction that reflects, and urges critically inclined viewers to reflect on, contemporary forms of entertainment that include film as well as TV series, online platforms, pornographic websites, and video games that, on our side of the screen, already simulate violent, often misogynistic, and racist fantasies that, as *Vice* suggests, are, nolens volens, constitutive of the digital age. "No laws," we are assured, are limiting this world of pure entertainment. And so, for the duration of the film, Michaels encourages spectators to suspend disbelief, relax, lower the critical guard, and accept the welcome to VICE and, by extension, the welcome to the digitized world of violent simulations it alludes to.

## The Riddle Reloaded

Reflecting on a specific case study that already belongs to a "traditional" twentieth-century medium such as film, allows us to reevaluate the pros and cons of an ancient riddle on the psychic effects of representations of violence that are no longer limited to cinema but are constitutive of a plurality of new digital media in the twenty-first century. With respect to the traditional defenses of aesthetic representations of violence, the pros are familiar; they are not deprived of convincing arguments, which are implicit in the very genre of fiction (from Latin, *fingere*, "to shape or form" but also "to feign").

After all, *Vice*, just like the violent online simulations the film alludes to, dramatizes an entertaining illusion that should not be confused with reality, if only because as a sf film, it is not even based on a transparently realistic representation of reality. As we decide to go to the cinema, watch a film on our flat screen, or, more likely, stream it directly from Netflix on a computer, tablet, or smartphone, we are clearly invited into a fictional world of make-believe that few in the digital age would mistake for reality itself. Actors like Bruce Willis are lavishly paid to impersonate roles; no real transgressions are normally committed on the set—though unintentional killings are not unheard of. Above all, as we watch the movie from an aesthetic distance, we certainly are not breaking any laws—at least not in a free, democratic, and pluralist world not plagued by censorship. If spectators feel like imaginatively partaking in scenes of violence whose origins are as old as the dawn of aesthetics, which films like *Vice* invite us to contemplate, and video games like *Cyberpunk 2077* allow us to actively simulate, there should indeed be no consequences, as the film's trailer promises. Perhaps, then, what was true for tragic spectacles in the past remains true for the violence internal to contemporary films and games in the present: the fictional images on-screen are but shadows or phantoms that a minimally alert spectator has learned since childhood not to confuse with the real world—if only because they are mere copies, appearances, or simulacra that should not be mistaken for reality itself.

And yet, as the ancient Greeks were the first to suspect at the dawn of philosophy, representations of violence, no matter how false in appearance, call for careful diagnostics of their affective powers to generate effects in spectators nonetheless—be they good or bad, therapeutic or pathological. Thus, the counterargument goes, if the trailer stages violent cinematic actions that are fictional, illusory, and, in this epistemological sense, not real, that is, false, and far removed from reality, the powers of fictions can also trigger affective impressions on spectators that are clearly felt, experienced, and, in this psychological sense, have real embodied effects, again—for both good and ill. In revisiting the ancient riddle of the effects of violent representations, or simulations, from a contemporary perspective, my focus will thus not be moral, let alone moralistic, but instead diagnostic and interpretative.

Media change historically, generating new forms of simulation, but the philosophical problem is far from new. We will thus be in good intellectual company in the pages that follow. A respectable genealogy of thinkers engaged with the heterogeneous problematic of *mimesis* (imitation and representation, but also impersonation, identification, influence, reproduction, simulation, among other meanings) has been diagnostically attentive to what we call (new) media violence. Already Plato, for instance, critiqued representations of violence in literary classics like the *Iliad* for dramatizing models of behavior that promote violent affects and sexual transgressions. He did so not only because these mythic tales did not tell what he considered to be the truth about the gods (moral and epistemic reasons), but also because he worried such spectacles generate contagious effects on the irrational part of the soul (psychological and pedagogical reasons). Conversely, Plato's most influential student, Aristotle, in an agonistic inversion of perspective that is not deprived of mirroring continuities with his teacher, defended tragedies like *Oedipus Rex* that stage an exemplary case of violent actions and sexual transgressions that reach into the present. Aristotle defended tragedy not only for encouraging rational, cognitive, perhaps even philosophical thoughts; he also considered that the pathos tragic violence generates has purifying effects he grouped under the concept of "catharsis," an enigmatic concept that will inform a number of subsequent theories and methods—including the "cathartic method" that gave birth to psychoanalytical theories predicated on an Oedipal myth.

Over two millennia later, due to genealogical vicissitudes we shall have to trace in some detail, such myths are still with us, giving us interpretative keys that inform, or misinform, contemporary perspectives. For instance, the fantasies the *Vice* trailer represents in the illusory sphere of cinematic fiction seem specifically constructed to trigger in the audience what René Girard would call "mimetic desires." The desire to see the movie in the first place and get a taste of such lawless, utopian, and transgressive representations of vice—albeit at two removes; but perhaps also the desire to be in the prestigious position Julian Michaels dramatizes as a fictional character, and Bruce Willis impersonates as an actor qua cinematic star in reality—an imaginary identification that, the trailer assures, allows you to "have anything you want."

Once such perspectives are considered in the company of a long genealogy of thinkers of violence and mimesis that goes from antiquity to modernity reaching into the present, an affective and conceptual Pandora's box is reopened and a plurality of more insidious diagnostic questions that go beyond good and evil evaluations naturally emerge. For instance: Who is the "you" that is the subject of this "want"? And if Michaels addressing "you" clearly intends to include all viewers of the film, do *you* really want it? After all, films like *Vice*, and the kinds of entertainment the images in the background refer to (robberies, dance, sex, etc.), target a specifically male, often white, privileged, and digitally connected audience. Consequently, the mimetic mechanisms surreptitiously at play in the film's trailer already structure viewers' desires, beginning, middle, and end, on prescribed cinematic (male/white) models that designate other (female) subjects as privileged "objects" of desire.

Do *we*, then, consciously—that is, intentionally—want to be affectively involved in a patriarchal, misogynistic, and phallocentric transgressive utopia that, as the film will soon confirm, can quickly turn into a violent dystopia? Or should we consider such forms of entertainment (film, internet websites, video games) as legitimate virtual resorts that allow for transgressive experiences that can be put to social, progressive, and perhaps even emphatic or therapeutic social use? More generally, are we the conscious subjects of the desires these (new) media intentionally elicit in the sphere of fiction? Or are we rather being unconsciously subjected to fictional actions that trigger deeply felt, embodied reactions that threaten to blur the line dividing fiction and reality, online and offline behavior? Above all, and to echo diagnostic preoccupations that are already internal to the plot of *Vice*: Do simulations of violence serve a therapeutic, medical, or, to use this ancient concept, cathartic function that gets violence out of people's systems? Or, alternatively, do these simulations have the potential to bleed across the screen dividing the world of entertainment from "this world" via a pathological form of affective contagion?

## An Ancient Quarrel

As these questions indicate, this cinematic fiction brings us very quickly to the heart of an ancient yet also modern and still contemporary quarrel over the effects of aesthetic representations of violence on spectators. This quarrel, like all good quarrels worth revisiting, is Janus-faced, for it looks in opposed directions. On one side, it looks back to the origins of western aesthetics and reopens an ancient contest, or agon, that posits Plato's hypothesis on the contagious effects of representations of violence (or affective hypothesis) contra Aristotle's hypothesis on their cathartic effects (or catharsis hypothesis); on the other side, it looks ahead to contemporary quarrels on network-based (new) media violence that, despite the numerous innovations in the media that allow for increasing degrees of immersive participation—or perhaps because of it—continue, to this day, to oscillate, pendulum-like, between these competing hypotheses. If my linguistic reproduction of *Vice*'s cinematic welcome was far removed indeed from the original cinematic fiction, it may at least have succeeded in subliminally foregrounding one point that, despite the oscillations of perspectives, will remain central throughout this study on violence and the unconscious: namely that, for good and ill, fictional representations or simulations of violence may not always remain confined within the autonomous sphere of fiction; they can also generate affective, embodied, and unconscious effects on viewers and users that call for new diagnostic investigations in the digital age.

Confronted with this Janus-faced quarrel, my mimetic hypothesis will thus also be double; and this doubleness is already reflected in the two-part structure of this study that form a diptych on violence and the unconscious. My argument will unfold in two separate but related volumes that both mirror and invert perspectives on the double problematic of violence and the unconscious. The mirroring titles of these volumes reflect two competing conceptions of the unconscious that offer different perspectives on the effects of representations of violence throughout the ages. The first is titled *Violence and the Oedipal Unconscious*, volume 1, *The Catharsis Hypothesis*; it establishes a genealogical connection between a conception of catharsis that originates in classical antiquity in Aristotle's thought and, via a series of genealogical vicissitudes I shall consider in detail, provides a key to the so-called Freudian "discovery" of the unconscious that finds in *Oedipus Rex* a paradigmatic and universal case study that continues to cast a shadow on contemporary culture. The second is titled *Violence and the Mimetic Unconscious*, volume 2, *The Affective Hypothesis*, and its starting point is equally ancient: it originates in Plato's critique of mimesis and, via a series of equally complex genealogical turns, finds its contemporary version in recent discoveries in the neurosciences that contribute to a return of attention to a relational, embodied, and performative conception of mimesis internal to homo mimeticus. The competing genealogical perspectives on the relation between violence and the unconscious differ significantly and will eventually lead to antithetical conclusions. And yet, like all mirroring confrontations, the advocates of each tradition know their respective counterparts, reflect on one another, and will help us reevaluate the value of their hypotheses on catharsis and contagion. Hence the need to tell both sides of a Janus-faced story of violence and the unconscious via a diptych on catharsis and contagion before coming to any rushed diagnostic conclusion.

At the level of method, both volumes share two general mimetic principles that inform both the catharsis and the affective hypothesis and give intellectual unity to this double argument. On one side, I draw on a longstanding tradition of transdisciplinary theorists of mimesis in order to take some genealogical distance from the still controversial topic of media violence. This genealogical distance will allow me to trace the theoretical vicissitudes of two antagonistic but related concepts (catharsis and contagion) that, while fundamental to the debate on (new) media violence, have rarely, if ever, been reevaluated from a *longue durée*, genealogical perspective. This perspective is long for it considers major thinkers of violence and mimesis that go from antiquity (Plato and Aristotle) to modern(ist) theories of the unconscious (Bernays to Nietzsche, Freud to Bataille) to contemporary theories of violence (Girard to Lacoue-Labarthe, Arendt to Cavarero), among others.

At the same time, theoretical reflections on contagion and catharsis will be shadowed by specific examples of (new) media violence involving genres as diverse as theater, film, reality TV, and video games (like *Cyberpunk 2077*), stretching to include (new) fascist insurrections triggered by conspiracy theories and anticipated by TV series (like *Black Mirror*). On the other side, we will articulate a genealogy of the contagion and catharsis hypothesis internal to disciplines as diverse as continental philosophy, psychology, psychoanalysis, aesthetics, literary theory, media studies, digital humanities, cultural studies, literary theory, and political theory. Together, these perspectives stretch to include recent turns to affect, embodiment, and mirroring reflexes constitutive of what I call the mimetic turn or *return*; they will also open up two related but competing conceptions of the unconscious—the Oedipal and the mimetic unconscious—on which contemporary debates on media violence often rest, if not explicitly at least implicitly so. Once joined, we shall see that these two cathartic/affective hypotheses on violence and the unconscious provide broader, not always completely new, but nonetheless revealing, illuminating, and perhaps even original genealogical foundations to account for the riddle of (new) media violence *Vice* invites us to revisit. A methodological point should be clear from the outset. As my subjective opening, interpretative case study, and imaginary and rather unorthodox questionnaire already implicitly suggested, this study is not intended as an empirical, quantifiable, sociological contribution to what is an already widely discussed and still controversial topic in the social and empirical sciences. While the debate on the effects of impersonations, representations, and simulations of violence is still ongoing and difficult to answer unilaterally given the protean diversity of new media, the different forms of violence at play in the digital age, and the methodological difficulty in proving direct causal effects between (new) media violence and behavioral violence, at least one point looks increasingly certain: the line dividing fiction and reality, violent representations online and violent insurrections offline, imaginary actions and embodied reactions in a world increasingly immersed in simulations of violence that are also violent simulations, is becoming increasingly porous, generating heterogeneous affective continuities that might spill over and beyond the screen of digital representations that connect and disconnect digital users hooked on a plurality of digital screens. Disturbing homologies can potentially emerge as the heterogeneous violence we *see* from an exterior aesthetic distance generates a violent pathos already at play in the real world. Sometimes this violence can even be lethal for actors on cinematic sets, as real guns can still be legally used in the United States to simulate fictional scenes with all too real effects—already an alarming indication that the line dividing fiction and reality can be thin and porous at best. More regularly, however, the pathos of fictional violence might contribute, if not to directly trigger, cause, or determine, at least to partially influence, normalize, or even numb viewers and gamers, to violent models of behavior that increasingly affect new generations in the digital age.

Furthering a modernist theory of mimesis inaugurated in a trilogy of books started in *The Phantom of the Ego* (2013), subsequently developed in *Conrad's Shadow* (2016), and brought to bear onto the present in *(New) Fascism* (2019), in this diptych on *Violence and the Unconscious* I shall step farther back to the origins of theories of *mimēsis* in classical antiquity to leap ahead and provide steps toward a new theory of imitation for the future. In order to do so, new concepts will have to be created that expand the reaches of our modernist mimetic theory to a generalized theory of homo mimeticus. For instance, while desires remain imitative, a future-oriented theory cannot be restricted to mimetic desire alone. Instead, I propose the concept of *mimetic pathos* to indicate that all affects are mimetic, for both good and ill. Thus, I rely on a double perspective attentive to both the infectious and experiential power of affect or pathos to generate what I call *pathologies*, on one side, and a critical account or logos on this pathos considered from a genealogical distance I group under the rubric of *patho-logies*, on the other. Catharsis and contagion will thus serve as the conceptual links that both connect and disconnect pathologies from patho-*logies*. In the process, the catharsis hypothesis and the infective, contagious or, as I shall call it, affective hypothesis also set the stage for a theoretical contest, or *agon*, that traverses the history of western aesthetics and organizes this book in two related, sometimes competing, and ultimately symmetric and mirroring arguments. Since the mirroring continuities between the cathartic and affective hypotheses are as significant as the inversion of perspectives that mirroring reflections usually entail, I shall qualify this agon in terms of *mimetic agonism*. Catharsis contra contagion: this is the genuine mirroring antagonism I will be struggling with in the diptych that follows. The ambition? Contribute to a new theory of homo mimeticus that is already facing some of the main challenges of the twenty-first century.[1]

Last but not least, this genealogy of violence and the unconscious will lead me to go repeatedly beyond fictional representations. I shall thus investigate scenes of crimes that increasingly blur the line between representations of violence and real violence via classical but also modern and contemporary examples, or case studies, some of which are quite recent, that continue to emerge as I write these prefatory lines. We live in a hypermimetic world haunted by new and heterogeneous forms of violence that may metastasize online before bleeding offline; or, vice versa, they might start offline before being disseminated online and subsequently retroacting offline, generating spiraling feedback loops that call for new diagnostic operations.

This mimetic or, better, hypermimetic spiral includes the much-discussed issue of media violence and the mass shootings that continue to plague countries deprived of basic gun regulations but are not limited to them. In the age of progressive movements like Black Lives Matter (BLM) and #MeToo, on one side, and violent insurrections constitutive of (new) fascism and authoritarian wars on the other, it is crucial for new generations of theorists of mimesis to broaden the scope of investigation and include emerging phenomena that are not limited to (new) media violence but cast a revealing light on the relation between violence and the unconscious more generally. As this Janus-faced argument unfolds, I shall thus take care to look back, genealogically, to the foundations of theories of catharsis and contagion from antiquity to modernity while also keeping an eye on the present. Especially in the second volume, I shall increasingly put genealogical lenses to use to propose close readings of police murders of ethnic minority populations, especially African Americans; sexual assaults on women; conspiracy theories online that give rise to (new) fascist insurrections offline; and role-playing video games, among other recent manifestations of violent pathologies that cast a long shadow on the contemporary world.

As an introductory gesture, let me thus step into the detective's shoes, so to speak. My aim is to supplement the fictional diagnostic internal to the plot of *Vice* from a broader genealogical perspective attentive to the enigmatic relation between violence and the unconscious from antiquity to the present.

# Introduction

## Mimetic Studies

From antiquity to modernity, artistic media have changed dramatically over the centuries and have reached increasing powers of affection; and yet this does not mean that the untimely question about the influence of art should continue to be left unanswered in the contemporary period. As we transition from *Violence and the Oedipal Unconscious* to *Violence and the Mimetic Unconscious*, we should take a moment to pause and recognized that Plato's untimely question at the dawn of mimetic studies about the influence of art has not lost any of its relevance in the digital age.[1] On the contrary, it is more urgent and pressing than ever. From cinema to TV, publicity to sitcoms, video games to virtual simulations, artistic impressions can obviously no longer be limited to "high" classical genres like Greek tragedy or the modern novel but should stretch to include contemporary forms of popular entrainment that, for some time, have already been migrating online. Given the insidious nature of such aesthetic influences, we thus accept the challenge: in an agonistic move inspired by Nietzsche, I shall attempt to answer Plato's great question about the moral influence of what the founding father of philosophy called, for lack of a more encompassing term, *mimēsis*: namely, an influence that is not only moral but also psychic, and concerns not only the formation of good subjects but also the transformation of homo mimeticus.[2]

To give this untimely question a more specific genealogical focus, I restrict the question of artistic influence in general to the already broad problematic of the influence of violent media, or (new) media violence, in particular. This contemporary problematic continues to convoke the ancient but resilient and far-reaching debate about the cathartic and contagious, therapeutic and pathological effects of fictional violence. As our argument now begins to tilt from the catharsis hypothesis to the contagion, or affective, hypothesis, our diagnostic perspective changes sides, but the methodological principle that guides this Janus-faced inquiry remains fundamentally the same. Adopting a genealogical approach attentive to the process of displacement and transformation of aesthetic theories remains the necessary first step to reevaluate the relevance of cathartic and/or contagious hypotheses for the contemporary hypermimetic media that all too visibly cast a shadow on homo mimeticus. It also urges us to reload Plato's ancient question on the moral influence of art from a genealogical yet present-oriented and perhaps even future-oriented perspective constitutive of what I propose to call new mimetic studies.[3]

## Reloading the Question

Let us recall that our first step in *Violence and the Oedipal Unconscious*, volume 1, *The Catharsis Hypothesis* was to trace a genealogy of the "catharsis hypothesis" via exemplary texts by ancient (Aristotle), modern (Freud), and contemporary (Girard) thinkers. Despite their numerous differences and innovative turns, these figures are genealogically connected precisely via their interpretations of the riddle of catharsis we considered in detail. They also contributed to the birth of an Oedipal conception of the unconscious that, if not necessarily in medical practice, at least in abstract theory, had an enormous success in the modernist period, both within and beyond academia. In the process, the Oedipal unconscious disseminated a generalized medical conception of the purgative effects of representations of violence in the twentieth century that to this day continues to inform—or, more often, disinform—popular culture.

Located in proximity of the origins of aesthetic and thus mimetic theory, the catharsis hypothesis has continued to puzzle classical scholars from the Renaissance to the present. Still, due to its Freudian and post-Freudian rearticulations, and for a series of vicissitudes discussed in volume 1, it eventually became synonymous with the discovery of the unconscious tout court—that is, an Oedipal unconscious that finds a door to discharge violent, pathological, often traumatic affects that need to be consciously acknowledged, perhaps reenacted, and at least re-presented in order to be worked through and, as the legend goes, eventually cured. While such a hypothesis had much success in theory, we saw that it had less efficacy in practice. Eventually, even its most outspoken theoretical advocates who turned this hypothesis into a clinical "cathartic method"—and, later, into a "mimetic theory"—abandoned it, leaving the agonistic contestation between the catharsis and the affective hypotheses for others to resolve.

After this genealogical detour via the labyrinth of cathartic interpretations and the theories of the unconscious they engendered, I return to the problem with which we started from the other end of the theoretical spectrum. In the present volume, I now reframe the problematic of the influence of representations of violence on human behavior by tracing a genealogy of its conceptually related but opposed perspective that finds in the hypothesis of contagion an alternative, equally ancient, long-standing, and, as we shall see, more realistic starting point. My mimetic hypothesis, first articulated in *The Phantom of the Ego* (2013), is that the ego, I, or subject is far from being self-enclosed, autonomous, and impermeable to outside influences. On the contrary, it is relational, porous, and suggestible to an unconscious imitation, or will to mime, constitutive of a mimetic unconscious that manifests itself via affective contagion.[4] If we saw that the triangular configurations internal to both Oedipal and mimetic theories promoting a cathartic hypothesis need serious updating in light of recent critiques on multiple fronts, the mimetic unconscious is currently receiving growing attention in a digital age increasingly under the spell of hyper-contagious new media.

Despite the numerous insights offered by mimetic theory, it is becoming increasingly clear that in the digital age, the dynamic of affective contagion cannot be restricted to the triangular logic of mimetic desire alone—though these desires continue to be triggered by new algorithmic media that tap into the mimetic unconscious; nor is violence always the effect of a crisis of difference that requires a scapegoat in order to be discharged—though violence continues to be discharged against innocent victims, most notably women and racial minorities, without cathartic relief for survivors. Finally, the theological underpinnings of mimetic theory that privilege not only a trinity of concepts (mimetic desire, mimetic rivalry, scapegoat) but also a Christian religious figure over other, no less innocent but more contemporary sacrificial victims, also need updating. We need a less theological or, as Georges Bataille would say, a-theological foundation.

To that end I propose not to replace let alone erase but rather to supplement or transfer the valuable insights of mimetic theory in a more generalized theory of homo mimeticus that rests on new, interdisciplinary, and a-theological conceptual foundations. If the logic of romantic agonism we saw as internal to mimetic theory erased influential predecessors that accounted for the laws of imitation in the past, the logic of mimetic agonism that informs new mimetic studies acknowledges and confronts these predecessors in order to go further and confront hypermimetic crises in the present. Moreover, we have seen in volume 1 that the increasing tendency toward hyperspecialization in the humanities are out of sync with the transdisciplinary problems of our age. (New) mimetic studies joins forces with a number of different disciplines, or logoi—from philosophy to aesthetics, literary studies to media studies, crowd psychology to anthropology, feminism to decolonial studies, environmental studies to political theory—in order to provide a correction to this hyperspecialistic tendency. Its aim is to account for emerging pathologies of homo mimeticus that can go from emotional contagion to (new) fascism, posthuman identifications to plastic metamorphoses, psychic dispossessions to new media violence, among others, via a plurality of logoi on mimetic pathos. The concepts of mimetic pathos, pathos of distance, patho(-)logies, hypermimesis, and the mimetic unconscious provide steps toward a new theory of imitation whose hinge pivots from the Oedipal unconscious to the mimetic unconscious, catharsis to contagion. Its general ambition is to continue to further mimetic studies that are already underway.[5]

To carry out this delicate overturning of perspectives from catharsis to contagion, then, I shall revisit a select number of influential theorists—from antiquity to modernity to the contemporary period along with corresponding case studies—that provide mirroring counter arguments and alternatives to the thinkers we have considered in volume 1. Despite the antithetical perspectives at play in our shift from the Oedipal to the mimetic unconscious, I suggest that what was true for the catharsis hypothesis in the twentieth century remains equally true for the affective hypothesis in the twenty-first century. In a far-reaching move that stretches from antiquity to modernity, postmodernity to the present, both perspectives help us reflect critically on the theories convoked to account for the relation between violence and the unconscious, informing discourses on (new) media violence as well. Stepping back to ancient theories might also be a way to lay new foundations for contemporary mimetic studies. My genealogical wager is, in fact, that a classical diagnostic of contagion paves the way for a conception of the mimetic unconscious that has been neglected in the past century; and yet it anticipates recent scientific rediscoveries of mirroring reflexes that rest on empirical, quantifiable foundations still in need of a qualitative, philosophical, and genealogical supplements in the present century.

For the reader who starts this investigative journey with volume 2, let me briefly recall a fundamental insight that guides both sides of our Janus-faced investigation. If we take some distance from contemporary evaluations of (new) media violence, it is in fact sobering to remember that the catharsis/contagion debate is not new, let alone original. It has haunted philosophers for a long time, has a long and complicated history that traverses heterogeneous discourses in western thought, and continues to explicitly—and, more often, implicitly—underscore contemporary discussions on the powers of affects, algorithms, and the unconscious. Before proffering any judgments on such a polarized riddle—one so popular that it makes cameo appearances in contemporary blockbusters while continuing to puzzle academic research on the subject—genealogy teaches us to be modest and prudent. Hence the need to first take a step back to the emergence of theories of catharsis and contagion in classical antiquity, trace their consolidation in the modern and contemporary period via exemplary representatives in emerging human sciences—from psychoanalysis to mimetic theory, crowd psychology to physio-psychology, affect theory to the neurosciences, all of which inform mimetic studies—and test each hypothesis on the basis of recent developments in critical theory in conjunction with empirical sciences that will help us properly address, reframe, and begin to solve the riddle of (new) media violence from the angle of our theory of homo mimeticus.

If we adopt genealogical lenses that look back in order to better see what lies ahead, I think it is safe to say that conflicting evaluations on the good and bad mimetic effects of representations of violence can ultimately be traced back to the joint origins of philosophy and aesthetic theory in Plato's *Republic* (c. 380 B.C.) and Aristotle's *Poetics* (c. 335 B.C.). These two foundational, agonistic, and in many ways complementary philosophical texts not only set the conceptual stage for a debate that will leave long-lasting traces in the history of philosophy and the human science more generally; they also continue, to this day, to implicitly inform polarized discussions about the cathartic and contagious effects of representations of violence on human behavior. What was true for Aristotle with respect to catharsis will now apply to Plato concerning contagion: both figures remain our patron guides in our Janus-faced genealogical investigation.[6] They provide broad shoulders on which my understanding of homo mimeticus rests. If I repeatedly look back to them, it is to better see what lies ahead of us into the future. There is, in fact, still much to learn about the logical and pathological powers of mimesis from the very thinkers who established conceptual foundations on mimesis that traverse the ages and inform new mimetic studies as well. They did so, among other ways, by introducing two concepts—contagion and catharsis—that have been interpreted from competing diagnostic perspectives that reach into the present.

And yet, at the same time, for contemporary theorists writing in the wake of psychoanalysis, affect theory, the digital turn, and recent discoveries in the neurosciences, the answers to such ancient and always new questions reloaded by contemporary new media vary dramatically not only according to philosophical orientations on violence now complicated by social, political, and economic agendas; they also vary according to the model of the unconscious these theorists explicitly or, more often, implicitly rely on. Hence the need to reinscribe the catharsis and now affective hypotheses on media violence in the competing theories of the unconscious that are genealogically connected to them—if only because the modern hypothesis of the unconscious is born out of an ancient quarrel, or mimetic agon, between cathartic and contagious hypotheses.

As one of the opening epigraphs already suggests, among the moderns, Nietzsche's diagnostic of artistic influence will lead us to return to the foundations of mimetic studies in Plato's thought, where the Janus-faced problematic of contagion and catharsis originated in the first place. And once again, looking back, genealogically to an untimely and far-reaching thinker will not only give us the necessary critical distance to re-evaluate the value of these hypotheses; it will also put us in a position to look ahead to contemporary (new) media such as cinema, TV series, reality shows, and video games that increasingly blur the line between reality and show. How? Via simulations that are not simply disconnected from reality—what Jean Baudrillard calls "hyperrealism." Rather, they performatively bring new realities into being that risk rendering violence "banal," commonplace, and thus unthought—what I call "hypermimesis" (chapter 1). To give specificity to my diagnostic, concrete contemporary examples of hypermimetic violence will punctuate this second volume in view of both providing case studies for new mimetic studies and bringing the affective hypothesis closer to home.

For instance, the performative logic of hypermimesis calls attention to the power of fictional violence to generate mirroring mechanisms in reality, pathological mechanisms that, as the rise of anti-violence movements like #MeToo and Black Lives Matter (BLM) recently made clear, continue to be predominantly directed against gendered, sexual, and racial minorities. A close reading of police murders captured on camera in the United States (for example, George Floyd and Rayshard Brooks) will supplement diagnostics of gender violence internal to our cinematic case study from the perspective of racial—or, rather, racist—violence (chapter 4). Conversely, the power of political leaders qua TV show personalities (Donald Trump) to rely on new media conspiracy theories to generate violent, (new) fascist insurrections (the storming of the U.S. Capitol on January 6, 2021) provides an example of a new type of hypermimetic violence I call "(new) fascism" (chapter 3) While hypermimesis is not restricted to the traditional problematic of media *representations* of violence, this concept and the practices that ensue will have to be taken increasingly seriously for their affective, contagious, and violent effects.

Examples are revealing mimetic categories. They will allow us to put competing theories to the test in ways that are, as Giorgio Agamben notes, "neither universal nor particular" but reveal a "singularity" that is valid for other cases as well.[7] As our cinematic opening in the prologue intimated, these examples will go from the pathos internal to film violence back to tragic representations that set the stage of the debate on media violence. They will also go beyond representations of violence to include recent cases of sexist, racist, and political violence that could easily be categorized under the rubric of social injustice, yet, as our examples of police murders of African Americans captured on video and (new) fascist insurrections generated by online conspiracies will make clear, cannot easily be detached from the problematic of (new) media violence. On the contrary, they urge us to reflect further on the looping effects that may start with forms of online violence that generate violence offline, as well, a patho(-)logical loop through which new mimetic studies circulates.

If our genealogical focus is primarily on the effects of aesthetic representations of physical, emotional, and symbolic violence, be it real or staged, represented or enacted, fictional or historical, it is not in any attempt to define what violence "is" or is supposed to "be." Rather, it is because aesthetic representations or simulations have performative, or, as I call them, hypermimetic, powers that they can potentially—that is, in specific contextual circumstances—lead from psychic aggression to physical violence, hyperreal simulation to mimetic reenactment. These powers are thus not only performative in the linguistic sense, as in performative speech acts that were central to doing things with words during the linguistic turn; they also do things with affects, minds, bodies, as well as objects (such as weapons), via a performative mime-act, or will to mime, shot through with violent pathos constitutive of homo mimeticus.

The affective hypothesis was embryonic in the Oedipal unconscious and the rivalries it tends to generate already discussed by mimetic theory, but it requires an alternative door to the unconscious to be fully developed for the heterogeneous field of mimetic studies. This book will thus foreground an embodied conception of the unconscious that has mirroring reflexes as a *via regia*. Renewed critical attention to embodied, affective, and performative reflexes is now central to a number of new critical turns (the affective turn, the performative turn, the new materialist turn, among others) that are currently contributing to the *re*-turn of attention to mimesis—or mimetic turn.[8] In the process, this reevaluation of the powers of mimetic contagion will open up an alternative pre-Freudian but also post-Freudian genealogy of the unconscious that is based not on a repressive or catharsis hypothesis but on a contagion or affective hypothesis. In short, if the focus on catharsis was instrumental in the discovery of an Oedipal unconscious that still in-*forms* mimetic theory, the focus on contagion paves the way for the rediscovery of the mimetic unconscious central to expanding the genealogical reach of mimetic studies.

We have seen in volume 1 that the origins of mimesis in bodily dance and mime were still internal to Aristotle's reframing of mimesis as the representation of an action. What we shall see in volume 2 is that mimesis continues to remain seminal for future anti-Platonic philosophical physicians such as the young Nietzsche, as he posits both a visual (Apollonian) *distance* and an affective (Dionysian) pathos at the heart of his account of the birth of tragedy, for instance. My general hypothesis in *Violence and the Mimetic Unconscious* is the following: it is only when the two sides of mimesis—affective and representational, Dionysian and Apollonian, embodied and visual—are provisionally joined that this Janus-faced concept's (un)timely relevance to account for violent pathologies that move from fictional shadows to material subjects, visual representations to human bodies, becomes fully apparent.

The two sides of mimesis have tended to be disjointed in contemporary debates in critical theory and the humanities more generally. Unsurprisingly so, since metaphysical theories of representation are often up against theories of embodiment and affect, just as transcendence is opposed to immanence, or Being to becoming—and vice versa. Yet in order to understand the main thrust of a contagious or affective hypothesis whose philosophical origins go back to Plato, it will be crucial to realize that both perspectives operate jointly. Plato's complex argument contra mimesis is often reduced to the metaphysical trope of the "mirror" and the debased copies or images of reality it re-presents (presents again); yet, considered from the point of view of the creator of concepts, Plato's critique of mimesis actually begins by foregrounding the figure of the actor, or *mimos*, and the dramatic characters it impersonates on ancient stages, casting an affective shadow that continues to inform modern and contemporary stages, screens, or internet platforms as well. As with respect to the catharsis hypothesis, this critical move entangles the philosophical physician in the mimetic powers she sets out to denounce via a paradox that is not deprived of logical or, better, patho-*logical* insights.

A theory of homo mimeticus then continues to play a decisive role in this double diagnostic of violence and the unconscious. It provides a qualitative, interpretative, and philosophical supplement to the growing number of quantitative empirical studies on (new) media violence. And it does so by inscribing this timely problematic in the longer genealogy of untimely thinkers that go from antiquity (Plato) to modernity (Nietzsche, Charles Féré, Georges Bataille) to the contemporary period (Girard, Hannah Arendt, Philippe Lacoue-Labarthe, Adriana Cavarero, Marco Iacoboni). These and other heterogeneous thinkers of mimesis call attention to the dynamic interplay between fictional violence and unconscious behavior; they also lend credibility to the affective hypothesis on (new) media violence that blurs the line between fiction and reality and call for a mimetic turn to be properly reevaluated.

## The Mimetic Turn

For some time, a mimetic turn has been haunting different strands of critical theory—albeit under different masks and conceptual personae. In the wake of the waning of the linguistic turn at the twilight of the past century, the dawn of the present century has seen a growing concern with the protean manifestations of mimesis that go beyond realistic representations to affect minds and bodies, individuals and collectives, precarious bodies and the body politic. Be it under the rubric of identification in psychoanalysis, affective contagion in affect theory, mimetic desire in mimetic theory, imitation in sociology, influence in psychology, simulation in media/game studies, mirror neurons and brain plasticity in the neurosciences, different turns to affect, ethics, performance, new materialism, embodied cognition and the brain, among other emerging perspectives, testify to a *re*-turn of attention to the protean concept of what the ancient grouped under the rubric of mimesis.[9] If Walter Benjamin influentially claimed at the dawn of the twentieth century that language seemingly brought about an "increasing decay of the mimetic faculty,"[10] I shall argue that new media in the twenty-first century trigger an exponential growth of hypermimetic faculties still in need of diagnostic evaluations. This is what new mimetic studies aims to do.

Indeed, mimesis is the Janus-faced concept that will allow us to reevaluate the affective hypotheses contra the catharsis hypothesis from a genealogical distance. This is perhaps unsurprising, since both are mimetic concepts—which does not mean that they can be contained within the autonomous sphere of aesthetic representation. The problematic of (new) media violence is, in fact, mimetic, but not only in the traditional sense that media violence simply represents, or realistically mirrors, a type of violence that has its pre-existing origins in the social world—though it does that too. If the increasing realism animating the aesthetics of video games is an important factor, as we shall consider in chapter 5, our vector of analysis is not limited to mimetic realism. Hence, it does not presuppose a transparent mirroring connection that goes from reality to fiction, the original to the copy, by assuming that "the media" in their heterogeneity simply "*re*-present" (present again, for the second time) a violent and equally heterogeneous world in which we live. From this naively referential mimetic perspective, it would be all too easy to deduce that if the media represents violence, it is because the world is a violent place, which it is, but not because of this billiard-ball representational model. According to this view, the potential cause is reframed as a consequence—and the case is closed before being opened.

And yet inversions of perspectives are not without performative effects, which leads to a second, more complex, yet more productive understanding of homo mimeticus. Supplementing the realistic view of mimesis that dominated literary accounts of representation of reality in the past century and is increasingly inadequate to account for the insidious and quite protean powers of new media in the present century, I propose a more embodied, affective, and, above all, performative theory of mimesis. The driving *telos* of the book is in fact to overturn traditional vectors of analysis that frame art as a representation of reality. Instead, our vector goes from fictional representations on the side of art to mimetic subjects on the side of life, rather than the other way around, revealing the so-called human original to be impressed, for better and worse, by fictional copies.[11] Interestingly, since classical antiquity mimesis has been considered in its double manifestations as both poison and cure—what the Greeks called a *pharmakon*.[12] This diagnostic duplicity is equally constitutive of the catharsis/contagion debate: catharsis is on the side of the cure whereas contagion on the side of the poison. My mimetic hypothesis, then, is that media representations or simulations of violence generate destabilizing pharmacological, or, as I call them, patho(-)logical, double effects that continue to prove difficult to theorize, recognize, let alone measure; yet, in specific contextual circumstances, they can either potentially contribute to a cathartic release in spectators in need of being entertained, or help legitimize already diffused forms of social violence, often against women, racial, and sexual minorities as well as undocumented immigrants deprived of legal rights. These fictions can also erect models of behavior, types, and exempla that, over time, repetition, and habits of consumption, have material, embodied, and deeply felt effects on an impressively imitative, plastic, and suggestible creature, or homo mimeticus.

This double genealogical focus on both violence and the unconscious filtered by the ancient problematic of mimesis provides this study with a specific, rarely discussed, and thus innovative perspective. In fact, despite the growing number of discussions on media violence, no study exists as yet that places the problematic of mimesis, understood as both representation and behavioral imitation, at the center of contemporary debates. This is unfortunate and somewhat surprising. Time and again, we shall see that both catharsis and contagion on which the debates on (new) media violence turn are concepts intimately entangled with the long and complex history of mimesis. As such, they also encourage theorists to rethink traditional conceptions of subjectivity on which the effects of (new) media violence are impressed—for good or ill. If dominant accounts of media violence still tend to implicitly privilege the traditional view of an autonomous, self-sufficient, and predominantly conscious, fully rational and intentional subject (the subject of *Aufklärung*, or *Homo sapiens*), genealogical lenses lead us to pay close attention to a relational, porous, suggestible, and disarmingly open conception of a phantom of ego that is prone to unconscious influences and mirroring reflexes (the subject of mimesis or homo mimeticus).

Furthering a mimetic turn that originates in philosophical and literary modernism whose sources of inspiration reach back to classical antiquity and ultimately concern the *re*-turn of mimesis in the present and future,[13] I shall continue to take a genealogical detour via some foundational texts in western thought on the question of violence and the unconscious. This detour focuses on influential philosophical authors who have remained in the shadow of contemporary discussions on (new) media violence so far; yet they set the philosophical foundations of the debate on the relation between violence and mimesis that originates in antiquity (Plato), supplement the problematic of the unconscious in modernity (Nietzsche, Freud, Féré), and reveal the protean powers of mimesis in the contemporary period (Arendt and Lacoue-Labarthe, Girard and Latour, affect theory and the neurosciences). Foundational figures in philosophy and the humanities more generally but rarely discussed in any detail in the social sciences, these, among other exemplary theorists of catharsis and contagion, will help us develop an informed genealogical account of the role of contagion in the debates on (new) media violence and beyond. A reevaluation of these and other theories of violence and the unconscious, in turn, will also allow us to unearth the entangled philosophical, aesthetic, and psychological foundations of the twin concepts of catharsis and contagion whose agonistic confrontations are perhaps more far-reaching than previously realized. In fact, we have seen in volume 1 that the catharsis hypothesis gives birth to an influential theory of the unconscious that still latently informs discussions on violence in the humanities (psychoanalysis); conversely, the affective hypothesis central to volume 2 paves the way for the discovery of mirroring principles (mirror neurons) that are constitutive of the mimetic *re*-turn.

In sum, the mimetic turn is attentive to the agonistic relation between catharsis and contagion, as well as to the role these concepts play in the discovery of the unconscious—all problematics constitutive of mimetic studies. The latter will thus allow us to fill a gap in discourses on (new) media violence for a number of reasons that I schematically enumerate as follows: first, mimesis is the very aesthetic/philosophical concept on which the debate on the good and bad effects of representation of violence rests, going from classical antiquity to modernity to the present; second, mimesis is intimately connected to both the concepts of catharsis and contagion, that is, the very concepts that are routinely convoked in debates on media violence without a full awareness of their related yet conflicted genealogical relation; third, both catharsis and contagion play a significant role in the discovery of two distinct—Oedipal and mimetic—conceptions of the unconscious that continue to latently inform contemporary debates in mimetic theory and now mimetic studies as well; and fourth, mimesis is a protean concept that manifests itself under different disciplinary masks, which allows us to address the multiple contagious manifestations of (new) media violence and trace previously unnoticed continuities between theories of aesthetic representation, dramatic impersonation, cinematic identification, televised shows, stretching to include hypermimetic phenomena such as reality TV, fake news, video game simulations, and the mirroring reflexes they might generate in real life. Hence the need for a qualitative, transdisciplinary, interpretative field of mimetic studies that does not aim to replace but, rather, to supplement empirical and quantitative studies.[14] Our methodological hypothesis is that stepping back to the origins of the debate on media violence will allow us to leap ahead to the present. In this genealogical long jump, we shall account for contemporary manifestations of violence and the unconscious that a long genealogy has taught us to expect and sometimes even anticipate.

Now, since this mimetic turn is actually a *re*-turn, genealogical lenses urge us to step back to important precursors of the past century in order to push our diagnostic further in the present century.

## The *Re*-Turn of Mimesis: Precursors

After a century of benign neglect, the ancient problematic of mimesis, traditionally restricted to aesthetic representation and copies of imaginary ideal worlds, is currently returning to the forefront of the critical scene—albeit under different masks and conceptual personae.

To provide a genealogical distance that is often missing in recent innovative turns, perhaps still driven by a romantic desire of originality, which is legitimate but often obscures important precursors,[15] I start by turning back to two theorists of mimesis who, often in an agonistic relation, developed their thoughts at the twilight of the past century and will help us further the mimetic turn, or *re*-turn, at the dawn of the twenty-first century.

So far history has not been too kind to the French philosopher and literary theorist Philippe Lacoue-Labarthe. He is often remembered as a shadow of other, more known thinkers. He is in fact routinely associated with deconstruction, due to his elective affinities with Jacques Derrida and Jean-Luc Nancy, and rightly so for he was part of a community of thought and life.[16] And yet this is the moment to stress that Lacoue-Labarthe is an original thinker in his own terms who was very attentive to a long genealogy of thinkers in mimetic studies. As a careful reader of Plato and Diderot Nietzsche and Girard, among others, Lacoue-Labarthe offers a diagnostic of the performative powers of literature that not only supplements Girard's theory of mimetic desire; he also draws specifically on a theatrical aesthetics to reveal contagious mechanisms that start with literature but generate performative effects outside the text that continue to be at play in more visual media as well and are now constitutive of mimetic studies. "For 'literature,'" writes Lacoue-Labarthe in an agonistic confrontation with Girard, "far from simply reflecting [and we should add, purifying] (as Girard always seems somewhat tempted to think) a prior generalized mimetism, is on the contrary *what provokes mimetism*."[17] Literature and art more generally not only reflect or represent the same mimetic structures of desire and rivalry to be framed in a universal mimetic theory; it also provokes or triggers new forms of mimetism constitutive of the protean metamorphoses of homo mimeticus.

This is true of linguistic media like literature and the theater central to Lacoue-Labarthe's deconstructive theory of a mimesis without a model; yet this performative mechanism is even more explicitly at play in new media under the lens of new media studies. Cinema, film, TV series, and video games that rely on language, but also on images, sound, and immersive digital simulations not to simply reflect an all too human or, perhaps, posthuman mimetism—though they continue to do that, too, and increasingly well.[18] Rather, they trigger a destabilizing mimetism, which, as Lacoue-Labarthe shows, can have passive, contagious, and violent consequences (as in the case of fascist violence), while also paradoxically fueling active, creative, and productive effects (as in the case of the aesthetic creation).[19] What we still need to clarify is how, exactly, mimetic spectacles that are far removed from the laws of imitation still manage, perhaps more efficiently than ever, to provoke mimetism in spectators. This mimetism includes desire, as Girard suggests, but stretches to encompass the more general sphere of affect, or mimetic pathos, thereby providing alternative foundations for a generalized theory of mimesis, the unconscious, and the contagious patho(-)logies central to mimetic studies, old and new.

To be fair to Girard, we have seen that he will eventually agree with Lacoue-Labarthe on the power of art not only to represent mimetic truths at the foundation of culture, but also to provoke mimetic effects, including contagious effects that potentially lead to violent destinations.[20] True, these two latest advocates of mimetic studies of the past century belong to two different and agonistic theoretical traditions that should not be conflated: one is on the side of sameness and referentiality (Girard), the other is on the side of difference and linguistic mediation (Lacoue-Labarthe). Still, when it comes to the question of mimetic violence, the differences between the two are perhaps less marked than their agonism makes it appear to be.[21] An understanding of the paradoxical logic of what I call mimetic agonism encourages us to put both perspectives to use to supplement each other and continue promoting a mimetic turn, or *re*-turn, in the present century.

This operation should come quite naturally, since we are now conscious of the shared genealogies that inform both deconstructive and mimetic theories of violence and the unconscious. After all, as we have seen in volume 1, Girard, like Lacoue-Labarthe, inherits his pharmaceutical diagnostic of violence from the same intellectual model—namely, Jacques Derrida and what he calls his "brilliant" account of the Platonic *pharmakon*.[22] Having played a key role in the organization of the 1966 Structuralist Controversy conference and having attended talks by eminent philologists like Jean-Pierre Vernant who, as we have seen, insisted on the "ambiguity" of the figure of the *pharmakos*,[23] Girard is thus inevitably attentive to both the cathartic *and* the contagious sides of violence. Having stressed Girard's defense of the catharsis hypothesis in *Violence and the Oedipal Unconscious*, it is now the moment to recognize that the affective or contagion hypothesis is, in many ways, the best-known side of Girard's Janus-faced account of the good and bad effects of representations of violence.

The journal devoted to Girard, *Contagion*, is thus aptly titled. It calls attention to Girard's diagnostic of the violence of mimesis, which, in many ways, forms the alpha and omega of his mimetic theory: from the contagious nature of "appropriative desire" to the "mimetic rivalries" that ensue at the interpersonal level, from the collective "crisis of difference" Girard posits at the origins of culture that, thinking of Oedipus again, he often compares to a "plague," to the "escalation of violence" he prophesies at the end of times, both contagion and violence or, rather, the contagious nature of violence constitutes the driving telos of his mimetic theory. If sacrifice and the scapegoat mechanism it reproduces are designed to "quell violence within the community" (*VS* 30) via the cathartic mechanism we saw Girard eventually abandon like Freud before him, he is fully aware that violence has contagious properties built in it that spread like the plague or catch on like a fire. Thus, already in *Violence and the Sacred* (1972), Girard recognizes that "the slightest outbreak of violence can bring about a catastrophic escalation" (30). And he adds: "Violence is like a raging fire that feeds on the very objects intended to smother its flames" (31). This double realization echoes ancient diagnostics that will bring us very quickly back to the origins of philosophy.

Girard may be Aristotelian in his view that tragic representations of violence generate catharsis; yet he remains Platonic in his recognition of the danger of mimetic contagion. Thus, building on a long Platonic suspicion of affective contagion, Girard unequivocally writes that "the only way to avoid contagion is to flee the scene of violence [*s'éloigner*]" (28). Plato, as we will soon confirm, would not only have fundamentally agreed that *distance* serves as an antidote to mimetic pathos; he would have gone further by saying that the only way to avoid contagious pathologies is not simply to flee the scene but to ban violent theatrical spectacles altogether.

Despite Girard's romantic agonism that leads him to set up a distance from Plato's theory of mimesis, or rather because of this agonism, his mimetic theory remains anchored in ancient Platonic foundations. As he recognized, in a rare tribute to the founder of mimetic studies:

> Paradoxically, it was Plato's more immediate contact with the nature of tragic inspiration, his most acute intelligence that motivates his philosophical hostility to drama. He recognized in tragedy a formidable breakthrough [*percée redoutable*] into the opaque and dangerous origins of social values, as something posing a challenge to the very concept of civic order. (*VS* 293; trans. modified)

Girard, then, wholeheartedly agrees with Plato about the dangers of mimetic contagion. On the shoulders of the ancients, we shall go further in acknowledging our debt. The philosophical thesis we shall unpack in our genealogy shall in fact be the following: Plato's breakthrough into the past is also a mirror in which our unconscious violence is reflected in the present and likely in the future as well. Now, given the Janus-faced structure of the Platonic pharmakon, Girard pays as much attention to both the contagion as to the catharsis hypothesis. Although he does not explicitly state it, Girard does not advocate between Plato's critique of mimesis and Aristotle's defense of poetry. Rather, he implicitly urges new theorists of mimesis to articulate the dynamic interplay between the therapeutic and the poisonous sides of what I call mimetic patho(-)logies—at least in theory.

And yet, in practice, in a characteristic move of agonistic differentiation, Girard remains consistently severe with Plato's theory of mimesis. As with

Freud, so with Plato: a mimetic proximity calls for an agonistic distance. As he puts it, Plato "refuses to look at the scapegoat mechanism," or "refuses to look at the victims of his society."[24] Girard's emphasis on Plato's "refusal" mirrors his discontent with Freud's "banish[ing] mimesis" (*VS* 173). Far from seeing the truth, Plato refuses to even look at it; far from theorizing repression, Freud takes the side of banning—a deft but perhaps too neat a mirroring inversion to be fully true. What this mirror does, instead, in a self-referential reflection on Girard is to unmask his own agonistic stance toward the models he so severely critiques, a mimetic stance I qualified as *romantic* agonism out of which mimetic theory was born. Girard's emphasis on differentiation might aim to retain the myth of originality, yet his theory of imitation does not do full patho-*logical* justice to the antagonists' argument—as mimetic agonism aspires to do for mimetic studies.[25]

If mimetic theory remains haunted by the romantic myth of individual originality, mimetic studies relies on genealogical lenses in order to open up a plurality of perspectives that acknowledge precursors of the past in order to go further in the present. A more sympathetic genealogist of mimesis would in fact have pointed out that Plato's account of Socrates in the *Phaedo* already foreshadows the theory of the scapegoat, or pharmakos. Already before Christ, who, for Girard serves as the ultimate scapegoat and sparks a tradition of *imitatio Christi* in which images of violence like the Crucifixion are put to mimetic use,[26] Socrates also provides an exemplary model of innocence that paves the way for future diagnostics of sacrificial victims—as Lacoue-Labarthe judiciously notices.[27] Alternatively, a feminist perspective would point out that the roles Plato attributes to female characters, like Diotima in the *Symposium*, are certainly infected by a patriarchal bias that plagued classical culture reaching into the present, yet also dramatize women as figures of wisdom who can be put to progressive, nonviolent, and democratic political use—as Adriana Cavarero perceptively points out.[28] Instead, in a rivalrous move driven by a still romantic anxiety of influence Girard critiques in theory but may not have fully overcome in practice, he opts to turn Plato's critique of violence against the father of mimetic studies himself, as he writes: "The Platonic rejection of tragic violence is itself violent, for it finds expression in a new expulsion—that of the poet" (*VS* 295). Plato's expulsion of violent spectacles and poets from his utopic city is, of course, fictional,—yet such a fictional move can be turned into a scapegoating mechanism to attack the author that proposed it.

This is a mirroring move that mimetic studies should be careful not to reproduce. In fact, once the spiral of diagnosing the violence internal to rejections of violence as itself violent is set in motion—and Girard is the first to know this in theory—the contagious cycle continues to spread like a fire. If only because we are ourselves at risk of designating, at one remove, Girard's diagnostic of Plato as itself violent, and so on, in an endless, spiraling regress of mimetic accusations that fuels, rather than quells, the vortex of violent actions and unconscious reactions. This rivalrous move not only promotes the violence the mimetic theory seeks to counter; it also goes against the grain of Nietzsche's genealogical imperative to stimulate "amicable and fruitful exchanges" between traditionally competing fields.[29] Above all, it prevents a full, detailed, and rigorous exploration of the diagnostic logos that informs Plato's condemnation of contagious pathos that calls for patho-*logical* supplements in the digital age. Affect theory, as we turn to see, provides a supplementary perspective constitutive of the mimetic turn, or *re*-turn.

## Affective Turn, Mimetic *Re*-Turn

In recent years, the emergence of affect theory and new materialist approaches in the humanities contributed to shifting the focus of attention from concerns with linguistic mediation and discursive formation that dominated the rise of theory in the second half of the twentieth century toward more immanent diagnostics of embodied and contagious influences that account for processes of becoming (other) constitutive of the twenty-first century.[30]

To be sure, the affective turn was not explicitly advocated under the ancient rubric of mimesis. Understandably so, due to the idealist metaphysical baggage of a concept that tends to be reduced to the sameness resulting from adequation to ideal Forms rather than immanent material processes, stable essences rather than processes of becoming. And yet this new turn implicitly contributed to tilting an old understanding of mimesis previously confined to the sphere of arbitrary relations between signs and referential reality toward a more immanent, embodied, and relational diagnostic of nonlinguistic forms of "mimetic communication" central to the formation, deformation, and transformation of subjectivity.[31] In the process, the affective turn also fostered a return of attention to (new) materialist thinkers that find in Spinoza and Nietzsche important precursors.

Spinoza occupies a privileged place in affect theory, and his influence should inform mimetic studies as well. In particular, his insistence that "the human body can be affected in many ways, whereby its power of activity is increased or diminished"[32] relies on a conception of affect (*affectus*) understood as a body's capacity to affect and to be affected that is thoroughly mimetic in its contagious dynamic: the affect of the other penetrates the body of the self, generating the same affect, be it gay or sad. This realization led Spinoza to be critical of free will, especially when the will is entangled in violent emotions. Thus, he writes, for instance, that "we are by no means free in respect to what we seek with violent emotion."[33] As we shall see, this limitation of free will applies to violent emotions with the willpower to flow from representations or simulations on the side of new media to bodies and guns on the side of life, via what I call the "mimetic unconscious" and political theorist William E. Connolly calls "visceral register."[34] Connolly and I agree that both operate in subliminal ways below conscious awareness and are in this pre-Freudian but also post-Freudian sense *un*-conscious.

The affective turn, then, also calls for new diagnostics that explain why, exactly, a body can affect and be affected in the first place—a vital question for our problematic as well. For instance, it led affect theorists to investigate the "philosophical/psychological/physiological underpinnings" of affective contagion that can be turned to "political/pragmatic/performative ends," including violent ends.[35] As we shall give specific substance to these perspectival patho-*logical* underpinnings, genealogical lenses will reveal the centrality of mimesis to account for the riddle of contagion and the banality of violence it entails (chapter 1). This is especially true if we zero in on an immanent, rather than transcendental, conception of mimesis that originates at the dawn of philosophy in Plato's dialogues (chapter 2), received intense physio-psychological scrutiny in the modernist period in Nietzsche's writings (chapter 4), and is returning to the forefront of discussions in the neurosciences with major implications for cultural life and political theory as well (chapters 4 and 5). Above all, mimesis continues to be relevant to account for the power of images to incline bodies toward performative, political, sometimes liberating but also potentially violent ends.[36] A return to the beginnings of mimetic studies, then, can not only pave the way for innovative theoretical turns. It can also account for the power of bodies *to be affected mimetically* by other bodies but also objects, images, spectacles, and digital simulations.

Affect theory shares some fundamental and so far insufficiently noted productive correspondences with mimetic studies. Sailing past the Scylla of realism and the Charybdis of subjectivism, cultural critic Brian Massumi, for instance, on the shoulders of a materialist tradition in process philosophy that goes from Deleuze to Bergson, Nietzsche to Spinoza, turned the focus of critical attention to an imperceptible affectivity of the body that is not only represented in order to "make sense" but that itself *senses* the world, and with different degrees of intensity. These sensations are not subjective, conscious, and identifiable because these properties, for Massumi—echoing Deleuze, echoing Spinoza—belong to "emotions" rather than "affects." Affects are, in fact, considered pre-subjective, fluid, visceral, and generative of intense forces that are not under the volitional control of consciousness and are thus, in our specific sense, *un*-conscious. Hence, Massumi writes: "The vast majority of the world's sensations are certainly nonconscious," and he specifies that "nonconscious is a very different concept from the Freudian unconscious (although it is doubtless not unrelated to it)."[37] Indeed, the nonconscious or unconscious are related for they share a genealogy tied to ancient catharsis/affective hypotheses; yet they are different concepts nonetheless that call for a sense of psychological discrimination.

The nonconscious explored by affect theory has immanent aspirations. It does not set up a boundary between distinct emotional ties such as desire and identification in order to channel the protean power of affects to impress bodies within familial triangular structures framed in a stabilizing metapsychology; nor does it posit the hypothesis that bringing nonconscious affects to consciousness or dramatizing them in family theaters of representation can serve as cathartic cures. As Deleuze and Guattari put it in *Anti-Oedipus* (1972), paving the way for affect theory: "The unconscious poses no problem of meaning, solely problems of use. The question posed by desire is not 'What does it mean?' but rather '*How does it work?*'"[38] This will, indeed, be our question with respect to contagious and violent affects as well; unsurprisingly so, given the shared genealogies that entangle the affective turn with the mimetic turn—though in chapter 4 we will add an untimely Nietzschean principle whose physio-psychological genealogy has largely escaped attention so far.

The connections between anti-Oedipal theorists and theorists of mimesis are indeed rooted in a shared genealogy. Thus, siding *with* Nietzsche, but also D. H. Lawrence and Henry Miller, *contra* psychoanalysis, Deleuze and Guattari specify that "hypnosis and the reign of images" have the power to generate the Oedipalized symptoms that psychoanalysis pretends to cure: "depression and guilt used as a means of contagion" (*AO* 125), they write. These contagious means also trigger violent neurotic effects they characterize in mimetic speech as follows: "Let me deceive, rob, slaughter, kill! but in the name of the social order, and so daddy-mommy will be proud of me" (291).[39] The therapy, in other words, has contagious effects, and this mimetic contagion is inscribed in the repressive hypothesis itself. Thus, directing their unmasking genealogical machine against the myth of Oedipus, Deleuze and Guattari follow D. H. Lawrence in suggesting that the repressive hypothesis brings about what it aspires to repress:

> The law tells us: You will not marry your mother, and you will not kill your father. And we docile subjects say to ourselves: so *that*'s what I wanted. . . . It is not a question of the return of the repressed. Oedipus is a factitious product of psychic repression. It is only the represented, insofar as it is induced by repression. (125)

Psychic theories have performative effects. They are implicated in the production of the very logos that aspires to be a cure in theory yet generates pathological effects in practice—contributing to "making madness," to use Mikkel Borch-Jacobsen's expression.[40] Genealogical lenses shall lead us to trace a similar patho(-)logical dynamic back to Plato. It is thus not surprising that echoing Lawrence but also Nietzsche, these anti-Oedipal theorists reinscribe psychoanalysis in an ancient metaphysical tradition as they define it as "the new avatar of the 'ascetic ideal'" (291). Clearly, for Deleuze and Guattari, like Nietzsche and Lawrence before them, the therapy is entangled in the performative production of the sickness it aims to cure. Or, to put it in our language, the patho-*logy* serves as the model for a performative pathology to emerge.

That mimesis cannot be dissociated from the contagious dynamics of affects that flow from self to others is clear. Deleuze and Guattari focus on the productive nature of desire they posit as an alternative to negative accounts of desire predicated on lack. They write contra Hegel, Freud, and Lacan. These are foundational moves that reoriented philosophical discussions in the 1970s in light of what Roberto Esposito calls a "generalized anti-Hegelianism" whereby "difference and repetition have taken the place of the identical and of the negative."[41] Mimetic studies will further this line of inquiry, but we should first realize that these anti-Hegelian thinkers are not as radical as they could be. After all, they continue to retain the Hegelian, Freudian, and Lacanian focus on desire as the main door to account for the whole spectrum in the affective life of a depersonalized subject. Perhaps this privileged focus on desire, which, as we have seen in volume 1, was still dominant in the French intellectual context of the 1960s that equally shaped Girard's theoretical focus on mimetic desire, might betray a residual influence of the Hegelian theories they set out to overturn.

Mimetic studies do not aim to develop a unifying theory of imitation with transhistorical, universalist aspirations; nor does it rest on a single theorist who ties mimesis to the vicissitude of triangular desires—no matter how insightful that theorist continues to be. Instead, I shall join forces with a plurality of heterogeneous thinkers attentive to the unconscious powers of affective contagion. An untimely genealogist of the unconscious of Nietzschean inspiration like Michel Henry, for instance, while not focusing explicitly on mimesis, comes very close to our theory of homo mimeticus. In fact, he also considered "immanence and affectivity" as the essence of life and rightly notes that "affectivity fills the totality of the Nietzschean landscape, it is everywhere."[42] In fact, the French phenomenologist equally considers the "force," "hyperpower" (*hyperpuissance*) (*GP* 249), or, better still, the "pathos" of Dionysus animating "the endless play of its suffering and joy" (10) as the most immediate manifestation of a nonrepresentational unconscious. Paving the way for the affective turn, Henry also posits that "superficial thoughts are the thoughts of mediation" (396). He thus implicitly calls for a nonrepresentational theory of mimesis like ours to account for the unconscious power of affect to go beyond a phenomenology of auto-affection, opening up the ego to that relational pathos that entails the capacity to be affected—by others. This operation entails both a mirroring and an inversion of Henry's phenomenology: a mirroring because his genealogy rightly acknowledges that "only one who primitively digs in one-self as a Self and, thus, auto-affects oneself is susceptible of being affected by whatever else [*affecté par quoi que ce soit*]" (280–81); and an inversion because my mimetic hypothesis is that only a being who is primitively affected by an intimate and privileged other (e.g., parent, friend, model, lover, partner)—what I call, echoing Pierre Janet, a *socius*—remains a relational being who is mimetically affected by whomever or whatever else.[43]

Pioneers of affect theory, like Deleuze, Guattari, and, we now add, Henry, pave the way for a genealogy of an anti-Oedipal unconscious that is no longer based on a dated reading of Freud but anticipates some of the more recent *re*-turns of attention to affect, embodiment, and contagion. Although they do not generally foreground the concept of mimesis as such, their work is truly immanent and affirmative—read Spinozist and Nietzschean—and in line with the genealogy that follows. Interestingly, Deleuze and Guattari will later acknowledge (with Gabriel Tarde, for instance) the centrality of what they call affective flows of "microimitation" in the generation of contagious fluxes. While Deleuze and Guattari remain opposed to the (Platonic) concept of mimesis as stabilizing image or form for its vertical (tree-like) ontology (or dominant mimesis), they specify the horizontal dynamic of rhizomatic contagious flows via a (Tardian) notion of the unconscious I qualify as minor mimesis, as they write:

> Tarde was interested in the world of detail, or of the infinitesimal: the little *imitations* . . . a microimitation does seem to occur between two individuals. But at the same time, and at the deeper level, it has to do not with an individual but with a flow or a wave. *Imitation is the propagation of a flow.*[44]

Imitation is, indeed, the propagation of a flow. And this imperceptible mimetic flow is the affective life at the palpitating heart of homo mimeticus as well. Although it is rarely mentioned, there is thus a mimetic principle at the genealogical sources of the anti-Oedipal nonconscious. Hence our choice to qualify it as the *mimetic* unconscious.

Already for Deleuze and Guattari, then, this unconscious generates contagious flows of mimetic becoming that transgress the boundaries of subjectivity. This flow of affective mimesis does not fit within triangular configurations, or visual representations, that frame and stabilize the ego in an Oedipal drama, or an ideal *imago*. Instead, the mimetic unconscious multiplies connections, proliferates flows, transgresses mind-body and self-other dualisms, and triggers processes of becoming other that immediately affect, by way of contagion, the visceral materiality of a porous mimetic subject that is currently returning on the theoretical scene. We are in fact in good company in affirming this view. Jane Bennett, for instance, recently joined forces in a "vibratory *encounter*" with the mimetic turn in her new materialist "return to the question of the I" via an affective "influx & efflux" that emerge in the process of "riding" the waves of Walt Whitman's poetic lines.[45] Bennett and I fundamentally agree that the I or ego is a "porous," "plastic," "phantom," "working to destroy individuation" in affective and material ways that often remain "unconscious, vague to the bearer."[46] Why? Because this ego is open to what Bennett now also calls the "pathos of sympathy" or "feeling-with that respects the distance" and "partake[s], both conscious and unconsciously in an atmospheric of mimetic inflection," riding both good and bad influences.[47] Similarly, supporting this mimetic-affective-materialist turn, William Connolly, in his exploration of the visceral level of cultural life, not only taps into the Nietzschean tradition of the unconscious; he is also explicitly critical of what he calls, thinking of psychoanalysis, a "heavy explanatory theory." He writes, for instance: "much of perception and thinking is prior to consciousness, even without introducing a repression hypothesis to make that point."[48] Indeed, why introduce a repressive hypothesis to make a progressive political point? It is much more efficient to rely on an immanent diagnostic of affects that operate below the threshold of consciousness and perception, are physio-psychological and pre-subjective in nature, and have the (will to) power, or pathos, to induce contagious states of depersonalization.

Deleuze and Guattari, thinking of Nietzsche, speak of a subject "which has been abandoned by the ego" (*AO* 22). I call this process of mimetic depersonalization, that finds in Nietzsche a privileged case study, "phantom of the ego." What Massumi does not fully tell us, Deleuze and Guattari begin telling us, and genealogical lenses reveal, is the following point: this relational, anti-Oedipal, and embodied non/unconscious in which, thanks to flows of affects, realities "pass into each other" (*PV* 8), breaking down ontological boundaries between subject and object, mind and body, self and others, humans and nonhumans, at different speeds and with different degrees of intensity, is not only *post*-Freudian in its anti-Oedipal orientation. It is also directly in line with a *pre*-Freudian discovery of the power of movements to generate mirroring sensations we shall have to trace in some detail in the pages that follow.

Consciously or unconsciously, then, recent developments in different schools of critical theory and continental philosophy are currently joining hands and can be productively aligned with mimetic studies. In fact, they open up alternative doors to the unconscious in touch with the fluxes of imitation that traverse it, rendering psychic life open, porous, and thus vulnerable to the outside, for good and ill. Given this Janus-faced orientation, it is thus no accident that both affective/mimetic traditions pay close attention to actors as paradigmatic examples of phantom subjects without proper qualities who are endowed, paradoxically, with a will to mime that generates highly contagious, mimetic, sometimes therapeutic but also potentially pathological effects on both individual bodies and the body politic at large.

## The Will to Mime

Before we turn to consider the affective hypothesis in more genealogical detail, an introductory account of the power of actors to affect bodies and minds, via mimetic pathos, or the will to mime, is still in order. Perhaps more explicitly than other artistic figures, actors have served as paradigmatic examples for mimetic studies, old and new, because they dramatize both the visual (Apollonian) and embodied (Dionysian) powers of mimetic contagion. Such a focus might thus best serve to supplement this introduction with a genealogical specificity that will inform all the chapters that follow. It will also allow us to clinch the connection between the affective turn and the mimetic *re*-turn. The case of the actor, from which mimesis, by the way, derives its conceptual identity (from *mimos*, meaning "mime" or "actor"), allows us to detect underlying imperceptible continuities between different genealogies of contagion that are often neglected due to agonistic movements of differentiation but run like an undercurrent through key figures in the genealogy of the mimetic unconscious that drive our investigation.

Just like Nietzsche, on the shoulders of Plato, had turned to the case of Wagner to diagnose the tyrannical power of the actor over the crowd in the late 1880s, so Massumi, on the shoulders of Deleuze, turns to the case of Reagan as a paradigmatic example to theorize the unconscious power of affect in the late 1990s (*PV* 39–44, 46–67). More recently, furthering a Nietzschean/mimetic tradition, I turned to the case of Trump to account for the contagious continuities between TV shows and political shows.[49] The media are indeed different: we have moved from the theater to the cinema, TV reality shows to political shows to new media that rely on algorithms to amplify the powers of affection (chapter 3). Given such shifts in the aesthetic medium, it is tempting to change conceptual messages as well. Thus, the ancient rhetorical concept of pathos tends to be replaced by the contemporary concept of affect. And yet, in shifting terminology we should be careful not to erase the genealogical traces of previous diagnostics. This is sometimes the risk with new turns. For instance, alluding to a psychological tradition that goes back to mesmerism and culminates with hypnosis, Massumi stresses that what is at play in affective contagion is not at all an attempt to "mesmerize the masses" or trigger "emotive identifications" (*PV* 40)—if only because emotions are subjective, identifiable, and on the side of being, whereas affects are pre-subjective, unidentifiable, and prone to becoming.

Fair enough. But this ontological binary between priests of being and advocates of becoming, theories of mesmerism and identification on one side and theories of affect and contagion on the other might not always be clear cut. Could it be that suggestive genealogical continuities flow between these entangled traditions and concepts? The media have certainly changed and have increased their power of affection exponentially, yet the dramatic strategies at play remain tied to hypnotic forms of (will to) power that Nietzsche, for one, rooted in the Greek concept of pathos. Thus, he defined the will to power as "not a being, not a becoming, but a *pathos*—the most elemental fact from which a becoming and effecting first emerge" (*WP* 635; 339). For Nietzsche, the philologist trained in classics, pathos is not simply an emotion and certainly cannot be reduced to a sad passion restricted to *penthos* (suffering). Rather, Nietzsche has the ancient Greek understanding of pathos as the "most vital moment in religion and art, feared by others as an enticement to sacrilege and irrationality."[50] Thus understood, pathos goes beyond good and evil for it can be as much the cause of joy and of suffering. And yet, for our topic we shall have to consider that Plato linked pathos to the part of the soul "that is in command of dictators, madmen and criminals"[51]—a diagnostic Nietzsche, this time with Plato, tied to actors as well; that is, histrionic figures who, via new media, cast a spellbinding shadow on contemporary politics (chapter 3). Mimetic pathos is indeed a fluid, turbulent, and thus mobile concept from which our theory of homo mimeticus unfolds.[52] This theory brings us back to the mimetic unconscious and defines the movement of pathos of distance in the soul that oscillates between activity and passivity, rhetorical receptivity and pathological capacity to impress and be impressed, or, if you prefer, affect and be affected—often inducing a spectrum of altered states of consciousness in which homo mimeticus is particularly vulnerable to violent pathos.

That a mimetic pathos has already taken possession of affect theory is clear. The figure of the actor qua "genius" was, in fact, central to a romantic conception of artistic inspiration. If it finds its origins in Plato's ironic account of enthusiasm in *Ion*, it continues to implicitly cast a shadow on contemporary turns as well. Brian Massumi contributes to resuscitating this tradition as he diagnoses a popular U.S. mimetic figure under the rubric of what he ironically calls a "genius": namely, former U.S. president qua actor Ronald Reagan. Massumi is particularly attentive to Reagan's early career as an actor qua mime. He considers this actor along cinematic lines that are explicitly Deleuzian and future oriented in theory, yet implicitly root affect theory in a long genealogy of mimesis in dramatic practice. For Massumi, in fact, the case of Reagan did not rely on the power of a linguistic discourse, or logos, to play his role as an actor from a visual distance; nor was he in full possession of his theatrical craft, or *techne*, to intentionally manipulate his bodily gestures, expressions, and tone so as to generate pathos in the audience. Instead, as a second-rate actor Reagan "politicized the power of mime" for, Massumi adds, "the genius of the mime is also the good fortune of the bad actor. Reagan's gestural idiocy had a mimetic effect" (*PV* 40, 41). And, needless to say, since this actor was swept into office not once but twice, this mimetic effect was contagious.

The shadow of mimesis thus falls on the mime amplifying his acting willpower, or mimetic pathos. At one remove, this shadow equally informs the diagnostic internal to affect theory. Speaking of this voice that was not good in reading but had an intense effect as the actor spoke dramatically, that is, in mimetic rather than diegetic speech, Massumi says: "It was the embodiment of an asignifying intensity doubling his every actual move and phrase, *following him like a shadow of a mime*" (41; my emphasis). The mimetic actor is thus no longer fully himself when he speaks. He is shadowed, animated, perhaps even (dis)possessed by another who is not fully other for this shadow traverses the porous boundaries that divide self from others, doubling the mimetic actor's intensity and will to power to affect and infect others. Reagan, in other words, was possessed by a will to mime with the power or pathos to dispossess others as well.

The diagnostic is accurate, perceptive, and innovative, but it is certainly not original. The echoes between affective contagion and mimetic contagion are loud; the continuities between affect theory and mimetic studies are clear. We are in fact told that this actor is a man "without content" (*PV* 42)—Robert Musil would have said "without qualities." We are equally told that he "was nothing" (42), that he was "no one" (56), and that it is precisely this lack of proper qualities that, paradoxically, "will allow Reagan to enter innumerable bodies of other 'fellows'" (55). Philippe Lacoue-Labarthe, echoing Diderot's *Paradox of the Actor*, would have said that this "*mime de rien*" is nothing in himself, is a subject "without properties," and is thus "improper," and paradoxically for this reason, "the more the artist (the actor) is nothing, the more he can be everything."[53] Affect theory, revisited from the angle of mimetic theory now expanded via mimetic studies attentive to new media, generates a feeling of déjà vu. This is, in fact, a modern paradox of mimesis that is still our paradox, precisely because it rests on the shoulders of an ancient theory of mimesis that, via multiple iterations, reaches into the present. To put it in more classical parlance, we could say that Reagan, the actor (or *mimos*), *impersonates* a role via a dramatic mimesis that convinces not so much by what he says at the level of the message (or logos), nor by an artistic craft (or techne) he controls. Rather, the genius of the actor relies on the untidy intermixture between a visual identification with an ideal (Apollonian) image seen from a distance and an immanent receptivity to a bodily (Dionysian) pathos.

We are thus back to the foundational concept of "pathos of distance" that provides the second conceptual step in our theory of homo mimeticus, giving it a distinctive movement rather than a stable form. This double perspective of the actor's will to mime, in fact, generates a conjunctive disjunction that oscillates between pathos and distance, affect and vision, and was indeed at play in Reagan's acting method. On one side, his initial acting strategy early in his career consisted in "envisioning the mental picture of the author's character" (Reagan qtd. in *PV* 47), thereby approximating Diderot's anti-affective theory of acting based not on sensibility or pathos but on a distant and reflective contemplation of an "ideal model" (*modèle idéal*) or "great phantom" (*grand fantôme*).[54] On the other side, for Reagan, this mimetic drive turns an affective, embodied, and intensely felt pathos that provides a decisive turn in his acting and, arguably, political career—what he calls "the most challenging acting problem in my career" (qtd. in *PV* 52). Since this "acting problem" sheds light on the contagious dynamic between violence and the unconscious we shall be diagnosing in the chapters that follow, let us replay it in slow motion.

In his early days, Reagan was given a challenging role that stretched his mimetic faculty beyond its limits for he had to play a divided subject. All acting entails a form of psychic division, but this role asked literally for a bodily split. "A whole actor would find such a scene difficult," admitted Reagan in his first autobiography; and he adds, in a self-critical mood, "giving it the necessary dramatic impact as half an actor was murderous" (*PV* 52). Asked to impersonate a young man in a movie titled *King's Row* (dir. Sam Wood, 1942), Reagan needs to dissociate himself from himself—or, rather, from his body. In the scene in question, in fact, his character, Drake McHugh, wakes up and finds out he lost both his legs, which have been amputated. The half actor feels the need to double his mimetic strategy to live up to the role of half a man. In fact, in the weeks spent preparing for the scene, Reagan recalls being obsessed, perhaps even possessed, by this cinematic phantom in his daily life. He not only "consulted physicians and psychologists" and "rehearsed the scene before mirrors" (53) from a visual distance that relied on the mediation of a mirror image; he also felt the urge to "find out how it really felt, short of amputation" by drawing on the "cauldron of emotions" (53). That is, a cauldron animated by the physio-psychological turbulence internal to his embodied, affective, and mimetic unconscious to the point of rendering the phrase he had to give voice to automatic. A pathos of distance, in short, had been set in motion—if not consciously, at least unconsciously so.

**FIGURE 2.** Ronald Reagan starring in *Kings Row* (dir. Sam Wood, 1942).

Driven to exhaustion by this oscillation, the decisive turning point emerges from the practice on the set triggered by a visual "deception." The setting is rather crude: it consists in a mattress with a hole, a blanket to cover it, and a prop underneath that allows for the actor's lower body to disappear from sight, leaving the half mime lying in bed to contemplate his missing legs for a whole hour. Simply meant to hide Reagan/McHugh's legs from the spectators' vision so that the cinematic representation *looks* realistic from the outside, this crude device operates on the actor's body at the affective level of his mimetic unconscious from the inside. The line splitting what this divided self sees from what he feels, mind and body, fiction and reality, mimetic representation and mimetic pathos, begins to blur; and this blurring generates an affective contagion in which the actor feels increasingly divided, split, amputated—to the point of becoming overwhelmed by the divided character he is impersonating. "Gradually, the affair began to terrify me," Reagan reminisces. And then suddenly, as he finds himself terrified, in an altered state of consciousness that blurs the distinction between psyche and soma, vision and sensation, being oneself and becoming someone other, he hears the magical string of words: "Lights!" "Quiet please!" "Action." If not Reagan "himself," his mimetic unconscious is now ready to play the role of a divided man—as he exclaims, with horror: "Where's the rest of me?"

"There was no retake." As Reagan reminisces: "I had put myself, as best I could, in the body of another fellow" (53). The shadow of mimesis had indeed fallen on the actor's ego, turning it not so much into a melancholic self but into a phantom of the ego instead.

Reagan's mimetic strategy is, indeed, double. The image of the divided other he imagined, doubled by the missing legs he does not see, has the power to induce in his physio-psychology the affective horror of the amputated figure he mimes. This spiraling interplay of distance and pathos, visual mimesis and bodily mimesis, *psycho*-logy and *physio*-logy, triggers a mirroring patho(-)logical illusion that may be cognitively false but is truly felt with pathos. Neurologists are familiar with analogue visual-somatic effects: not unlike the "mirror box" used by neuroscientists for patho-*logical* ends to relieve amputated patients from phantom pains trick their brains into feeling real relief by having them massage the remaining arm while looking in a mirror where they see the phantom arm being massaged,[55] so, in a mirroring inversion that puts the patho-*logy* to cinematic use, not seeing the legs via an optical illusion, leads the mimetic actor to the truly felt pathological anguish of feeling amputated. As we shall see, the discovery of mirror neurons in the 1990s not only confirms an ancient connection between visual mimesis and affective contagion; it also lends empirical support to physio-psychological

theories of the mimetic unconscious that posited, already in the 1880s, that
the sight of movements outside has the power to generate a physio-affective
contagion truly felt inside (chapter 4). Whether that contagion has the
power to break the screen of representation, violently affecting bodies and
minds of spectators, remains to be seen, and perhaps felt.

The point for now is that the mimetic strategy of impersonation not only
worked for Reagan in a cinematic fiction; it also worked in the sphere of politics. In the long run, it even paved the way for future apprentice presidents
that relied on the strategies of the actor with the mimetic pathos, or will to
mime, to generate real manifestations of insurrecting violence (chapter 3).
Time and again, we shall see that the actor's ego dissolves not because he is
nothing in itself; he dissolves because it is physically haunted by a mimetic
shadow of yet another shadow that dispossesses the "original," leaving but
a phantom of a phantom behind, possessed by a mimetic pathology. Yet
according to a paradoxical logic, or patho-*logy*, that genealogical lenses have
rendered us sensitive to, such subjects without qualities, or phantoms without proper egos, are not deprived of contagious powers to affect and infect
others nonetheless—triggering if not the physical violence of the amputation
itself, at least the pathos of this horror for spectators who, sitting in armchairs
with legs well in sight, can contemplate from a cinematic distance.

At one additional remove, the mimetic paradox that leads an increasing distance to amplify the power of pathos might return with a contagious
vengeance in the digital age.[56] In fact, actors' will to mime no longer requires
a cinematic set. It is now amplified by a multiplicity of personalized social
media and distributed on screens via avatars endowed with the potential to
infect mimetic bodies generating violent, and potentially virally contagious
pathologies as well.[57] Affect theory, in fact, has launched a call to "rethink
body, subjectivity, and social change in terms of movement, affect, force, and
violence" (*PV* 86). New mimetic studies redoubles and ramifies the call by
placing the diagnostic of violence and the unconscious in a longer genealogy attentive to the paradox of the actor. If we agree with affect theory that
the pathos internal to the will to mime operates via an "action at a distance"
(43)—or "*action à distance*" as Gabriel Tarde already said[58]—our point is that
a tradition of thinkers of mimesis not only fully agreed with this diagnostic;
they also paved the way for it, allowing us to anticipate phantoms to come.

Stepping back to the birth of theories of mimesis, the genealogy of contagion that follows will continue to further the mimetic turn by incorporating affect theory into new mimetic studies.

Plato contra Aristotle; the catharsis hypothesis contra the affective hypothesis: the artistic manifestations of the debate change historically, and so do the theories of the unconscious that mediate them. Yet the fundamental theoretical agon on the good and bad effects of violent representations continues to resonate through the ages, opening up new riddles for new generations of theorists to solve. Hence the urgency for new genealogical operations that look back to the mimetic patho-*logies* of the past to better diagnose the mimetic pathologies that cast a shadow on the present and future.

Let us then return to the fictional crime in the cinematic case study with which we started in order to reload the problematic of (new) media violence from the angle of the affective hypothesis under the lens of new mimetic studies. Whether its mimetic or, rather, hypermimetic powers generate patho(-)logies constitutive of the digital age is what we turn to diagnose.

# CHAPTER 1

# The Banality of Violence

## A Taste of Hypermimesis

After a genealogical account of the development and transformation of the concept of catharsis constitutive of *Violence and the Oedipal Unconscious*, we are now in a position to confirm that the protagonist of Brian Miller's science fiction (sf) film *Vice* (2015) is not alone in expressing a suspicion toward the therapeutic properties of the catharsis hypothesis. A long tradition of interpretations of Aristotle's *Poetics* expresses similar doubts. The protagonist of *Vice*, Detective Roy Tedeschi is equally not alone in voicing concerns about the contagious effects of representations of violence, for the affective hypothesis is even more ancient than the hypothesis of catharsis. In Plato's *Republic*, Socrates asked Glaucon an untimely question we reproduced as an epigraph, for it has not lost any of its relevance today and will guide us in our investigation: "Have you not observed that imitations, if continued from youth far into life, settle down into habits and second nature, in the body, the speech and the thought?" (*Rep.* 395d). In a different, more contemporary fictional scenario, had Socrates asked the same question to Tedeschi, the latter would have likely answered with a firm "Yes, I have observed the powers of imitation." And so, we can only assume, did contemporary parents attentive to their children's mimetic faculties reloaded in the digital age.

This imaginary fictional dialogue between Plato's philosophical alter ego (Socrates) and a sf cinematic character did not take place at the dawn of philosophy; yet this does not mean it cannot be reenacted at its twilight. After all, sf is increasingly considered a far-reaching philosophical genre that is conducive to critical reflections on technological innovations that mimetically affect and potentially infect present generations. As Hannah Arendt recognized in *The Human Condition* (1958), sf deserves philosophical attention as a "vehicle of mass sentiments and mass desires."[1] This popular genre does not simply represent mass desires from a futuristic aesthetic distance. Rather, sf mediates or channels "mass sentiments" via the generalized vehicle of a mass medium generating mimetic and contagious effects that spread rhizomatically, like a fungus, across the body politic.

We should thus immediately specify that such mass sentiments and desires are not narrowly realistic in the sense that they transparently reflect desires in the so-called real world—they need a hermeneutical effort to be brought to the fore; nor are these sentiments mimetic only in the sense that the mass imitates the desires of a model restricted to a triangular dynamic that leads to rivalry and violence—for the mass, as Arendt well knew from her work on totalitarianism, is directly vulnerable to the more general mimetic pathos of contagion with direct political consequence, including violent consequences. Rather, increasingly in the digital age, mass sentiments are projected onto fictional futures via technological mediations that are already constitutive of the contemporary human, or posthuman, condition. While new digital technologies do not offer representations of reality that transparently mirror the outside world (realism), they should not be hastily grouped under the postmodern rubric of a "simulation" that no longer rests on the logic of imitation (hyperrealism). Whether they are at play in films, TV shows, reality shows, or video games, these hyperreal simulations, which often display violence in order to capture the increasingly saturated attention of users and spectators, have the disconcerting power to retroact, via spiraling feedback loops, on the material bodies and psyches of homo mimeticus. They may also generate a "punitive rage," which, as Mark Pizzato puts it, can potentially "overflow the enclosed space of fictional becoming and the film's ostensibly moral resolution—with further acts of violence outside the cinema (or home video theatre), as preemptive strikes or vigilante vengeance."[2] As we shall have occasions to confirm via contemporary case studies, this spiraling loop can generate an interplay of hyperreality and reality, fictional actions and bodily reactions, that is not simply mimetic but, as I call it, hypermimetic.[3]

At the beginning of our genealogy, we already experienced a taste of violence via an imaginary participation in the cinematic fantasies that *Vice* induced. We now step back to reevaluate the fuller motion picture so as to better diagnose the pathological effects of hypermimesis from a cinematic distance that will foreground the affective hypothesis we will trace to the end. A brief comparison with modern genealogists of violence like Nietzsche and Georges Bataille will help us foreground the diagnostic that informs this study as a whole: namely that violence cannot be easily peeled off from aesthetic theory, if only because it is the pathos of violence that may have given birth to tragedy and continues to animate new aesthetic forms of entertainment and the strange pleasure they entail.

If our diagnostic started with an interpretation of a fictional case study in order to theorize the relation between violence and the unconscious, we shall also take care not to constrain the diagnostic to fictional representations alone. In fact, the problematic of contagion calls for sociopolitical distinctions that cannot be dissociated from the problematic of (new) media violence. In Brian Miller's sf crime thriller, the violent fantasies are, in fact, specifically directed toward women; and this choice reflects the reality that women are disproportionally subjected to violence in the real world as well. Our opening case study dramatized a gendered bias that is constitutive of contemporary forms of "entertainment" (from film to video games) more generally and will inform the chapters that follow. And since the detective retrains the rather traditional role of the white male hero of this rather traditional Hollywood plot, we shall balance the fictional diagnostic with a feminist perspective on (new) media violence.

At the same time, the detective's critical take on police practices within the film calls for a different supplement directed against racial minorities as well.[4] The number of police murders of African Americans in the United States—from Freddie Gray to George Floyd to Breonna Taylor, among many others—were all too real. Yet their capture on video reveals that these brutal police murders might not be dissociated from the problematic of (new) media violence that inflects racist and violent forms of daily policing practices for many minorities (African Americans but also Hispanics, Asian Americans, and immigrants more generally). These brutal police practices risk, in fact, to render violence "banal," in Hannah Arendt's specific sense that they have become so ordinary, commonplace, and widely enforced that they generate an "inability to think" she considered in the context of antisemitism but applies to racist violence more generally. It belongs to the category of "evil."[5] The phrase "the banality of violence," then, does not downplay the horror of violence. On the contrary, it aims to supplement Arendt's account of evil with contemporary forms of racist and sexist discriminations that, while not the same as antisemitism under Nazism, share the same psychological "thoughtlessness" in the violence they still generate for minorities today. Such an inability to think at the level of thought, or logos, stems perhaps from a prior dispossession generated by a contagious affect or pathos that triggers a specific taste for (new) media violence.

## Contagious *Vice* and Artificial Tastes

Given the diagnostic turn that entangles media violence with issues of gender and race, a clarification is now in order. If I opened this book by giving voice to Julian Michaels's (Bruce Willis's) highly questionable fantasies at play in the VICE resort, it was not only because Bruce Willis tends to generate an automatic unconscious identification in male viewers for whom, since the 1980s, he served as a model of seduction, hypermasculinity, and heroic actions that often lead to violent cinematic actions. Starting with his early debut in the TV series *Moonlighting* (1985–1989) to popular action/crime films series like *Die Hard* (started in 1988), from *Pulp Fiction* (1994) to *Surrogates* (2009), which anticipates the problematic of androids and online entertainment further explored in *Vice* (2015), among others, the power of cinematic models to unconsciously trigger mimetic mechanisms of identification in the audience should not be underestimated given the centrality of affective mimesis for cinema as an art. Edgar Morin writes in his pioneering study: "Film comes to life for the spectator if the latter projects his/her own psychic states onto actions and characters, their needs, fears, passions; in a world s/he identifies with the hero's problems."[6] Projection and identification, or to put it in a more classical language, mimesis, is thus at the heart of the contagious pathos that blurs the line between fiction and reality for *spectators*.

Still, I relied on this mimetic strategy because I wanted readers of this book *not* to start the investigation by automatically thinking critically about violence from a safe distance that the medium of critical writing already mimetically encourages. Rather, I wanted readers to start engaging with the problem of violence and the unconscious by lowering the critical guard somewhat and approximating the position, and thus disposition, of someone who is being entertained. It's easy to take critical distance from violence when we consciously think about it; less so when, due to a suspension of disbelief, we allow our mimetic unconscious to experience its pathos. Despite the rationalist spell cast by the flattering self-designation of *Homo sapiens*, we should not forget that we are also *homo ludens* and thus open to an agonistic mirroring identifications that are not reducible to the logic of representation and are constitutive of homo mimeticus as well.[7] This is indeed the disposition viewers experience as they feel the violence at play in virtual/violent cinematic fantasies the medium of film mimetically induces. As we do not think only with our minds but also with and *from* our bodies, I consider it crucial for new mimetic studies to draw on this experiential affect, or pathos, to subsequently develop an affectively informed critical diagnostic from a distance. That the identification with a male actor is gender biased and triggers violent male fantasies within the film is clear enough. But this gender bias is equally central to the problematic of (new) media violence outside the film. My methodological wager, then, is that such a violence, which often operates below conscious awareness, needs to be confronted via a Janus-faced perspective that is attentive to both the immediacy of affect and the mediation of thought, pathos and distance, as well as the unconscious patho(-)logies it entails.

One of the fundamental theoretical assumptions that guides our diagnostic evaluation of both catharsis and contagion is that a partial emotional participation in the pathos of violence characteristic of aesthetic experiences, no matter how problematic, might be a necessary presupposition to adequately evaluate the pathos of violence from a proximate distance. This is, in many ways, a contemporary transfer of the "pathos of distance" (*pathos der Distanz*) internal to Nietzsche's genealogy of morals to the genealogy

**FIGURE 3.** Ambyr Childers and Charlotte Kirk as "artificials" in *Vice* (dir. Brian Miller, 2015).

of violence and the unconscious we pursue. It calls for clinical observers who are at least partially implicated in the affects (*pathos*) they diagnose as a pathology; and precisely because of this affective participation, they are in a position to develop mimetic patho-*logies*—that is, critical accounts (*logoi*) on mimetic affects (*pathoi*) that reevaluate the complex interplay between media violence and the unconscious. Having partially felt this mimetic pathos of violence and recalled its powers of affection and infection, we can now return to a more clinically detached yet still affectively involved observation of our cinematic case study. If *Vice* is predicated on a plot structured on an imitation of a violent action, the diagnostic of mimesis it promotes reaches beyond the screen of representation to address the violent digital pathologies it metaphorically alludes to.

The VICE resort is specifically designed for male, predominantly white and wealthy human clients to unleash all kinds of violent, sexualized, and sadistic fantasies onto so-called artificials. Designed as idealized, embodied, and highly aestheticized female androids, artificials are played by real actresses that provide a degree of aesthetic realism originally characteristic of the old medium of cinema. These types also point to stereotypes at play in new computer simulations and video games increasingly close to cinematic realism. That realism is part of the appeal of the VICE resort is clear. As the promotional advertisement announces, its aim is to provide "the most

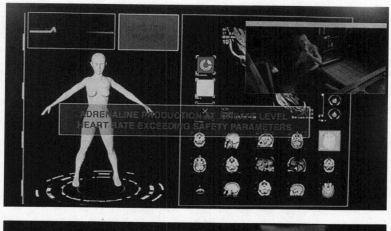

**FIGURE 4.** "Physical" violence and "simulated" violence in *Vice* (dir. Brian Miller, 2015).

realistic experience possible" as a form of "pure entertainment" that does not require the mediation of a screen, at least for clients within the film. At the same time, it also allegorically alludes to violent simulations constitutive of contemporary video games that, for the moment, are not directed against cyborgs and still require the mediation of a screen.

As figure 4 suggests, the violence the film denounces at the level of the message finds a mirroring counterpart in violent eroticism or, as Nietzsche would call it, "voluptuous cruelty."[8] This cruelty is amplified by the cinematic medium: close-ups, high-angle shots, the character's open mouth. At one remove, it can be routinely played out via video games that tend to have no consequences for the computer simulations yet might have mirroring effects on gamers we shall consider. As the plot unfolds, in fact, spectators soon find out that such entertainment includes rape and murder. These violent actions prefigure controversial video games such as the banned *Rape Day* (2019) or the much-awaited *Cyberpunk 2077* (2020), violent games that allow for a first-person interactive participation in the pathos of violence that *Vice* represents from a cinematic distance. The film sets the stage, so to speak, both aesthetically and theoretically.

Within the plot of the film, initially no harm ensues. The androids' physical damage is effectively repaired, their memories are erased, and they are subsequently rebooted and put to entertaining use, in a revolving cycle of mechanical reproduction that continues undisturbed—until a real, rather than artificial, girl is actually killed by one of VICE's clients. To the possibility that the VICE resort serves as a cathartic outlet of pent-up violent pathos, the film opens up the alternative hypothesis that the opposite may be true instead: simulated forms of violent games used for realistic entertainment could blur the boundary that divides artificial from real experiences, fiction from reality. This leads to a criminal investigation within the cinematic fiction, which, at one further remove, we aim to pursue in the sphere of theory. There is, in fact, a theoretical conflict, or *agon*, internal to *Vice* that structures not only the entire plot of the film but also our genealogy of violence and the unconscious. And this agon generates a dramatic, affective, as well as theoretical tension between the catharsis and the affective hypothesis that is worthy of a classical play. Its philosophical reach goes from classical antiquity to modernity into the present.

Within the plot of the film, the violence in question is depicted as "most realistic," but as a sf movie *Vice* is obviously not concerned with a nineteenth-century conception of mimetic realism that faithfully represents the real world as it already exists—though the metaphorical parallels with a contemporary, digitized, and violent media environment are numerous and obvious. Nor is the film exemplary in its imitation of a complex action based on the classical Aristotelian principles of aesthetic unities that, as we saw in volume 1, find in *Oedipus Rex* a paradigmatic model—though a reversal of fortune and a tragic recognition continue to be at play. And yet this does not mean that *Vice* is deprived of mimetic, mirroring, and illuminating patho-*logical* reflections that urge new generations of theorists to reflect *on* contagious and affective pathologies that promote violence not only in fiction but also in our "real," though increasingly virtual and digitized, world.

Despite the shift from high culture to low culture, or perhaps because of it, *Vice* continues to serve as an illuminating contemporary case study to diagnose massively diffused forms of entertainment characteristic of the digital age. It also allows us to foreground the affective hypothesis that will occupy us. If the term "vice" is traditionally used to indicate a moralistic, perhaps even religious, condemnation of the type of violent practices that films like *Vice* depict (sex, aggression, rape), the film's title is not without ambivalences. In fact, it also serves as a luring advertisement for transgressive practices that are constitutive of (new) media entertainment in general that tend to have violence and eroticism as a common denominator. At one remove, for spectators, the ambivalence internal to the title *Vice* urges critical reflections that are neither narrowly moralistic nor solely critically detached. Rather, it sets up a mirror to spectators that reveals how we might already be partially complicit with the violence represented. It might also foster a critical logos on the affective potential of the film itself and, by extension, violent films and entertainment more generally, to generate contagious pathologies. There is thus a reflective, patho-*logical* insight nested in the "scene of violence" at play in *Vice*, which, as media theorists have pointed out, is constitutive of the history of cinema tout court.[9] It also provides a starting point for theoretical accounts of the mimetic patho(-)logies that supplement cinematic approaches to violence by theorizing not only visual but also affective, embodied, and immanent experiences of violence with realistic human androids that are meant to reflect (on) the full-immersive, ubiquitous powers of hypermimetic forms of entertainment characteristic of the digital age.

Just like so many sf movies that dramatize fictional second lives in parallel digitized worlds—from *The Matrix* (1999) to *Surrogates* (2009), *Avatar* (2009) to *Her* (2014) to *Black Mirror* (2011–2019)—the VICE resort is a thinly disguised metaphor for human or, as increasing number of scholars prefer to call them, posthuman activities that are now played out vicariously, via mimetic avatars, on different kinds of digital interfaces that have the power to upload all too human "vices" in virtual second lives: from full-immersive computer-generated (CG) 3D films to internet pornography to video games, among other forms of entertainment. In this more general metaphorical sense, then, *Vice* depicts a world of affective immersion and participation in representations of violence that set up an unflattering mirror to the contemporary entertainment industries and, at one remove, to the world that is being entertained.

Despite the progress of civil rights movements and ideology critique in the second half of the twentieth century, violence is still overwhelmingly directed against women and racial/sexual minorities in the twenty-first century—both within films and in social life. Such an ongoing reenactment of misogynistic, sexist, racist, phallocentric, and violent discrimination constitutes what media theorists Cynthia Carter and Kay Weaver call "the wallpaper of everyday life."[10] And this wallpaper is porous. Far from remaining within the confines of representation constitutive of more traditional, less ubiquitous, and ritualized genres like the theater that gave rise to cathartic theory, (new) media violence allows for a more pervasive form of affective participation with the power to infiltrate everyday life. Incipient in the transition from cinema to TV in the consumer culture of 1950s, these interactive forms of participation intensify with the onset of the internet at the dawn of digital culture of the 1990s, and now create a ramified social network of spectacles, but also interactive games, and online practices that are already "entertaining" new generations born in the digital age.

Our cinematic case study is fictional and futuristic in orientation, yet the diagnostic that emerges from *Vice*'s representation of the effects of virtual violence on real violence is nonetheless realistic. Or, better, it dramatizes the contemporary problematic of hyperreal simulations that have the power to retroact on reality to influence mimetic behavior—or hypermimesis. *Vice* holds theoretical interest for it articulates the (hypermimetic) continuities between virtual violence and real violence, the sphere of hyperreal actions (simulations) that are fictional and the sphere of real, bodily reactions (imitation) that are not under the full control of consciousness and belong to an embodied, relational, and immanent unconscious that has mimesis as a via regia (mimetic unconscious). Whether the film's diagnostic is also realistic in its evaluation of the cathartic/contagious powers of hypermimetic violence in the digital age is what we now turn to find out.

## Get It Out of Your System

Despite the German and Italian aspirations of his last name, Detective Tedeschi (meaning German in Italian) may not be a philosophical physician of the caliber of a German thinker like Nietzsche who incidentally made Italy his privileged destination. And yet the diagnostic of the actor who plays this role (Thomas Jane) born in a city notorious for its crime scene and racist violence (Baltimore) may not be deprived of empirical foundations that are in line with Nietzsche's genealogical suspicion of catharsis discussed in volume 1. As Tedeschi starts investigating the crime (murder) that spilled from the VICE resort into the real world, involving the killing of a real rather than "artificial" girl, he enters the world of violent simulations for an undercover investigation that leads us rather quickly to the theoretical agon we have been tracking from the beginning. Having now reached the middle, we can reevaluate it to the end.

If we replay a scene where Tedeschi walks up to the owner of the resort, Julian Michaels (Bruce Willis), who introduced us to this dystopian resort with "no laws and no consequences," our genealogy of violence and the unconscious puts us in a position to know why the detective's initial diagnostic sounds familiar, simple, and persuasive. He says: "You'd think that if people could commit any crime they could think of, they'd get it out of their system." We now know the reasons of this hypothesis's "intuitive appeal"[11]: from its obscure origins in Aristotle's *Poetics* to its medical recuperation by Viennese philologists (Bernays) and philological physicians (Freud and Breuer) to the mass phenomenon of Hollywood blockbusters that went global since at least the 1950s, the catharsis hypothesis has, indeed, come a long way. Thanks to the success of psychoanalysis in the twentieth century and its dissemination by the cultural industries, the idea that an affective or bodily participation in violent acts tied to sex and murder—be it real or imaginary, represented, or reenacted[12]—may have a purgative effect that evacuates the affective pathology from one's system has infiltrated the globalized postwar culture. True or false, the catharsis hypothesis is thus constitutive of the twentieth and twenty-first centuries' collective cinematic imaginary, and is, nolens volens, part of what people would normally think—at least in the twentieth century.

And yet, even such industries know better in the twenty-first century. They have, in fact, more up-to-date diagnostics to offer millennials who were welcomed, from birth onward, into the age of the Internet of Things. Thus, Tedeschi immediately complicates the diagnostic via an alternative possibility that we have already encountered, and to which we now set out to give genealogical substance. He continues, "But these people get a taste [of violence], and they just can't get enough." The diagnostic could not be more direct; the paradigm shift to think about violence and the unconscious could not be clearer. The cathartic therapy does not work in this cinematic fiction. It is unattained, and thus neither consoling nor redeeming. It is certainly not therapeutic. Tedeschi offers, instead, an inversed hypothesis that does not rest on the theoretically elusive concept of catharsis but on a deeply felt pathos against the dangers of contagion:

> People go in there and get to freak out and do . . . whatever they do, and then they keep going in there, and then they keep going in there, and then . . . they bring that shit out in the real world. It feels normal to them, you know?

To put it in more clinically detached, less hysterical and vulgar, and more specific terms, we could translate the diagnostic as follows: repeated engagement in violent forms of entertainment online that require a form of active participation, such as in video games, may not generate cathartic effects after all. Rather, they have, in specific social circumstances we shall have to investigate, the potential to trigger an addictive compulsion to repeat violent actions that are entertaining in games, yet do not remain confined within the hyperreal sphere of simulation. On the contrary, having been normalized via addictive repetitions online, these simulations can potentially bleed into the "real" yet increasingly digitized world via hypermimetic feedback loops that deserve new diagnostic investigations. Of course, the detective's diagnostic concerns fictional characters who partake in VICE (the resort); yet, at one remove, he is also addressing viewers of *Vice* (the film). Let us take the diagnostic closer to home.

Our cinematic case study suggests that when it comes to representations of violence, the line dividing the fictional from the real world, visual entertainment to embodied practices, is thin and porous at best. It is also clear that these representations of violence no longer follow the laws of purgation of the same by the same based on what used to be a homeopathic, therapeutic, and cathartic principle. On the contrary, what VICE/*Vice* (the resort for clients and, at one remove, the movie for viewers) reveals is a propagation of the same by the same based on a pathological, addictive, and contagious principle. What this principle indicates is an escalating, spiraling, and hyper-mimetic dynamic that blurs the line between fiction and reality in a way that is at least double. First, within the diegesis, violence is not formally contained within the resort, but transgresses the boundary between artificial and real experiences—hence the murder of an "artificial" girl turns into a murder of a real girl. And second, at the extra-diegetic level of the network society the film *Vice* alludes to, it illustrates how violent artificial experiences online may affect behavioral attitudes that have real consequences—hence exposure to media violence generates a "taste" for real violence. In sum, physical and affective participation in violence in the world of *Vice*, now understood at all its levels (i.e., the resort, the film, the virtual world it represents, and the violence that spills into the real world), does not get violence out of people's system. On the contrary, it generates an addictive, normalizing, involuntary, and in this sense *un*-conscious "taste" for more violence instead in a media-contaminated, violence-addicted, population that, eventually, "just can't get enough."

The diagnostic is not flattering, yet this does not mean that it is false. Philosophical physicians working with more traditional media had, in fact, already called attention to the contagious tendencies lurking behind the birth of aesthetic entertainment. The drives at play in *Vice* are not only representative of violent forms of entertainment in the digital age; they also tie this age back to a much longer genealogy in western thought we shall have to convoke. This tradition suggests that to witness fictional representations of violence and suffering is a source of aesthetic pleasure. Better still: perhaps this accursed share is even at the origins of aesthetic pleasure.

## Birth of Entertainment: Out of Violent Pathos

The playful analogies between Detective Tedeschi and the German philosopher who serves as our genealogical mediator between the ancients, the moderns, and the contemporaries in matters of catharsis and contagion is not deprived of a serious genealogical point. Nietzsche, in fact, goes as far as positing low violent drives at the origins of "high culture" itself. Starting in *The Birth of Tragedy* (1872), he controversially suggests that the source of that noble genre par excellence, which is Greek tragedy, lies in what he calls "the tremendous phenomenon of the Dionysian" (1; 18): namely, a "physiological" ritual phenomenon that, Nietzsche specifies, is encountered "epidemically" in its "barbarian" (from Greek *bárbaros*, non-Greek) form (2; 39), is animated by what he calls a "horrible mixture of sensuality and cruelty" (2; 39), and finds, in the ritual "dismemberment" (*sparagmos*) of the god, its most violent ritual manifestation. There is, then, an embodied (Dionysian) ritual at the source of suffering (pathos), which the Greeks mediated via the filter of (Apollonian) representation on the stage. Nietzsche would have been well-positioned to know that for a classical philological tradition that goes back to Herodotus, Dionysus's *sparagmos* was considered the "god's secret *pathos*."[13] This is why Nietzsche, going against an idealist/moral tradition in philosophy, controversially argues that "cruelty is one of the oldest festive joys of mankind," a violent joy that is first enacted in sacrificial rituals and is then represented in aesthetic "spectacles of cruelty."[14] These spectacles occupy a privileged place in western aesthetics. They were in fact dramatized in myths, epics, and in that violent genre par excellence that, to this day, continues to serve as a source of inspiration for cathartic/contagious theories: namely, Greek tragedy.

A genealogy of violence and the unconscious, then, bring us back to the classical genre from which the catharsis hypothesis originated; but this time the scale is clearly tilted in favor of an affective hypothesis. From the origins of his career onward, Nietzsche is in fact concerned with the shift from physical violence to aesthetic violence, from a Dionysian mimesis based on ritual "intoxication" to Apollonian mimesis based on visual "images." Still, in a mirroring inversion, the continuities cut both ways and can equally flow beyond visual representations to reach embodied realities. Thus, later, in *On Genealogy of Morals* (1887), Nietzsche is more specific in his diagnostic, this time not of "barbarian" but of highly "civilized" moral and aesthetic values. In order to support his hypothesis that "pleasure in cruelty need not have died out," he gives the classical example of "tragic sympathy" (II, 7: 49), which, as we have seen, is at the foundation of Aristotle's cathartic hypothesis.[15]

Contra Aristotle, and in an unflattering evaluation of an all too human taste for violence that goes from Apollonian (aesthetic) distance back to Dionysian (ritual) pathos, Nietzsche now specifies:

> To witness suffering does one good, to inflict it even more so [*Leiden-sehen tut wohl, Leiden-machen noch wohler*]—that is a harsh proposition, but a fundamental one, an old, powerful, human all-too-human proposition, one to which perhaps even the apes would subscribe (II, 6: 48).

Perhaps apes would subscribe. After all, the continuities between ape brains and human brains are rooted in our evolutionary nature and are known to concern violent behavior, as well, as primatologists like Jane Goodall confirmed.[16] Sf films such as *The Planet of the Apes* sequel dramatically amplified this point via a nonrealistic genre. But in all fairness to apes, in the natural world their cruelty is not considered deliberate, does not come anywhere near the genocidal practices of humans, and, above all, does not turn into ritualized aesthetic spectacles with the potential to amplify mimetic tendencies. What Nietzsche calls the "pleasure of *cruelty*" and "unspeakable happiness at *the sight of torment*" is an all too human reality manifest in the centrality of violence in aesthetic fictions.[17]

Nietzsche is not alone in his diagnostic. Along similar lines, but with a clearer focus on the type of sexualized violence dramatized in our cinematic case study, Georges Bataille ties eroticism and violence in a gordian knot as he claims that "in essence the domain of eroticism is the domain of violence, of violation."[18] Both erotic and violent experiences, in Bataille's view, are Dionysian experiences that trouble the boundaries of individuation, introducing mimetic continuities at the heart of discontinuities. These transgressions also generate paradoxical movements of "attraction and repulsion" that are constitutive of sacrificial rituals and, Bataille crucially adds—via Hegel but with Nietzsche in mind as well—constitute the "primary theme [*thème premier*] of *representation* (of art, festivals, spectacles)."[19] Prior to Girard, and furthering Nietzsche, Bataille already establishes a continuity between the violence of sacred experiences and the violence at play in aesthetic experiences, sacrificial rituals and aesthetic representations.

And yet Bataille does not propose a catharsis hypothesis structured around an Oedipal triangle. Instead, he furthers a mimetic hypothesis that oscillates, pendulum-like, between attraction and repulsion, proximity to pathos and visual distance. As noted, after the shift from mimetic desire to *mimetic pathos*, the double movement of *pathos of distance* is the second distinguishing conceptual feature of our theory of homo mimeticus. As for Nietzsche before him, but from a distinctly anthropological perspective, for Bataille, in fact, religious rituals that culminate in the killing of a sacrificial victim give birth to aesthetic rituals. More precisely, the violence at play in aesthetic representations like Greek tragedies for the ancients and, more recently, novels for the moderns, rest on spectators' mimetic identification with the victim that attracts viewers/readers toward the pathos of death—while allowing them to remain at a distance, on the side of life. Thus, Bataille specifies the source of the horror and fascination at play in Greek tragedy by saying: "It is a question, at least in tragedy, of identifying with whatever character who dies, and to believe that we die with him [or her], while remaining alive" (HMS 337). Identification with the tragic hero is here not geared toward the catharsis of pity and fear that can be put to therapeutic or social use. On the contrary, the "subterfuge" of tragic spectacles generates an intensification of pathos constitutive of a sacred fascination for the horror of death, a "sacred horror" humans mediate from a representational distance characteristic of what Bataille calls "classical subterfuges, spectacles or books, to which the multitude recurs" (337).

Clearly, what Bataille says of the identification with the sacrificial violence at play in ancient and modern representations—from tragedies to novels—in the past is even more visible in the representations of violence in the present. The popular success of cinematic genres like horror movies and slasher movies in the past century, and now the transfer of violent and erotic matters to the digital via action role-playing video games, does little to disprove the excessive reality of what Bataille called our "accursed share" (*part maudite*). If Bataille coined this concept to account for an "excessive force translated in the effervescence of life" via experiences of expenditure at play in sacred festivities, eroticism, sacrifice, and artistic representations thereof,[20] new media put the nonproductive (or heterogeneous) side of this general economy to restricted (or homogeneous) capitalist use. These new genres and media are in fact specifically devoted to representing the violence of sacrifice in view of intensifying the visceral movements of "attraction and repulsion" to the point of horror,[21] allowing for a degree of proximity to the pathos of death, while retaining the safe distance characteristic of entertainment. Violence is thus not only sacred but profane; not only internal to sacrificial (ritual) experiences but above all to inner (aesthetic) experiences. And since aesthetic spectacles are doubly safe in the sense that neither the tragic hero(ine) nor the spectator actually die, Bataille exclaims in an ironic inversion of genres: "But it's a comedy!"

Contemporary spectacles of death can indeed be comic and entertaining in the sense that protagonists can be far from being high and noble but can be low and base instead, thereby conforming to a defining Aristotelian characteristic of comedy. They are certainly entertaining given the massive success of (new) media and genres that rely on violence to capture the audience from early age: from cartoons to horror movies, slasher movies to video games. Still, in the digital age a fundamental doubt remains: are these spectacles of violence really contained within the spectacle, or subterfuge, of representation—as Bataille suggests? Or is a supplementary inversion of perspective also in order—as Nietzsche indicates?

Notice that, like Girard after him, Bataille is attentive to the sacrificial origins of aesthetic representations of violence that lead from sacred violence to aesthetic violence; but, again like Girard, he is less attentive to the mirroring countermovement that leads violent representations to have a contagious effect on spectators' behavior. Perhaps because in the essay in question, his focus was more on Hegel's fascination with death than on Nietzsche's diagnostic of contagious intoxication; or perhaps because Bataille still lived in an age in which spectacles had not yet pushed representations of violence to extremes via new media and genres specifically geared toward reinforcing an identification not so much with the tragic victim of violence, or *sacrifié*, but with the perpetrator of violence, or *sacrifiant*—think of action/war movies and, especially, video games; or perhaps for other heterogeneous reasons. In any case, Bataille left this path unexplored. And yet this does not mean that his general account of "mimetic communication" that relies on the power of identification to blur the boundaries between self and others, fictional violence and sacrificial violence, should not be explored further via the angle of new yet no less contagious media under the lens of new mimetic studies.[22]

A film like *Vice* encourages us to pursue this path. In fact, it does not take ritual violence but digital violence as a starting point of critical reflections on the effects of the latter on spectators. In the process, it not only confirms a diagnostic of human violence that a Nietzschean genealogy considers "old" and "fundamental"; it also adds a theoretical supplement to our genealogy of violence and the unconscious that cuts both ways: on one side, it indicates that the type of sexual/murderous violence at play in the film does not rest on the tragic laws of mimetic representations that elicit pity and fear with cathartic, purifying, and therapeutic effects—a hypothesis we already saw Nietzsche critique. Rather, it follows the laws of mimetic contagion that illustrate violent, pathological influences that reach beyond representation to influence human behavior—a view we will see Nietzsche promote.

But the diagnostic of *Vice* cuts even deeper as it links representations of violence and violent actions, fiction and reality, the screen and the brain. It thus brings evaluations of the effects of (new) media violence up to date with contemporary preoccupations with the performative powers of increasingly aggressive, eroticized, and murder-oriented digital representations and simulations. While empirical studies have noticed that erotic films can actually generate more aggressive behavior than violent films,[23] a Bataillean perspective also warns us that the entanglement between erotic and violent drives might not be easy to disentangle in an eroticized/violent media environment that rests on both drives (see figure 4). Since both sexual and aggressive arousal are tied to sadistic imaginary pleasures, it should follow that films that join violence and eroticism are likely to amplify a taste for violence in the real world—though this correlation continues to arise controversies we shall return to.

For the moment, suffice to say that the drives at play in *Vice* are representative of violent forms of entertainment in the digital age; they also tie this age to a much longer genealogy in western thought that we are beginning to uncover. This genealogy of contagion suggests that to witness fictional representations of violence and suffering not only does one good; it might also generate the desire to inflict suffering in real life. Simulations, in other words, may not be narrowly mimetic (realistic) from an aesthetic point of view, yet they have the potential to promote mimetic (contagious) effects from a behavioral perspective.

Welcome to hypermimesis!

## Hypermimesis

This porous interplay between fiction and reality, virtual images and bodily actions, violence seen and violence felt, should give future-oriented mimetic theorists pause. In fact, it suggests that we are no longer confined within the sphere of mimesis understood as "representation of reality," which, as Erich Auerbach famously suggests, is characteristic of western aesthetics, from Homer to modernism.[24] Nor have we entered a "hyperreal" world of postmodern "simulation" that, as Jean Baudrillard announces, "is no longer based on imitation" for it generates "models of a real without origins or reality."[25] Both realism and hyperreality remain of course part of our heterogeneous media. Still, they are no longer sufficient to account for the disconcerting interplay between hyperreal simulations that have nothing to do with realistic representation; if only because they have the power to retroact on reality to generate mimetic or, better, hypermimetic effects.

The theoretical principle that emerges from our cinematic case study captures the spiraling dynamic of hypermimesis that should be a central concern for new mimetic studies in the twenty-first century. It suggests that the sphere of virtual simulation (or hyperreal) linked to fictional and virtual scenes of violence is never fully disconnected from the material reality of the body; if hypermimesis stretches the logic of imitation to the extreme, it is far from engendering the "liquidation of all referents," as Baudrillard postmodern interpretation suggests.[26] Quite the contrary, having distorted like a surreal mirror the real world, but never having fully abandoned its relation to referents, hyperreal simulations are endowed with a hypermimetic supplement that has the power to retroact, via a spiraling feedback loop, on the material world, generating all too real effects with a vengeance.

If the mirror of (new) media violence has performative properties that may cause imaginary identifications, or aha jubilations, at the level of the child's development or ontogenesis, it does not conform to a mirror stage restricted to the formation of a pre-Oedipal I. In fact, exposure to violence in the sphere of fiction for adults does not lead to imaginary formative experiences predicated on an Oedipal unconscious that originates in western tragedies and culminates in the flickering signifying jouissance of a neon Coca-Cola ad in Baltimore—as Jacques Lacan suggested in a scene we shall return to. More realistically, our Baltimore detective suggests that the mirror of (new) media is likely to foment embodied and material addictions that lead to a taste for violence with the potential to induce tragedies in social life instead—as routinely exemplified by episodes of police violence in the United States. Hence again, as simulated actions on the screen contribute to triggering violent reactions in the world, fictions risk becoming realities, artificially simulated tastes risk becoming real hypermimetic tastes—and, to echo the detective, we simply "can't get enough."

To be sure, *Vice* may not be a film that will be remembered in the history of cinema for its exemplary imitation of a carefully crafted, complex, and original action (or *muthos*). Film scholars will easily recognize that it does not escape more traditional laws of mimesis, if only because it is largely based on adaptations of previous sf films, most notably Michael Crichton's *Westworld* (1973). Yet this does not mean that it is deprived of a certain diagnostic logos on the circulation of violent pathos in the age of the Net. It is perhaps not accidental that this myth of a violent frontier world has recently been reloaded as a TV series with the same unoriginal title, *Westworld* (2016–2022, created by Lisa Joy and Jonathan Nolan), a return symptomatic of a pathology that is far from cathartically cured.

While *Westworld* (both the original film and the TV series) dramatizes guests' participation in fictional, cinematic genres such as the western that allow the unleashing of violent actions that go from murder to rape, *Vice* dramatizes a world of virtual fantasies characteristic of the Net. In both fictional worlds, the line between reality and fiction progressively blurs and, within the diegesis, real (rather than artificial) characters are killed. Tellingly, the degree of sexual and physical violence intensifies as we move from the cinematic world of *Westworld* to the TV series to the internet-based world of *Vice*—a symptom, perhaps, of humans' increasing addiction to violence whereby increasingly heavier doses are needed to feel its pathos. What seems certain, among other things, is that this patho-*logy* describes tastes with the power to spill from the virtual into the real world along lines that are not based on a billiard-ball causal logic and are neither narrowly realistic nor abstractly hyperreal. Rather, they are representative of real, hypermimetic symptoms unpredictably triggered by violent fictional worlds.

Hypermimesis, then, designates a world in which the distinction between fiction and reality, virtual effects and material effects, no longer holds. In a spiraling recoil, hyperreal simulations that are far removed from reality fold back via new media into the material world, giving form to "realities" that may have originally appeared in fictional representations, yet can also be reproduced by bodily actions and reactions with the potential to inject more violence in the immanence of daily life. Neither only fictional nor solely real but born out of the dynamic interplay between fiction and reality, hypermimesis is currently transforming humans' highly plastic and adaptable tastes, generating contagious pathologies with the power to spread virally. Thus, *Vice*'s Baltimore-born Detective Tedeschi suggests that a repetition of a violent action in the virtual world can involuntarily, and thus unconsciously, turn into a "taste" for violence in the real world.

Is it accidental that Brian Miller chose Thomas Jane, an actor born in Baltimore, to play the role of the detective for this film? Perhaps. As you will recall from volume 1, this is the city that hosted the famous Structuralist Controversy conference in 1966 that disseminated poststructuralist ideas about the arbitrariness of the sign that applied to mimesis as well. This is, of course, a coincidence. Tedeschi is not French and lacks the profile of a high theorist. But when it comes to the problematic of violence and the unconscious, a city like Baltimore is not entirely arbitrary for it points to a referential reality as well. As a popular TV series like *The Wire* (2002–2008, created by David Simon) dramatized, Baltimore is a gritty, highly segregated, and violent city plagued by criminal activities like drug-dealing, gun-related violence, and, last but not least, police corruption and violent forms of racial discrimination that often go as far as murder. This type of violence does not tend to remain confined within popular series like *The Wire* to be enjoyed from a safe representational distance. Without being naively realistic, this violence has a referent in the real pathos of everyday life. Police violence against minority groups is a case in point. For instance, as the police murder of Freddie Gray in Baltimore made visible in 2015 what had always been clear to African Americans and other ethnic minorities: namely, that racist structures have remained firmly in place, inflicting physical violence in reality for a significant part of the African American population in horrifying ways I shall return to.

Moreover, the powers of TV series now go beyond representation for they can generate performative hypermimetic effects in which fictions, including violent political fictions, can serve as models to mimic in an increasingly mediatized political reality. As more recent political-thriller TV series like *House of Cards* (2013–2018, created by Beau Willimon and fictionally set in Washington, DC, but shot in Baltimore) have indicated, fictional political shows have the power not only to anticipate violent political realities; they perhaps also served as models for apprentice presidents in search of examples to imitate in order to turn the political itself into a fiction not deprived of violent effects. Aggressive TV shows, I argued elsewhere, paved the way for the politics of violence in 2016 as the host of a reality *show* titled *The Apprentice* (2004–2017) put the hypermimetic powers of a mimetic actor to use and abuse.[27] The paradox of being nothing and wanting to possess everything was indeed at play for the whole world to see as the elected (apprentice) president and leader of the Free World turned politics itself into a TV *reality* show.

Following up on this hypermimetic line of inquiry via the case of *House of Cards*, which was aired prior to Donald Trump's election in 2016, one cannot help but notice that the analogies between Frank Underwood (played by Kevin Spacey) and Donald Trump's corrupt ascension to power are numerous and striking. The spectacular lies, endemic corruption, sexual scandals, manipulation of media, cast of the First Lady, and ruthless ambition for power and domination that drives *House of Cards* were on full display in the *White House* itself during the entire 2016–2020 Trump presidency, generating an ongoing reality TV show that rendered the fictional series somewhat obsolete. Given that Trump was himself the host of a reality TV show and given his habits of media consumption, it is perhaps not unlikely that *House of Cards* served as a model for the apprentice president to imitate in an abysmal presidential reality. Conversely, the blurring of fiction and reality took place on the front of fiction as well. In 2017, as *House of Cards* was still ongoing, Kevin Spacey, whose fictional crimes as Frank Underwood go unpunished in fiction, was accused of sexual assault in reality, leading to his dismissal from the series the same year. Interestingly, in 2018 Spacey starred in a YouTube video titled "Let Me Be Frank" in which, under the mask of Frank, he blends his fictional role with the real accusations of sexual assault in order to implicate the audience in the pleasure they took in his (fictional/real?) crimes. Not leaving spectators off the hook, he says, breaking the fourth wall not unlike Willis in *Vice*: "And you loved it!"[28]—driving this hypermimetic point home. On both sides of the political/fictional divide (which is no longer one), it is difficult to find a clearer manifestation of the powers of hypermimesis.

Now, to give further substance to the performative powers of hypermimesis, let me turn to some tragic examples from the city of Baltimore to start foregrounding what should be obvious in the twenty-first century: namely that Black lives matter.

## Black Lives Matter: Tragic Examples

The mirroring parallels between reality *shows* and *reality* shows begs the question: how can fictions become a reality? Does the fiction serve as a model for reality to simply imitate? Or, rather, does reality "itself" already operate on the mode of fiction? And if both principles are already at play, does this dynamic interplay between reality and shows apply to the problematic of (new) media violence as well? What is certain is that TV reality shows are symptomatic of a hypermimetic spiraling feedback loop between shows and reality that blurs the line between the copy and the model, fictional representations and material referents, and is still in need of theorization. They point to a transgressive excess of violent mimesis, or hypermimesis, that far exceeds structuralist concerns with the subject of the linguistic signifier at play during the linguistic turn, generating unconscious principles with the potential to trigger murders in the city central to the mimetic turn.

While each country inflects the problematic of (new) media violence differently depending on specific social, cultural, political, economic, and juridical norms, including, of course, the crucial issue of gun regulations, the United States stands out on the issue of gun-related violence for both its lack of regulations and the number of deaths that ensue from guns ready at hand. It is thus crucial to realize that a gun is not a passive object in the hand of a subject. On the contrary, it urges us to reconsider agency across the subject/object, human/nonhuman divide. As Bruno Latour has argued, guns are not simply objects to be manipulated by volitional human subjects in full agentic control; rather, they are endowed with an agentic power of their own, which he groups under the category of "actant." Actants are part of a network of "technical mediation" whose effect is to distribute agency beyond the human/nonhuman divide.[29] As numerous social theorists have long noted, gun-related violence is not only on the rise in the United States but is so endemic that it is considered a public health issue comparable to

an epidemic infection.³⁰ Given the qualitative and interpretative rather than
quantitative orientation of this study, let me supplement the diagnostic with
some specific case studies that can help bring the hypermimetic dynamic of
technical mediation internal to this epidemic via some examples closer to
home.

Popular "wisdom" on the conservative front defensive of rights to bear
arms might object: it is only an example. But in philosophy, examples should
not be dismissed as merely singular, nonrepresentative, or anecdotal cases.
On the contrary, examples are representative while retaining the specificity
of their singularity. In this sense, they hold a paradoxical logical status that
is not unrelated to mimesis. In fact, both examples and mimesis open up an
in-between intellectual space to articulate the relation between sameness and
difference or, if you prefer more traditional categories, the universal and the
particular. As Giorgio Agamben puts it, the "force" of the example stems
from being "a singularity among others, which stands for all of them and
is valid for all . . . Neither universal nor particular, the example is a singular
object that, so to speak, shows its singularity [*mostra la sua singolarità*]."³¹
And this singularity (uniqueness but also strangeness) opens up a space in
between the logic of the same (the universal) and the logic of difference
(the particular). In this sense, examples may initially not appear central to
a problem, for they stand by—*Bei-spiel*, Agamben notes, plays (*spiel*) on the
side (*bei*). And yet, as the examples we have already encountered confirm,
by playing on the side, so to speak, they have the power to bring a plurality
of other cases to the center of attention. Examples of violence that are as
theoretical as they are practical make clear that gun-related violence is deeply
entangled with (new) media violence. They also reveal a banality of violence
that has become all too common in the United States and shows how an
inability to think violence can be triggered by mimetic reflexes that emerge
from the complex interplay of (new) media representations on the one hand,
and a plurality of contextual material factors on the other. As we will see, the
agentic powers of guns do not operate on cathartic principles but trigger a
contagious hypermimetic dynamic instead.

Linguistic theories found in the 1966 Structuralist Controversy conference a privileged locus of dissemination in a city that, fifty years later, is
still notorious for racist violence. I thus step back to this mythic scene of

theoretical origins in Baltimore to leap ahead to alternative lines of theorization that go beyond structural/linguistic models. My goal is to account for patho(-)logical examples of hypermimetic violence relevant for new mimetic studies today.

## From Jouissance to Black Lives Matter

Baltimore 1966/2015. As we have seen in volume 1, there were many illustrious contributors who attended the Structuralist Controversy conference organized at Johns Hopkins University in 1966. Still, with respect to the problematic of the unconscious, one name stood out from the program. In his contribution to the symposium, French psychoanalyst Jacques Lacan took the stage to reiterate a linguistic conception of the unconscious that may have been in line with Freud in theory but was more directly aligned with structuralist concerns with the arbitrariness of the sign in genealogical practice. The focus was, in fact, on a linguistic subject of the signifier driven by lack, or a *manque à être*, whose unconscious desires were far removed from embodied realities and closer to linguistic theories. As Lacan famously proclaimed, in a phrase that was much echoed in the (post)structuralist era, the unconscious is "structured as a language."[32]

The phrase was known in Paris but less so in Baltimore. A repetition was de rigueur. Thus, reiterating his structuralist position by claiming that structure and language are "the same thing," while inscribing it in a repressive hypothesis whereby thoughts are "barred from consciousness," Lacan took the stage to clarify his theory of the unconscious to his Baltimore audience. As he put it, the "unconscious has nothing to do with instinct or primitive knowledge" because, he specified, "words are the only material of the unconscious" or "words . . . are the object through which one seeks for a way to handle the unconscious."[33] To be sure, this structuralist focus on interpretation of words is still indebted to Freud's "talking cure" predicated on the cathartic method. But for Lacan it also leads to a linguistic conception of the subject of jouissance. And as philosophical commentators like Mikkel Borch-Jacobsen and Philippe Lacoue-Labarthe have convincingly shown,[34] this subject owes much to the violent struggles for recognition and pure prestige internal to the Hegelian/Kojèvian account of the master-slave dialectic that was dominant in the 1960s and will later inform Girard's theory of mimetic desire as well.

With some historical distance, then, we cannot misrecognize Lacan's use of mimetic tactics in line with more materialistic and everyday conceptions of the unconscious. In fact, Lacan proceeds to inscribe the tragic pathos of jouissance in a structural polarity that oscillates from "birth to death" and entails both "pain and pleasure"—affects that, as we have seen, have a long genealogy in cathartic theories based in ancient tragedies. Yet Lacan also reassures his disoriented American audience with a local, contemporary analogy supposed to bring the logic of unconscious desires closer to home. Comparing the *sujet de la jouissance* to a linguistic sign he saw in the streets of Baltimore, Lacan concluded his talk with a personal observation: "When I came here this evening I saw on the little neon sign the motto 'Enjoy Coca-Cola.'"[35] This is, of course, a particular example. Still, it displays a theory of desire with universal ambitions. And what we see is that the detour via the linguistic abstractions of the subject of the signifier driven by an ontological lack brought Lacan back in touch with the down-to-earth reality of the subject of desire driven by a neoliberal-induced consumer-oriented lack. What Lacan saw on the way to the conference was a flickering Coca-Cola neon sign, appearing and disappearing. What he misrecognized was a mirroring reflection of a linguistic truth, or *alētheia*, high above, designed to induce mimetic desires available to all in a capitalist culture driven by materialistic dreams in abstract theory. What he failed to see is that such dreams are not really enjoyable in a segregated, racist, and materially deprived social reality in the streets of Baltimore in daily practices—which leads me to mirror the scene and inverse perspectives via an equally personal yet rather different experience.

Fast-forward fifty years later. From 2013 to 2016 I held an appointment as a visiting scholar at Johns Hopkins University in Baltimore. My host institution was the legendary Humanities Center that hosted the 1966 conference and changed the landscape of critical theory during the linguistic turn. Neon Coca-Cola signs were still in sight but, not unlike the poststructuralist theory of the unconscious that accounted for it, they had somewhat lost their glamour. Segregation, racism, poverty, crime, and the violence that shadows them were, in fact, way more visible and tangible in the streets of Baltimore. To be honest, they made a stronger impression than capitalist

signs above; or, rather, they revealed the illusory nature of those signs. I was
in touch with the reality below on a daily basis, cycling back and forth from
the carefully trimmed lawns of Johns Hopkins's Homewood campus to the
less privileged, segregated areas on the north/west side of Baltimore where
we lived—namely, areas that are less abstract and ideal in orientation, yet
effectively provided more immanent and referential, less imaginary, and
more realistic sources of inspiration for an alternative theory of mimesis I
was already developing at the time.

It is perhaps no accident that this theory of homo mimeticus had the
general concept of pathos rather than the restricted focus on desire as a main
entry. It also recognized the role of both "mimetic sexism" and "mimetic
racism" in the propagation of a type of violence that is often unconsciously
projected onto subordinate others, yet as a number of modernist writers
already showed is constitutive of the dominant self.[36] Now, furthering this
genealogy of the unconscious from a down-to-earth yet no less theoretical
perspective attentive to the embodied dynamic of violence in the present,
I suggest a change of examples to better mirror a type of violence that has
been neglected in the sphere of high theory yet never left the streets of social
practices. The latter encourage us to replace, pace Lacan, the symbol of
Coca-Cola's jouissance and the linguistic/capitalist desires it metonymically
signifies, with the reality of Freddie Gray's pathos and the embodied/racist
violence it represents.

Freddie Gray, a twenty-five-year-old African American man, was arrested
by the Baltimore Police Department on April 12, 2015, and belatedly charged
for possession of a pocketknife. Gray died on April 21 due to "injuries to his
spinal cord" inflicted by the officers during the arrest.[37] If neon signs can be
replaced in an endless chain of signifiers to be posted on restaurant chains,
what the example of Gray shows is that a Black human life is an irreplaceable
singularity that nonetheless expresses a widely pervasive, violent, and racist
pathology. The name Freddie Gray, not unlike Eric Garner, Breonna Taylor,
Atatiana Jefferson, Rayshard Brooks, George Floyd, and so many others
too numerous to mention, is not only metonymic of countless murders of
African Americans at the hands of police in a racist reality; police violence is
equally reproduced in reality TV shows like *Cops* (1989–2020) that disproportionally target African Americans, Latinos, and other ethnic minorities
in terms that are both mimetic and hypermimetic. Such shows, in fact, not

only represent a violent racist reality that plagues American culture, racial minorities in general, and African Americans in particular (mimesis); they also serve as models for violent racist practices to be reproduced by cops in reality, leading to the spiraling perpetuation of additional murders (hypermimesis).

While direct causation is difficult, or rather, impossible to prove empirically, examples can reveal that the link between racist TV shows and racially based crimes may not be altogether arbitrary. Having run for over three decades, *Cops* was finally canceled a few days after cop Derek Chauvin killed George Floyd on May 25, 2020. Floyd was arrested for having used a twenty-dollar counterfeit bill. Chauvin held his knee over Floyd's neck for over eight minutes, irresponsive to the latter's plea, "I can't breathe," uttered more than twenty times.[38] The murder was captured on camera and went viral, exemplifying double patho(-)logical effects. On the side of pathology, Floyd's brutal murder reveals yet again a racist epidemic of violence that is far from new, for it is structurally endemic to the United States and is present in European countries as well, most visibly contra undocumented immigrants but not only. The killing of Floyd stood out for being filmed on video, capturing a murderous racist violence that is pervasive in the world of TV shows; yet it also brought the real pathos of death to bear on a singular living person in reality. The cancellation of *Cops* was thus not arbitrary. It was a belated, long overdue, and radically insufficient response to the realization that an uneasy hypermimetic correlation exists between TV realty shows and real police murders that continue to plague racist cultures. And yet, at the same time, and without contraction, the pathology of racist violence generated a shared sympathy (*sym-pathos*, feeling with) that also spread hypermimetically as BLM movements joined forces across racial, cultural, and national borders to counter racist violence in the United States and across the world.[39] This is an affirmative illustration that violent pathologies may not generate cathartic cures yet can give rise by a positive contagion to therapeutic patho-*logies*. That is, anti-racist patho-*logies* that rely on the interplay of shared pathos and critical logos that, thanks to new media, spread hypermimetically, generating sympathetic responses at a distance.

True, the cases of Freddie Gray and George Floyd are singular examples of pathologies of racist violence with a high potential to bleed from fiction to reality; yet they also encourage a more general reflection on the patho(-)

logies of violence that go beyond linguistic models in order to address hyper-mimetic phenomena that, for better and worse, generate mimetic pathos (suffering but also sympathy) in real life. In the process, as it crosses the line between fiction and reality, the shared pathos of racist violence manifests an unconscious dynamic that is not merely linguistic and based on the interpre-tation of words barred from consciousness. Rather, it is based in the bodily mimetic instincts that Lacan, not unlike Freud before him, foreclosed from his psychoanalytic theory,[40] yet find in "primitive" (from Latin *primus*, "that come first") yet complex affective reactions that affect all subjects a danger-ous but not deterministic trigger to violent actions in social life.

While there is widespread agreement in the condemnation of such hor-rors, it has not been sufficiently stressed that many of these police murders are not only indicative of a structuralist racism that plagues U.S. culture in general and is mediated by a racist ideology that infects the police system in particular. They are also likely to be triggered by reflex bodily reactions that are operative on an immediate, automatic, and unconscious level most visibly at play in childhood yet continuing to be displayed in adults as well—most tragically as police officers pull the trigger based on models of unconscious aggression that might have been seen in fiction yet have all too real mur-derous effects. For the moment let us zoom in on this type of reflexes via one additional example that considers the complex interplay between (new) media violence, gun mediation, and unconscious hypermimetic triggers.

### Hypermimetic Triggers

Baltimore 2016. It is one year after the killing of Freddie Gray. Picture an immigrant family with two small children, one attending a local public school in West Baltimore. The family is racially mixed and so is their cultural location, in the sense that they live in a small and predominantly (white) segregated neighborhood and send their five-year-old son to a (Black) segre-gated local public school—just across the segregating road.

Coca-Cola ads are not a particular source of jouissance as the father walks his son to school in the morning—for the joy is in the short walk itself, the narrow shortcut between overgrown hedges, fresh air hitting their sleepy faces, wet leaves bending to caress their cheeks. Still, the stark contrast between the upper-middle-class white households and the public school on the African American side of the street brings to mind what had happened to Freddie Gray, just a year earlier. While holding his son's hand and passing the house of the only other racially mixed couple they know in the neighborhood, dad is juggling conflicted thoughts. Segregation still plagues this city. *The Wire* is not so far from reality, after all, and the material effects of racism show through the cracks. The cracks of the decaying school are worrisome enough, but even deeper, more worrisome, is the spirit of demoralization many who came to the United States as adults feel viscerally after a few months in the country—Coca-Cola signs notwithstanding. Lacan didn't stay long enough to feel this pathos, he thinks. Or maybe the French psychoanalyst didn't venture far enough from his hotel where, as the legend goes, he was busy making phone calls back to Paris the conference organizers would have a hard time to pay. Who knows?

As the father and son approach their destination and wait at a streetlight to cross the street, the irony of the school's name (Thomas Jefferson School) to designate a segregated public school in the twenty-first century, hits harder than usual that morning. Other thoughts start to bubble up too. Was it wise for the father to disregard his university colleagues' surely well-meant advice to sign up for a private school? True, these are the same colleagues who cautioned against cycling through Black neighborhoods that are materially poor, yes, but at least spiritually alive. They are also the same who advised against joining Black protests after the murder of Freddie Gray—protests that generated social unrest, yes, but an unrest geared toward staying alive. The paradoxes of white, privileged academics teaching in the humanities show through the cracks too. Still, Thomas Jefferson School is not Johns Hopkins; the infrastructures are crumbling, the classroom is literally a container, and pedagogically, well, the problems go even deeper. How is the son supposed to learn to write full sentences (the homework assignment on the first week of class) if he hasn't even been taught the alphabet? "Private school" is easy to say. Who can afford it? Plus, they didn't come to America to be complicit with a type of segregation he had been naive enough to think at least partially overcome in the twenty-first century. No, he won't cross that line; he will keep crossing the street. These were mixed feelings for a mixed family at a familiar crossroads.

Child and father cross the road, then, but they are forced to stop. The access to the school is blocked. A teacher reports to a small gathering of concerned parents: "There has been an accident. The school is closed today." The son looks up and smiles. The other children did not look displeased either, but a feeling of unease was palpable nonetheless. Still, finding the school closed was not extraordinary. It had been shut down regularly throughout the winter—what back in Europe was called "snowing" is dramatically renamed "snowstorm" here: an excuse to shut down the school system for weeks on end simply because the infrastructures are lacking to clear the streets? he wonders, but that's another story. In any case, the dad—whom by now you will have identified—thought it was a routine dysfunction in a dysfunctional system. The system was dysfunctional enough, but snow was not the problem this time. Once back home, an email had arrived in the meantime, notifying parents that there had indeed been "an accident." It had nothing to do with the weather. It was serious. A preschooler had died that morning. After the initial shock, he asks about the type of "accident." It was this family's third year in Baltimore. Hearing gunshots was not unusual in the neighborhood. It turned out that it was indeed a "firearm accident."

The child was not in the same class as his son, but in a parallel class. The proximity of the tragedy brought the pathos home with an avalanche of questions. How can a four-year-old be involved in a "firearm accident"? Did the shooting take place at the school? At home? In the streets? These were the initial questions that were running through the father's head, but he manages with difficulty to contain his composure since his son is in sight. He tries to answer the email with some critical distance. Writing becomes difficult on such occasions. He can only think of a practical question: Could you please give me some more details about the type of 'accident'"? The counselor's reply came fast. He reassured the father by saying he had joined a discussion with some of the older children at school that very morning; they could discuss the accident and "share their thoughts about what death means." Some students, though, had the same down-to-earth, apparently less philosophical but no less meaningful question. As he reported, "a student in that group asked if the child shot himself with a gun, and the counselors did say that he died from an accident with a gun, but that they did not have more details to share about the death." What we could do, he continued, was "join the parents with our thoughts and prayers."

The details of the accident were not given directly to either students or parents. They found out indirectly, via a local newspaper—in a shockingly crude line that read as follows: "The boy grabbed a gun and shot himself around 10:40 a.m. inside a home in the 400 block of North Athol Avenue, according to the Baltimore Police Department."[41] The identity of the dead boy's father doubled the pathos. The child was a son of a policeman. The boy had found a loaded gun in the house—"not the officer's service weapon," a spokesperson for the Baltimore Police Department tried to reassure readers. The news failed to be reassuring. As the gunshots kept intensifying that spring, the immigrant family was ready to migrate back, closer to home. They left Baltimore for good in the summer of 2016.

This is, again, "just" an example. Still, it is a particular case that reveals a larger endemic problem in the United States. It makes clear, among other things, that the pathos of this local Baltimore tragedy does not require deep interpretations of familial dreams, or neon signs, in order to be properly contextualized. It requires some critical distance and sense of discrimination that goes beyond the familial tragedy to account for broader sociopolitical tragedies. A number of interpretations were already in circulation. Officials called this an "accident," as the schools announced via a euphemistic effort intended to downplay this tragic horror. The newspaper specified that the "boy shot himself," seemingly reporting the facts objectively, while actually relying on a phrase that (absurdly) implies a conscious intention of self-murder on the side of the four-year-old child. While well-meaning but pedagogically unprepared teachers had discussions with their students about the "meaning of death" in general, waxing philosophical, the example of the children has something to teach us: they encourage us to ask empirical, factual-based investigative questions like: How can a policeman leave a gun loaded and unsecured in his private home? Why is such a gun accessible to a four-year-old? And what happened once the loaded gun was in his young hands?

As Bruno Latour pointed out, a gun is not simply a passive object or a "neutral tool" in the hands of an all-powerful agentic subject. Rather, it is a "mediating technology" that has agentic properties of its own that have the power to alter the actions of the subject holding a gun as it enters into a composite, gun-subject relation with agentic properties that emerge from this human-nonhuman relation. As Latour puts it: "You are different with a gun in hand; the gun is different with you holding it. You are another subject because you hold the gun; the gun is another object because it has entered

**FIGURE 5.** *Top:* Cartoon violence (Daffy Duck, Warner Bros.). *Bottom:* Video game violence.

into a relationship with you."[42] If such distributed agency applies to adult subjects trained in dealing with weapons (say, a policeman), it applies even more so to children who not only lack training but may not have full conscious awareness of the danger a real weapon entails.

This composite gun-child assemblage that distributes agentic power across the human/nonhuman divide leads us to ask further, more interpretative, contextual questions pertaining to mimetic studies. If we do not consider the gun-child composition in isolation, but place it in a social context, we are left to slow down and ask: Why does a four-year-old find the gun interesting to pick up in the first place? Where does the idea of pointing the gun to his body—and pulling the trigger—come from? Had the boy seen such gestures performed before on TV against fictional characters (cartoons)? Had he previously enacted such gestures with fictional guns (video games)? And if so, had he been encouraged to unconsciously mimic such gestures? Perhaps even to consider such gestures harmless because painless—maybe even funny because performed by comic and likable characters that encourage identification? Most of these questions are destined to remain unanswered. The child is no longer here to tell us. But other children can be asked, perhaps starting with our own. There is, in fact, growing recognition that violence in apparently innocent, entertaining genres like cartoons is less harmless than it appears to be, precisely because it contributes to normalizing deadly forms of violence under the mask of comic entertainment.

If we now zoom out of this specific yet culturally revealing tragedy and we situate it in a more global context, it is clear that so-called accidents like this one are symptomatic of a wider social pathology. Prominent in the United States, gun-related "accidents" and "crimes" are linked to systemic racism, poverty, lack of basic social rights such as education and health care, radically amplified by a disconcerting lack of basic gun regulations, all of which make the number of individual shootings shockingly pervasive, including shootings of children.[43] If we consider that these real cases are shadowed by a viral dissemination of fictional representations of violence available on TV, film, and video games for children to consume in high doses from their early years of life, the conditions for triggering hypermimetic spiraling feedback loops leading from fictional violence to real violence are dangerously in place.

There are a number of objective symptoms pointing in that direction. If we locate this subjective, qualitative experience in a broader quantitative context, the statistics for the United States alone are alarming.[44] Despite powerful corporate interests to deny the effects of media violence on children and the epistemic impossibility to prove direct causation, the general theoretical view on the long-term effects of this exposure is worrisome, cannot be beneficial, and leads to the following diagnostic: "It is widely agreed that viewing violence has serious and negative consequences for children in both the short and long term."[45] Cartoons, in particular, thrive on violence and, before the onset of video games, were "consistently rated the most violent of all programs on television."[46] They remain problematic despite their comic dimension, or perhaps because of it. In fact, cartoons not only can serve as a model for young children to mimic—as any slightly attentive parent routinely notices; they also promote a vision of violence as painless, funny, and perhaps even desirable given the lack of physical consequences it entails in fiction. Among the reasons that render children a vulnerable target of (new) media violence is their "inability to distinguish fantasy from reality; and their imitating even fantasy cartoon depictions of violence, their inability to distinguish between justified and non-justified violence and susceptibility to identification with violent characters."[47] This emotional identification is dangerous for young viewers. It can even be deadly if these viewers have access to real weapons. The genealogy of this hypothesis goes all the way back to the origins of mimetic studies in Plato's *Republic*. With rather classical examples in mind, the latter already suggested that scenes of violence should not be told or dramatized in front of children for mimetic reasons: children not only learn through imitation; they are also not in a position to fully distinguish between reality and fiction.

Without acknowledging this genealogical connection to lend philosophical support to their empirical findings, contemporary social theorists are, indeed, rediscovering an ancient pedagogical lesson: namely that violent gestures performed by heroic fictional characters, be they epic, tragic, or comic, have the power to induce mimetic gestures in children, which, over time and repetition, become habitual, automatic, and unconsciously inscribed in their "nature," turning it into more violent, aggressive, destructive, and potentially self-destructive second nature. To be sure, direct causation between (new) media violence and real violence continues to elude definitive empirical proof; children respond differently to representations of violence, and the most immediate trigger, as these Baltimore-based cases suggest, concerns gun regulations, education, and socioeconomic and racial disadvantages.[48] And yet, together, these two examples, one of intentional and conscious racist police violence and the other of not-conscious childhood self-inflicted violence, urge new genealogists of violence to look deeper into the spiraling hypermimetic interplay between violent simulations of fictional violence and a racist, all too real violence. As we shall confirm, via another example of police murder, this violence can become an automatic, pre-reflective reflex, and can be unconsciously triggered in adult police officers as well.

The detour via the reality of gun-related violence brings home the ancient realization that fictions can, indeed, have tragic consequences, which does not mean that these tragedies generate cathartic effects. On the contrary, they are symptomatic of a contagious dynamic rooted in a conception of hypermimetic violence we need to further diagnose.

## Hypermimetic Violence

If we now return to our cinematic fiction after this foray into the reality of racist violence the film does not represent, we can go further and double down on our diagnostic with a gendered perspective on the patho(-)logies of hypermimesis and the banality of violence it entails. In *Vice*, Detective Tedeschi, in fact, swims against dominant corporate interests that protect the VICE resort for economic reasons. His suspicion is that a repetition of a violent action against artificial female cyborgs in the resort and the world of virtual entertainment VICE represents, can quickly turn into a "taste" for violence against real women in everyday life. His diagnostic suspicion could be summed up via the following mirroring principle: tell me which simulation games you play, and I will tell you which actions you could potentially reenact; show me how you act in reality, and I will tell you which simulations games you play in virtual reality.

The hypermimetic continuities between fictional violence and real violence illustrated in *Vice* debunk dominant notions of the unconscious based on a catharsis hypothesis that dominated the past, Freudian century. They also articulate an affective hypothesis that is currently finding a confirmation in the social sciences and the neurosciences in the twenty-first century. Rowell Huesmann, for instance, in a detailed review of the literature on media violence and social violence over the past fifty years, sums up his findings as follows: reviewing

the actual scientific evidence that has been collected on the effects of media violence, the psychological process that have been identified as causing its effects, and the exact role that imitation plays in the process, it becomes apparent that media violence is stimulating violent behavior.[49]

If such studies are not as well known as they deserve to be, it is perhaps because such diagnostics are as untimely as they are unfashionable. They fly in the face of popular understanding of a dominant model of the Oedipal unconscious that dominated the past century and, nolens volens, helped promote a catharsis hypothesis that is still with us. More problematically still, such studies reopen the dossier on a mimetic unconscious that goes against powerful corporate, economic, and political interests to put violence to neoliberal profit. The lesson is, of course, as old as the history of civilization. Violence, just like sex but with different social implications, is a key ingredient for "good" fictions. And the "proof" that these fictions are considered "good" by many, is that they sell. Ergo, violence is also the key ingredient for good profits as well.

We should not be surprised that the cultural industries that sprang up in repressive, puritan, and capitalist-oriented societies in need of compensatory entertainment, effectively put a model of the unconscious based on repressed sexual and murderous wishes to capitalist profit. In this narrow sense, then, the Oedipal unconscious applies to a puritanical culture that, after a brief window of sexual liberation in the 1960s, continues to be predicated on covert and not so covert forms of sexual suppression and the phantasmal violence it entails. Nonviolent, consensual sexuality continues to be largely repressed—or, better, censured—in mainstream Hollywood. Seeing a nipple would be the horror, but a decapitated body? Fine. What should surprise, however, is that the most graphic forms of violence characteristic of a plurality of cinematic genres (action movies, horror movies, slasher movies) prominent in the 1980s and 1990s, which are now at play in realistic and rather cinematic video games we shall return to, are not subjected to similar regulations and are part of viewers' regular media diet.

In our so-called civilized societies, the same *pudeur* that leads a culture to render consensual sexual intimacy taboo by veiling it behind a virtual window does not seem to equally apply to violence. As Cynthia Carter and Kay Weaver also point out, "what is extraordinary about the evident acceptability of so much film violence is that censorship laws deter against the explicit depiction of consenting sex, but permit the screening of explicit and graphic violence."[50] The same modesty that applies to human body parts a classical culture considered beautiful does not seem to apply to bodies that, in a gun-obsessed culture, can be shot to death, blown up, massacred, and torn to pieces via an aesthetic that privileges what the Italian feminist philosopher Adriana Cavarero calls "horrorism," by which she designates "a disgust for a violence that . . . aims to destroy the uniqueness of the body."[51] Horrorism based on the violence of physical "dismemberment" is all too real in the case of terrorism. At one remove, in the sphere of aesthetics, scenes of dismemberment make the horror of the Dionysian *sparagmos* a ritual everyday experience routinely available from early age and in high doses.

The fact that this striking double standard concerning pornographic violence and bodily beauty is not regularly noted is symptomatic of the degree of normalization that media violence has undergone. More recently, in the aftermath of the digital revolution and the transfer of what Bataille called our "accursed share" to the internet, the proliferation of an untidy intermixture of both violence and sexuality has been uploaded on pornographic websites that are highly heterogeneous and should not be unilaterally subjected to moralistic critiques, though age restrictions certainly apply. As I said at the outset, my argument is not moralistic but genealogical, and thus diagnostic in its concern with subject formation and transformation. Still, many of these sites dramatize violent misogynistic practices that are likely to serve as models for teenagers and influence sexual aggressions in real life.[52] It is as if the latent eroticism at play in patriarchal forms of phallocentric violence against women constitutive of Hollywood classics, resurfaces with a transgressive vengeance in the sphere of internet pornography, which does not mean that this is a classical return of the repressed driven by an Oedipal unconscious.

Interestingly, and somewhat paradoxically, such transgressions are also the driving force behind those very movies that set out to denounce the perverse effects of sexualized violence. *Vice* is, once again, a case in point. The film's anti-violent *message*, in fact, rests on an aestheticization of violent actions at the level of the *medium*. Thus, while Detective Tedeschi condemns the leak of violence from the artificial world of VICE into the real world, leading film spectators to unconsciously identify *with* social justice contra misogynistic and phallocentric violence, the movie *Vice* actually represents brutalities inflicted on eroticized "artificial" girls and filmed with an I-camera point of view that puts the viewer in the position of the aggressor, for real spectators to feel "shocked" or, as the owner of VICE prefers to say, "entertained." The title *Vice* is thus well chosen: it points simultaneously to the sickness and to the diagnostic, to the disease and to the remedy, or, in our language, the pathology (or sickness) and the patho-logy (i.e., a critical discourse on mimetic pathos). To be sure, *Vice* might not be a cinematic classic that will stand out in the history of film for its aesthetic value. Still, it generates a patho(-)logical paradox worthy of a Platonic pharmakon. If this pharmakon lies at the origins of media studies' concern with epic spectacles, it is still in search of a diagnostic for new media studies attentive to digital spectacles.

Before continuing to look ahead to new evidence that confirms the hypermimetic power of (new) media contagion, it is thus necessary to look back, genealogically, to theoretical origins of this hypothesis first. My assumption is that only by doing so can we understand the strange and rather counterintuitive idea that what we are now used to evaluating as poetic virtue could, at the origins of aesthetic theory, be considered the source of an all too human vice.

Exits the fictional detective; enters the original philosophical physician.

# CHAPTER 2

# Vita Mimetica

## Platonic Dialogues

The philosophical diagnostic of the power of contagious violence to spill from aesthetic representations into the so-called real world does not originate in contemporary movies. Rather, it can be traced back to an agonism between philosophy and literature in classical antiquity, a mimetic agonism that should now be reloaded to include post-literary media as well. Its first systematic formulation precedes Aristotle's defense of poetry in the *Poetics* (335 B.C.), directly in-*forms* or, rather, inspires the latter's conception of catharsis, and goes back to the very origins of philosophy in general and of aesthetic (read: mimetic) theory in particular.

Unsurprisingly, the origins of the affective hypothesis can be traced back to Aristotle's teacher, intellectual father, and exemplary philosophical model. Plato was, in fact, a model worthy of imitation not only for his first, most influential, and brilliant student but also for a chain of subsequent philosophers who reach, from antiquity to modernity, into the present—thereby lending support to Alfred Whitehead's often-quoted definition of European philosophy as a "series of footnotes to Plato."[1] If this genealogical point is true for Plato's influence on western philosophy in general, it is especially true for his diagnostic of *mimesis* in particular. He is, so to speak, the founder of mimetic studies who, with some updating, can still partially orient, without determining, the future of new mimetic studies as well. In fact, Plato's critique of the irrational, contagious, and pathological effects of mimetic spectacles on the audience, doubled by Aristotle's counter-ideas about mimesis's rational, philosophical, and cathartic potential, still provide the two main shoulders on which the mimetic patho(-)logies constitutive of our theory of homo mimeticus stand—in order to look further ahead.

Fully aware that the dynamic of agonistic contests can have productive patho-*logical* effects, Plato called his most influential pupil, *Pôlos*, the Foal, arguably because a foal kicks its mother while drinking its milk—a telling metaphor for the contradictory push-pull internal to what we called "mimetic agonism."[2] The catharsis hypothesis we explored in volume 1 is, in fact, the logical kick Aristotle directs contra Plato's diagnostic critique of mimesis; yet this does not mean that the milk of Plato's patho-*logy* is deprived of nourishing value for the breeding of philosophical foals. Countered by a chain of defenses of poetry that go from Aristotle to Longinus, Philip Sidney to Percy Shelley, the affective hypothesis continues to flows via a panoply of modern and contemporary thinkers from Rousseau to Nietzsche, Bataille to Girard, Deleuze to Connolly, Massumi to Cavarero to Gallese among others, albeit under different names or conceptual personae: from Dionysian mimesis to mimetic communication, affective contagion to mimetic inclinations, mimetic influences to mirror neurons and other contemporary avatars of mimesis that are currently contributing to the mimetic turn. At play in different strands of critical theory, the *re*-turn of attention to mimesis calls for a new transdisciplinary field of studies I call mimetic studies. His founder deserves special attention, especially since he first developed the contagious hypothesis against which the catharsis hypothesis pushed to be born.

Despite the immanent, materialist, and embodied telos of this *re*-turn of attention to homo mimeticus, if we follow the genealogy of the pathologies of contagion and the therapeutic patho-*logies* it generates, the traces are numerous, yet they all ultimately lead back to the dawn of philosophy, in Plato's (anti-)mimetic thought. Unlike Aristotle, Plato did not write a treaty on poetry or poetics. Still, he can be credited for laying the conceptual foundations of aesthetics before Alexander Baumgarten rediscovered it for the moderns in the Romantic period. If Aristotle set the foundations for the catharsis hypothesis in the *Poetics* (c. 335 B.C.), he did so in agonistic opposition to Plato's prior articulation of the affective hypothesis in the *Republic* (c. 375 B.C.). Speaking of literature but with an oral theatrical culture in mind, the classicist Penelope Murray formulates this agon as follows: "Is it dangerous in that it encourages emotions and feelings that ought to be kept in check, or is it therapeutic in that it allows us to vent our emotions in a harmless way?"[3] If Murray crucially specifies that "literature" should now "of course include television and film," we should add that it should include new digital media and video games as well. This untimely aesthetic question, which we are still pursuing in the digital age, is at the core of an influential philosophical dialogue that has tended to be marginalized in contemporary aesthetic theory, perhaps because its title points so clearly to politics rather than aesthetics, misleading readers to "form expectations that the title promises."[4] Yet as classicists have long recognized, if we do not allow the title to cast a shadow, or magnetic spell on thought, and we take the trouble to carefully read Plato's *Republic* itself, it becomes quickly apparent that it "opens with an examination of the nature not of politics but of poetry" (*PP* 3).[5]

As we will see, poetry, literature, or, better, *mimēsis*, as Plato understands it, is at the heart of political but also ethical, psychological, pedagogical, and only ultimately metaphysical questions that form and transform the *vita mimetica* of subjects aspiring to live in a just city.[6]

## Dawn of Mimetic Studies

Books 2 and 3 of *Republic* deserve special attention in our genealogy. Rarely read, let alone studied, except by classicists, not only do these books introduce the concept of "*mimēsis*" for the first time on the philosophical stage, setting the foundations for mimetic studies in general; they also inaugurate the problematic of the contagious effects of representations or, better, dramatizations of violence and the mimetic pathos it generates in the souls of the guardians and, by extension, spectators and citizens, more generally generating what Plato considers pathological effects. Plato was, in fact, fundamentally aware that epic and tragic narratives like Homer's *Iliad*, Hesiod's *Theogony*, or Sophocles's *Oedipus Rex* dramatize fictional characters whose violent and transgressive actions (war, murder, incest) provide bad ethical models, examples, or types for spectators to imitate in real life.[7]

Contrary to what is often repeated in philosophy and literary studies alike, mimesis for Plato is not confined to the formal sphere of aesthetic images, shadows, or phantoms of reality—mimesis as visual "copy" or "representation." Rather, it stretches beyond the wall of representation to include the immanent and embodied sphere of the actor's dramatic performances—*mimēsis* from *mimos*, "actor," and, even prior to it, "performance."[8] That is, theatrical impersonations that have a contagious and thus mimetic effect on the psychic life of the guardians in particular and of spectators in general, threatening to turn their ego into a copy, shadow, or phantom of other egos—mimesis as behavioral imitation, or homo mimeticus.

For our genealogical investigation, it is crucial to stress at the outset that in the *Republic*, the problematic of mimetic impersonation and the psycho-ethical concerns it entails both precede and inform the issue of mimetic representation and the metaphysics it founds. Plato, in fact, inaugurates the problematic of mimesis in Books 2 and 3 not on the ground of an ontological theory that situates artistic representations as "shadows" or "phantoms" at three removes from original intelligible ideas, or Forms—we will have to wait the end of *Republic*, in Book X, for this idealist, transcendental, and metaphysical distinction to be fully sketched out.[9] On the contrary, Plato inaugurates his discussion of mimesis on the basis of a much more real, embodied, and thus immanent concern with the pedagogical effects of violent dramatic spectacles on the formation of subjects in general and on impressionable creatures, such as children, in particular.

As our opening epigraph already suggests, subjectivity, for Plato, can be impressed, formed, and transformed by exemplary fictional models that were not confined within a book, but were primarily impersonated by actors on dramatic stages. This also means that Plato's primary concerns with mimesis—in Books 2 and 3, but perhaps also in the *Republic* tout court—might be *ethical* and *psychological* perhaps more than *epistemic* and *metaphysical*. This is an unfashionable hypothesis that tends to remain at the margins of philosophy, but it has not gone completely unnoticed. Philippe Lacoue-Labarthe, for instance, in his penetrating commentary on the first books of *Republic* in "Typography" puts it trenchantly. For Plato, he says, "the question of mimesis has something to do with what must be called a *psycho-logy*," and he specifies: it "is not, as is repeated endlessly, principally a problematic of the lie, but instead a problematic of the *subject*" (*T* 98, 121).[10] That Plato's initial concern is first and foremost with subject formation, or deformation in childhood, is especially apparent from the literary examples he convokes. After having vividly depicted scenes of violence—the battles of the gods in Homer's *Iliad* or the castration of Cronos in Hesiod's *Theogony*, for instance—Socrates asks Glaucon a question that, over two millennia, continues to guide new mimetic studies as well: "Do you not know, then, that the beginning in every task is the chief thing, especially for any creature that is young and tender? For it is then that it is best molded and takes the impression that one wishes to stamp upon it" (*Rep.* 377b). The media have changed since, generating a far more pervasive and immersive network of impressions, but the plastic subject matter under the pressure of such stamps remains essentially the same. Hence the urgency to reload this untimely question.

Now, since the form of the Socratic dialogue, as the Swiss historian Jacob Burckhardt also noted, is a constitutive part of the Greek agonistic spirit,[11] we shall not only notice the centrality of mimetic agonism in Plato's thought from a safe critical distance; we shall also actively engage in a mimetic agonism ourselves. This Socratic question, in fact, might prompt contemporary readers up to date with recent developments in mimetic studies to risk an answer of our own: yes, we know about the plasticity of the human subject; it molds not only the psyche but the brain as well. We also know that brain plasticity present at the beginning of human life continues to form and transform adult life, middle to end.[12]

A genealogical inversion of perspectives from mimetic representations to mimetic subjects, images to bodies, written simulations to dramatic impersonations is, thus, in order to properly account for Plato's specific psychological, pedagogical, and ethical concerns with the influence of mimetic models in general, and the contagious violence internal to tragic and epic dramatization in particular. This diagnostic, in fact, does not only concern the abstract mediated ontological relation between aesthetic representations and ideal Forms, sensible copies and intelligible originals whose metaphysical Truth is reserved for philosophical and religious minds ready to espouse Plato's idealist ontology that locates true life in an alternative afterword. It rather concerns a more immanent question about the affective, formative, and transformative powers of dramatic spectacles on human psychology, fictional characters on real characters, shadows on egos, whose ethical and political implications are of direct interest to responsible inhabitants of the ancient, modern, and contemporary city. That is, a (hyper)mimetic city increasingly surrounded by false yet nonetheless performative and transformative spectacles that infiltrate the psychic life of the ego, turning it into a phantom of the ego. Hence the mimetic turn or *re*-turn to homo mimeticus aims to shift the focus of analysis from metaphysics to ethics and psychology, verticality to horizontality, transcendental intelligible forms to immanent affective impressions, mimetic impressions that already in-*form* (form from the inside) the *Republic*—beginning, middle, and end.

To see more clearly into the formative power of mimetic shadows, let us start with the middle of the *Republic* and take a closer look at what is often considered the founding scene, or myth of philosophy in general and aesthetic theory in particular. That is, an allegorical myth that paradoxically relies on mimetic strategies to relegate the powers of mimesis to the status of illusory shadows, while at the same time pointing to the reality of magnetic chains that, perhaps more than ever, threaten to imprison homo mimeticus in a mythic cave. This scene of origins sets the stage for a mimetic life, or vita mimetica, that is, perhaps more than ever, part of our human and posthuman condition today. It is thus worth reconsidering this influential myth in both its liberating and subjugating sides by attending to both the logos and the pathos that animates this vita mimetica. Since this is a double life, I shall do it in two parts.

## Vita Mimetica I: The Logos of Liberation

The Allegory of the Cave that opens Book 7 of the *Republic* is arguably Plato's most famous and influential myth. It serves as matrix, soil, or perhaps womb out of which philosophy is born. It attracted numerous influential commentaries in the history of philosophy, from Heidegger to Badiou, Arendt to Irigaray, Blumenberg to Cavarero, reaching, via film, into popular culture, from *The Truman Show* (1998) to *The Matrix* (1999). Hence, it continues to remain a productive starting point that speaks to theorists of hypermimesis facing the digital age, especially since what is at stake in the cave is not only the question of the "essence of truth" or *alētheia* constitutive of Plato's philosophical logos and the unveiling or unconcealment it entails;[13] the myth also dramatizes the contagious powers of mimesis animating Plato's philosophical critique of mimetic pathos. It ultimately urges genealogists of mimesis to be attentive to both the logos and the pathos of Plato's myth in order to account for both the theoretical and affective side of simulations.

The Allegory of the Cave tends to be convoked every time a philosophy teacher wants to introduce the general contours of Plato's idealist thought and perhaps philosophical thought tout court. And rightly so, for it dramatizes in a compressed allegorical fashion, at least three main fundamental principles in Plato's idealist philosophy that orient the discipline. I summarize them schematically: first, it introduces Plato's conception of philosophy as a difficult ascending path of liberation from the chains of the sensible world of darkness and ignorance that progressively allows the philosopher to contemplate the luminous and intelligible sphere of ideas in general and the idea of the Good in particular—the ex-prisoner contemplating spellbound the luminous but also blinding sun outside the cave; second, it illustrates Plato's idealistic critique of the sensible, material, and phenomenal world known through bodily senses as a mere simulacrum or copy of the intelligible world deprived of true ontological being—the simulacra of animals and men behind the prisoner's back and the phenomenal world of the cave more generally standing for the city, or *polis*; and third, the Allegory of the Cave foregrounds Plato's critique of artistic representations, simulations, or projections in terms of deceitful appearances that are at three removes from truth (the sun), depend on a mechanism of projection (the fire and the puppets), and should be dismissed as illusory representations of reality—the shadows on the wall and the aesthetic phantoms they primarily stand for.

The myth is clear, intelligible, and perhaps attainable for the idealist philosopher within the allegory endowed with a blind faith in the afterworld. Of course, already at the time of Plato, regular citizens within the city never actually broke loose of the material chains of life, let alone of the aesthetic spectacles that entertain them—they are, in fact, not inclined to abandon the cave and are actively hostile to self-proclaimed liberating figures. There is, in fact, a strange and little-discussed power at play in those binding chains. This was true then and remains true now. Starting in the modern period, scientific progress increasingly questioned the reality of immutable ideas predicated on a religious adequation between being and thought. Hence, the production of knowledge increasingly turned the focus of attention back to the immanent materiality of this world—the only one we have.

Still, the Allegory of the Cave continues to speak, perhaps more than ever, to contemporary generations who are increasingly spellbound by new media, from cinema to TV, digital simulations to video games, among other projections of phantoms that are in a relation of adequation with the cave's shadows. As contemporary philosophers of Platonic inspiration like Alain Badiou, for instance, made clear, sf blockbusters like *The Matrix* (1999) reload the distinction between the apparent world and the real world for the digital age so effectively that even for self-proclaimed Platonic philosophers, the film, that is, the mimetic simulation, can serve as a "preparation for Plato."[14] This is an irony that Plato, the maker of myths, would have been the first to appreciate. In the process, it also reveals Plato's ongoing relevance to account for digital shadows that are far removed from reality, indeed, yet cast a binding spell on the ego nonetheless.

The illusory nature of mimetic representations, the critique of the phenomenal world, and the ideal of intelligible truth it entails, as a chain of commentators noticed, is center stage in the Allegory of the Cave. Yet it is only half the story or, rather, myth. If only because the powers of mimesis are Janus-faced and look as much toward the abstraction of a philosophical logos based on a theory of intelligible ideas (both *theōrein* and *idein* are linked to seeing) as toward the immanence of an artistic pathos operating in the darkness of the cave qua Greek polis. As Hannah Arendt has noted, the ontological narrative of liberation from the illusory, phenomenal world constitutes the driving telos of the myth and traditionally lead the philosophical subject toward what she critically called "*vita contemplativa*" characteristic of the life of the philosopher.[15] Contra this philosophical tradition, Arendt is critical of this vertical narrative of abstract ascension and directs her political gaze to the fact that the ex-prisoner feels compelled to return to the cave. This is a political gesture that allows her to reinscribe, if not the myth itself, at least her thought back in the "*vita activa*" characteristic of the world of action in the political life of the city, or polis. Thus, Arendt claims that "the doctrine of ideas as presented there [in the parable of the cave] must be understood as its application to politics, not as the original, purely philosophical development."[16]

This remains, indeed, the driving telos of our reading of the myth as well. We are in fact concerned with the immanent, material, and embodied effects of the shadows on the psychic and political life of citizens. And we are in good company too. Furthering Arendt, the Italian feminist philosopher Adriana Cavarero recently added important notes on the political implications of the Platonic allegory for a surging democracy that is attentive to the patho(-)logical powers of mimetic inclinations. Cavarero perceptively notes that Plato is not only a philosopher; he is also an "artist [who] knows how to arrange the light of the scene" for he "imitates the artists but he also makes sport of them. Homer is his favorite target."[17] A mimetic agonism is indeed at play at the origins of philosophy that cannot easily be dissociated from its main artistic contestant—if only because a mirroring dramatization is constitutive of the birth of philosophy "itself."

On the shoulders of these incisive political and philosophical reframings of the founding myth of philosophy, we add a patho(-)logical supplement. Plato's mimetic agon with Homer, in fact, also leads to a refined diagnostic understanding of the affective powers of mimesis with aesthetic, pedagogical, as well as political implications relevant to (new) media violence as well. Put differently, there is much at play in the myth Plato dramatizes, under the mask of Socrates, that concerns a more immanent, embodied, and aesthetically oriented imitative life. There is, thus, what I shall call a vita mimetica at play in the Allegory of the Cave, and by extension in Plato's thought and western philosophy tout court, that has tended to remain in the shadows and that deserves to be center stage in the digital age. Located in the space between the *vita activa* and the *vita contemplativa*, action (*praxis*) and contemplation (*theōria*), politics and philosophy, but also ethics and psychology, the vita mimetica is an aesthetic life attuned to both affect (pathos) and discourse (logos), politics and ethics, and focuses on the patho(-)logical power of simulations to cast a magnetic spell on homo mimeticus. This spell is imperceptible, truly immanent, and tends to escape specular transcendental theorization. If the vita mimetica has tended to remain in the background of both philosophy and politics so far, we need to adopt the lenses of mimetic studies first sharpened by Plato to bring its immanent powers into the foreground.

There is a paradox of mimesis at the origins of Plato's thought that many have noted and that the logic of mimetic agonism allows us to clarify. In his dialogues in general and in the Allegory of the Cave in particular, Plato relies on the same mimetic strategies in his own narrative practice that he vehemently denounces in his philosophical theory: not only myth, allegories, and dramatic heroes are constitutive of the content of his tale; the very narrative form of the dialogue in which Plato does not speak in his proper name but in the name of another are equally constitutive of the powers of mimesis he denounces in poets in his theory, yet he puts them to *re*-productive philosophical use via the paradoxical dynamic of mimetic agonism in his mythic narrative.

Closer attention to this paradox allows us to reevaluate his account of the vita mimetica at play in the Allegory of the Cave. "He," Plato, that is, Socrates, puts it to his interlocutor, Glaucon—Plato's brother—in dramatic terms that stage the double powers of mimesis in mythic terms:

> Picture men dwelling in a sort of subterranean cavern with a long entrance open to the light on its entire width. Conceive them as having their legs and necks fettered from childhood, so that they remain in the same spot, able to look forward only, and prevented by the fetters from turning their heads. Picture further the light from a fire burning higher up and at a distance behind them, and between the fire and the prisoners and above them a road along which a low wall has been built, as the exhibitors of puppet shows have partitions before the men themselves, above which they show the puppets. (*Rep.* 514a–b)

Picturing this mythic scene in every detail is not as easy as it appears. Glaucon, for one, cannot help but notice that this is a "strange image" populated by "strange prisoners" (515a). Hence a good dose of imagination, and perhaps even affective participation, is required to picture it adequately and thus reflect on it clearly within the dialogue itself. At one remove, readers are encouraged to do the same. Notice the paradox: a pathos is already presupposed to grasp the logos mediated by the myth. This is perhaps why Plato deploys considerable narrative efforts and creative ingenuity to depict, in cinematic detail, a mythic scene of origins in which prisoners, we are told, are compelled by exterior physical devices ("fetters") that immobilize their bodies ("legs and necks") to look in one direction only, placing them in a bodily position, which is also an affective disposition, that blinds them to the reality of the theatrical *dispositif* at their back (the "fire" behind them and the "exhibitors of puppet shows").

Once the stage is set and impressed in our minds and senses, the steps toward a philosophical liberation are easier to follow. A prisoner (perhaps Plato "himself") is released and "compelled to stand up"; he looks around, sees the ingenious mechanism of projection, and recognizes the illusory nature of the shadows cast on the wall. As he does so, he still does not want to leave. We are told that he needs to be led "by force" and led through an ascending path that is "rough and steep" by "someone" (perhaps Socrates "himself"?) who "would drag him out in the light of the sun" (515e) in an illuminated yet paradoxically blinding environment that will dramatically overturn the cave-dweller's Weltanschauung inside out. In fact, in a scene that mirrors the scenario within the cave, what this ex-prisoner sees outside in a puddle are first the "shadows" or "reflections of men and other things" (artistic representations), then the "things themselves" (the world of phenomena), then the "appearances in the heavens" (the world ideas), and only at the very end does he see the sun itself (the supreme idea of the Good) (516a).

Now, in a mirroring inversion that in-*forms* both western metaphysics and Christian religion, Plato will endow "appearances in heaven" with the reality of the true world of Being, will denigrate the phenomenal world of "things themselves" to phantoms, and, at an additional remove, will dismiss the artistic "reflections" thereof as false shadows or phantoms of phantoms caught up in the changing world of becoming. Light versus darkness, high versus low, intelligible ideas contra illusory phenomena, intellect contra the senses, freedom versus bondage, true ideal Being contra false material becoming: the fundamental dualism that will orient western thought is clearly staged—on mythic foundations.

Much has been said about the content (logos) of this mythic scene from an ontological perspective that is attentive to the illusory powers of mimesis understood as visual representation far removed from reality. Understandably so, since the erection of an idealist metaphysics is, after all, the driving telos of the vertical development of Plato's dialectical logos. The mirroring reflections are plural: just as the prisoner ascends the difficult path toward the sun representing the idea of the good, so, at one remove, the reader progresses through the equally difficult dialectical path of the *Republic* toward the ideal of the just city; just as the prisoner outside the cave sees reflections of intelligible ideas on the surface of the water, so the reader, at the end of *Republic*, is made to see via the trope of a "mirror" (*Rep.* 596d), which duplicates "all things" including "all plants and animals, including himself" (596c). Hence the phenomenal world is debased as an illusory reflection, or "appearance" of the intelligible world of ideas Plato considers true "reality" (596e) .

In an ironic but also agonist twist, then, Plato puts a mimetic myth and the mirroring reflections it entails to philosophical use to unveil a world of illusory shadows that are mere phenomenal phantoms, or artistic phantoms of phantoms. The inversion of perspective Plato had dramatized via the dramatic power of myth in Book 7 is thus subsequently rearticulated via metaphysical concepts in Book 10. It is, in fact, only at the end of *Republic* that Plato formalizes a vertical metaphysical hierarchy, or "divided line," that goes from the intelligible Forms or ideas to the phenomenal world, to the artistic world of artistic representations, "phantoms of phantoms" at "at the third remove from the truth" (*Rep.* 602c). Thus, as the phenomenal world is turned into a metaphysical fiction, "appearances in the heavens" are turned into intelligible, universal, and eternal realities. They are supposedly attainable to the few who have followed Plato's metaphysical ascension to the very end. At the other end of the history of metaphysics, you will remember, Nietzsche will reverse once again the mirroring evaluation by revealing the ideas themselves as a mimetic fiction. Thus, he will call this philosophical narrative of ascension a "fable"—an adequate depiction of the original myth Plato "himself" narrates.[18]

Now, despite the growing decline of faith in such an ideal "afterworld" (*Hinterwelt*), we are beginning to suspect that phantoms far removed from reality remain particularly insidious in a digital age increasingly under the spell of a plurality of digital simulations. These hyperreal simulations, as Jean Baudrillard also noted on the shoulders of Nietzsche, may no longer rest on the logic of imitation qua representation in theory; and yet Nietzsche, on the shoulders of Plato, was also in a position to see that they continue to form, transform, and deform the beliefs, opinions, and practices of homo mimeticus, including violent practices with material effects.

Plato's reliance on a mimetic device par excellence such as myth in order to picture, or, rather, dramatize, his critique of mimesis is not only the source of a contradiction or *aporia* as it has long been noted. It also operates on a mimetic agonism that reveals Plato's acute sensitivity to the affective power, or pathos, of these illusory shadows to performatively produce all too real

effects—that is, contagious effects not deprived of both logical and pathological consequences he takes seriously in his thought, or logos. The myth is,
in fact, Janus-faced about the powers of mimesis: if it depicts a pathological
state of bondage, spellbound confusion, and lack of knowledge at the level of
its allegorical content, it also mediates a narrative of liberation, which Plato
thought best conveyed via a mimetic rather than purely conceptual form. No
matter how contradictory the gesture may be at the level of Plato's logos, his
reliance on both mythic and mimetic devices is constitutive of Plato's *pathology*, which realizes that the mimetic disease calls for a mimetic cure—what
he also calls a "*pharmakon*" (poison and cure).[19] Thus, Plato borrows the
power of fictional shadows (Socrates as an echo of Plato's voice) to break
the spell of contagious pathologies and cast a counter patho-*logical* spell on
Glaucon and, at one further remove, on readers as well. Due to his Janus-
faced poetic-philosophical sensibility and the mimetic agonism with Homer
that informs it, Plato takes quite seriously the psychic, ethical, and pedagogical powers of a mimetic and mythic pharmakon we group under the rubric
of patho(-)*logy*.

If we now shift perspective from the content of Plato's thought to pay
closer attention to his choice of narrative form, a different, more duplicitous,
and in our view more complex story begins to appear. This marginalized story
of a vita mimetica in the cave was left in the shadows in the past but has not
lost any of its contemporary relevance today to account for the contagious
powers of simulations in general and of violent simulations in particular in
the present and future. There is, in fact, an interesting mirroring interplay
(and inversion) between Plato's mythic narrative and the mythic content
it conveys. Plato's myth stages a double conception of mimesis understood
both as visual representation and dramatic impersonation that reflects the
two-sided critique internal to his myth. At first sight, Plato simply appears
to *represent* a mythic scene of origins that depicts the prisoners in the cave,
the shadows on the wall, and the puppet show behind their back in vivid,
representational, almost pictorial terms. We are even tempted to say that he
depicts the cave as a painter would represent a landscape: he paints a fictional
image he considers allegorically true to unmask the illusory nature of artistic
shadows.

But, of course, Plato, just like his main antagonist, Homer, is not a
painter. They both work with words rather than with colors, drawing on

poetic, mythical, narrative, and eminently mimetic strategies that betray Plato's youthful poetic ambitions and the mimetic agonism with the poets it led to. Despite Plato's oscillating evaluations of poetry that lead him to celebrate it as a divine form of inspiration in dialogues like the *Phaedrus*, dominant philosophers under the spell of his metaphysics have tended to take Plato's exclusion of the poets from the ideal *Republic* literally. They trusted perhaps too much his philosophical logos and ignored his narrative skills. Yet a minor tradition of classicists going from Nietzsche to Pater, Wilde to Havelock to Murray, among others like to recall Diogenes Laertius's claim that Plato burned his poems upon meeting Socrates, which does not mean that he could not turn his poetic gift into a new genre of writing—a dialogic genre he called philosophy.

Historically true or not, Plato's assimilation of narrative strategies from his agonistic model, Homer, is real and visible for all who can read. It is also constitutive of a mimetic agonism that in-*forms* his Janus-faced evaluation of mimesis. Plato, in fact, writes contra mimesis via mimetic means, turning mimetic agonism into a philosophical strategy that is constitutive of the origins of philosophy tout court, reaching via an exemplary chain of thinkers, into the present. As Nietzsche was quick to recognize, what "in Plato is of special artistic significance in his dialogues is mainly the result of a rivalry [read contest] with the arts of the orators, sophists, and dramatists of his time."[20] Due to the re-*productive* paradox of mimetic agonism, then, Plato's critical distance from orators and dramatists betrays a mimetic proximity to them. In fact, he draws on the power of mythic narrative in general and mimetic narrative in particular to propose a dia-*logos* that goes beyond muthos—via eminently mimetic means that rely on both representational mimesis and dramatic mimesis.[21]

These two notions of mimesis internal to Plato's narrative medium are at play at the level of the myth he dramatizes. Interesting for our topic is that they generate doubling effects that, at a second look, are perhaps less rational and more violent than they first appear to be. In fact, while this myth is often understood in terms of an intellectual liberation of sensorial illusions at the level of philosophical logos, the *muthos* itself stages a rather different story: namely, a story of childhood subjugation, prison-like immobilization, and subsequent liberation whose violence is at least double. In fact, the prisoners are submitted to two antagonistic, rivalrous, and quite brutal forces that provide the underlying agon to this myth and drive its narrative/ philosophical development. On the one hand, we have the power of false shadows on prisoners who, we are told, are "prevented by fetters from turning their heads" and are thus reduced to complete immobility; on the other hand, we have the power of the liberator who frees one prisoner from these chains, for sure, but also, Plato/Socrates specifies, "compels" him to look at the fire, "drags" him outside "by force," and "does not let him go before he had drawn him out into the light of the sun" (*Rep.* 515e). If we join both sides, we have a liberating, rational, and intelligible myth in abstract theory; but the dynamic dramatized in narrative practice is far removed indeed from a picture of balanced rationality, agentic freedom, and deliberate philosophical reflection characteristic of the *vita contemplativa*. It rather points to an irresistible human tendency to fall, body and mind, under the binding spell of visual dramatizations with the disconcerting power to chain the prisoners to an all too mimetic life, or vita mimetica, it is difficult to break free from.

Why is the pull of myth so strong? What is at play in those mesmerizing shadows that the ideal picture of rational thought who is the philosopher is reduced to dragging the apprentice philosopher out of the cave by sheer physical force? Let us take a closer diagnostic look at the affective, embodied, and perhaps unconscious powers, or pathos, at play in those subjugating chains that tie spellbinding prisoners to the vita mimetica. This takes us to her affective second life.

## Vita Mimetica II: The Pathos of a Life in Chains

Traditionally, philosophical interpretations of the Allegory of the Cave have tended to remain in the shadows of pure practitioners of the *vita contemplativa* primarily concerned with the essence of truth in the luminous world outside the cave. Building on less traditional, but not less illuminating, political accounts attentive to the *vita activa* inside the cave, such as those of Hannah Arendt and, more recently, Adriana Cavarero, we shall see, or, better, feel, that disconcertingly effective invisible powers are animating the vita mimetica Plato took the trouble to depict, narrate, and dramatize.

Reframing the Allegory of the Cave from the angle of mimetic contagion opens up different questions that are not reducible to metaphysical

ideas or ideals. These questions include, for instance: What kind of shad-
owy projections does this allegory stage? Wherein lies the power of those
shadows not only to subjugate the bodies and minds of prisoners but also to
chain them? If the entire myth is allegorical, what are the chains allegorical
*of*, anyway? And how can these chains be broken? The myth provides initial
stabilizing answers to the liberating side of the story, especially if we consider,
with Cavarero, that the "story" is not deprived of "strong biographical traits"
that entangle Plato's and Socrates's life and death in Athens.[22] The liberator is
presumably Socrates, the liberated prisoner Plato himself, and the liberating
force that drags the latter on a difficult ascending path that leads away from
the dark, artificial illusions inside the cave (read the phenomenal and artistic
world) toward luminous realities in the transcendental sky of ideas (read the
intelligible world) is nothing less than what Plato/Socrates calls "the power
of dialectic" (*Rep.* 511b). That is, a rational, intellectual, and discoursive
power that stings, like a gadfly, dispels opinions, and, as the myth itself says
in a realistic moment, will eventually lead prisoners back in the cave to "kill
the man who tried to release them" (517a) upon his return to free them. The
power of logos is thus not only a constraining vertical intellectual force that
leads to a new birth in the high sphere of the *vita contemplativa* directed
toward the sky of intelligible ideas; it can also trigger real physical violence in
the immanent, changing, and political world of embodied creatures engaged
in the vita mimetica. The gap between the ideal of the *vita contemplativa* and
the reality of the vita mimetica is significant. It can lead from a mythic fiction
to the pathos of real death, as Plato's *Apology* and *Phaedo* make clear.

Such a disconcerting loop between fiction and reality is constitutive of
what we call hypermimesis. If it is characteristic of the digital age, incipient
manifestations of hypermimetic powers were already present in the classical age. One particular example is worth mentioning. Prior to Plato's myth
in *Republic* (375 B.C.), and prior to Socrates's trial in 399 B.C., the death of
Socrates was foreshadowed by Aristophanes's comic play *The Clouds* (423
B.C.). The indirect reference to the death of Socrates qua liberator in Book
7 of the *Republic* calls to mind the earlier comic dramatization of Socrates's
death in *The Clouds*. Aristophanes, in fact, concludes his satirical portrayal of
Socrates by staging a disciple named Strepsiades who, for "Socrates' sake . . .
cast out the gods," repents at the divine offense, and decides to avenge himself
by burning down Socrates's house. Here is how the play ends:

Socrates: Dear, dear! I'm choking to death, most miserably.

Chaerephon: And I'm burning to death, most wretchedly.

Strepsiades: Why did you outrage the gods with your studies? Why pry into the seats of the moon? Chase, strike, beat them, for many reasons, but most because they insulted the gods.

Chorus: Lead out now. Our performance, we may state, has this day proven adequate.[23]

The comic performance proved more adequate to the tragic reality than Aristophanes probably intended, opening up questions that are still with us: How can a fiction precede reality? Do fictions serve as a model for life to imitate? True, in fiction Socrates dies by burning on a dramatic stage whereas in reality he dies by self-poisoning in his Athenian cell. No direct causation can indeed be established, especially since over twenty years passed between the comic play and the tragic reality. Yet the correlation is striking nonetheless. In fact, Aristophanes's play foreshadows Socrates's real death in ways that are not based on simple representation, for the fiction precedes reality. Still, it generates a theatrical simulacrum of Socrates that may not be deprived of performative effects: the fiction may have made a lasting impression on the popular imagination, and perhaps also on the evaluation and trial of Socrates. This, at least, is what Plato "himself" seems to think.

A few decades after *The Clouds* was staged, and following Socrates's trial and death, the claim that Socrates offended the gods was indeed used as the main angle of attack in his defense, which Plato dramatized in the *Apology*. The reasons that led up to Socrates's trial with a charge of impiety and corruption of the youth were doubtless multiple, complex, and cannot be reduced to a singular and direct cause; yet it is significant that Plato mentions Aristophanes's *Clouds* at the opening of Socrates's *Apology* as part of accusers who "tried to fill your minds with untrue accusations" with the power to influenced public opinion.[24] Is it a historical accident that the fictional dramatization of Socrates in *The Clouds* anticipated his accusation of impiety in real life? Or, rather, did the comic performance contribute to disseminating a view of Socrates in fiction, which may have not been realistic yet had the power to retroact on reality (directly) fueling his accusation in real life, perhaps even (indirectly) contributing to reproducing a real tragedy that culminated in Socrates's sacrificial expulsion from Athens, as well as his imprisonment and death?

Plato does not say it explicitly and the burning incident is not addressed, though it was probably still on the minds of the jury members. What is clear is that Socrates's opening reference to Aristophanes in his apology implicitly suggests that, for Plato at least, the second hypothesis may be closer to the truth. Sure, the accusations may not have been true to reality, but Socrates in the *Apology* suggests that they make lasting impressions on the audience, nonetheless, especially since such theatrical shows, he specifies, "took hold of so many of you when you were children," that is, at "the most impressionable age."[25] Thus he lists the "playwright" Aristophanes among his most "dangerous accusers" (18c), treating the power of his fictional stamp seriously and reminding the audience: "You have seen it for yourselves in the play by Aristophanes, where Socrates goes whirling round, proclaiming that he is walking on air, and uttering a great deal of other nonsense about things of which I know nothing whatsoever" (19c). These deep impressions cannot be detached from Plato's critique of mimetic power, if only because we have already seen him tie his critique of mimesis precisely to such impressionability to fables told in childhood in *Republic*. The plastic malleability of the impressionable subject is currently returning to the theoretical scene via a conception of brain plasticity that cannot easily be peeled off from a long-recognized plasticity of a mimetic subject.[26] What we must add is that even this malleable impressionability of children Plato compares to a "wax that can be impressed with a stamp" in a discussion on education in Book 2 of the *Republic* stems from his theatrical opponent. It is, in fact, Aristophanes who, before Plato, uses the trope of the wax to qualify the plastic malleability of a child "to mold yourself as in wax"—yet another confirmation that a mimetic agonism with and contra poetry and drama is constitutive of the birth of philosophy and mimetic studies.[27]

Let us now return to the Allegory of the Cave with this theatrical example vividly in mind. The moving shadows on the wall and the puppet show that projects them may not be true to reality. Granted. They do not even attempt to realistically represent reality for they are an "illusion." Granted again. And yet, they make a lasting, spellbinding, and real impression on the spectators, depriving them of their freedom of movement but also of thought. As many have noted, the entire *dispositif* of the puppet show in the cave bears multiple and obvious resemblances with a theatrical show; and the analogy is brought home for contemporary readers as it is even closer to a movie theater. A doubling of identities, an entertaining stage, and a mesmerized audience; or, a doubling mechanism of projection behind, a wall animated by shadows in front, and a public down below. Be it a theater or a movie theater, the cave's allegorical reference is clear. This is especially true since, as Plato had anticipated in Book 3 of the *Republic*, theatrical spectacles have the power to impress the psychic life of subjects from childhood on—and these impressions continue to be at play in cinematic spectacles.

Still, open questions remain. For instance, since theatergoing in ancient Greece was not a compulsory activity designed for slaves but a formative activity for free subjects, why are the cave-dwellers said to be in "fetters"? Clearly, the chains, not unlike the puppets or the shadows, have an allegorical meaning that should not be taken literally, lest one mistakes the genre of the allegory altogether. They call for a hermeneutical or interpretative effort that takes seriously the diagnostic potential of the allegory. In fact, if the puppets have been generally interpreted as allegorical of the phenomenal world, the shadows of the artistic world, and the sun as the supreme idea of the Good, the chains themselves and the violent subjugation they symbolize have received less interpretative attention by mainstream commentators who usually take them *à la lettre,* as part of the cave's furniture. These mysterious chains allude to mimetic powers that are not only representational but affective, not primarily visible but invisible and thus not easily subjected to theoretical (from *theōrein*, to see) contemplation from visual a distance. Still, this does not mean that an imperceptible mimetic pathos is not at play in the cave, animating the powers of false shadows. Let us consider these spellbinding powers more closely.

Just like the ascending, liberating pull that drags the prisoner out of the cave is metaphorical of the ascending movement of Socratic dialectic, so the chains that keep prisoners down in bondage from childhood on, forcing them to "look forward only" and preventing them from "turning their heads," must be metaphorical of a competing, antagonistic, and rather powerful pull, which Socratic dialectics is pulling away from. Just as light is opposed to darkness, high to low, outside to inside, freedom to bondage, along other binaries that structure this myth, so the power of philosophical logos must be opposed to a competing and rather binding power, or pathos. That the powers of mimesis Plato himself deploys as a philosophical patho-*logy* (cure) continue to play the main role as a mythic pathology (poison) is confirmed by the dual mimetic nature of the puppet show itself. Let us take a closer look.

The powers of the shadows are double as they are as much based on visual and auditive mimesis. First, the shadow-play dramatizes representations of "human images and shapes of animals" (*Rep.* 7.514c) on a platform in front of spectators in terms that are visual, representational, and, in this sense, mimetic. But as Plato's mise an abyme alerted us, there is a second, less perceptible but not less effective and affective notion of mimesis at play in the cave. In fact, these shadows are not only seen; they are also heard. Or better, they are both seen moving and heard speaking in a synchronic inter-play that brings them to life. It is, in fact, crucial to realize that the prisoners mistake the shadows for human and animal forms not only because they visually resemble these forms (mimesis as adequation or *homoiosis*); they are misrecognized because these forms also speak like humans, or at least appear to (mimesis as participation, or *methexis*). The chains are thus all the stronger as both vision and orality are simultaneously at play in the theater of the cave. In a narrative detail that is easy to miss yet gives affective specificity to the mimetic power of these shadows, Socrates tells us that the false impression of reality is amplified by an "echo" in the cavern that doubles the puppeteers' speech behind, leading the prisoners/spectators to believe "the passing shadow to be the speaker" (515b) in front. The shadows, in other words, appear *animated*: that is, given a soul, or *anima*. They move and speak, or appear to speak—as in an animation.

How, then, are the shadows animated? An audio-visual attention to the *vita mimetica* in the cave that goes beyond contemplation and action puts us in a position to offer what is perhaps an original, yet still mimetic, all too mimetic answer. The shadows are animated by a voice that is not originally theirs but that speaks in their name instead. What we are now in a position to begin to see—or, better, hear, and perhaps also feel from a distance—is the following point: this mimetic confusion of the shadows and the puppets, the "copy" and the "original," which is already a copy of the original idea, is not only problematic because it sets up a visual illusion at three removes from reality (the shadows alone are sufficient to make this rather basic ontological point). Rather, they are problematic because as any child knows, and so many philosophers seem to have forgotten, speaking shadows projected on a wall are endowed with a magical power of animation to generate affects that flow, by way of a sympathetic identification or mimetic pathos, from the animate shadows to the spellbound spectators. If the medium of the theater does not make this shared pathos palpable enough, try cinema.

As film theorists have long recognized, Plato's Allegory of the Cave provides an apt conceptual frame to reflect on the magnetizing power of cinema as well. They have not only returned to the Platonic myth to develop "meta-psychological" speculations about the "cinematic apparatus";[28] they have also called attention to cinema's power to induce in spectators what sociologist and film theorist Edgar Morin calls "imitation-hypnotic states" that are constitutive of what he aptly calls "the soul of cinema."[29] From a different but related perspective, Marshall McLuhan extends this Platonic diagnostic by taking the powers of mimesis beyond cinema to an age of mass media that is not without echoes with the Allegory of the Cave. Drawing on Eric Havelock's "splendid work *Preface to Plato*" in order to support the claim that "any technology gradually creates a totally new human environment," McLuhan turns to diagnose what he calls the neuronal "extension of man" generated by (cool) electronic media that via "the intensification of one sense [vision, for instance] by a new medium can hypnotize an entire community."[30] For the prophet of media theory, numbness is one of the effects of this hypnotic/mimetic unconscious: "We have to numb our central nervous system when it is extended and exposed, or we will die. Thus, the age of anxiety and of electric media is also the age of the unconscious and apathy."[31] If numbness is an effect of the mimetic unconscious, violence is potentially another. Thus, McLuhan, thinking of a "typographic spell" that has the power to generate what he does not hesitate to call "a massacre of the innocents," concludes mimetically that "we become what we behold."[32]

With these timely insights from modern media, we are better positioned to capture the untimeliness of Plato's critique of ancient media. What gives moving shadow a soul are unconscious, mimetic states that are essential to the magical efficacy of cinema to turn "shadows" into what we have become accustomed to calling animated figures, that is, figures with an *anima*, or soul. For better and worse, then, fictional animations like cartoons, cinematic protagonists, or video game avatars, have powerful formative and transformative effects. This is true for all kinds of publics who partake in the vita mimetica, for instance, by sitting in a dark room in a relaxed state, staring in one direction, immobilized, and spellbound by shadows on the screen that generate all kinds of affects. But it is equally true for more contemporary activities, like binge-watching TV series, surfing the internet, or playing video games.

From different perspectives, then, we can begin to sense how an underlying and so far largely uncharted genealogy of the vita mimetica first dramatized in the cave brings the ancient Platonic lesson of the contagious power of art to bear on the present. This type of affective contagion whereby mimetic gestures represented on a stage or, at one remove, on a screen, are endowed with an unconscious power to break through the wall of representation and affect spectators in a crowd, real or virtual, is strikingly relevant for an immersive digital culture. As a new generation of film and media theorists is becoming increasingly aware, virtual spectacles are not simply mimetic in the sense that they represent reality—though they continue to do that too. Rather, they are hypermimetic in the sense that they have the power to affect and infect the body, mind, and attitudes of spectators, contributing not only to informing conscious, rational subjects from a distance but also to *forming* unconscious, mimetic, and potentially violent subjects driven by pathos.

Despite the radical shifts of perspectives on mimesis, consistently in Plato's poetics, it is this affective confusion of identities between the actor and the poet, the shadow and the puppeteer, the rhapsode and Homer, that Plato's dialectic—in theory if not always in practice—violently opposes. Why is that so? And wherein lies its danger? If we link the echo in the cave to the shadows on the wall and see/hear them come to life, animated as in a cinematic projection that turns a silent film into a talkie, we should now be in a position to answer these marginalized yet fundamental questions. Because these talking shadows have a magical, immobilizing, or hypnotizing effects on the prisoners/spectators, magnetizing effects that Plato, in a related dialogue titled *Ion*, compares, yes, to a "chain."

Is this a genealogical coincidence? Let us briefly compare these mimetically entangled dialogues.

Ion is a reciter of poetry, or rhapsode, who specializes in Homer. He just won a poetic contest, or agon, but Plato stages a different scene, and the poor rhapsode is no match for Socrates. He is no philosopher and serves as the latter's punching bag. Plato's argument is that Ion recites Homer well but does not know what he is saying. He lacks both knowledge (*epistēmē*) and poetic craft (*technē*) but supplements this lack via a state of inspired (dis)possession that is not deprived of contagious qualities. As Socrates explains, Ion's passion for reciting Homer stems from a state of "enthusiasm" in which Ion is no longer himself; he is divinely possessed by another (*en-theos*, in the God) and thus speaking in the name of another. Remember that as a rhapsode, Ion did not read Homer in isolation; he recited the *Iliad* and the *Odyssey* for a public in the theater, generating an enthusiastic contagion that flows from Apollo to the Muses, the poet to rhapsode, stretching to magnetize spectators as well. Socrates explains this divine power via a magnetic analogy. He compares it to "the power in the stone Euripides called the magnet, which most call 'stone of Heraclea.'"[33] And in a metaphorical language that is not without echoes with the vicissitudes of the cave, Socrates continues:

> This stone does not simply attract the iron rings, just by themselves; it also imparts to the rings a force enabling them to do the same thing as the stone itself, that is, to attract another ring, so that sometimes a chain is formed, quite a long one, of iron rings, suspended from one another. (*Ion* 533d–e)

There is, indeed, a magnetic power at play in poetry, as Plato states in his inaugural poetics. This power does not remain confined to the sphere of visual representation. On the contrary, it flows, like magnetism, through a vertical chain that finds in the rhapsode a key middle ring on the way to magnetizing spectators as well. And so, via such a dramatization, spectators find themselves magically attached to a long chain that is endowed with magnetic, affective, contagious, and binding properties. Like a magnet, the reciter of Homeric poetry on the stage in fact has the power to spell-*bind* spectators. That is, binding them with a spell to a fictional spectacle that generates an intoxicating affect or pathos—including a violent pathos that does not generate cathartic sympathy but mimetic contagion instead. As Cavarero also recognized: "The magnetic chain, which comes down from the Muse to Homer and to the *raphsod* [*sic*] keeps them imprisoned with invisible bonds." And she perceptively adds: "So the prisoners in Plato's cave are not so bizarre!" (RC 16).

My reading is in agreement with Cavarero, which I consider one of the most perceptive and philologically sound account of the phenomenology of aesthetic attachment internal to the Platonic cave I know of. My only *différend* concerns a rather specific but, for my argument, important point, which might be useful to register before returning to the issue of violence and the unconscious. Cavarero's sophisticated attunement to the magnetic powers of orality leads her to consider "bizarre" Plato's "idea of substituting the horizon of listening [central to *Ion*] with that of vision" (RC 16) central in the Allegory of the Cave. Cavarero, with her characteristic attention to sound, registers the presence of the echo in the cave, but stresses that in the shift from *Ion* to the allegory, Plato introduces visual tricks to keep the prisoners static. As she puts it, with characteristic ironic and thus Socratic distance:

> To keep the prisoners immobile, with their eyes fixed on their visions, the philosopher needs tricks and devices [*trucchi e marchingegni*]. The magnetic power of the Muse, which chains the listening to the story, must be replaced by an artificial harnessing of the gaze with chains and projectors [*rudimentali macchine di proiezione*]. (16)

Thus, Cavarero concludes, "the same chains, as if in a somewhat awkward conjuring trick, pass ambiguously through a metaphoric significance to a realistic one" (16). I fundamentally agree with the general thrust of Cavarero's argument: her attention to orality offers a decisive contribution to the mimetic turn and new mimetic studies more generally. It is in fact undeniable that in *Republic* Plato privileges the specular model to theorize the destabilizing powers of mimesis at play in the cave (he will do the same with the trick of the mirror in Book 10). Cavarero's ironic distance toward what she calls "rudimentary projection machines" (an irony lost in translation) is thus well-taken to critique the rather laborious specular machinery Plato stages to dramatize his speculative metaphysics.

At the same time, I would like to stress that poetry was still staged, performed, enacted on a theater in the fourth century B.C., and was thus animated by *both* oral *and* visual powers. The magnetic powers of the Muse are thus given a visual supplement in the cave to further account for the power of art in general and of the theater in particular to magnetize or chain spectators in affective terms constitutive of the vita mimetica. My hypothesis is that it is not orality alone, neither visuality alone but, rather, the dynamic interplay between voice and vision, mimetic language heard and mimetic bodies seen (including gestures and facial expression), that animates the powers of mimesis that spell-*bind*, or chain, spectators to those animations. The chains are allegorically all too powerful and immobilizing precisely because they are magnetized by the dynamic interplay of orality and visions, echoes and shadows, or, to use Nietzsche's categories, Apollonian imitation and Dionysian imitation. There is thus a visual supplement in Plato's drama-tization of the cave worth taking seriously—especially when what is at stake are spectacularly violent animations that, as we stressed, are endowed with a power of magnetization that reaches a predominantly visual, yet still orally connected culture, which is, incidentally, not unlike our digitally mediatized hypermimetic culture.

That the danger of violence is internal to poetic madness and the chain of dispossession it entails is already clear from the genealogical influences at play in *Ion*. Socrates, in fact, compares the type of contagious frenzy that flows like magnetism from Apollo to the poet, the rhapsode to the audience to an intoxicating state of "Bacchic transport" that is characteristic of Dio-nysian rituals. Socrates gives ritual substance to the analogy of the magnet as follows:

> as the worshiping Corybantes are not in their senses when they dance, so the lyric poets are not in their senses when they make these lovely lyric poems. No, when once they launch into harmony and rhythm, they are seized with the Bacchic transport, and are possessed—as the bacchants, when possessed, draw milk and honey from the rivers. (*Ion*, 533e–534a)

Plato may have burned his poems but didn't forget the poetry and tragedy that impressed him in his youth. For those who tend to read Plato as the antipode of Nietzsche, or vice versa, here is a philological surprise: There is a Dionysian contagion at the heart of Plato's poetics. For Plato, just as for Nietzsche after him but with an inversed evaluation, tragic and epic poetry has the power to break the wall of representation and generate contagious intoxications on the side of life. And as for Nietzsche, already for Plato, such a contagion flows like magnetism through a chain of mimetic rings that go from Apollo to Dionysus and calls to mind an intoxicating violence that culminates in a body torn to pieces, or *sparagmos*.[34] Such violent scenes of dismemberment were familiar to a Greek audience who would have understood the dangerous implications of this Dionysian analogy; they might however no longer be familiar to a modern readership that is perhaps numbed by an excess of violent spectacles. Let us thus reconsider the ritual scene of violent dismemberment Plato has in mind so as to account for the dangers of poetic (dis)possession and the violent contagion it entails—a danger Plato foregrounds in *Republic* but only alludes to in *Ion*.

## Dionysian Frenzy

Socrates's reference to bacchic frenzy, dispossession, and the mention of "milk and honey" it entails is an unmistakable allusion to a tragic play that culminates in a visceral scene of contagious violence: Euripides's *The Bacchae* (405 B.C.).[35] To a Greek audience of *Ion* (the name of a play by Euripides as well), the bacchants, dancing in a state of possessed frenzy, would have brought to mind vivid mythic scenes of Bacchic violence, rendering such violence difficult to detach from Plato's diagnostic of magnetic contagion.

This Dionysian tragedy may not be as famous as *Oedipus Rex*, but it is well known. And if Oedipus is the paradigmatic play on which the catharsis hypothesis rests, *The Bacchae* provides classical foundations to develop the affective hypothesis. The shift between classical plays thus also signals a move from an Aristotelian-Freudian hypothesis still internal to mimetic theory to a Platonic-Nietzschean hypothesis animating new mimetic studies. The plot is already familiar. A play devoted to the powers of the god Dionysus and the refusal of his cousin, King Pentheus, to pay tribute to him, the tragedy stages an agon between sacred and political powers that culminate in a frenzied ritual of (dis)possession that leads to a body torn to pieces. Picture the scene: Pentheus's mother, Agave, is followed by other Maenads up to the mountains in a state of intoxicating enthusiasm. Not being "herself" but divinely possessed, she captures her son who had been spying on their Dionysian rituals from a distance:

She was mad, stark mad,
possessed by Bacchus. Ignoring his [her son Pentheus] cries of pity,
she seized his left arm at the wrist; then, planting
her foot upon his chest, she pulled, wrenching away
the arm at the shoulder—not by her own strength,
for the god had put inhuman power in her hands;
Ino, meanwhile, on the other side, was scratching off
his flesh. Then Autonoë and the whole horde
of Bacchae swarmed upon him. Shouts everywhere,
he screaming with what little breath was left,
they shrieking in triumph. One tore off an arm,
another a foot still warm in its shoe. His ribs
were clawed clean of flesh and every hand
was smeared with blood as they played ball with scraps
of Pentheus' body.[36]

This is of course a mythic fictional scene rather than an actual histori-cal scene. Still, it was thought to harken back to the origins of Dionysian rituals.[37] Once impressed on the audience via a dramatic impersonation, or performance, the pathos of this scene of violence was not likely to be forgot-ten. It provides an exemplary scene of ritual dismemberment that modernist figures like Nietzsche, Bataille, and, later, Girard and Cavarero will posit at the origins of tragic art, and, in a different form, might still be at play in contemporary art.

For a Greek readership of *Ion*, the implications of the analogy between poetic possession and ritual possession via the trope of Dionysian frenzy dra-matized in *The Bacchae* would have been double for it operates both at the level of the content (or message) and at the level of form (or medium)—with clear entanglements between the two. At the level of the message, such irra-tional states of dispossession can lead to violence, not pity, toward so-called detached spectators, as the case of Pentheus's body torn to pieces confirms within the play; at the level of the medium, such intoxicating violence is extremely contagious, as the sacrificial frenzy that takes possession of the Maenads suggests.

Now, what Plato's trope of the magnetized chain in both *Ion* and *Republic* implies is that at one further remove, spectators in the theater are exposed to the same magnetizing power. Not unlike Pentheus within the play, they are not positioned at a safe distance from tragic and epic spectacles. On the contrary, this violent Dionysian pathos can potentially be transmitted, via a possessed actor, dispossessed rhapsode, or animated shadows, to the viewers as well. The property of the magnetic chain is in fact to introduce an affective contagion that flows from fiction to life, mimetic representations to mimetic subjects, and by extension violent fictional actions to violent embodied reactions. That such subjects are prone to violence is also clear. We should not forget that Plato specifies that spectators of visual projections in the cave would not refrain from killing "the man who tried to release them" (*Rep.* 7.517a). Is it an accident that Plato is also careful to specify, in an oblique allusion to *The Clouds*, that such a liberating figure would "provoke laughter" upon his return to the vita mimetica?

Perhaps. What the Platonic myth contextualized within these tragic and comic plays reveals is nothing less than the specific contagious dynamic in which an aesthetic medium transmits a contagious pathos to a theatrical audience. Despite the different perspectives Plato dramatizes, he always points to the same mimetic strategy in the end. Not unlike the talking shadows of Book 7, or the poet/actor of Book 3, the rhapsode in *Ion* does not speak in his own name but speaks in the name of fictional characters, always pulled by epic or tragic strings. And it is on the basis of this dramatic impersonation that affective continuities between mimetic fictions and mimetic subjects have the power to cast a magnetizing spell that not only deceives spectators about reality; they also, and for us more important, affectively *bind* spectators to fictional exempla and types endowed with the magnetizing pathos to make lasting subliminal impressions and chaining the public to such fictional projections. If such fictions include comedies like *The Clouds* that arguably played a role in Socrates's imprisonment or comprise tragedies like *The Bacchae*, which Plato alludes to in *Ion*, the Allegory of the Cave suggests that it is this mimetic-contagious-magnetic-hypnotic chain and the pathos (not only suffering but all dispossessing affects more generally) it conveys that, in a mirroring inversion, the logos of Socratic dialectics sets out to pull away and break free from.

If we now step back to sum up the genealogical insights that emerge from these two related Platonic dialogues that dramatize the contagious effects of violent spectacles on the vita mimetica, we can both see and feel how this artistic "chain" manages to set subjects in "fetters." The metaphor of a magnetic "chain" that ties spectators to actors or rhapsodes in *Ion*, echoed by the "fetters" that focus the prisoners' attention to the shadows projected in the cave of *Republic*, suggests the following conclusions: first, this magnetic force points to a Janus-faced conception of mimesis understood not only as visual representation but also, and above all, as dramatic impersonation in which both voice and vision play a joint role. To put it in Plato's mythic terminology, this force not only relies on the illuminating and musical powers of Apollo at the top of the chain but connects spectators at the bottom to the dark chthonic powers of Dionysus and the bodily intoxication it entails. This Apollonian/Dionysian double notion of mimesis is not purely exterior but also interior, not only visible but also invisible, not only oral but embodied, not solely illusory but truly contagious. Or, better, it is contagious because the joined powers of Apollonian and Dionysian mimesis blur the line between exterior and interior, fictions and reality, art and ritual, shadows and spectators, leading subjects caught in the snares of a magnetic-hypnotic-mimetic spell to mirror, if not fully consciously, at least unconsciously, the animating shadow-play they both see and hear in a mimetic fiction in their embodied, magnetized, and mimetic life.

The vita mimetica, then, brings us back to the ancient quarrel between philosophy and poetry with which we started. In the process, it restages the affective hypothesis from a dramatic perspective attentive to the powers of mimesis on the side of life.

## The Ancient Quarrel Revisited

The case of this mimetic subject is serious. And Plato, under the mask of Socrates, plays a serious role to diagnose it. He adopts the role of a "physician" who, he says, "treats the body [*soma*] with the mind [*psyche*]" (*Rep.* 408e). This is, indeed, what we could call—echoing Lacoue-Labarthe—a psycho-*logist*, or someone who gives a rational account (logos) of the soul (psyche). But since, strictly speaking, the dualist distinction between the "body" and the "soul," psyche and soma, does not apply to this physician of the soul, we could also call him—echoing Nietzsche—a "philosophical *physician*" (*GS* 2; 35). This physician of the soul, or philosopher of the body, is concerned with a specific case of mimetic sickness: namely, a cultural sickness generated by the contagious effects of mythic fictions in general, and violent characters, or types, in particular, both of which have the power to turn human nature into what Plato calls, "second nature" (*Rep.* 395d).

Already—or, better, especially—for Plato, then, mimetic models play a key role in the formation, deformation, and transformation of the subject. As Pierre Hadot puts it, anticipating Foucault, for Plato "the care of the self [*souci de soi*] is not opposed to the care of the city [*souci de la cité*],"[38] if only because by transforming the former the latter is transformed as well. Hadot's conception of ancient philosophy as a way of life rightly notes the formative power of the Platonic genre of the dialogue. As he puts it: "the dialogue teaches them [interlocutors] to place themselves in the shoes of the other [*à la place de l'autre*], and thus to overcome their own point of view."[39] What we add is that the mimesis Plato opposes in theory is both the medium (the dialogue) and the message (the allegory) philosophy reloads in practice to counter the spellbinding power of mythic models Plato considers pathological but can be turned to patho-*logical* use. The philosopher may have left the cave in theory but continues to rely on lessons he gather from the vita mimetica he aimed to leave behind.

Now, what was true of the shadows in the cave was already true for the mythic shadows at play on theatrical stages. The shadows of men and animals projected on the wall are intertwined with the powers of mimetic representations to attract spectators, just as theatrical spectacles in a culture still partially dominated by orality attracted Athenians to the theater generating mass phenomena that could include up to seventeen thousand spectators.[40] As M. F. Burnyet puts it, if you want to identify the contemporary version of Plato's target to bring his diagnostic home, a change of perspective is in order: "Think pubs and cafés, karaoke, football matches, the last night of the Proms. Think Morning Service at the village church, . . . Above all, think about the way all this is distributed to us by television, the omnipresent medium at work in every home."[41] And if this does not bring the critique close enough, think of new media that, in the digital age, envelop daily lives in a plurality of screens, from computer screen to laptops, smartphones to tablets to video game screens.

Plato's concern should now ring close to home. His critique of mimesis is not limited to false representations of reality at the level of content; it is primarily concerned about the real impressions such representations have on the psychic, ethical, and political development of subjects. This is why Socrates, with war scenes in the *Iliad* under his lens, says, for instance, that "the battles of the gods in Homer's verse are things that we must not admit into our city either wrought in allegory or without allegory" (*Rep.* 378d–e). And with the tragic affects generated by the Trojan War in mind, or "Trojan *pathē*" (380a), which includes suffering, sorrow, calamities, and above all the passion or pathos of the tragic hero Achilles that elicits a magnetizing identification,[42] he specifies: "Nor again must mothers under the influence of such poets terrify their children with harmful tales" (378d). Mothers, then, should be cautious with the tales they tell their children. And perhaps we ought to include fathers as well in this discussion. Why exclude them from the battle—or, should I rather say, dialogue?

And so, modern parents with a taste for dialectics might, at this point, be tempted to join the discussion. Let's imagine, for a moment, we're still in democratic Athens where philosophical discussions took place with strangers encountered on the marketplace, or agora. An attentive listener would perhaps jump in and reply to the venerable teacher: "By Zeus, Socrates, I disagree with your diagnostic! Why should tales of violence be so harmful? Surely fictional violence is better than real violence, is it not?" And having listened to his dialogues before, they would remind him: "After all, is it not you, of all Athenians, who claimed that fictions are not realities, but simply shadows, or phantoms of reality?"

**Socrates:** I cannot deny it, the lover of wisdom would be forced to admit.

Emboldened by this initial success, a parent would press on:

**Parent:** And didn't you say that these phantoms are not once but twice removed from reality?

**Socrates:** Yes, that is what I have often said.

**Parent:** And if something is not real, Socrates, doesn't it follow that it is a mere appearance or illusion, like those fluttering shadows at the bottom of a cave you told us about?

Socrates: I do recall that scene.

And now, feeling triumphant, the parent turned into an apprentice philosopher would proceed to quote at length from Books 7 and 10 of the *Republic* to drive the point home and remind old Socrates of the idealist ontology he had seemingly forgotten.

After listening patiently to the Allegory of the Cave, feeling once again pity for the chained prisoners spellbound by mere shadows they mistake for realities, and following the adventure of the heroic figure who abandons the cave, ascends to search for the true source of intelligible light, and then heroically returns to unmask the poetic wizards responsible for the puppet show and reveal the painful truth to the prisoners, Socrates would, once again, see clearly and would perhaps reply: "You're right, by the dog. You have learned my idealist ontology well." And so, the modern parent qua apprentice philosopher, in an instant of hubris, would feel, for a moment, to have surpassed the ancient teacher. But for a moment only. For old Socrates has been holding an ironic twist up his sleeve that allows for a dialectical turn. Thus, facing the parent-philosopher in us, he retorts.

Socrates: My dear fellow, you are a careful reader, and you dramatize a vivid scene. But have you not noticed that in order to prove the truth of your argument [logos], you have also resorted to a tale [muthos]—that is, a fiction, a shadow, or, in your own words, a lie far removed from reality?

Parent: You're right, Socrates. I had not thought of it.

Socrates: So [patiently continuing], either your argument, just like mine, rests on fictional foundations—in which case, we are both far removed from the truth. Or [he adds, with an ironic smile], there is indeed something powerful, formative, and magically effective in such mythic tales—in which case, we are both mirroring the truth. Now tell me: which option do you consider true?

And so, the aspiring philosopher, returned to the humble role of respectful parent ready to learn from the venerable teacher, would have to concede:

"I think the second option is true, Socrates. The second, most definitely."
After this humbling experience, Socrates would then set out to explain that
tales cannot simply be dismissed as illusory fictions, for they can be put to all
kinds of uses and abuses.

Contemporary parents who translate this diagnostic to account for the
influence of new media might readily agree that violent simulations cast a
shadow on our digital culture as well. The projection mechanisms at play
in the cave may need some updating to account for hyperreal simulations
in the age of the internet, as films like *The Matrix* (1999) make vividly clear.
And yet the ancient lesson about the contagious powers of mimesis remains
instructive for hypermimesis as well. Shadows continue, in fact, to be projected, not at the bottom of mythic caves that resemble a theater, or a movie
theater, but on all kinds of walls, screens, digital interfaces, or black mirrors
that turn the surrounding world into a game of shadows, produce real spells
on mesmerized spectators and users that are constitutive of human or, rather,
posthuman behavior.

Already for Socrates, then, children are especially vulnerable to the
spellbinding power of violent myths, a hypermimetic power now reloaded
via cinema, TV, and, increasingly, video games, among other simulations. As
he continues, this time in a diagnostic that I quote truthfully from Book 2
of *Republic*, and should be intelligible not only to the scholars but also to
all concerned parents who are now hopefully fully involved in the discussion: "Don't you understand, I said, that we begin by telling children fables,
and the fable is, taken as a whole, false, but there is truth in it also?" (*Rep.*
377a). And after stressing how impressed children can be by fictional models
that have the power to "mold" the characters of souls that are, as Sophocles
already stressed, wax-like and "take the impression that one wishes to stamp
upon it" (377b), "he"—Socrates, that is, Plato—continues, in a concerned
parental tone: "For the young are not able to distinguish what is and what is
not allegory, but whatever opinions are taken into the mind at that age are
wont to prove indelible and unalterable" (378d). This is a basic and fundamental pedagogical insight that not only has withstood the test of time; it has
also gained in diagnostic relevance in direct proportion to the increasingly
realistic power of (new) media and the repetitive and prolonged exposure to
formative but also deformative fictions and the violence they impress on new

generations. The detour via the origins of mimetic studies in classical antiquity was worth the efforts to reload new mimetic studies in the digital age.

Speaking of contemporary media, social theorists have in fact returned
to this ancient Platonic insight. For instance, Potter notes that "children
younger than 5 are likely to have difficulty in distinguishing fantasy from
realty-based programming. . . . Thus, violent television content has a different
effect on younger children than it does on older children."[43] Plato would have
concurred. And yet, what his diagnostic adds is that these different stages
in childhood might not be as clear cut as contemporary theorists imply, if
only because first impressions can have lasting consequence on the plasticity
of the psyche, or brain, of spectators born in bondage, under the spell of
magnetizing fictions generating mimetic and contagious continuities that
flow below the boundaries of linguistic discontinuities and continue to shape
adult attitudes, expectations, and habits as well.

This, then, is the cultural and educational background that lies behind
Plato's critical diagnostic suspicion of mimesis, a background condensed in
the Greek word *paideia*, which means both "education" and "culture." With
this frame in mind, we can better understand why after a lengthy list of
passages from Hesiod's *Theogony* and especially Homer's *Odyssey* and *Iliad*,
which include, among other violent acts, castration, manslaughter, rape,
and filicide, Socrates opens Book 3 by saying that "we must further taboo in
these matters the entire vocabulary of terror and fear [φοβερός]" (*Rep.* 387c).
This may be a sensible idea in theory that each responsible parent is likely to
privately implement to different degrees, but it leads to tyrannical solutions
at the public level of the polis. To be sure, the censorship Plato proposed
not only failed in practice; it also had the pathological effect of discrediting
the logos that led to his diagnostic of mimetic pathos in the first place, leading generations of theorists to politely throw out the diagnostic of mimetic
contagion along with the tyrannical solution.

And yet, a sense of genealogical discrimination calls for a reevaluation
of Plato's critique of mimesis. Jonathan Dollimore, for instance—hardly a
defender of puritan moralism—proposes an incisive recuperation of Plato's
insights on art, which he puts to progressive social use, as he states: "If Soviet-
style [Platonic] censorship proved to be as counter-productive as it was
oppressive, . . . Plato was only the first of many to correctly infer that art can

threaten ideals of rationality and civilized human conduct."[44] With Dollimore, I agree in retaining Plato's diagnostic of mimesis, especially the insight
that "in drama we are not just moved by what we see, but we 'passionately'
identify with it."[45] What Plato's patho-*logy* also invites us to consider is that
terror and fear does not lead to any reassuring catharsis. On the contrary, it
generates a pathos that flows from the actor to spectators. As Socrates reiter-
ates in Book 10, when spectators are confronted with "a hero who is in grief,"
they "accompany the representation with sympathy," generating a *sympathein*
(shared pathos) that spreads contagiously, like a magnet, "even among the
very best of us" (*Rep.* 605d), attracting the irrational part of the soul to the
point of (dis)possession. In sum, once reframed within the general economy
of his theory of mimesis, our affective hypothesis is confirmed: Plato's quarrel with literature is not only based on the metaphysical problematic of
false representations (or mirror) of reality organized on a vertical hierarchy
to be theorized from a rational distance constitutive of his idealist logos
(transcendental thesis); it is also about the ethical, psychic, and pedagogical
problematic of affective impersonation characteristic of the actor (or mimos)
and the magnetic-mimetic-hypnotic-mirroring contagion endowed with the
spellbinding power to transmit mimetic pathos to the audience (immanent
thesis).[46]

A pathos of distance, then, animates Plato's diagnostic of contagion.
And once confronted with Aristotle's mimetic agonism toward his intellectual father, a mirroring inversion of perspectives in the patho-*logy* is bound
to ensue. Thus, in a final passage of the *Republic* that must have pricked Aristotle's mimetic ears and probably motivated him to write his own original
reply in the *Poetics*, "Plato," still wearing his Socratic mask (contrary to his
anti-mimetic advice, he rarely lets go of it, and if so, only to put on another
mask), notoriously concludes Book 10 by sending mimetic poetry in "exile"
so long as "she is unable to make good her defense" (*Rep.* 608a). Aristotle's
catharsis hypothesis in the *Poetics is* the defense aspiring to counter Plato's
affective hypothesis in the *Republic*. Or, to use Plato's analogy to describe
his ambitious pupil, catharsis is the youthful and rebellious kick against the
maternal fear of mimetic pathos.

This mimetic agon had far-reaching consequences for philosophy in
general and mimetic studies more specifically. To this day, contemporary

discussions of violence continue to take this ancient theoretical quarrel as a starting point for discussions related to the patho(-)logical effects of representations of violence. As Girard also recognized,

> Plato found it impossible to believe that tragic discord or tragic violence could ever become synonymous for harmony and peace. That is why he rejects with horror those patricidal and incestuous impulses to which Aristotle (and Western culture in general, not excluding the psychoanalysts) assigned a certain "cultural value." (*VS* 295)

An ancient quarrel between philosophy and poetry caused, at one remove, a quarrel within philosophy itself. And this quarrel stretches (via psychoanalysis and mimetic theory) to present debates on catharsis and contagion that concern not so much poetry and literature but the multiple avatars thereof (film to TV, internet platforms to video games). These, at least, are the psychological, ethical, and pedagogical implications that inform Plato's theoretical exclusion of poetry in the education of the youth at the dawn of mimetic studies.

And yet, in practice, genealogical lenses made us see that the quarrel was never as clear cut. Not only poetry, in its protean manifestations, never ceased to cast a spell on the western imagination, reaching massive audiences that had never even heard of, or cared about, old Platonic bans. Over the centuries, this philosophical exclusion of mimesis via a mimetic dialogue was either not taken seriously and considered an exercise in utopian writing based on a performative contradiction; or those who did take Plato, the ironist, seriously, simply found the exclusion of illustrious poetic figures such as Homer and Hesiod puzzling, violent, and offensive. In the wake of modern follow-ups on Aristotle, from Philip Sidney's *An Apology for Poetry* (1595) in the Renaissance to Percy Shelley's *A Defense of Poetry* (1840), in the Romantic period, advocates of high culture, especially literary critics, tended to take Plato's critique of poetry more than seriously—they took it personally. Hence, due to a passion for tales developed in childhood, many naturally tended to automatically side with Aristotle's defense of poetry, interpreting such Platonic passages as a tyrannical, totalitarian, and violent exclusion of poetry tout court from the western literary canon. Being ourselves not immune to the magic of mimesis and having just resorted to some mimetic dramatizations to mediate the ironic pathos of Socrates's dramatic logos, we obviously fundamentally sympathize with artists' poetic craft, on the one hand, and with the general thrust of Aristotle's defense of poetry and its numerous modern avatars, on the other.

These defenses, in fact, continue to inform our literary education in at least three different but related senses: first, censure is not a viable solution not only because it is radically at odds with democratic values but also because this repressive strategy might actually backfire and trigger an increased desire for what it censures. Taboos, Bataille taught us, tend to trigger violent transgressions.[47] Second, there is a strong philosophical potential in poetic media that, despite the changes in medium, has not lost its diagnostic power. As Aristotle influentially argued, fictions continue to serve as a starting point for further theorization by providing myths that are specific in their narrative articulation, mimetic in their structural organization, and provide exemplary case studies of probable and necessary sequences of events that have, if not universal and transhistorical value, at least philosophical and theoretical purchase. And third, what Plato calls "poetry" and up to the last century we called "literature" now occupies already such a marginal, fragile, and precarious place in contemporary educative systems increasingly informed and transformed by new digital media that concerned parents should be happy if literature continues to be read at all these days—let alone Homeric poetry!

For these and other reasons, scholarly allegiances in this "ancient quarrel" between poetry and philosophy, which itself rests on a mimetic agon between the Janus-faced hypotheses of catharsis and contagion, tend to be set in advance. This privilege for poetry is even accentuated for those who claim to operate within a Nietzschean tradition of thought. In fact, Nietzsche, in *On Genealogy of Morals*, puts it dramatically as he calls Plato "the greatest enemy of art which Europe has so far produced," and sums up the mimetic agon at the foundation of western culture as follows: "Plato versus Homer: that is the complete, the real antagonism" (II: 25, 129).[48] More than two millennia after Plato, then, genealogists of morals are naturally inclined to celebrate Homer contra Plato as the origin of our golden literary heritage, rather than of dark human vices—no matter how violent and bloody this heritage is.

And yet, a deeper understanding of the paradoxical logic of mimetic agonism allows us to see that the antagonism between the philosopher and the poet, exclusions of poets and defenses of poetry, is never as clear cut as it appears to be. Plato, as we have seen and heard, may have been opposed to mimesis in theory, but made ample use of mimetic strategies in practice (dramatic dialogues, mythic tales, theatrical masks, agonistic confrontations, scapegoating mechanisms), and his position on the powers of mimesis is more complex than it is often said to be. Before automatically siding unilaterally with Aristotle's defense of poetry and the cathartic kick he did not fully articulate, it is necessary, then, to be more specific in the reevaluation of the truth and falsity of Plato's (anti-)mimetic thought for contemporary mimetic studies and education more generally. This entails going beyond secondhand understandings of Plato qua philosophical tyrant, in order to further disentangle the diagnostic reasons that in-*form*, firsthand, his critique of mimetic violence.

It should be clear by now that poetry as we understand it today is *not* what Plato has in mind in his critique of mimesis, but we still need to contextualize this crucial point further to bring Plato's diagnostic inside our homes. His conception of "poetry" is not the same as what we now group under this term, as we teach or attend a course on, say, Romantic or modern poetry, or simply read a poem in a book or online. Poetry in the fourth century B.C. was not primarily read. It was, rather, performed as a dramatic spectacle that was enacted, and thus embodied, on a theatrical scene for a large audience that would assemble in the theater to witness dramatizations of tragedies, comedies, and epics. True, the Greek alphabet had been invented as early as the eighth century and a cultural elite was literate; yet, as the classicist Eric Havelock influentially argued in *A Preface to Plato* (1963), in fourth-century Greece the major source of information and affective entertainment was still an "oral culture" in which the poet had a prestige way superior to the philosopher, for theatrical "poetry" rather than theoretical "poetics" served as manuals of conduct that provided models for actions.[49]

Now, it is within this dominant theatrical, oral context that thrives on pathos and which puts the logos of the philosopher in a position of disadvantage, if not entirely to sleep, that Plato, who admits to being "very conscious of her [poetry's] spell" (607c), made the following patho-*logical* observation about the violent pathos generated by his main antagonist, Homer:

> so long as she [poetry] is unable to make good her defense we shall chant
> over to ourselves as we listen the reasons that we have given as a counter-
> charm to her spell, to preserve us from slipping back in the childish loves
> of the multitude (*Rep.* 607e).

Thus, as poetry is banned from the ideal city, a philosophical logos aspires
to take the educative place of poetic pathos. Philosophy is the countercharm
to the spell of poetry, which does not mean that this antidote is deprived of
poetic charms.

If we return to what is arguably *the* conceptual protagonist of *Republic*,
that is, mimesis, we notice that even in the context of his famous metaphysical critique of mimesis as a copy of a copy, Plato's target is not simply the
*content* (or message) of epics or tragedies and the epistemic falsities they
convey—though it is certainly that too. His target remains also, and perhaps
above all, the dramatic *form* (or medium) that channels such spectacles and
the pathos thereof from the theatrical stage to what he calls, giving a psychological account of the chained prisoners, "the nondescript mob assembled in
the theater" (*Rep.* 604e). The public goes to the theater to be moved, for theatrical pathos speaks to the "fretful part" (604e) of the soul. But what is moving, we now know, affects both hearing and vision—stretching to impress
all the senses. It is thus not only a question of listening to a poetic recital or
of seeing a theatrical representation from the outside but also of feeling the
tragic/comic effects of theatrical impersonations from the inside. This is the
lesser-known side of Plato's critique of mimesis. It has been overshadowed
by the philosopher's ontological concerns with mimetic representations as
false copies far removed for true Forms discussed in Book 10, which have the
painter (not the actor) as a paradigmatic artistic example; and these concerns
with duplication were reproduced, at one additional remove, by literary critics' understandings of mimesis qua realism.[50]

And yet, at a closer look, even in Book 10, Plato continues to have these
psychological, ethical, and pedagogical concerns with affective contagion
in mind that have the actor (or *mimos*) as the paradigmatic type. Thus, in a
revealing passage that casts an illuminating backward light on Book 3, Plato
speaks of the irrational power of mimetic dramas on spectators' soul, including souls of otherwise "intelligent and temperate disposition" (604e). He

does so, once again, by diagnosing how the mimetic affects flow from the stage to the crowd, generating a hypnotizing effect on the spell-*bound* prisoners. Desire is part of this magnetic bond, but so are other manifestations of mimetic pathos, such as "sex, and anger, and all the appetites and pains and pleasures of the soul" (606d), including, of course, the violent pathos triggered by scenes of war central to Homer's poetics in general and to the *Iliad* in particular. Hence the urgency to expand the focus on mimetic desire to include mimetic pathos more generally, or rather, absorb the Oedipal problematic of desire in the more general economy of affect, or pathos. Hence again, Plato condemns a type of mimetic subjectivity that, under the spell of actors, is led to "imitate the *pathos* of others" (604e) so that it becomes a *sym-pathos*. Plato, in other words, knows what every actor, public speaker, or political leader knows. Namely that the defining characteristic of a "mob" is to be prey to contagious affects—especially violent ones—that spread mimetically and unconsciously from self to others, generating a mimetic pathos with the power to turn egos into phantoms or shadows of egos. The countercharm that fixes the gaze on a hypnotic sun rather than on hypnotic shadows is, again, called philosophy.

To be sure, the driving telos of Plato's philosophy is on the ascending paths of dialectics that leads the rational part of the soul outside of the cave to contemplate the world of intelligible ideas. Yet we are now in a position to realize that this movement of intellectual liberation characteristic of the *vita contemplativa* is not an action; it is a reaction against the powers of false shadows to generate spellbinding effects on the irrational part of the soul at play in the vita mimetica. There is, thus, a mirror relation between these two opposed worlds: light is opposed to darkness just as a white horse is opposed to a black horse—but both sides are constitutive of the same divided soul. If the *Republic* is an ascending, dialectical, and rational path that leads readers toward the sun and the metaphysical idea of the Good it entails, it is also a diagnostic that makes us feel the dark magnetic pull of the poetic antagonist Plato is up against. Since this pull tends to be left in the shadow of dominant rationalist accounts concerned with the *vita contemplativa*, in the company of advocates of the *vita activa*, we inversed the telos of the journey and read Plato to better understand the spellbinding power of the vita mimetica.

We might not have been fully aware of it, but thus reframed Plato has been encouraging us to enter into the labyrinth of the unconscious, a mimetic unconscious based on an affective hypothesis in which the same is not cured by the same but generates more of the same instead. This contagious pathology concerns also desire, as Girard recognized, but was never limited to it, no matter how mimetic desire is and continues to be. An affective supplement to mimetic theory is thus needed to expand the diagnostic to the more general sphere of mimetic pathos and the pathologies it entails. Pathos is, indeed, a spellbinding force that takes possession of the ego, dispossesses it of its rational control, and via heterogeneous, magnetizing, and highly contagious affects that—from laughter to grief, sympathy to desire, love to ressentiment, fear to panic, joy to anger to other violent manifestations of pathos—generate good but also bad effects now under the lens of mimetic studies.

## Concluding the Dialogue: The Rhetoric of Mimesis

Having reframed the quarrel between philosophy and poetry from the angle of dramatic mimesis and the pathos it entails, we are in a position to conclude our formative and perhaps transformative dialogue on the vita mimetica. If Plato is drawn, like a moth, to the *vita contemplativa*, Socrates, to his risk and peril, returns to the cave, due to his pedagogical concerns with education (*paideia*) constitutive of the vita mimetica. Perhaps because he is not deprived of hypnotizing skills himself, Socrates is fundamentally aware of homo mimeticus' receptivity, from childhood onward, to contagious affects that operate on what he calls the "irrational" part of the soul, below conscious awareness, and are in this sense unconscious. At the end of *Republic*, in Book 10, he continues, along lines I now faithfully reproduce:

> And does not the fretful part of us present many and varied occasions for imitation . . . especially by a nondescript mob assembled in the theater? . . . By all means.

> And is it not obvious that the nature of the mimetic poet is not related to this better part of the soul . . . , if he is to win favor with the multitude, but is devoted to the fretful and complicated type of character because it is easy to imitate?

It is obvious. (*Rep.* 604e)

And a little later Socrates continues:

> And so, in regard to the emotions of sex and anger, and all the appetites and pains and pleasures of the soul which we say accompany all our actions, the effect of poetic imitation is the same. For it waters and fosters these feelings when what we ought to do is to dry them up, and it establishes them as our rulers when they ought to be ruled, to the end that we may be better and happier men instead of worse and more miserable.
>
> I cannot deny it, said he. (606d)

While the catharsis hypothesis taught us to downplay this contagious principle in the twentieth century, can we still continue to downplay it in the twenty-first century? In a sense, yes. After all, turning one's back to an inconvenient truth is a widespread reaction immune to rational arguments. The case of Thrasymachus already illustrates this point at the opening of *Republic*, acting like a "wild beast" (336b), dramatizing with anticipation the desire of the cavemen to "kill the man who tried to release them" (517a). This will to kill was thus at play within the Allegory of the Cave itself—and, at one remove, in Athenian reality as well, as the death of Socrates confirms. And yet, for those familiar with the power of actors to establish models of behavior, including racist, sexist, and militaristic models that spread contagiously in the body politic, it is becoming clear that mimesis, no matter how (un)realistic the message, produces real hypermimetic affects at the level of the medium. And this brings us to a last, and arguably most far-reaching, step in Plato's diagnostic reflection on the power of contagion.

With this (con)textual frame in mind that took us to the final message encoded in the *Republic*, we are in a better position to reevaluate, at a slower diagnostic rhythm, a key formal distinction concerning the medium Plato introduces at the beginning and has been implicitly informing his critique of contagion, as well as ours, all along. It is in fact crucial to stress that in Books 2 and 3 Plato does not ban poetry in toto; nor is he solely concerned with the problematic content of poetry (what he calls logos)—though this epistemic concern will continue to inform his critique of poetry as an illusory shadow.

Rather, and somewhat less readily perceptible, when the concept of mimesis first appears in Book 3 of *Republic*, and thus enters the philosophical scene for the first time, Plato, strictly speaking, does not speak only as a philosopher or as a psychologist—though he is both. He also speaks as what we now call a literary critic attentive to the power of words to animate shadows. Plato, under his Socratic mask, is, in fact, concerned with poetry's formal qualities of expression (what he calls *lexis*) of texts that, as we have seen, were dramatized on the stage for the crowd or, if you prefer the cinematic myth, projected on a wall of a cave. This shift from the "what" to the "how" of poetic speech, logos to lexis, inaugurates not only the field of literary studies *as* mimetic studies. I shall go further and say that on this formal shift of emphasis hinges Plato's entire diagnostic condemnation of the contagious properties of mimetic pathos tout court that runs—beginning, middle, and end—through the *Republic*, opening an alternative door to the unconscious that reaches into modernity, informing new mimetic studies as well.

Plato's assumption is deceivingly simple and can be summarized as follows: the form or mode of expression (lexis) cannot be dissociated from the content (logos) because *how* the actor (mimos) speaks—that is, in which narrative mode or diction he or she speaks—determines the affective power of *what* he or she says.[51] *Lexis* not only mediates logos but forms it and performs it. And, unsurprisingly, *mimesis* is the link in the chain that mediates between formal, semantic, and affective elements. In fact, in his account of narrative modes and the effects they generate in Book 3 of *Republic*, Plato's target is not poetry in general but what he calls "imitation" (mimesis). And since this is the first time mimesis is introduced in *Republic*, and by extension Plato's thought and philosophy more generally, genealogists are encouraged to slow down and consider closely this incipient moment of emergence at the dawn of philosophy that continues to inform the mimetic turn today.

Not speaking in his proper name, but in the name of another, namely, Socrates, "Plato" sets up a formal difference between "imitation" (mimesis), "pure narration" (diegesis), and what he calls "mixed style," which relies on a mixture of both diegesis and mimesis. The typology depicted in this inaugural poetics is the following: in simple narrative or diegesis, "the poet himself is the speaker and does not even attempt to suggest to us that anyone but himself is speaking" (*Rep.* 393a): this is a third-person, indirect speech characteristic of the dithyramb. In imitation or mimesis, on the other hand, "the poet delivers a speech as if he were someone else" (393c): this is a first-person, direct speech characteristic of tragedy and comedy. Mixed style is based on an interplay between mimesis and diegesis and is characteristic of the epic. There are thus different narrative modes of diction in which "poetry," in the broad Platonic sense of literature, can be recited, and *only one* is banned at this stage.

Glaucon is slow to grasp such a discerning literary point, which is thus likely to have been unknown prior to Plato and will influence Aristotle's *Poetics* as well.[52] While Aristotle reproduces these Platonic narrative distinctions, he does not weave them in his poetics concerned with the rationality of mimetic plots. For those who inherit Plato's concern with mimesis's irrational potential, they raise some further diagnostic questions. For instance: why is mimetic lexis so dangerous? What distinguishes it from diegesis not only at the level of content or logos but at the level of affect or pathos? And why does this formal distinction between mimesis and diegesis matter so much that it actually coincides with the first conceptual appearance of mimesis in *Republic*, and by extension in the history of philosophy and aesthetics?

These questions fall under the concerns with what the ancients called rhetoric. And since rhetoric taps into the affective pathos characteristic of homo mimeticus, it goes to the very foundations of mimetic studies as well. Rhetoric is of course attentive to not only what is said but also how, by whom, and to whom it is said. Hence, to uncover these foundations it is crucial to recall the previous rings in our argument on the vita mimetica, including the magnetic power of shadows, the oral culture that pervades them, and above all the theatrical dimension of the scene. The critique, in fact, is explicitly addressed to mimetic power, but the direct target is actually the actor, or rhapsode, who gives voice to mimetic speeches on theatrical stages that resemble the famous cave.

For instance, in the example of mimetic speeches in the *Iliad*, "he," Homer, that is, a reciter of Homer, like Ion, "*makes us feel* that not Homer is the speaker, but the priest," for instance, thereby "deliver[ing] a speech as if he were someone else, . . . assimilate[ing] thereby his own diction as far as possible to that of the person whom he announces as about to speak" (*Rep.* 393b–c). Or take another example of mimetic speech, one in which an actor or rhapsode does not narrate events such as a battle between the gods, or a war scene from a narrative diegetic *distance*. Rather, and crucially, in mimetic speech, the actor in the role of, say, Achilles would *impersonate* his anger, his refusal to join his companions, and eventually his heroic deeds in battle that culminate in the killing of Hector, whose body he attempts to tear to pieces, and so on. This actor would indeed impersonate the role with pathos, using his voice, for sure, but also his body, gestures, and facial expressions. The implications of this dramatic point for the vita mimetica are far reaching: in simple narration (diegesis), the actor speaking in the third person preserves a linguistic distance from the fictional character that allows for a distinction between self and other, actor and role, to subsist; in mimetic speech (mimesis) the actor speaks in the first person, impersonating a role linguistically but also *affectively* so that the fictional character's affect (pathos) becomes a shared or *sym-pathos* that binds subjects by spell-binding them.

You will have heard the echo with the Allegory of the Cave. Just like in mimetic speech, the speaker (say Homer, a rhapsode, or an actor) does not speak in his/her proper name but in the name of a fictional other (say Chryses or Achilles), generating fictional shadows or phantoms, so the shadows on the wall are endowed with the voice of someone who does not speak in his/her proper name but in the name of the shadows instead. Or, to put it with Plato's narrative categories, the shadows are spoken via *mimesis*, not *diegesis*. This narrative and aesthetic point makes us see and hear that Plato's critique of mimesis may be explicitly addressed to the painter and the illusory representations he creates that visibly deform true reality, yet the direct target is actually the poet, actor, or rhapsode, who gives voice and body to poetic speeches and movements with effects that imperceptibly form and transform the spell-bound subject. No wonder allegorical chains are needed to make the affective, contagious, and transformative powers of mimesis visible.

True, not unlike Homer at the beginning of the *Iliad*, Plato does not speak in his proper name (diegesis) either but speaks in the name of another (mimesis). Undisturbed by this aporia for it emerges from his mimetic agon with Homer, he implicitly indicates how mimesis can be put to patho-*logical* use, as Socrates presses on:

And is not likening oneself to another in speech or bodily bearing of him to whom one likens oneself?

Surely.

> In such case then it appears, he and the other poets effect their narration
> through imitation. (*Rep.* 393c)

With the figure of the actor or rhapsode hiding behind the mask of the poet, we are now in a position to understand the full power of mimetic lexis to generate a chain of mimetic contagion that flows from the stage to the spellbound spectators. From the very beginning, in fact, mimesis is already double and opens up the possibility for protean transformations: it is a formal narrative device (mimesis as lexis) that serves as the medium for the actor (mimos) to give bodily and affective expression to mimetic fiction (mimesis as representation), which in turn generates contagious affects that become shared with spectators via an identificatory *sym-pathos* (mimesis as pathos) with magnetizing properties. Poets who narrate through imitation make it possible for actors on the stage not to be themselves but to make spectators feel that they become other—namely, the characters they impersonate in speech, body, and affective expression.

The mechanism is simple but not less effective for that. It is based on a linguistic distinction that is not confined to content or language (logos) but affects via form or diction (lexis) the body and the soul of spectators with affect (pathos). In fact, the actor speaking in mimetic speech does not only "assimilate thereby his own diction as far as possible to that of the person whom he announces as about to speak" (*Rep.* 393c) thereby *appearing* to speak like someone other and generating a deceitful illusion. By the same linguistic mimesis, a bodily impersonation ensues whereby the actor is "likening oneself in speech and bodily bearing" (393c), becoming someone other and generating a truthful affective contagion. Picture the scene: if the mimos impersonating Achilles weeps and hits his chest and we see him weeping and hitting himself, his sorrow is contagiously passed on to us and we feel like weeping with him; if he is triumphant and we see him raising his arms, our muscles tighten in glory as well; and if he gives vent to violent affects, no matter how opposed to violence we are in theory, our blood stirs, our muscles tighten; we might even feel the unconscious urge to reenact such a violence in practice—though we have been trained to conceal this urge.

This mimetic reenactment, then, taps into the soul's irrational part, generating mirroring unconscious reflexes. Unlike a transcendental mirror held up by a painter used to establish abstract metaphysical dualities, the figure of the actor is endowed with concrete mirroring powers that can be put to self-critical use. Reagan was of course not the first to point that out; neither are contemporary affect theorists. It was Plato who, while busy erecting an ontology of Being, was still up against a poetic world of becoming whose magnetic power he intimately felt, dramatized, and theorized. Hence, he set up an immanent mirror embodied by an actor with the power to cut across binaries that divide representation and identification but also self and other, mind and body, fiction and reality, art, and life.

The experience of mimetic contagion is, indeed, Janus-faced: it viscerally connects vision and affect, representation and impersonation, inspiration and intoxication. Or, to echo the divinities Plato convokes, the experience of mimetic contagion flows from Apollo to the Muses, from the poet to the rhapsode to the spectators, inducing a state of contagious intoxication characteristic of Dionysian rituals. The mimetic medium, then, channels the contagious affects expressed in the mimetic message, generating affective sameness where rational distance should be preserved.

We were wondering: why do mimetic spectacles generate a type of unconscious contagion with the potential to spill from the sphere of mimetic representation to the sphere of mimetic behavior? Why does Plato seemingly conflate different forms of imitation in his fluid, dynamic, and rather protean concept of mimesis? The answers should be fully in sight by now. They do not rest on the hypothesis of catharsis but rest on the one of contagion. Schematically, the diagnostic can be summarized in the following four points. First, Plato's critique of poetry does not target a reading practice but a performative, theatrical practice that is expressed by actors who impersonate exemplary, sometimes noble but often violent characters—hence the focus on the protean figure of the mimos who often stands in for the poet. Second, his ethical condemnation does not concern, as is often assumed, poetry in general but concerns mimetic poetry, by which he means literary models that rely on first-person direct speech, such as tragedy and comedy, and partially the epic—hence the need of establishing a poetics that distinguishes among narrative modes (lexis). Third, the use of mimetic or dramatic mode, Plato notices, allows for a type of theatrical imitation that is not simply linguistic; rather, it stretches to affect and inflect the actor's tonality, mimicry, and bodily gestures—hence the need for Plato's poetics to stretch from narrative to include the actor's expressions and bodily gestures (soma) that operate on the irrational part of the soul (psyche). Last, it is this mimicry of the actor made possible by mimetic speeches that is responsible for triggering the public's collective impulse to unconsciously imitate, as if under a magnetic spell, such gestures and the affects in mirroring terms that impress the soul and the body, turning nature into "second nature"—hence the importance for this poetics to include not only personal psychology but collective psychology as well.

In the end, mimesis operates as both the level of content and form, logos and lexis, vison and orality, message and medium—if only because the mime mediates contagious affects on the basis of a mimetic medium. This is an untimely diagnostic that is rarely mentioned by mainstream commentators of *Republic*, yet it has not lost any of its relevance today. A key measure of its untimeliness can be gauged by the following genealogical point: it is even adapted by self-proclaimed *anti*-Platonic philosophical physicians like Nietzsche who are in a relation of mimetic agonism with the father of philosophy in general and with his critique of mimesis in particular. As is well known, Nietzsche generally virulently opposes Plato's ontology based on an understanding of mimesis as simple (Apollonian) mirroring *representation*. Less known is that this anti-Platonic philosopher adopts Plato's psychology based on an understanding of an unconscious mimesis as affective (Dionysian) *contagion*.

And here is where Plato's ancient psychology returns, via the logic of mimetic agonism, to the (anti-)Platonic philosophical physician with which we started in order to propose a diagnostic of Dionysian intoxications that reach from antiquity into the present.

# CHAPTER 3

# Dionysian Intoxications

## Cults, Conspiracies, Insurrections

Friedrich Nietzsche is arguably the most *anti*-Platonic thinker in the history of philosophy. He may thus appear to be an unlikely partner to mediate the affective hypothesis initiated by Plato in antiquity for the modern and contemporary period. Consistently in his corpus, in fact, Nietzsche affirms the primacy of life in this world rather than a faith in after-worlds, posits immanence contra transcendence, connects reason to unreason, privileges aesthetics over metaphysics, roots the mind back to the body, among other overturning gestures that are explicitly directed contra Plato and the idealist tradition he inaugurated. And yet, if we look beyond textbook introductions to philosophy, we quickly realize that Nietzsche's perspectives are never unilateral and call for important genealogical or, in our language, patho-logical qualifications. The dynamic of mimetic agonism that finds in Nietzsche a paradigmatic modernist example taught us to recognize that behind a violent philosophical opposition directed contra an intellectual antagonist at the level of philosophical logos often hides a strong affective impression that is rendered manifest at the level of *patho*-logies—that is, critical discourses attentive to the logic of mimetic pathos.

If we adopt genealogical lenses, Nietzsche's intellectual relation to Plato in general and to the latter's critique of contagious mimesis and the potential violence it entails in particular is more ambivalent than Nietzsche's antagonistic stance often suggests. As he puts it in *Ecce Homo* (1908): "I attack only causes that are victorious."[1] And what cause could be more victorious than Plato and the Platonism that dominated over two millennia of western thought? Further specifying his agonistic method of attack, Nietzsche who, in his youth, had fought a duel, continues his account of this agonistic dynamic as follows: "The strength of one who attacks has in the opposition he needs a kind of *gauge* [Maß]; every growth reveals itself in the seeking out of a powerful opponent—or problem; for a philosopher who is warlike also challenges problems to a duel" (*EH* 7;47). As discussed in volume 1, this intellectual opposition is part of a mimetic agonism Nietzsche inherits, in the company of Jacob Burckhardt, from the ancients and puts to productive patho-*logical* use for the moderns and, at one remove, for the contemporaries as well.[2] For Nietzsche, in fact, an agonistic form of conceptual violence contra a previous influential theory, or opponent, is not a negative but an affirmative move. Why? Because it considers the latter "a worthy enemy, against whom one can test one's strength" (*BT* 17–18). Here we find another confirmation that mimetic agonism is a philosophical strategy to develop a critical logos on the dynamic of mimetic pathos. We can continue to put it to use for solving ancient, modern, and contemporary riddles that, to this day, continue to oscillate, pendulum-like, between competing contagious/cathartic hypotheses.

Given the intellectually productive dimension of this agonistic method, we should recall that for genealogists of violence, mimetic agonism and the "pathos" that animates it depart in original ways from dominant conceptions of the unconscious. If it is based on an ambivalent relation with a previous model, this pathos does not simply generate psychic pathologies but also patho-*logical* diagnostics that cannot be contained with an Oedipal familial drama and the repression of desire it entails, as Freud theorizes it; nor does it fit within a triangular structure of mimetic rivalry triggered by mimetic desire, which leads to ressentiment, rivalry, sacrificial violence, ritual death, and the negation of life as Girard's agonistic overturning of Freud's Oedipal model understands it—though it can certainly do that as well.[3] Rather, and for us more important, the mimetic agon for Nietzsche finds a gauge in influential theories or logoi inherited genealogically from the past, which are put to logical rather than pathological use in view of turning affective negation into conceptual affirmation, mimetic rivalry into original creation, psychic sicknesses into therapeutic cures, contagious pathologies into diagnostic patho-*logies*. Or, to put it in Nietzschean terms, mimetic agonism finds in the dyadic (rather than triangular) dynamic of the duel with and against the opponent a way to put "*aggressive* pathos" (*EH* 7; 47) to philosophical and creative use.

Mimetic studies will continue to rest on broad shoulders, but innovations are urgently needed in order to catch up with our fast-changing times. Nietzsche, for one, urges philosophers to be daring. This entails not to simply accept "concepts as a gift, nor merely purify and polish them, but first to make and create them, present them and make them convincing" (*WP* 409; 220). Mimetic agonism, as I defined it, is nothing less and nothing more than the fundamental principle that contributes to philosophy's main vocation: namely, the creation of new concepts vital to solving ancient and modern problems that are still with us today—from Dionysian contagion in classical antiquity to modern crowd behavior, to the powers of new media to trigger violent insurrections that cast a shadow on the future of democracy, among other (hyper)mimetic manifestations of unconscious violence we shall also consider.

Contemporary political events like the storming of the U.S. Capitol on January 6, 2021, will serve as an example of how (new) media can be put to violent political use in the digital age. In a striking illustration of the powers of hypermimesis, it also reveals how real political violence was anticipated by cinematic fictions, most notably by future-oriented TV series like *Black Mirror* (2011–2019, dir. Charlie Brooker), as the episode "The Waldo Moment" (2013), will make clear.

But let us proceed in genealogical order.

## Dionysian Contagion: Ancient Intoxications

In volume 1, we have encountered Nietzsche's critical stance contra Aristotle's cathartic hypothesis. What we need to add now is that Nietzsche's suspicion of catharsis leads him to both lean on and supplement Plato's affective hypothesis. The Platonic foundations of Nietzsche's diagnostic of contagion run deep and become most visible in the context of the agonistic confrontation between cathartic and affective hypotheses on the influence of tragic art. This is how Nietzsche's diagnostic of the influence of art on spectators continues in *Human, All Too Human* (1878) in a section we already partially considered, titled "Old doubts about the effect of art." Let us now restitute it in its entirety:

> It might be that in every individual case pity and fear would be attenuated and purged [*entladen*] by tragedy: nevertheless, they could on the whole become greater under the influence of tragedy, and Plato would still be correct in asserting that tragedy on the whole makes people more fearful and susceptible to emotion [*rührseliger*]. The tragic poet himself, then, would necessarily acquire a gloomy, fearful view of the world and soft, sensitive, lachrymose soul; it would likewise correspond to Plato's opinion if the tragic poets and the entire community [*Stadtgemeinden*] that especially delights in them would degenerate into ever greater excess and licentiousness. (*HH* 212; 140)

Plato contra Aristotle, contagion contra catharsis: the agon between the catharsis and affective hypothesis does not stop with ancient quarrels but reaches major advocates of modern quarrels as well. Already in his early period, Nietzsche, in fact, makes clear that he is ready to side *with* Plato contra Aristotle in order to warn the moderns about the potentially pathological effects of mimetic spectacles on the audience. The diagnostic is worth repeating: a drive may not be discharged (a better translation of *entladen*, the same verb Jakob Bernays had used to explain catharsis)[4] but, rather, *intensified* through its satisfaction. Consequently, for Nietzsche, tragic pathos could not only amplify fear and other affects constitutive of an immanent ontology (what Michel Henry calls "the pathos of Being and its suffering—that is life" [*GP* 12]); it can also infect cities and entire communities via scenes of unbridled immoderation and, perhaps, violent degeneration that infect, by way of affective contagion, the body politic. We shall return to such scenes of degeneration via some modern and contemporary examples, both fictional and real.

What is certain is that Nietzsche is not alone among modern philosophers in siding with Plato, contra Aristotle, in view of calling attention to the contagious properties of theatrical spectacles. While a number of modern predecessors could be enlisted, a Platonic thinker Nietzsche is often antagonistic to, Jean-Jacques Rousseau, is worth mentioning as further indication that mimetic agonism continues to be generative of diagnostic patho-*logies* of mimetic contagion. The influence of Plato is present everywhere in Rousseau's writings and is particularly visible when it comes to the question of education and the critique of modern civilization it entails. But it is probably in the *Lettre à d'Alembert* (1758), a text specifically devoted to the negative effects of the theater in general and comedy in particular, that Rousseau sides contra his French contemporary, in order to state his clearest opposition to the catharsis hypothesis that, under the spell of neoclassicism, continues to inform advocates of *les Lumières* (the Enlightenment). For Rousseau, in fact, the "the general effect of [comedic/theatrical] spectacles is" not to purge but rather to "augment natural inclinations and give new energy to all kinds of passions."[5] Mimetic passions are fueled rather than purged by dramatic spectacles; drama does not diminish but augments the all too human predisposition for pathos.

If Nietzsche expressed his suspicion of catharsis inspired by the solitude he found in the Swiss Alps in his hikes in upper-Engadin, Rousseau writes from the perspective of his Swiss city of Geneva; and yet the diagnostic is essentially the same. In fact, the latter also worries that "passions that are overstimulated [*trop irritées*] could degenerate into vices" (*LA* 68). We are thus back to the detective of *Vice* who turns out to have been not only Nietzschean but Russeaustic. In fact, Rousseau sets out to explicitly disqualify the catharsis hypothesis in favor of the affective hypothesis as he continues: "I know that the poetics of theater pretends to accomplish the opposite result: to purge [*purger*] passions by exciting them, but I have difficulties of conceiving of this rule" (68). And he concludes by saying that "the only instrument that can be used to purge passions is reason and I already said that reason has no effect in the theater" (69). Nietzsche will not go as far as Rousseau in his Platonic faith about the power of reason over affect, logos over pathos. And yet he fundamentally shares Rousseau's diagnostic suspicion of the catharsis hypothesis and the endorsement of the affective hypothesis that ensues.

Plato, Rousseau, Nietzsche. These are only three thinkers in a long philosophical chain, yet they are exemplary thinkers and acute psychologists nonetheless. Given Nietzsche's general antagonistic relation to Rousseau, which redoubles his antagonism to Plato, the specific focus on the catharsis/contagion quarrel continues to reveal surprising continuities with the founder of mimetic studies. The Platonic foundations of Nietzsche's diagnostic of mimetic contagion are operative from the beginning of his philological career. The power of art in general and of mimetic artists in particular to influence spectators by disrupting the mental screen of (visual) representation via the (bodily) and intoxicating power of dramatic impersonations is a familiar theme to the author of *The Birth of Tragedy* (1872). It is constitutive of the Dionysian "pathos and drunkenness" that, for Michel Henry and Georges Bataille before him, "is the eternal essence of living life" (*GP* 15).[6] Of course, the early Nietzsche celebrates the mimetic phenomenon Plato tends to condemn, but the diagnostic of contagion is strikingly similar, and significant philological continuities between the father of philosophy and its influential modernist antagonist can be found flowing underneath the obvious metaphysical discontinuities that divides them.

In his first book, Nietzsche had in fact famously relied on two divinities, Apollo and Dionysus, to provide mythic conceptual masks to account for two classical yet still modern facets of mimesis. If Plato, in Book 10 of the *Republic*, had identified mimesis as visual representation or copy at two removes from reality via the figure of the painter, or the trope of the mirror, Nietzsche, via the mediation of Schopenhauer, substituted the illusory sphere of Apollonian representation instead. Conversely, if Plato, in Book 3, introduced mimesis as a dramatic impersonation characteristic of the poet, or actor on a theatrical stage, Nietzsche substitutes the figure of the Dionysian reveler that, in his view, still animates the tragic chorus with its power to mediate a contagious mimesis to spectators in the theater. And again, like Plato before him, he renders this contagion via "the analogy of intoxication [*Rausch*]" (*BT* 36) and the "strange rapture" and "frenzied" dispossession of identity it entails, as Nietzsche's classicist friend, Erwin Rhode, also puts it in *Psyche*.[7]

But the genealogical connections go deeper. Notice, in fact, that the (anti-)Platonic philosopher gave aesthetic and philosophical flesh to an ancient Platonic link between the Apollonian sphere of poetic inspiration, on one side, and the Dionysian sphere of ritual intoxication, on the other, a mimetic, contagious, or, better, magnetic link already theorized by Plato via the trope of the magnet and the chain that ensues. As we have seen, in *Ion* Plato had in fact originally tied the enthusiastic and dispossessed figure of the rhapsode to Apollo, the god of music. What we must add now is that he also paved the way for the Apollonian-Dionysian connection that, for Nietzsche, gives birth to tragic art. How? By metaphorically linking, via a "mighty chain," the Apollonian-inspired rhapsode to a frenzied ritual dispossession of identity that he, Plato, had already compared to the Dionysian bacchants or Corybantes when they dance in a state of manic frenzy and are not in their senses. Plato, then, opened up a perspective that will be evaluated positively by the tradition of the sublime (ancient and modern);[8] and under the rubric of the Dionysian, this tradition will continue to inform the early Nietzsche as well.

Furthermore, if Plato is generally critical of states of mimetic dispossession, this is the moment to recognize that just like Nietzsche after him, he is far from unilateral in his evaluation of this ritual mimesis and the contagious madness it entails. For instance, in *Phaedrus* Plato, always under the mask of Socrates, will speak appreciatively of "madness" (*mania*) as he sets out to articulate a typology that distinguishes between four types of mania, linking them again to familiar divinities: namely, poetic madness (inspired by the Muses), erotic madness (inspired by *Eros*), prophetic or divinatory madness (inspired by Apollo), and, last but not least, ritual or telestic madness (inspired by Dionysus).[9] Interestingly, and to complicate our genealogy further, in the context of ritual/Dionysian madness, Plato turns out to be also an advocate of the cathartic hypothesis. While he is generally critical of the mimetic excess, contagious frenzy, and pathological contagion internal to telestic rituals, he is also ready to recognize that it can be put to patho-*logical* use. Thus, in *Phaedrus* he writes that via Dionysian madness, "rites and means of purification were established, and the sufferer was brough out of danger, alike for the present and for the future" (244e). Who said that Plato was unilaterally opposed to catharsis? As always in matters of mimetic agonism, the opposition is far from clear cut; it can even serve as a gauge to develop new patho-*logies* for contemporary advocates of mimetic studies.

In many ways, Plato is here paving the way for Aristotle and the catharsis hypothesis the latter develops in *Politics* with and contra Plato; he also puts us in a position to confirm that what is true for *mimēsis* remains true for mania: genealogical lenses reveal that important continuities exist between the catharsis and the affective hypotheses. Perhaps because they are two sides of a Janus-faced conceptual/affective coin. Plato's duplicity is, in fact, symptomatic of a perspectival thinker who likes to overturn diagnostics in order to reveal that the mimetic pathology can be the source of patho-*logies* as well (and vice versa). As Gilbert Rouget puts it, for Plato, mania and the contagious dispossession it entails "is at one and the same time sickness and healing of sickness, which should not surprise us."[10] Indeed, it does not. Plato's pharmacological perspectives change depending on the context and problem in general and the type of mimetic madness in particular, often promoting a perspectival evaluation of Dionysian patho(-)logical powers Nietzsche will subsequently further in the modernist period.

Despite their oscillating evaluations of Dionysian contagion, or rather because of them, both Plato and Nietzsche fundamentally agree that its affective power relies on the infectious register of dramatic mimesis, which includes mimicry, impersonations, speaking out of other bodies, which, as we have seen, include "speeches and tales" such as in tragedy or the epic. What we must add now is that Plato's critique of mimesis, like Nietzsche's after him, includes "song and tunes" constitutive of the contagious and intoxicating properties of mimesis qua "*mousikē*." That is, a more general aesthetic rubric that originally refers to Apollonian gifts from the Muses, including but not limited to what we now group under the rubric of music for it included dance and poetry as well. Uploaded by new media that have performative effects, mousikē is again entangled with the vicissitudes of the catharsis/affective hypotheses constitutive of Dionysian gifts of ritual intoxication.

Music cannot be confined to traditional definitions of mimesis understood as representation; yet it has contagious properties a genealogical tradition that goes from Plato to Nietzsche considers in need of patho-logical evaluations that cut both ways. Plato was, in fact, fundamentally aware of the formative powers of music. Hence, in Book 3 of *Republic* he follows up on his diagnostic of dramatic mimesis with the realization that

> education in music is most sovereign, because more than anything else rhythm and harmony find their way to the inmost soul and take strongest hold upon it, bringing with them and imparting grace, if one is rightly trained, and otherwise the contrary (401d).

Unsurprisingly, Plato's pharmacological evaluation of the contagious effects of dramatic mimesis applies to music as well, stretching to include and, paradoxically, endorse violent forms of mousikē. He qualifies his diagnostic as follows. Since it is a question of education of the guardians that need to be trained for war, the latter should "fittingly imitate the utterances and the accents of a brave man who is engaged in warfare . . . and who, when he has failed, either meeting wounds or death or having fallen into some other mishap, in all these conditions confronts fortune with steadfast endurance" (399a–b). For Plato, then, in the case of education in warfare, music can be put to violent use by inducing a mimetic identification with exemplary heroes. For a Greek readership it would have been difficult not to think of heroes like Achilles. That is, a hero Plato had critiqued in his dramatic theory of mimesis for appealing to the irrational side of the soul. And yet, in his musical theory of mimesis, Plato changes perspective and implicitly approves of heroic, warlike models that are ready to confront death in warfare practices.

Conversely, philosophical physician that he is, Plato sets out to purify the many-stringed instruments like the harp and the flute or *aulos*, that is, the musical instrument most often associated with Dionysian rituals and the "possession trance" it generates.[11] In this context, he even offers yet another cathartic suggestion that is likely to have inspired his agonistic pupil qua *Pôlos* as he has Socrates state: "we have all unawares purged the city which a little while ago we said was luxurious . . . Come then, let us complete the purification" (399e). Cathartic and contagious hypotheses central to mimetic studies can thus not be dissociated from musical studies for both mimesis and music are constitutive of mousikē. There is even a cathartic telos that orients Plato's diagnostic of mimesis, an indication that theoretical patho-logies that are aware of both cathartic and contagious principles may have in themselves a purifying intellectual, if not necessarily medical, value.

Nietzsche is, in any case, true to Plato when he establishes a mimetic continuity between tragedy and music. Given his controversial thesis that the paradigmatic example of mimetic art is born "out of the spirit of music" (the subtitle of *The Birth of Tragedy*), he does for the moderns what Plato had done for the ancients: he opens up mimesis to non-representational yet nonetheless contagious Dionysian influences that, under the recent rubric of affect, performativity, and embodiment, are increasingly recognized as constitutive of our contemporary mimetic condition. We are thus in a position to see that the continuities between the modern prophet of Dionysus and its ancient forefather are more significant than their mimetic agonism often leads critics to believe. Both thinkers do not hesitate to praise mimetic forms of dispossession that Plato grouped under the rubric of madness, going as far claiming that "the greatest blessings come by way of madness" (*Phaedrus* 244a)—a Platonic phrase Nietzsche will be quick to echo (see *BT* 21).

And yet, this mirroring relation with Plato also means that Nietzsche is also far from unilateral in his evaluation of Dionysian mimesis and the contagion it generates. If he continues to celebrate it for *aesthetic* reasons, he will turn increasingly critical of Dionysian mimesis and the contagious madness it entails for *psychological* but also *ethical* and *political* reasons. We have seen, for instance, that in *Human, All Too Human*, Nietzsche had already spoken of a type of pathological contagion that can affect and infect the "entire community [*Stadtgemeinden*] that especially delights in them" leading the community "to degenerate [*ausarten*] into ever greater excess and licentiousness [*Zügellosigkeit*]" (212; 141). Nietzsche is here joining the physio-psychological language of "degeneration" with the moral language of "licentiousness" to make a diagnostic point that not only concerns past-oriented Greek communities threatened by Dionysian frenzy and the violence it entails. His use of the term *Stadtgemeinden* suggests that his diagnostic is equally present-oriented: it points to what is better translated as "municipalities," which, as a site of electoral decisions, has an unmistakable political connotation relevant to the modern but, as we shall see, also contemporary period.

That Nietzsche's diagnostic preoccupations with Dionysian contagion are increasingly entangled with broader ethico-political preoccupations with the decline of modern culture is confirmed repeatedly in his career. For instance, in his "Attempt at Self-Critique" written in 1886 to supplement the diagnostic of *The Birth of Tragedy*, the former self-proclaimed prophet of Dionysus returns to critically reevaluate what he now calls a "rhapsodic book" (*BT* 3; 19) and the youthful celebration of Dionysian intoxication it entails. To the initiated, Nietzsche is saying between the lines that he may have been enthusiastically inspired as he composed his first book—he was perhaps closer to a rhapsode than to a philologist. Acknowledging that "the name Dionysus was added as one more question mark" in his celebration of life as an aesthetic phenomenon, Nietzsche now changes patho-*logical* perspective as he considers it a "difficult psychological question" (4; 20) that he had not fully answered or properly evaluated. Speaking in favor of the hypothesis of contagion, he now convokes the modern pathological language of "neurosis" to account for a type of "degeneration" that, again, is not only individual but collective, not only past oriented but present and, perhaps, also future oriented. Thus, Nietzsche asks, in a diagnostic arrow directed toward the future: "Is [Dionysian] madness perhaps not necessarily the symptom of degeneration [*Entartung*], decline [*Niedergangs*], and the final stage of culture?" (4; 21).

Perhaps. What is certain is that with increasing insistence in his later period, Nietzsche will repeatedly turn his diagnostic lenses to critique the contagious, infective, and pathological dynamic he had previously grouped under the rubric of the Dionysian question mark. He does so by focusing on theatrical figures qua agonistic models such as Richard Wagner who rely on the powers of theatrical mimesis to cast a spell on crowds. Nietzsche's mimetic agonism with Wagner and the crowd psychology it entails is already a landmark of modernist mimetic studies.[12] Schematically for our purpose, here is the general outline of his mimetic agonism: in his early period, Nietzsche sides *with* Wagner *contra* Plato to celebrate the contagious powers of Dionysian mimesis and the intoxication it entails for aesthetic reasons; in his later period, Nietzsche overturns perspectives and sides *with* Plato *contra* Wagner to critique the contagious powers of mimesis internal to the collective "herd" or "crowd" for psycho-political reasons. This is a typical overturning of perspectives constitutive of Nietzsche's complex evaluation of mimetic patho(-)logies. Thus, in *The Case of Wagner* (1888), Nietzsche frames his former model in an agonistic configuration that allows him to sharpen his patho-*logical* diagnostic of contagion: that is, he takes Wagner as a psychological case study (not unlike Freud will later do with the case of Anna O., Dora) to account for his magnetic-hypnotic-mimetic will to power to induce contagion in an ego that is part of a mass. In the process, he opens up a physio-psychology of the unconscious that has a theatrical, suggestive, and contagious rhetoric as its starting point. As he puts it, Wagner relied on "theatrical rhetoric, a means of expression, of underscoring gestures, of suggestion," which, together, qualify him as a "master of hypnotic tricks," "an incomparable *histrio*, the greatest mime," who relies on "hypnotism by means of music" in order to move and "persuade the masses [*Massen*]."[13] Mime, hypnosis, suggestion: there is indeed an interesting genealogy of the unconscious internal to Nietzsche's diagnostic of the case of Wagner that looks back to the origins of mimetic theory in mime and paves the way for suggestions that are still operative today. Let us take a closer look.

Wagner, the former avatar of Dionysus, is now characterized by a mimetic power, or "pathos," that, via the medium of a theatrical rhetoric characterized by gestures and expressions, has the will to power to generate what Nietzsche calls "suggestion." That is, what a pre-Freudian tradition of the unconscious defined as "a peculiar aptitude for transforming the idea received into an act."[14] That for Nietzsche these suggestions are not only aesthetic and for-mal but have violent cultural implications, is indicated between the lines. In fact, he goes as far as claiming that the crowd under the suggestive spell of Wagner, whose ideology, he reminds us, includes German nationalism and antisemitism, capitulates to the will to power of what Nietzsche now calls, drawing on a political register, a "leader" (*CW* 156). The German term Nietzsche uses is ominous: he calls this leader a "*Führer*."

There is indeed an embryonic critique of fascist violence internal to Nietzsche's psychological diagnostic of Wagner's aesthetics in general and of the crowd's tendencies to fall under the spell of an authoritarian leaders endowed with will to power in particular. What we must add is that when Nietzsche, in "Attempt at Self-Critique," returns to reevaluate the false pow-ers of Dionysus to generate what he calls "visions and hallucinations shared by entire communities [*Gemeinden*] or assemblies at a cult [*Kultversam-mlung*]" (*BT* 4; 21), he is speaking of the powers of Dionysus in classical antiquity in genealogical terms that remain rooted in an aesthetic tradition that has mimetic contagion as its main focus. At the same time, if we recall the philological fact that *Gemeinden* in German implies a *political* assembly that, Nietzsche warns us, can turn into a religious "cult," the intended echoes with his larger critique of modern crowd behavior—in the cult of Bayreuth for instance—are loud and clear. The psychic subjugation to a tyrannical leader it implicitly entails are also hard to miss. In many ways, Nietzsche is in fact relying on his aesthetic education in the contagious powers of mimesis to pave the way for crowd psychology, a fin de siècle discipline that emerged to account for mass contagion, collective behavior, and violent insurrections, which, in the digital age, are fully constitutive of the problematic of new media violence.

## Mass Contagion, Modern Pathologies

Due to his Janus-faced genealogical lenses, Nietzsche was in an ideal position to establish a bridge between ancient and modern accounts of mimetic contagion. With increasing intensity in his middle and, especially, later periods, he joined his philological insights in the ancient dynamic of Dionysian contagion with his psychological insights in the modern problem of psychic contagion and applied them to account for the eminently mimetic problematic of the crowd. He thus anticipates the emerging fin de siècle discipline of crowd psychology, which should be reloaded by new mimetic studies for the digital age—if only because it continues to cast light on the contagious dynamic of unconscious violence that is increasingly manipulated by (new) mass media in need of diagnostic evaluation.

Founding figures of crowd psychology like Gustave Le Bon and Gabriel Tarde posited the laws of imitation and the contagion it generates at the heart of the social along lines that are often seen as anticipating Freud who is an "heir" of this tradition.[15] While this diagnostic is historically correct, Freud also aimed to go beyond the language of "contagion," "hypnosis," and "suggestion" that was already internal to Nietzsche's diagnostic of the *Masse* and informed crowd psychologists as well. He did so by promoting an Oedipal theory of the social bond, which, as we have seen, was structured around the binary split between desire and identification. Interestingly, the theory of mimesis Freud was supposed to leave behind is currently returning to the forefront of the theoretical scene: it is in fact part of what Christian Borch calls "an alternative history of sociology" that casts new light not only on the psychology and sociology but also on the violent "politics of crowds."[16] In particular, crowd psychology provides if not entirely original at least mimetic epistemological foundations supporting Nietzsche's untimely insight that the language of contagion, hypnosis, and suggestion is most apt to capture the strategies leaders qua *Führers* (will) use to influence mass behavior, including the trigger of violent behavior. This is an area of mimetic studies that speaks directly to present pathologies of contagion in urgent need of diagnostic reevaluations.

Drawing on the metaphor of contagion from Pasteur's discovery of microbes rather than from ancient Dionysian principles, Gustave Le Bon, in his influential and ideologically problematic *Psychologie des foules* (1895), transferred the psychological language of hypnotic suggestion from individual to collective psychology, therapeutic practices to social practices. He did so to account for modern psychological mechanism that include violent, unconscious phenomena. As he puts it in the "Preface" of the book: "The substitution of the unconscious action of crowds for the conscious activity of individuals is one of the principal characteristics of the present age."[17] This unconscious has mimetic contagion rather than dreams as a *via regia*; its symptoms are not latent in Oedipal dreams but manifest in crowd behavior, which he diagnoses as follows: "the disappearance of the conscious personality, the predominance of the unconscious personality, the turning of feelings and ideas in an identical direction by means of suggestion and contagion, the tendency to immediately transform the suggested ideas into acts" (*C* 8), including aggressive and violent acts. Nietzsche's insights on the powers of suggestion had indeed proven untimely—and so did his political warning. The crowd's unconscious propensity for violence is especially clear as it falls under the spell of a prestigious leader (Le Bon's *meneur*, a term Freud will translate as *Führer*) who has mastered the rhetoric to induce mimetic contagion in crowds and publics, including repetition, use of images rather than words, affirmations rather than explanations, and violent passions.

Consider this psychological fact: there is a disconcerting transformation of personality that can overcome an individual in a crowd once it is under the spell of a violent or tyrannical leader. While Le Bon's diagnostic is infected with a "mimetic racism/sexism" still rampant in the modernist period,[18] we need not throw out the baby of crowd psychology with the conservative ideological bath water that animates it. Le Bon characterizes the man of the crowd in terms that account for his vulnerability to unconscious violence, as he writes:

> He possesses the spontaneity, the violence, the ferocity, and also the enthu-
> siasm and heroism of primitive beings, whom he further tends to resemble

by the facility with which he allows himself to be impressed by words and images—which would be entirely without action on each of the isolated individuals composing the crowd—and to be induced to commit acts contrary to his most obvious interests and his best-known habits. (*C* 8)

Crowds under the spell of fascist leaders have indeed been known to commit violent acts, contrary to their interests in the past century. There is no reason to believe that such spells, as they are mediated by misrepresentations constitutive of new media, are not effective among (new) fascist leaders in the present century.

Mimetic studies provide untimely warnings contra ancient, modern, and still contemporary manifestations of unconscious violence. Notice, in fact, that this violence, which can all too easily be directed against sacrificial victims, or scapegoats, is not necessarily the product of a rivalry over a contested object of desire; nor is it a sacrificial outlet generated by what René Girard calls a "crisis of difference"—though both phenomena continue to be massively exploited by tyrannical leaders, old and new. In Le Bon's pre-Freudian account, violent actions and unconscious reactions are rather generated directly by the leader's contagious rhetoric itself, a mimetic rhetoric based on language, but, as Plato had already foreseen via the case of the actor, also bodily gestures and facial mimicry that operates vertically, from the top down, generating spellbinding effects whose contagious efficacy is amplified horizontally, from within the crowd as the violent pathos becomes a shared pathos. Tied both horizontally and vertically in this double bind, the man of the crowd no longer feels lonely and isolated but heroic and empowered, delegates responsibility to the leader, and is ready to commit irresponsible violent actions. Le Bon specifies:

> The violence of the feelings of crowds is also increased, especially in heterogeneous crowds, by the absence of all sense of responsibility. The certainty of impunity, a certainty the stronger as the crowd is more numerous, and the notion of a considerable momentary force due to number, make possible in the case of crowds sentiments and acts impossible for the isolated individual. In crowds the foolish, ignorant, and envious persons are freed from the sense of their insignificance and powerlessness, and are possessed instead by the notion of brutal and temporary but immense strength. (*C* 22)

Historical examples are not lacking, for Le Bon's manual to induce crowd behavior was not left unused. It found in Mussolini and Hitler attentive readers who would put such principles to horrifying violent practices; once reloaded via new media that infect physical crowds and virtual publics alike, these contagious principles continue to inspire what I call "(new) fascist" leaders endowed with the mimetic will to power to cast a shadow on the present century.[19]

A genealogy of the affective hypothesis via the ancient and modern vicissitudes of crowd behavior allows us to deepen the patho(-)logies of homo mimeticus that are Janus-faced: if we look back to ancient and modern principles, it is because a long-standing tradition in mimetic theory allows us to look ahead to account for and sometimes anticipate contemporary contagious principles that tend to be downplayed by quantitative-oriented studies but are now taken seriously by new mimetic studies. As Nietzsche, on the shoulders of Plato, had foreseen, there is an intoxicating power internal to Dionysian states of dispossession that can spread epidemically across communities, municipalities, and states. In the process, they generate hallucinatory phenomena characteristic of cultic rituals that, as the origins of Dionysian rituals make clear, are not deprived of unconscious forms of intoxicating violence. Crowd psychology should be an integral part of new mimetic studies for it confirms the violent potential of Dionysian rituals reenacted by tyrannical leaders qua *meneurs*, or *Führers*.

What we must add now is that the cultic "hallucinations" characteristic of collective forms of violent "degeneration" may still have sounded untimely at the twilight of the twentieth century. Still, they are currently manifest at the dawn of the twenty-first century, stretching via tyrannical leaders qua actors who rely on new hypermimetic media to cast the shadow of violence on contemporary communities as well.

## (New) Fascist Contagion: Trump Moment, *Waldo Moment*

Nietzsche's diagnostic principles on mimetic contagion apply to ancient spectacles and to modern rituals; yet looking back genealogically, via advocates of the affective hypothesis, allows mimetic studies to look ahead to the contagious pathos of violence mediated via new media representations or misrepresentations of reality as well. If modern media like radio and film relied on the powers of (oral/visual) mimesis to trigger unprecedented violence in the crowds of the past century, new social media like Twitter and Facebook not only generate an intensification, rather than purification of emotions that go viral online; they also trigger hallucinations via conspiracy theories characteristic of contemporary cults that are far removed indeed from reality yet are endowed with the magnetic, hypnotic, and contagious power to trigger violent insurrections offline.

Walter Benjamin influentially argued that the introduction of language and the distance it entails may have induced a "decay of the mimetic faculty" in the modernist period.[20] We now have sufficient evidence that this diagnostic needs to be updated for the contemporary, digital period. This is, in fact, the moment to recognize that the shift to the digital age, and the full immersion in the pathos new media manage to disseminate at unprecedented speed and with growing power of efficacy, is currently triggering an explosion of the mimetic—or, rather, hypermimetic—faculty. Contemporary examples are not lacking, both at the private or individual level and at the public and collective level. Individually, we all have examples in our households; think of new forms of technological addictions induced by new media: from compulsive social media checking to overuse of video games. Collectively, think of the ways the daily news's emphasis on violent threats can be politically manipulated to generate fear, anxiety, and anger online, which can in turn be used to justify violent aggressions offline: from the co-option of terrorist attacks on 9/11 to justify wars contra imaginary "weapons of mass destruction" to the racist discrimination routinely invoked to justify systemic violence that prevent minority groups to breathe, among other contemporary symptoms we have already encountered.

There is, however, a growing hypermimetic phenomenon with contagious and violent powers that still needs to be included in our diagnostic: namely, the powers of new media to generate conspiracy theories that originate online via new means of (mis)representing reality, yet do not remain confined to the (Apollonian) sphere of representation. Rather, they retroact via spiraling feedback loops on reality with a (Dionysian) vengeance generating mass-immoderation, degeneration, and insurrectionist violence. If such violence was once characteristic of mimetic cults, it is now at play hypermimetically, in communities and municipalities, stretching to affect and infect what were once bastions of western democracy.

Let us turn to some contemporary examples to evaluate the violent potential of hypermimesis on the unconscious of individuals, publics, and crowds.

### The Trump Moment: Insurrection, Conspiracy, Cultic Violence

The storming of the U.S. Capitol in Washington, DC, on January 6, 2021, provides a dark, harrowing, yet no less exemplary case study to account for the contagious side of Dionysian mimesis reloaded via conspiracy cults that spread online in the digital age and generate violent political intoxications offline. The context is different, but the genealogical connection with the contagious powers of mimesis our genealogy unearthed so far is direct. The conspiracy theory of "election fraud" that went viral through new media, asserting that Joseph Biden "stole the election," was not based on the simple logic of mimesis understood as realistic "representation" or mirror of reality, as a tradition that goes from Plato to Auerbach considered it. And yet this conspiracy should neither be ironically dismissed as a "hyperreal simulation" that has nothing to do with the logic of "imitation," as Jean Baudrillard diagnosed for the postmodern period.[21] Rather, a Nietzschean diagnostic of the Dionysian powers internal to conspiracy theories suggests that online conspiracies retroact performatively on the immanent materiality of political life, generating contagious, mimetic, or, better, hypermimetic actions and intoxicating reactions that emerge from the interplay between hyperreal simulations online and all too mimetic behavior offline.

Following Donald Trump's electoral defeat and refusal to concede to Joseph Biden as the forty-sixth president-elect of the United States, the mob assault on the U.S. Capitol concluded four years of Trump's catastrophic presidency amplified by a global pandemic with a theoretically foreseeable yet practically unforeseen insurrection qua domestic terrorist attack that led to five casualties, including a police officer. The assault was consciously triggered by a chameleon figure, or *histrio*, endowed with the theatrical ability to generate hypnotizing mass-identifications via a reality TV show (*The*

*Apprentice*, 2004–2017) in the sphere of aesthetic fiction, before changing scene and playing the role of an "apprentice president" who effectively turned politics itself into a fiction. A narcissistic authoritarian leader unable to face the reality of a democratic political defeat, the case of Trump confirms Nietzsche's untimely insight that one day, "'actors,' *all kinds* of actors will be the real masters" (*GS* 356; 303). In the process, this "master of hypnotic tricks" (Nietzsche's phrase) also provided a striking example of the powers of hyperreal simulations online that have nothing to do with faithful (Apollonian) representations of reality, yet have the property to induce truly felt, contagious, and violent (Dionysian) hallucinations offline, triggering hypermimetic intoxications in communities qua crowds Trump used as a political weapon contra democracy on January 6.

Unexpected by politicians and police alike who left the Capitol disarmingly open to the insurrection, the assault should not have surprised theorists of mimesis, old and new—if only because it brings together the main features of a diagnostic of Dionysian contagion we considered in the ancient and modern period, and now reaches via new media into the (new) fascisms of the present. On the shoulders of this Janus-faced genealogy of Dionysian intoxications that looks back to the past to look ahead to the present, warning the future as well, I schematically summarize these (hyper)mimetic principles in four points.

First, the insurrection required the organized assemblage of a crowd of supporters at a rally primarily composted of white supremacists and right-wing extremists whose unconditional adherence to the outgoing president and refusal to accept the nominated president-elect provided a shared consensus (*con-sensus*, feeling with) injected with violent anti-democratic potential. It was in fact conducive to spreading an intoxicating mass-contagion characteristic of a collective soul that not only wants power but wants to destroy democratic power tout court. Promoted under the dramatic hypernationalist banner of the "Save America March" with the explicit intent of assembling a highly mimetic, suggestible, and potentially violent crowd that could be put to (new) fascist use contra the Capitol and the democratic processes it symbolizes, the organizers of the rally demonstrated good insights in the contagious dynamic of what Nietzsche called "*Masse*," and a marginalized tradition in the social sciences called "crowd" (*foule*), operating on its

propensity to be spellbound by the violent mimetic rhetoric of an authoritarian leader.[22]

Second, the insurrection was catalyzed by the presence of a presidential
leader who relied on what Nietzsche called theatrical strategies characteristic
of the "actor" or "mime" in order to cast a suggestive spell on the crowd.
The crowd's affective identification, or hypnotic *rapport*, with the *meneur*
was already established due to Trump's double role as media personality
and political leader who, throughout his presidency, consistently relied on a
violent rhetoric to generate a state of permanent mass contagion in the collective soul of his base. This rhetoric should not be derided for its linguistic
simplicity but studied for its contagious efficacy. Its distinctive characteristics are well known to crowd psychology and should be assimilated by new
mimetic studies as well. They include aggressive affirmations rather than
rational explanations, repetitions rather than arguments, use of images rather
than thoughts, clear division between us and them, good and evil, right and
wrong, and a general awareness that violent emotions (anger, fear, resentment) work best to galvanize a crowd.

In the speech that incited the crowd to storm the Capitol, Trump's imple-
mentation of the strategies of crowd psychology were obvious and manifold.
In particular, he relied on the repetition of the Big Lie constitutive of his
conspiracy theory ("rigged election"), an unproven and hyperbolic affirmation of victory ("we won by a landslide"), an emotional appeal to patriotism
and love ("American patriots"), the direction of violence against scapegoats
(the "China Virus," "the weak Republicans," the "fake media"), a stubborn
refusal of facts ("we will never concede"), among other well-tested strategies
internal to crowd psychology, which are now constitutive of the first "Twitter
President" endowing his rhetoric with "contagious force."[23] Strengthened by
this affective support and by the resentment that animated it, Trump and his
closest associates whipped up the crowd's pathos to the culminating point of
suggesting a violent anti-democratic aggression contra the U.S. Capitol. They
did so explicitly by inciting the mob not to be "zeros but heroes" (Donald
Trump Jr.), by promising "trial by combat" (Rudolph Giuliani), and suggesting a violent insurrection that had performative effects: "We fight like hell,
and if you don't fight like hell you're not going to have a country anymore"
(Donald Trump).[24]

A suggestion deprived of referential foundations generated performative violent effects in reality nonetheless. The crowd of white supremacists driven by real material deprivations, grievances, and resentment amplified by an ongoing pandemic crisis was at this point galvanized and ready to turn the magnetic suggestion into a violent action. It paradoxically voiced support for the very figure who actively promoted the anti-democratic policies responsible for their grievances. Responding enthusiastically to Trump's rhetoric, they chanted in a collective chorus worthy of a Dionysian ritual: "stop the steal," "we love Trump," "fight for Trump," and so on. Members of the mob, which, in addition to white supremacists, included Far-Right extremists (Proud Boys), followers of online cults (QAnon), and, last but not least, armed veterans, including former federal agents (FBI), were also ready to put themselves on the line by physically fighting for Trump—against themselves.

Third, this paradoxical turn of events cannot be dissociated from the handheld recording devices that redoubled the event online, where the galvanization had initially started in the first place. Trump's speech, riot, and subsequent insurrection was in fact planned and announced well in advance via new social media like Twitter, Facebook, TikTok, and Instagram that effectively disseminated the conspiracy theory about "election fraud" by relying on what "conspiracism" does best: namely, promoting the idea that especially when it comes to big historical events (say, an election), but not only, official explanations inevitably hide a more occult, false, yet truly believed plot casting the conspiracy believer to be a victim of an evil plan. Summarizing the main features of conspiracy theories under the heading of "nothing happens by accident; nothing is at it seems; and everything is connected," in their informed overview of this growing heterogeneous phenomenon, Michael Butter and Pieter Knight confirm historically what we have all seen on January 6, 2021: namely that "the leaders of populist parties and movements frequently draw on conspiracy tropes, and their followers appear to be particularly receptive to them," specifying that "extremist violence" often ensues.[25] Equally well known is that "conspiracy theories can serve as a way to 'save-face' for those on the losing end of a situation, such as elections."[26] Gaining new momentum via the proliferation of new platforms of dissemination online, conspiracy theories can no longer be considered a marginal phenomenon confined to a few pathological cases. Rather, they play an increasingly important role in influencing public opinion in the digital age; they are also likely to play an increasing role in the spread of new media violence.[27] To put it our language, conspiracy theories turn the powers of the false to *patho*-logical use by generating fictions that rest on the logic of affect, or pathos, to dissolve not only the distinction between the real world and the illusory world but also violent linguistic suggestions and violent insurrectionist actions.

Last but not least, the powers of conspiracy theories to erode the epistemic foundations of long-standing democratic practices are complex and manifold, but the assault on the Capitol could not have succeeded without a simpler, yet not less violent, racist supplement. While the U.S. police force is traditionally overprepared to violently counter peaceful protests among ethnic minorities (from civil rights to BLM), in a mirroring inversion of perspectives it underestimated an announced violent insurrection among white majorities (from white supremacists to far-right extremists). For reasons that are still emerging as I write and are currently revealing Republican officials' complicity with the assault,[28] although the police force was warned of the danger of insurrection in advance, it remained understaffed, unprepared, and left the door practically open to an intoxicated mob allowing them to invade the Capitol, loot parts of the building, and take possession of the Senate chamber. In an eerie confirmation of the Dionysian genealogy we have been tracing, a figure dressed as a shaman and member of the far-right conspiracy cult QAnon only made the underlying link between ancient ritual cults and contemporary conspiracy cults visible for all the world to see.[29]

The storming of the Capitol made the hypermimetic powers of new media visible, urging new mimetic studies to expand the category of media violence. The enthusiastic readiness to turn a violent linguistic suggestion ("fight like hell") into violent ritual aggression, in fact, was already generated online via the conspiracy theory of "election fraud" before spilling—via the amplification of Trump's incendiary speech to the crowd—offline, generating violent insurrectionist practices contra democracy.

Importantly, the feedback loop between online and offline violence continued during the storming of the Capitol itself as the insurrectionists filmed not only Trump's speech but also their own terrorist attack, redoubling the event in the digital world. This digitized recording of a (new) fascist suggestion turned into terrorist action generated a parallel reality that, once again, did not simply (mis)represent reality according to the laws of realism; it also generated performative hypermimetic and patho(-)logical effects that cut both ways, both with and contra democracy: on the democratic side, the recordings online were instrumental in helping the police identify insurrectionists, track them down, and inflict severe penalties; on the insurrectionist side, these videos went viral and contributed to disseminating violent anti-democratic feelings that are not limited to the United States but are operative transnationally via a growing cosmopolitan network that connects (new) fascist movements across the world.[30]

To be sure, the insurrection eventually failed, and a lawful democratic election ensued. And yet the example of how conspiracy theories can easily lead to violent insurrections that reveal the fragility of democratic institutions left lasting traces in the history of democracy. They also left lasting traces online that can serve as possible models for future insurrections offline to imitate, in an hypermimetic spiral of endless regress.

In the end, the assault on the Capitol left many politicians shocked, caught security forces unprepared, and was considered unprecedented within the sphere of U.S. politics. And yet mimetic studies shows that its contagious dynamic has a long genealogy that warns us about the violent intoxicating powers of mimesis. Interestingly, even the hypermimetic dynamic that links digital simulation to bodily intoxication was anticipated, if not in the sphere of political theory, at least in the sphere of hypermimetic fiction. I have already argued elsewhere that Trump's success during his presidential election arguably stemmed from hypermimetic strategies of identification he mastered in his reality TV show and new media practices first, before putting them to violent pathological ends in the sphere of politics.[31] It is thus perhaps not surprising that one of the clearest mirroring diagnostics of the contagious powers of hypermimesis that can be put to patho-*logical* use in the interdisciplinary field of new mimetic studies also stems from an original TV show—or, rather, series.

Having traced the genealogical sources of the affective hypothesis back to Dionysian rituals, let us now look ahead to a future-oriented reflection on the Dionysian power of digital contagion that sets up an hypermimetic mirror to political violence.

"The Waldo Moment": Hypermimetic Mirror of Reality

The award-winning British TV series *Black Mirror* (2011–2019), created by Charlie Brooker, offers revealing future-oriented reflections for mimetic theory in support of affective contagion. A sf, dystopic, and future-oriented series on the performative powers of new digital technologies to affect human behavior offline, *Black Mirror* already received a number of philosophical commentaries that praised its diagnostic of new technologically induced pathologies, or "techno-pathologies," operative here and now.[32] Initially aired on Channel 4 in 2011, running for five seasons until 2019 and now available on *Netflix*, *Black Mirror* has a proven record not only to perceptively represent the contagious pathologies of the digital—from smartphone addiction to cyberattacks, video games intoxications to digital totalitarianism—but also to anticipate historical events yet to come. The series has thus philosophical potential, at least if we follow Michel Serres in his view that the primary vocation of philosophy is to anticipate, for as he puts it: "*philosopher c'est anticiper.*"[33] With respect to political contagion and the hypermimetic violence it generates, *Black's Mirror's* philosophical/anticipatory value is strikingly apparent in an episode titled "The Waldo Moment" (dir. Bryn Higgins, written by Charlie Brooker), an early episode that received poor reviews when it was first aired in 2013. Yet it should be re-viewed in 2022, if only because it anticipates violent insurrections in the sphere of fiction that few could imagine in the sphere of theory—let alone politics.

In an inversion of the original/copy opposition that would have pleased a deconstructive critic, "The Waldo Moment" provides patho-*logical* insights into the dynamic of hypermimesis that are most valuable for the future-oriented field of new mimetic studies. It tells the story of Jamie (Daniel Rigby), a frustrated comedian who impersonates a digital cartoon of an animated blue bear named Waldo. Originally modeled on Boris Johnson in the United Kingdom, Waldo relies on new media strategies that will be successfully used by Donald Trump to win the U.S. presidency in 2016. Thanks to Jamie's effective impersonation, which relies on tonality of voice but also facial expressions and gestures mediated via remote-controlled performance caption as well as other animation effects, Waldo moves beyond the comedy show to become an unpredictably competitive political candidate, getting support

**FIGURE 6.** "The Waldo Moment" (2013), season 3 of *Black Mirror* (dir. Charlie Brooker, 2011–2019).

from voters disillusioned with politics and in affective need of "comic" if not cathartic relief.

That this relief does not have primarily cathartic but rather contagious properties is soon made clear. While impersonating Waldo, Jamie draws on a rhetoric of violent accusations, vulgarity (curses), sexualized gestures (erections), obscene sounds (farts), and above all, a general aggressive attitude toward traditional political candidates who represent the status quo. Waldo operates in the hyperreal sphere of animation characteristic of a cartoon simulation; yet from the opening of the episode, it is clear he has the hypermimetic power to affect the immanent world of politics as well. This blurring of boundaries is accentuated by the fact that politics is already increasingly modeled on the sphere of aesthetic entertainment, which operates on the visceral sensations of physical crowds, TV publics, and, last but not least, internet users to cast a magnetizing spell on the contemporary polis—chaining spectators and users to black, mirroring screens.

"The Waldo Moment" exemplifies the kind of fictions with spellbinding powers Plato was already denouncing as pathological at the dawn of mimetic studies. Still as a hypermimetic pharmakon, the episode is not deprived of new patho-logical insights into the contagious dynamic of pathos. In particular, the episode calls attention to the role of linguistic disrespect, abuse, and rhetorical violence that is at play in contemporary politics. In the wake of Trump's presidential election in 2016, Waldo's strategies have become a staple of political rhetoric, generating a contagious reciprocal dynamic of violent "discursive abuse" that is constitutive of Alt-Right populism but, due to the mimetic laws of reciprocity, is not limited to it.[34] Waldo's blend of comedy and politics, in fact, animates both sides of the political spectrum as it equally informs satirical TV shows on the left that profit from the comic potential of tyrannical leaders via a structural ambivalence constitutive of "comic fascism."[35] What still needs to be recognized is that Waldo's rhetoric is not limited to linguistic accusations characteristic of political discourse that can be critiqued, or unmasked, from a hermeneutical distance. It also generates an affective contagion that operates on the crowd's and public's unconscious in performative terms that progressively lead from a rhetoric of linguistic violence online to actions of physical violence offline.[36] What Waldo's "crowd-pleasing" animation reveals is how thin and porous the boundary dividing fiction and reality, entertainment and politics, but also, and for us more important, verbal abuse and physical abuse can be in the digital age.

The powers of hypermimesis require new diagnostics, but in order to look ahead to violent pathologies to come, it is wise not to forget the ancient and modern lessons we learned from a long-standing genealogy of thinkers of affective contagion. Both illusory (Apollonian) shadows and embodied (Dionysian) affects are, in fact, at play in the logic of hypermimetic contagion "The Waldo Moment" foresaw in fiction and the Trump moment actualized in politics. On the Apollonian side, the figure of the animated bear points to the irrelevance of a real referent for the simulation to operate, grab attention, and take hold of the sphere of contemporary politics that is already modeled on entertainment. In fact, what gives momentum to the Waldo moment is not a political program or idea. Jamie readily admits that he is "not a politician," "can't answer serious questions," and that Waldo "doesn't stand for anything." Rather, what matters is what a producer says early on: "Twitter can't get enough of Waldo—loves him."

Needless to say, this diagnostic perfectly applies to the Trump moment as well, and so does what follows: liking, retweeting, commenting on short

**FIGURE 7.** Waldo contra politicians, "The Waldo Moment."

comic/hateful messages via social media whose format privileges comic/ vulgar characters that can go viral online, inducing an emotional contagion that takes root offline. In fact, Waldo's popularity grows further as a You-Tube video of an aggressive debate on a TV show, where the satirical blue bear attacks his political opponents, goes viral. This success online, in turn, provides the necessary number of supporters that allow Waldo to become a "serious" political contender.

There is an ancient mimetic lesson reloaded here for present times: in the digital age, the efficacy of any message, including a political message, does not stem primarily from its content, or logos. As a U.S. agent is quick to realize, Waldo "could deliver any brand of political content"—though the rhetoric of ad hominem accusations, which in the case of Waldo is initially not deprived of some referential truth, is effective in generating a violent pathos among "protest voters." The efficacy of the message stems, rather, from the medium in general and from the number of views it attracts online, generating a shared pathos of aggression that triggers a viral emotional contagion that infects the body politic as well. As a TV journalist puts it: "Cartoons don't play by the rules, and Waldo's open disdain for his opponents has clearly struck a chord." Struck in fiction, this chord resonates in reality as well.

Conversely, on the related Dionysian side, the presence of a physical crowd or public that is responsive to a rhetoric based on vulgarity and
accusations punctuates the episode beginning-middle-and-end staging an
escalation that progressively turns from linguistic abuse to physical abuse,
rhetorical violence to embodied violence. Thus, if Waldo initially relies on
the crowd of viewers to mediate and amplify his insults directed against his
main rival, the conservative MP Liam Monroe (Tobias Menzies), the episode turns physically violent as Jamie quits his position as operator only to
be replaced by his producer who manipulates the Waldo simulation in order
to turn the crowd against the original voice of Waldo by shouting: "500 quid
to the first man to hit him"—triggering a real beating.

"The Waldo Moment" teaches us that in an in increasingly digitized
world, the boundary dividing virtual actions and physical reactions no longer
holds and that the step between verbal violence online and physical violence
in reality is but a short one, especially if the crowd has already been attuned
to following the lead of virtual simulations. This hypermimetic principle
is confirmed at the end of the episode. Losing the election to Monroe and
coming in second—I told you this was a future-oriented mirror of reality—
Waldo gives the following order to his crowd of followers assembled to hear
the results: "Hey, hey! Everyone! 500 quid to anyone who can lob a shoe!"
And the hyperreal simulation produces a hypermimetic effect as the crowd
members start throwing shoes at the elected prime minister.

The blue bear may appear to be an illusory image far removed from reality. Still, its violent political powers are real, all too real. As the American
agent puts it, he is the "perfect assassin." While Waldo lost that particular
election at the local level, he wins a long-term political future that will overturn democratic politics at the global level. The episode ends ominously in
a not-distant, dystopian totalitarian future based in an Asian country but
digitally and globally interconnected in which the Waldo brand has been
adopted transnationally across the globe as a fictional figure to manipulate
and control the population.

How could such a totalitarian regime be implemented? As the U.S.
agent had prophetically put it: by channeling into the Waldo simulation a
"targeted hopeful message, energizing the disenfranchised without spooking
the middle via a new platform" that relies on Twitter among other new media
constitutive of (new) fascism and now under the lens of new mimetic studies.

**FIGURE 8.** The insurrection moment in "The Waldo Moment."

**FIGURE 9.** (New) Fascist dystopia, "The Waldo Moment."

As the episode's concluding shot suggests, the result is a transnational totalitarian regime that promises empty rhetorical slogans like "hope," "change," and "belief" mediated by hyperreal simulations on ubiquitous screens that have nothing to do with referential reality yet have the power to generate violent hypermimetic subjugations in practice.

"The Waldo Moment" aired in 2013. Compared to other episodes of *Black Mirror*, it received little initial attention—until the Trump moment that lasted from 2016 to 2020. Revisited in 2021 in the wake of the predictable, announced, yet still unexpected storming of the U.S. Capitol and the increasing spread of (new) fascist sentiments in Europe, China, Russia,[37] and across the world, it urges new generations of theorists to take the logic of hypermimesis seriously.

The hypermimetic interplay between the Trump moment and the Waldo moment is striking and theoretically revealing of the laws of contagion in the digital age. The spiraling dynamic between fiction and reality, digital violence online and political violence offline, requires multiple factors to come together, yet it follows hypermimetic principles we have encountered via the case of Trump, which the case of Waldo allows us to both mirror and supplement. I summarize these principles in guise of conclusion: first, the unlikely presence of a "likable" TV personality or cartoon with whom a regressive identification has already taken place in the sphere of entertainment—a compensation for real frustrations and grievances mainstream politicians prove unable to rectify in reality; second, an agonistic conflict between the traditional message of politics and the new media simulations is staged generating a tension between a linguistic communication based on reason (logos) and a mimetic communication based on affect (pathos). While the distinction between logos and pathos is porous at best in the context of political elections modeled on TV entertainment, the communicative logic of pathos triggers mimetic *patho*-logies via strategies that include the following use of affirmative, vulgar, sexualized, and embodied rhetoric that relies on gestures and mimicry more than thoughts and programs; accusations rather than dialogues; affirmations rather than explanations; lies rather than facts; and above all, a ramified network of new media platforms that shift the ground of political action from reality to hyperreality via social media like Twitter or Facebook, among other hypermimetic machines. Not concerned with the referential laws of factual representation but with the number of views and likes generated online, new social media powerfully reload the mimetic faculty of homo mimeticus in the digital age. There will be work for new mimetic studies in the future.

New media platforms are the decisive hypermimetic factor at play in the formation of political cults internal to (new) fascist moments, which "The Waldo Moment" allows us to further unveil. Due to the algorithmic logic that exposes new media users to contents that already appeal to established ideological orientations, coupled by length constraints at the level of the message or logos that are ideal to mediate a simple expression of violent affect or pathos, social media have the patho-*logical* power to increase the mimetic faculty exponentially, rendering it hypermimetic. They also generate bubbles of information that disseminate the most hallucinatory conspiracies that would have concerned only a minority of people in the analogic age but, due to the powers of hypermimesis, go viral in the digital age. Often grouped under the epistemic rubric of "post-truth," it has not been sufficiently noted that the hypermimetic power of conspiracies cannot be limited to the (Apollonian) lies, illusions, and misrepresentation of facts that misinform them at the level of content, or philosophical logos—although the traditional definition of "mimesis" as a false copy or representation of true reality continues to apply to the new media in question and remains obviously relevant to "post-truth" as well.

Less visible but not less efficacious, conspiracy theories derive their hallucinatory power of conviction at the level of the (Dionysian) affects they generate. As the case of Waldo reveals, these hypermimetic, contagious, and potentially violent affects increase exponentially with the number of views online, generating bubbles of information that lend increasing power to digital simulations that are not simply false in the representational Apollonian sense; rather, they are endowed with the Dionysian powers of the false in the affective sense.[38] Last but not least, the presence of a physical mob that has already absorbed the hallucinatory message in heavy doses online is but the most visible symptom of a cultic Dionysian force that spreads horizontally from self to others. It does so via hypnotic, mirroring, and contagious mechanisms that are familiar since the dawn of mimetic psychology, are central to the modern discipline of crowd psychology, and are now reloaded via hypermimetic new media. When operative together, these and other hypermimetic symptoms constitutive of (new) fascist movements have the power to generate a spiraling circulation that goes from virtual simulations to embodied realities and back, igniting a visceral, intoxicating turbulence that renders the violent symptoms of the unconscious manifest in embodied forms of aggression visible for all the world to see.

## The Hypermimesis Loop

Spectacular manifestations of hypermimesis generating a type of violence that
circulates from fiction to realty and back are not lacking in the twenty-first
century. Terrorist attacks provide a last example of the laws of hypermimesis.
A sociologist active in new mimetic studies, Christian Borch, for instance,
begins the introduction of a volume titled *Imitation, Contagion, Suggestion*
(2019) as follows: "The early twenty-first century has been characterized by a
tragic surge in terrorist events"; and after listing a number of recent manifestation of terrorist violence—from shootings targeting the Jewish community
to decapitation in the name of Muhammad, he specifies: "One of the truly
disturbing facets of such attacks is that, rather than being isolated cases, they
often mimic previous ones," generating a number of "examples of contagious
terrorism, in which one type of assault provides a template to be copied
subsequently."[39] On the basis of this sociological fact, Borch and the contributors to the volume convincingly set out to recuperate the marginalized
concept of "suggestion" in order to account for disconcerting phenomena of
mimetic contagion, including, as the example of terrorism indicates, violent
forms of contagion.

Furthering this line of inquiry, what is true for the contagious properties of real terroristic attacks taking place in the social world is equally true
for episodes of violence that are not witnessed firsthand. They are rather represented, at one or several removes, via aesthetic media that can be based
on realistic representations of violence (daily news, documentaries, YouTube
videos) yet, in the age of hypermimesis, become increasingly difficult to disentangle from fictional representations or simulations of violence (film, TV
series, video games). As figures like Jean Baudrillard controversially noted
with respect the horror of 9/11 that marked the beginning of the twenty-first
century with a terrorist attack: "we had dreamt of this event"; and in support of his oneiric hypothesis, he suggests that "the countless disaster movies
bear witness to this phantasy."[40] This is still a valid vector of analysis, but
the logic of bearing witness strangely conforms to the logic of representation
Baudrillard is up against. Rather than echoing postmodern claims that dissolve reality in the desert of hyperreal simulations, new mimetic studies pay
much more attention to the performative logic of hypermimesis. In fact, in
light of what we have seen so far, isn't it more logical that countless disaster

**FIGURE 10.** *Top: Fight Club* (dir. David Fincher, 1999). *Bottom:* Attack on Twin Towers, New York, September 11, 2001 (aarp.org).

movies do not simply bear witness to phantasies of destruction but, rather, contribute to their material realization?

Given the disconcerting similarity between disaster phantasies in which skyscrapers are spectacularly exploded by terrorist attacks—think of the end of *Fight Club* (1999, dir. David Fincher), for instance—and the collapse of the Twin Towers, we should indeed invert the diagnostic, especially if the fiction precedes the reality. Baudrillard got the logic of simulation upside down. Disaster movies do not only confirm or bear witness to phantasies. On the contrary, they have the power to serve as precursors, and thus as models, for violent hypermimetic horrors to be reproduced in real life. As the historian Yuval Harari also notices: "terrorists stage a terrifying spectacle of violence that captures our imagination and turns it against us. . . . Terrorist don't think like army generals. Instead, they think like theater producers."[41] Better still, terrorists think like film producers, and now, new media producers. This also means that like all film producers, these creators of pathos are likely to imitate violent models that are traditionally part of an aesthetic or fictional tradition but that increasingly, via the paradoxical logic of hypermimesis, inspire acts of violence in the "real" world as well.

If direct causation, once again, cannot be proved empirically, the mirroring analogy between fictional and real horrors is close enough to give new mimetic studies pause for thought. It also encourages genealogists of mimesis to revisit a psychological tradition that has the performative powers of suggestion as a via regia to the unconscious. This mimetic tradition now deserves to be reloaded to account for the specific dynamic of hypermimesis that has the power to turn a fictional suggestion into a real action, including violent terrorist actions. Contemporary examples will continue to unfold as the logic of hypermimesis increasingly erodes the line between fiction and reality, online and offline practices, providing new generations of scholars with case studies to continue theorizing the dynamic of hypermimetic contagion in the digital age in view of anticipating—and hopefully contributing to deflecting—horrors to come.

Nietzsche, who served as our main mediator between ancient, modern, and now contemporary Dionysian principles, did not have these examples in mind. Still, he was sitting on ancient shoulders that allowed him to see further into the future than most philosophers. He targeted the old Aristotelian riddle of the pleasure of tragic fictions redoubled by the pleasure of inflicting violence in historical reality by looking back to a Platonic diagnostic of mimetic contagion that crowd psychology would confirm in the modernist period and new mimetic studies would reload in the digital period. Nor did Nietzsche have contemporary neuroscientific findings at his fingertips that confirm the role of hormonal release (dopamine) or neuronal rewiring (neurons that wire together fire together) to support his hypothesis that repetition of pleasurable activities reinforces a mimetic drive to reproduce them, turning them into addictive habits—though he was reading the neuroscientific literature of his time carefully, as we shall also confirm. Still, his experiential and experimental perspectivism, which finds in the immanence of his body his greatest reason, is not deprived of diagnostic insights, patho-*logical* insights on the powers of hypermimesis to operate on an unconscious that does not have cathartic dreams as a *via regia*, but contagious, affective, and hypermimetic drives manifest in daily life.

Let us now turn to consider the specific dynamic that leads a psychic suggestion to trigger a motor action at the intersubjective level of the mimetic unconscious first, before returning to consider the logic of contagion at play in (new) media such as video games at the broader cultural level. It is this immanent door to the unconscious that we now turn to open.

# CHAPTER 4

# The Mimetic Unconscious

## A Mirror for Contagion

T he mimetic unconscious might seem a newcomer in the genealogy of violence that concerns us, but its sources of inspiration are more ancient than its most recent scientific confirmations make it appear to be. In the wake of a return of interest in affective contagion, embodied cognition, hypnotic influences, and mirroring reflexes that operate below conscious awareness, it is in fact only in recent years that a mimetic door to the unconscious has been opened, or, rather, reopened, in different strands of critical theory, continental philosophy, the social sciences, and the humanities more generally, now informing new mimetic studies as well. To be sure, these are fields in which the shadow of psychoanalysis still loomed large in the past century and will take some time to retreat in order to allow other theories of the psyche to come to the fore in the present century. Yet, before looking ahead to some of the most recent and exciting turns to affect, embodiment, and the brain that are constative of the mimetic turn or *re*-turn, lending empirical confirmation to the hypothesis of affective contagion, a step back is still necessary: genealogical lenses urge us to look back to precursors of the discovery of the unconscious in the nineteenth century that were marginalized in the Freudian period but, for reasons that will soon become apparent, should be recuperated for our post-Freudian age in the present century.

As the historian of psychology Henri Ellenberger has convincingly shown in *The Discovery of the Unconscious* (1970), hypnotic forms of affective contagion that were center stage in the late eighteenth and, especially, nineteenth centuries provided the via regia to the discovery of the unconscious. This discovery did not center on a single protagonist qua heroic explorer of the psyche. Instead, it was constitutive of a multiplicity of philosophical physicians who belonged to different schools of dynamic psychology attentive to altered states of consciousness including hypnotic swoons, affective contagion, suggestive influences, crowd behavior, and mirroring reflexes. Their diagnostics stretched to inform the psychic life of modernism as well. We have seen the role of this psychological tradition in the development of what Freud and Breuer called "the cathartic method" that paved the way for the Oedipal unconscious, as explored in volume 1. Let us now balance, mirror, and thus invert the genealogical diagnostic by focusing on the role of affective contagion in the rediscovery of the mimetic unconscious.

## Rediscovering the Unconscious

Legendary claims about the discovery of the unconscious had the unfortunate effect of casting a shadow on an entire psychological tradition attentive to the unconscious powers of emotional contagion that paved the way for a discovery that was not one. From its origins in Anton Mesmer's "animal magnetism" to Jean-Martin Charcot's physiological recuperation of "hypnosis" to access *la grande hystérie* at the Salpêtrière, from Hippolyte Bernheim's psychological approach to "suggestion" at the School of Nancy to Pierre Janet's "psychological analysis" (*analyse psychologique*) of the "subconscious" and the dissociation of personality it entailed that served as a model for psychoanalysis, to many other physicians of the soul already mentioned in volume 1 (Charles Féré, Alfred Binet, Joseph Delboeuf, among others), whose names might no longer be familiar to modern readers, a growing revisionist literature in the history of psychology is convincingly showing that these long-neglected figures paved the way for the so-called psychoanalytical discovery.[1]

Building on these informed historical studies that are still largely unknown outside the history of psychology is a decisive step to provide new psychological foundations for mimetic studies. In the process, I also expand this genealogy of the unconscious by engaging with a variety of perspectives, including modernist philosophical physicians, creative writers, as well as social theorists who belong to different disciplines such as anthropology, crowd psychology, and sociology, yet align themselves with the same pre-Freudian tradition of the cerebral, hypnotic, or suggestive unconscious. From Friedrich Nietzsche's diagnostic of theatrical "suggestion" to account for the case of Wagner in his later period to Joseph Conrad's dramatization of "possession trance" at the heart of the case of Kurtz, from Gustave Le Bon's analysis of the "age of the crowd" to Gabriel Tarde's inauguration of the "age of the public," from Émile Durkheim's anthropology of ritual "effervescence" to Pierre Janet "psychology of the socius," from D. H. Lawrence's dissolution of the "old stable ego" to Trigant Burrow's "social basis" consciousness" to Georges Bataille's analysis of nonlinguistic forms of "sovereign communication," among others,[2] there is an entire tradition of the mimetic unconscious that has been relegated to the margins of psychology, yet is now returning to the forefront of the theoretical scene.

I now join forces with a genealogy of contemporary thinkers that were still trapped within Oedipal dramas but aimed to go beyond Freud (Girard, Lacoue-Labarthe), and other philosophers who sidestepped the Oedipal hypothesis altogether (Deleuze, Foucault). This will allows us to reevaluate physiological or, as Nietzsche prefers to say, "physio-psychological" reflexes as an immanent backdoor to an embodied, intersubjective, and thus relational conception of the unconscious. I called this unconscious *mimetic* to signal its genealogical proximity to mimetic studies and the aesthetic tradition that informs it, from Plato onward. It also signals the all too human tendency to mirror others with one's body—and thus with one's soul—generating involuntary reactions, which, as our exemplary case studies will continue to demonstrate, include violent actions as well. Since these contagious forms of involuntary imitation often operate in subliminal ways, below the control of consciousness, they are, in this literal sense, *un*-conscious. Despite its Nietzschean inspiration, or rather because of it, the mimetic unconscious does not require a hermeneutic of suspicion that decodes latent Oedipal meanings repressed in individual dreams. Instead, it fosters a careful diagnostic observation of contagious, intersubjective, and bodily actions and reactions that are manifest in everyday life—including, naturally, violent (re)actions.

The symptomatic manifestations of the mimetic unconscious are plural. They include, but are not limited to, bodily reflexes, facial mimicry, affective contagion, entranced states, hypnotic suggestion, altered states of consciousness, and a generalized suggestibility to human as well as nonhuman or technological influences that affect human behavior below the threshold of consciousness, generating contagious symptoms nonetheless. Constantly operative at the level of habits, reflexes, and automatic patterns of behavior that operate at the relational and thus intersubjective level, the mimetic unconscious becomes particularly manifest in collective behavior characteristic of crowds, publics, and now, as we have seen, in the hypermimetic interplay between online simulations with the potential to spill offline. Historically, the violence internal to such disconcerting phenomena of mass contagion cast a shadow on fin de siècle Europe; it culminated with the rise of fascism and Nazism in the 1920s and 1930s, generating horrors advocates of an "enlightened" tradition in philosophy thought we had long left behind.

And yet outbreaks of mimetic contagion not only remain fully operative in the twenty-first century; they also threaten to escalate, amplified by new media that transgress the boundaries dividing private sphere and public sphere, reality and virtuality, fictional action and bodily reactions, generating fluxes of hypermimetic contagion that traverse the body politic with an increasing speed and power of affection. The mimetic unconscious helps us account for the efficacy of a type of contagion that is not located within an autonomous ego or volitional subject but, rather, emerges, shadow-like, from intersubjective forms of mimetic communication that are not limited to reason and language (logos) but include irrational and embodied affects (pathê)—or, better, oscillate, pendulum-like between pathos and distance, contagion and critique, in ways that are both enabling and disabling, pathological and pathological.

The mimetic unconscious goes beyond mind/body dualisms that dominated Cartesian consciousness and set up a clear-cut opposition between consciousness and the unconscious. Its symptomatic manifestations can thus be located on a continuous spectrum of degrees of psychosomatic awareness rather than at the far end of metaphysical dualities. Its defining characteristics can be summarized as follows: the mimetic unconscious is physio-psychological rather than purely psychological in origins; it is relational and intersubjective rather than monadic and subjective; it is collective and social rather than personal and familial. Better still, it cannot be rooted in the subject for it is part of a network of affective communication that brings the subject into being as a porous and plastic ego. This also means that the mimetic unconscious is anti-Oedipal and embodied rather than Oedipal and linguistic; its effects are not symbolic or imaginary but real and empirical; importantly, it deals with different degrees of consciousness rather than with a clear split or *Spaltung* between consciousness and the unconscious.

Given the collective manifestations of the phantoms it generates—from crowd behavior to public behavior to political behavior—this immanent, relational, and imitative unconscious opens up the ego to external political influences rather than to internal private dreams; it does not center on mimetic desire alone but considers that all feelings (fear, joy, sorrow, anger, disgust) as well as more impersonal and less identifiable affects (enthusiasm, horror, panic, frenzy) are mimetic, thereby finding in the more general concept of mimetic pathos a privileged starting point. Last but not least, its manifestations are immanent and material rather than ideal and transcendental; its effects are not theoretically postulated in an abstract "metapsychology" (Freud's term) but can be empirically measured via genuine forms of "physio-psychology" (Nietzsche's term). Above all, and crucial for this book, its multiple entry points hinge on an affectively contagious rather than a medically cathartic hypothesis.

Not unlike the catharsis hypothesis, the affective hypothesis does not claim to be completely new or original—and this applies to the mimetic unconscious it gives access to as well. Although some of its most insightful theorists wrote during the modernist period (ca. 1880–1950), theories of affective contagion are inscribed in a long and venerable historical, psychological, and philosophical tradition that goes from antiquity to modernity to the contemporary period. Its entire history still needs to be reconstructed, but we dealt with some of its most incisive advocates elsewhere. For our purpose it suffices to say that the diagnostic of homo mimeticus that emerges from advocates of the mimetic unconscious did not fare well in the Romantic era, which was anxiously concerned with claims of originality characteristic of individual geniuses. Nor did it concern critics under the spell of mythological obsessions with Oedipal dreams to interpret. And yet it is currently returning to haunt, like a phantom, the contemporary theoretical scene, providing a longer genealogical perspective to reevaluate the power of mirroring reflexes to generate affective contagion in the post-Freudian period.

Now, if we have seen in volume 1 that Freud's reliance on the cathartic method led him to the development of the repressive hypothesis and the Oedipal unconscious it entails, Nietzsche's promotion of the affective hypothesis led him to develop a pre-Freudian but also post-Freudian unconscious that had hypnosis, suggestion, contagion, and mirroring reflexes as a via regia. Theories of hypnotic suggestion have remained in the shadow of psychoanalysis in the past century. This is the moment to bring to light the relevance of this modernist immanent tradition of the unconscious for the present century.

## The Mimetic Unconscious: A Genealogy

Nietzsche's diagnostic of the mimetic unconscious relies on more than one discourse, or logos, to cast light on the contagious powers of mimetic pathos. Inverting perspective from a cathartic to an affective hypothesis, the self-proclaimed "philosophical *physician*" (*GS* 35) does not hesitate to turn to contemporary developments in the empirical sciences as a source of diagnostic inspiration. Given Nietzsche's aesthetic education, this is clearly not a reductionist move. On the contrary, it is perfectly in line with his anti-metaphysical critique of idealized conceptions of the soul (psyche) detached from the body (soma). As the agonistic movement of his mimetic patho-*logies* is set in motion with and contra Plato, and his diagnostic of a psyche rooted in bodily drives continues to ramify via an engagement with a multiplicity of modern logoi, Nietzsche increasingly draws from newly founded social and empirical sciences of psychology, or, better, physio-psychology, to sharpen his diagnostic lenses. This is why in *On the Genealogy of Morals* he gives the following advice to philosophers of the future: "it is admittedly just as necessary to secure the interest of physiologists and physicians in the exploration of this problem (of the *value* of previous evaluations)," which, he adds, "certainly require *physiological* investigation and interpretation prior to psychological examination" (*GM* I, 17; 37). The body, for Nietzsche, forms the soul; soma transforms psyche. This methodological claim explicitly applies to the value of moral principles, like pity, which he sets out to critique. And yet, since catharsis and the pity it is supposed to purify has been framed in increasingly moral interpretations in the modern period, his critique implicitly applies to the value of cathartic evaluations as well.

Nietzsche was as critical of moralizing interpretations of catharsis as purification as he was interested in psychosomatic accounts of contagious communication. Hence, in his genealogy of morality, he inverts perspectives to reevaluate how the body affects or, to use both a physio-psychological verb, *moves* the psyche. Nietzsche's reevaluation of catharsis is thus part of his broader project of reevaluation of all values, a diagnostic reevaluation that aims to counter dominant idealizing and moralizing tendencies in western philosophy that disconnect the psyche from the body, but also reason from affects, rational (Apollonian) distance from irrational (Dionysian) pathos. In the process, his patho-*logy* affirms an immanent tradition attentive to inner experiences in which bodily movements perceived outside have the power to generate involuntary movements felt inside, opening up an alternative, embodied, and relational door to the unconscious.

Nietzsche did not write a book on the unconscious or proclaim its revolutionary discovery. As a careful reader of Schopenhauer, he was aware that this concept had a long history. Still, his preoccupations with unconscious forms of mimetic communication run through his entire corpus, find in the affective hypothesis, rather than in the catharsis hypothesis, its guiding thread, and takes us beyond the "repressive hypothesis." By doing so, he paves the way for future genealogies of the self (*soi*) sensitive to the formative power of sexual practices and norms. As Michel Foucault showed in the first volume of *The History of Sexuality* (1976), the repressive hypothesis is firmly tied to bourgeois familial concerns that emerged in the seventeenth century and continued to inform future centuries as well. As he puts it, "the seventeenth century marks the beginning of an age of repression [*âge de repression*] characteristic of societies we call bourgeois, and from which we are far from being completely freed."[3] That psychoanalysis, as a form of "'*mise en discours*' of sex" and the "confessional" subjugating practices it entails, plays for Foucault a key role in the extension of the repressive hypothesis in the modernist and contemporary period, is clear. Thus, in the context of his genealogy of the multiplication of discourses on "un-natural" forms of sexuality embodied in literary figures like Don Juan that pave the way for his discussion of infantile sexuality, Foucault asks the following, ironic question: "let us leave it up to psychoanalysts to interrogate themselves to know whether Don Juan was homosexual, narcissistic or impotent."[4] This is clearly not a question Foucault considers worthy of genealogical consideration. If we recall that he inherited his genealogical method directly from Nietzsche, and that Nietzsche, to this day, is still routinely subordinated to Freud in matters of psychology (rather than the other way round), a genealogical reframing of the Nietzschean unconscious from the angle of contagion is long overdue.

Time and again, when it comes to furthering his psychological investigations, Nietzsche turns to France for theoretical inspiration. His predilection for a French tradition of moralist philosophers—from Montaigne to Pascal, La Rochefoucauld to Voltaire—is well attested by Nietzsche scholars, and so is his well-known debt to novelists qua psychologists like Dostoevsky and Stendhal.[5] And yet it has not been sufficiently stressed that Nietzsche's French influences were not limited to philosophy and literature. Given his affirmation that "psychology is once again the road to the fundamental problems" (*BGE* 23; 54), we should not be surprised that, writing in the 1880s, he turned to the same French psychological tradition that, a few years later, will impress the young Freud as well. Unlike Freud, however, Nietzsche did not fall under the spell of Charcot's legendary *leçons du mardi* that occupied center stage on the fin de siècle Parisian scene, a mimetic scene in which he ironically comments that people are "hardly anything anymore except psychologists!" (*CW* 5; 165). Hence, with his characteristic discerning instinct in matters of psychology, Nietzsche does not focus on dominant theoretical/theatrical figures who staged mimetic patients to display symptoms that confirm their theory. Not having traveled to Paris himself but preferring less crowded environments—from Upper-Engadin to Turin, Nice to Marseille—that allowed for individual walks and solitary meditations rather than crowded theatrical demonstrations, Nietzsche looks for inspiration in his body first and then in highly selective books that testify to what he often calls physio-psychology.

It is important to stress again that consistently in his work, Nietzsche thinks of himself as a "philosophical *physician*" (*GS* Preface, 2nd ed., 2; 35) who opens an immanent door to depth psychology and the unconscious that animates it. As he puts it, in a future-oriented diagnostic arrow that opens up two competing genealogies of the unconscious that will not be lost on future explorers of the soul: "a genuine physio-psychology has to struggle with unconscious resistances [*Widerstände*] in the heart of the investigator" (*BGE* 23; 27).[6] The diagnostic must have made an impression on Freud given his subsequent self-proclaimed efforts to overcome his own unconscious resistances to develop his version of depth psychology. Taken out of context, it would again be difficult *not* to automatically attribute this phrase, and the discovery that goes with it, to Freud.

And yet, a sense of genealogical discrimination doubled by an understanding of the paradoxical dynamic of mimetic agonism has taught us to be cautious in our diagnostic evaluations. After all, while Nietzsche considered sexual drives important, his theory of conflicting drives constitutive of the morphology of will to power is not restricted to sexuality; rather, it considers all drives and affects to be driven by a mimetic pathos. Similarly, although Nietzsche, as a philologist trained in classics, was well read in ancient tragedies, he did not privilege the case of Oedipus as a paradigmatic and symbolic case study to extrapolate a universal complex modeled on Sophocles's play. Both points are already clear if we restitute Nietzsche's diagnostic in its proper context. Notice, for instance, that Nietzsche speaks of "physio-psychology" not psychology proper. And if read on, it becomes quickly apparent that he has a rather different conception of *Widerstand* in mind than Freud's.

Nietzsche's psychology of the unconscious is not at all centered on the interpretation of incestuous and murderous Oedipal desires dramatized in dreams. On the contrary, for Nietzsche, his theory includes all "affects" (*Affekte*) or "drives" (*Triebe*), especially violent ones, that are constitutive of what he calls, anticipating Bataille, "the total economy of life." As Nietzsche puts it, these affects include "emotions of hatred [*Affekte Haß*], envy, covetousness, and lust for domination as life-conditioning emotions [*Affekte*] as something that must fundamentally and essentially be present in the total economy of life [*Gesamt-Haushalte des Lebens*]" (*BGE* 23; 53). Acknowledging this total affective economy entails overcoming resistances in a moralist, religious, and bourgeois culture, yet Nietzsche considers this overcoming central to his genealogy of unconscious violence rooted in what he calls "the development theory of the will to power" (23; 53). It is thus on this immanent, psychosomatic basis attentive to violent affects and drives constitutive of the will to power understood as a protean mimetic pathos that he proposes a backdoor to access the psychomotor reflexes mirroring reflexes that will have to wait a century in order to be *re*-discovered.

If we now go beyond Oedipal principles, genealogical lenses reveal that Nietzsche's concerns with "physio-psychology" were untimely but not fully original. He was writing during what Léon Chertok calls the "'golden age' of hypnosis,"[7] a period that, especially in France but not only, had revived Anton Mesmer's theory of magnetic fluids, or magnetism, that spread from self to others in contagious terms already metaphorically foregrounded by Plato's magnetic trope in *Ion* but also prefigured what James Braid called a "psycho-neuro-physiological" theory of hypnotism.[8] Nietzsche was not only fully aware of theories of hypnosis. As Marcel Gauchet puts it, he was also the "most acute witness" of the "physiological" or "cerebral unconscious" that dominated the second half of the nineteenth century, an immanent unconscious that due to its mirroring, relational, and socioaesthetic qualities I call mimetic.[9]

If we say that catharsis was a popular subject in the 1880s, this is the moment to note that theories of the mimetic unconscious were in the air at the same time and provided a viable and heterogeneous alternative to homogenous Oedipal triangles. Nietzsche was, in fact, a reader of Théodule Ribot's *La revue philosophique de France et de l'étranger*, an international journal that published pioneering work by prominent figures in philosophy, psychology, physio-psychology and emerging social sciences, such as crowd psychology and sociology. There, not unlike Freud a few decades after him, but with a distinctive genealogical awareness of the philosophical vicissitudes of mimesis and its entanglement with the unconscious, Nietzsche familiarized himself with the work of Jean-Martin Charcot on "hysteria," Hippolyte Bernheim on "suggestion," Charles Féré on "psycho-motor induction," and there are reasons to believe he had read articles by Pierre Janet on "automatism" and Gabriel Tarde on "imitation," among others.[10] This explains why the language of "hypnosis," "suggestion," and "imitation" punctuates his corpus and is at the heart of his analysis of mimetic phenomena such as mastery and slavery, the Apollonian and the Dionysian, will to power and crowd behavior—all concepts that are central to account for the dynamic of affective contagion.

Could it be, then, that hypnotic suggestion, which was for such a long time considered a riddle to be left behind, already looked ahead to theoretical solutions to the problem of unconscious imitation and the contagion it entails? "Interestingly," as Christian Borch notes, "the discursive repertoire of ICS [imitation, contagion, suggestion] has gained renewed traction since the 1990s and the early 2000s,"[11] urging new generations of theorists to take seriously the riddle of suggestion in the context of new mimetic studies. Nietzsche not only offers a confirmation of this mimetic hypothesis; he also urges genealogists of the future to revisit the psychomotor power of suggestion to trigger violent actions and reactions in order to go further.

## Suggestive Influences

In his physio-psychological meditations, we have seen that Nietzsche inscribes the *physiological* reflex of imitation in *psychological* theories of hypnotic suggestion, opening up a genealogy of the mimetic unconscious that is as past oriented as it is future oriented. This is the moment to add that he takes an empirical step further. Speaking of artistic spectacles, which have the theater, and thus an aesthetic representation based on a dramatic impersonation as paradigmatic medium, Nietzsche writes that art "exercises the power of suggestion over the muscles and senses" (*WP* 809; 427). The psychological notion of "suggestion" is here taken outside the confines of individual therapy to account for the broader effects of aesthetic representations on the minds and bodies of the audience. For Nietzsche, in fact, aesthetics, which is traditionally linked to perception by the senses (from *aisthēta*, "perceptible things") cannot be limited to the most distant, Apollonian, or, as Plato calls it, "sun-like" of the senses: namely, vision. Rather, aesthetics affects the more embodied, Dionysian, and darker senses including "muscles" as well. Artistic communication, in other words, is embodied communication. Thus, Nietzsche writes that the "aesthetic state possesses a superabundance of means of communication, together with an extreme receptivity for stimuli and signs," including, he crucially adds, the "language of gestures and

glances" (809; 437, 428). What was true for Plato remains true for Nietzsche:
there is an entire language of gestures and facial expressions at play in the
dynamic of mimetic contagion.

Nietzsche's immanent approach to aesthetics considers this superabundance of communication in itself neither good nor evil, neither moral or
amoral, peaceful or violent, for it includes sentiments like pity and empathy—though we have seen that for Nietzsche, tragic sympathy may not
be as moral a sentiment as neoclassical theories made it appear to be, and
includes cruelty, sadism, and other violent affects as well. Switching to one
of the theater's characteristically mimetic effects on the audience, Nietzsche
specifies, once again on the shoulders of a psychological tradition rooted in
physiology: "Empathy with the souls of others is originally nothing moral,
but a physiological susceptibility to suggestion" (809; 428). And thinking
of the case of Wagner's aesthetics, but with a larger critique of modern
aesthetics in mind predicated on theatrical spectacles that affect the crowd,
Nietzsche says that this suggestion is "merely a product of [a] psychomotor
rapport" (809; 428). Hypnosis, suggestion, rapport: here we find another
confirmation that Nietzsche was well read in contemporary psychology and
physio-psychology. These are, in fact, the concepts that, as Ellenberger has
demonstrated, are constitutive of the discovery of the unconscious. But if
Nietzsche is a faithful advocate of the hypnotic tradition of the unconscious
we have seen Freud reject in volume 1, he is also providing his own distinctive
rearticulation of competing schools of hypnosis to account for the suggestive
power of aesthetic representations to affect bodies and minds. What, then, is
suggestion, and how does it operate?

As the reference to "suggestion" indicates, Nietzsche relies on the French
physician Hippolyte Bernheim, of the School of Nancy, to give psychological substance to his *psycho*-physiological diagnostic of unconscious influence.
A medical internist by training, Bernheim claimed, contra the Salpêtrière
school lead by Jean-Martin Charcot, that hypnosis was not a pathological
nervous condition reserved to hysterical patients. On the contrary, in *Suggestive Therapeutics: A Treatise on the Nature and Uses of Hypnosis* (1880),
which Freud translated into German, Bernheim insisted that all people,
included educated and "very intelligent" people, are characterized by what
he called "susceptibility to suggestion" or, more simply, "suggestion" (*ST*
5, 15). Bernheim, in fact, argued that hypnosis (from *hypnos*, sleep) is a

misleading concept, for one does not need to be asleep to be unconsciously
influenced by others. It is thus as an alternative to hypnosis that he proposes
the more general notion of "suggestion" (*la suggestion*), which we already
saw Nietzsche echo and that Bernheim defined as "a peculiar aptitude for
transforming the idea received into an act" (137).[12] Suggestion, for Bernheim,
is thus a purely psychological notion akin to influence. But instead of being
limited to the influence of ideas, or *ideo*-logy, he adds a *patho*-logical supplement that speaks directly to affective contagion: he qualifies that suggested
ideas, just like images and gestures, are endowed with the (will to) power to
turn into actions.

For instance, suggestion accounts for patients in an altered state of consciousness induced by fixing a point or a pendulum who have an automatic
tendency to imitate the doctor's movements and turn their orders into an act.
"Lift your arm!" orders the doctor; and voilà, the arm goes up involuntarily,
as the caricature of Bernheim's theory often goes. But if one takes the trouble
to read Bernheim, it is clear that the distinction between consciousness and
the unconscious is far from being clear cut, that imitation takes place at
different levels of awareness, and that one does not need to be a mindless
automaton in a state of deep somnambulism in order to be under the sway of
suggestion. As he puts it, our thoughts, ideals, tastes, emotions, and actions
"may be suggested to our minds by others, and they are sometimes accepted
without being challenged" (*ST* 131); and he adds in a phrase that echoes
Nietzsche's diagnostic, or rather Nietzsche himself is likely to have echoed:
"Do we not all possess a certain cerebral docility which makes us obey commands?" (133)—including, as we have already seen, violent commands?

This is one of those untimely questions that was once internal to the fin
de siècle discipline of criminology and bears on the complex issue of free
will and responsibility. If the crime I commit was suggested by another, let
us say a powerful other—for instance, a leader or *meneur*—who, then, bears
responsibility for the violence that ensues? Even with the horrors of the
twentieth century behind, and in the wake of Hannah Arendt's diagnostic on
the "banality of evil," a dominant tradition in social theory, Arendt included,
failed to take seriously the "complexity of mimesis" that underscores so-
called banal evil actions.[13] This (hyper)mimetic complexity rests on a mimetic
unconscious that has suggestion as a *via regia*. Psychoanalysis's rejection of
suggestion discussed in volume 1 is not without deep ironies. Sigmund Freud

and, after him, Jacques Lacan may have been opposed to suggestion in theory, and yet they were successful in inducing a collective suggestion in practice: they managed to induce the idea that psychoanalysis discovered the unconscious and contributed to disseminating a philologically outdated notion of catharsis qua medical therapy that is, even today, hard to dispel. On the shoulders of a long tradition of philosophical psychologists (Nietzsche and Janet *in primis*), psychoanalysis rightly noted that we are not masters in our own house. Its focus on the unconscious was, however, limited. It restricted its manifestations to the sphere of dreams, neurotic symptoms, or slips of the tongue, all of which could be interpreted from a hermeneutical distance that puts the psychoanalyst, and later the literary critic, in a flattering position of masters of suspicion. Under the spell of hermeneutical mastery, it might be more difficult to recognize with Nietzsche and, before him, Bernheim and the tradition of the mimetic unconscious, that an all too human vulnerability to suggestion rends homo mimeticus a docile subject haunted by unconscious reactions in daily waking life. In specific circumstances, this phantom subject can easily capitulate to hypnotic masters endowed with the will to power to induce violent actions in our conscious daily life.

In the wake of Freud's denunciation of what he ironically called "the riddle of suggestion," this concept has been subjected to much critique.[14] This critique was not deprived of interest for its goal was to replace the riddle of suggestion with an Oedipal solution. It is ironic that the so-called science of the unconscious contributed to erasing the realization that humans are vulnerable to unconscious reflexes—an untimely diagnostic the tradition of the mimetic unconscious had already brought to the fore. More problematic is that from within this pre-Freudian tradition itself, the riddle of suggestion marked a break between the School of Nancy and the school of the Salpêtrière. It generated rivalries that are constitutive of the genealogy of contagion and catharsis we are tracing and contributed to dissolving interest in *both* hypnosis *and* suggestion in the twentieth century—all too mimetic states that now need to be revisited in light of rediscoveries in the present century.

Our genealogical mediator in these matters allows us to provisionally bridge these competing schools by considering both the psychological and physiological mechanisms internal to the powers of suggestion. Trained in classics but with an eye to modern psychology and one toward the future, Nietzsche can in fact help us see that the quarrel between the two modern schools of psychology and their founding agonistic figures—Charcot of the Salpêtrière contra Bernheim of the School of Nancy—like all quarrels based on mimetic agonism, is not as clear cut as it first appears to be. From agonistic discontinuities emerge underlying continuities that inform our genealogy of the mimetic unconscious. Notice, in fact, that Nietzsche speaks of *"physiological* suggestibility to suggestion" as well as "psycho*motor* rapport" (*WP* 809; 428) joining once again physiology with psychology. This should not be dismissed as a simple contradiction or as a misunderstanding of a psychological notion (suggestion) for a somatic notion (hypnosis). Rather, Nietzsche recognizes what recent historians of psychology concerned with rehabilitating suggestion in the twenty-first century have also pointed out. Mikkel Borch-Jacobsen, for instance, one of the most incisive contemporary advocates of Bernheim's theory of suggestion, writes: "The contrast between the somatic theory of hypnosis advocated by the Salpêtrière School and the psychological theory of the Nancy School is actually much less than it appears for they are both rooted in one and the same psycho-*physiology.*"[15]

Nietzsche would have fundamentally agreed. Hence his fluid oscillation between the two rivalrous schools. And in a mirroring move, he adds a supplement to this fundamental realization. Nietzsche's move is subtle, Janus-faced, and requires a genealogical effort to be brought to the fore. But the move is insidious, grounds the mimetic unconscious in an affective hypothesis, and there is something to be gained for *both* hypnosis *and* suggestion in this mirroring psycho-physiological operation. Schematically put: on one side, *with* the School of Nancy, *contra* the Salpêtrière, Nietzsche stresses the suggestibility of *all* subjects opening up his diagnostic of the unconscious to the *psycho*-physiological sphere of emotions, art, culture, and politics—thereby retaining the concept of the unconscious to account for influences beyond the control of the ego. On the other side, *contra* the School of Nancy, *with* the Salpêtrière, he focuses on the psycho-*physiology* responsible for the specific mirroring effects of motor inductions—thereby not letting go of the immanent powers of the unconscious to turn the ego into a phantom of the ego. This Janus-faced operation is both past oriented and future oriented. It remains, in many ways, our operation. Neither fully on the side of Charcot nor fully on the side of Nancy, but at the mirroring intersection where their theories meet and reflect on each other, Nietzsche gives away his genealogical source of inspiration in these psycho-physiological matters in a fragment from 1888 collected in *The Will to Power*. There Nietzsche specifies that this *"induction psych-motrice"* that grounds his conception of the unconscious in a reflex to imitate is actually indebted to what "Charles Féré thinks" (*WP* 809; 428).

This is the second time we encounter this obscure name in our genealogy of the discovery of the unconscious. It is thus the moment to recall that genealogy, as Foucault also specifies, echoing Nietzsche, is attentive to the "body" with its "weakness and strength" and must seek the "singularity of events" in "the most unpromising places"[16]—and, it should be noted, figures. Féré is such an unpromising figure. Who, then, was Charles Féré? What does he think? And in what way can the past concept of "psycho-motor induction," help us look ahead to contemporary preoccupations with the contagious influence of dramatizations of violence, which, as Nietzsche prefigured, operate on both senses and muscles in physio-psychological terms that might be at play in new media as well? These questions lead us to a discovery behind the scenes.

## A Discovery Behind the Scenes

Schooled at the Salpêtrière as an assistant of Jean-Martin Charcot, Charles Féré, unlike his master, was not in the limelight of the Parisian *scène* but was in the front line, nonetheless, working for the self-proclaimed Napoleon of neuroses. His presence is even recorded in what is arguably the most famous painting in the history of psychiatry: André Brouillet's *Une leçon clinique à la Salpêtrière* (1887), painted one year before Nietzsche mentioned Féré. Discussions of this famous scene often focus on the self-staged protagonist in the center, and the patriarchal display of power-knowledge it stages. I noted how this medical will to power is symptomatic of mimetic sexism elsewhere. Here I want to focus on the marginalized figure of Féré. He makes a cameo appearance in the background, the second to the left of Charcot, sitting in a pensive yet attentive clinical mood. Unlike his colleague, Paul Richer sitting on his right side, Féré is not taking notes. Perhaps because he might have a theory of his own in mind—we will never know. What we do know is that behind the theatrical scene that Charcot staged in his *leçons du mardi*, Féré was silently paving the way for, or, better, anticipating, an important discovery yet to

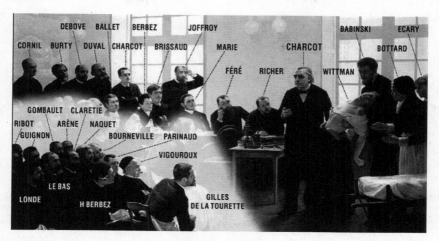

**FIGURE 11.** Reproduction of André Brouillet, *Une leçon clinique à la Salpêtrière* (1887; alchetron.com).

come. If he has so far remained in the background of the discovery of the unconscious, this is the moment to bring him to the foreground. It is high time for Féré to give a *leçon* of his own.

Author of books on magnetism, hypnosis, and the pathology of emotions, including criminal emotions, Féré was an empirical physician more attentive to immanent symptoms manifest in the body than to latent symptoms in need of interpretation. He was particularly interested in measuring the physio-psychological effects of movements on sensations, which, as we have seen, are at the center of Nietzsche preoccupations with unconscious communication central to aesthetic experiences as well. A book aptly titled *Sensation et mouvement: Études expérimentales de psycho-méchanique* (1887) must have made a strong impression on Nietzsche judging from how quickly and profoundly he assimilated it. In this book, Féré defines "*induction psycho-motrice*" as "the automatic reproduction of movements that we see performed."[17] It is indeed the source Nietzsche alludes in the 1888 fragment collected in *The Will to Power*.

But there is more. In a move that betrays an indifference to disciplinary *querelles* that simply oppose advocates of hypnosis at the Salpêtrière (led by Charcot) to advocates of suggestion from the rival School of Nancy (led by Bernheim), Féré associates this automatic process to what he also calls "mental suggestion" (*suggestion mentale*) (*SM* 16). The term would have found Charcot's disapproval for it is promoted by the rival School of Nancy, but Féré does not follow Bernheim's conception of suggestion *à la lettre*. Hence perhaps the need to create a new concept: namely, "psycho-motor induction." According to the physio-psychological dynamic internal to this concept, the operator (or *suggestioneur*) can rely on physiological movements that have the power to generate automatic motor reproductions in the person under suggestion (or *suggestioné*). Expanding Bernheim's notion of psychic suggestion, Féré redefines it as the "capacity to accept an idea communicated directly or indirectly by words, gestures, or by whatever sensorial stimulant."[18] Suggestion for Féré is thus not only a psychic force communicated by ideas that can turn into actions. It is a psycho-physiological force communicated by movements, gestures, sensorial stimuli—and, importantly for us, he adds, images too can generate automatic movements.

Picture the scene in which Féré would report this extraordinary finding to his supervisor, Charcot. The assistant might have noted to his supervisor: "*Cher Dr. Charcot*, I have a strange finding to report. I discovered with the help of a dynamometer that as a patient under suggestion observes a movement made by the doctor, this movement seen triggers an inner feeling in the patient so that the same movement is activated." "This seems a significant indication," Féré would continue, "that movement and sensations are indeed linked via a mirroring psychosomatic relation." And the legendary doctor might have replied: "*peut-être* [it's possible], *Dr. Féré*; though, as you know, only hysteric patients are prone to hypnosis—please stop calling it 'suggestion' and remember which school you are working for." And considering the possibility of a public demonstration, he might have added: "*et puis, mon cher assistant*, the patient's hand is not even moving . . . This is not at all a spectacular effect for the *leçons du mardi*, . . . ça va pas *du tout!*" And so Féré and his untheatrical patient would retreat again, behind the scenes.

And yet, offstage, Féré continued to experiment with dynamometers to capture an intersubjective relational power located between movements and sensations. In the company of Binet, Féré not only continued to confirm the mirroring effects of movements seen on inner sensations; he also gave a name to this disconcerting mimetic phenomenon. He called it "*induction psycho-motrice*" or "psycho-motor induction," a concept that accounts for a disconcerting power of movements to induce corresponding sensations in the psychic and somatic life of others. Thus, a few years later, not letting go of Bernheim's notion of "suggestion," Féré will write in *Travail et Plaisir* (1904): "motor images are particularly apt to emphasize suggestibility"; and he adds: "we know the frequency of *contagion by gesture* well both in normal and sick people."[19] For Féré, then, subjects don't need to be pathologically hysterical to unconsciously respond to motor images; normal people are vulnerable to "contagion by gesture" too: the motor images one sees, subliminally affect by a disconcerting physio-psychological contagion both the movements and the affects of the ego. How? via a contagious and unconscious mechanism that threatens to turn the ego into a copy, shadow, or phantom of the ego.

True, Féré's experiments themselves may have lacked spectacular theatrical effects. He was thus not in a position to give a *leçon* of his own back in the 1880s. Still, this physician of the soul had registered something important, or untimely, and thus out of sync with the trends of the time—because he was ahead of his time. Nietzsche, for one, was quick to sense the philosophical potential of this physio-psychological observation. Féré's addition of "gesture" or "whatever sensorial stimulant" as crucial to the dynamic of "contagion by gesture" is likely to have grabbed the philosopher's attention. If only because Nietzsche was already sensitive to the hypnotic effects of theatrical gestures and musical stimuli. Thus, convinced of Féré's method, he set out to reject the catharsis hypothesis on the basis of experiments with a dynamometer—as we have seen in volume 1. He also postulates the following more general and far-reaching contagion hypothesis on the power of art to affect, inflect, and influence bodies—as we are confirming in volume 2.

## Nietzsche on Psychomotor Induction

For Nietzsche, this discovery has groundbreaking implications for aesthetics in general and for his reevaluation of Plato's untimely question on the influence of the arts in particular. Let us thus read his reframing of Féré's discovery of contagion by gesture to the end. Nietzsche writes that "all art exercises the power of suggestion over the muscles and senses, *which in the artistic temperament are originally active*" (*WP* 809; 427; my emphasis). An artistic temperament, for Nietzsche, is always already a mimetic temperament. Why?

Because, as he had already made clear in his first book, artistic temperaments are animated by both Apollonian and Dionysian aesthetic principles, which find in both visual representation and bodily intoxication respectively their manifest drives. It is thus no wonder that for Nietzsche the sight of a physical movement or an aesthetic (Apollonian) representation is imbued with the power or pathos to go beyond visual images in order to affect and infect subjects prone to a bodily (Dionysian) intoxication. What Nietzsche says of the figure of the artist in *The Birth of Tragedy* equally applies, at one remove, to the spectators: "With reference to these immediate art-states of nature, every artist is an 'imitator' [*Nachahmer*] that is to say, either an Apollonian artist in dreams [*Traumkünstler*], or a Dionysian artist in ecstasies [*Rauschkünstler*], or finally—as for example in Greek tragedy—at once artist in both dreams and ecstasies" (*BT* 2; 38). What was true for Plato remains true for Nietzsche, albeit with an inversed evaluation: both visual and bodily sides of mimesis are indeed at play in the birth of tragic art endowed with the pathos to generate intoxicating movements and sensations in the audience.

These art-states of nature are acute in artists, but they are also deeply rooted in the affective life of homo mimeticus. We could thus say that the motor images that appear in the theatrical sphere of visual representations and culminate in tragic and thus violent scenes that generate pity and fear, once given body and soul by dramatic actors have the power not so much to purify these mimetic emotions. Rather, they can transmit, by psychomotor contagion, the violence of tragedy to spectators, potentially disseminating phenomena of mimetic intoxication that spread "epidemically," a phenomenon Nietzsche groups under the rubric of "Dionysian mimesis."

Later in his career, as Nietzsche introduces the concept of "psychomotor induction" to account for an embodied form of mimetic contagion, he frames his discussion in the context of his youthful considerations on artistic influence as he writes:

> All art exercises the power of suggestion over the muscles and senses, which in the artistic temperament are originally active. . . . All art works tonically, increases strength, inflames desires (i.e., the feeling of strength), excites all the more subtle recollections of intoxication—there is a special memory that penetrates such states. (*WP* 809; 427)

For Nietzsche art has power over muscles first, and souls second; or, better, it excites souls to intoxication, good and bad, precisely because it has a suggestive (will to) power over bodies and senses. It is thus based on this empirical and untimely mimetic principle that Nietzsche, with the case of the actor in mind but with a larger diagnostic of contagion underway, will speak of "a kind of automatism of the whole muscular system impelled by strong stimuli from within" (811; 429). Nietzsche's career-long attention to Dionysian forms of mimetic contagion rendered him extremely sensitive to the tremendous phenomenon of "contagion by gesture." Thus, he continues, in a fragmentary, exploratory mode: "*Compulsion to imitate*: an extreme irritability through which a given example becomes contagious—a state is divined on the basis of signs and immediately enacted—An image, rising up within, immediately turns into a movement of the limbs" (811; 429). Nietzsche, then, proposes a theory of affective contagion that draws on Féré's diagnostic of the "frequency of *contagion by gesture*," while at the same time extending this empirical insight to the sphere of dramatic, and thus aesthetic and mimetic, gestures. The detour via the physio-physiology of the mimetic unconscious brings us back to the aesthetics of mimetic contagion with an immanent principle to account for it.

Contagion by gesture, but also compulsion to imitate, psychomotor induction, and mirroring reflexes: these were untimely observations in the late 1880s. Even in the following century, these contagious principles did not lead psychologists concerned with the unconscious to provide an account of the mirroring physio-psychological dynamic that connects self and other, psyche and soma, vision and movement in their psychic theories. Quite the contrary. When such a mimetic hypothesis was mentioned by advocates of psychoanalysis, such as Sigmund Freud, it was usually to reject it.[20] Consequently, Féré's untimely diagnostic of the unconscious power of contagion by gestures continued to remain unknown in the twentieth century—a historical fact that can be measured by the number of scholars who have never even heard of his name.

Yet Nietzsche was also untimely in his psychological meditations. Thus, he notices that Féré ventures further in his diagnostic. The French physician adds physio-psychological qualifications that lend empirical support to the mimetic unconscious. For instance, Féré, in collaboration with Alfred

Binet, was intrigued by a patient who claimed that as he watched the doctor's hand move, he had the "feeling that the same movement is activated in his hand, even if the hand is completely still" (*SM* 14). It is worth stressing that in the 1880s in the context of the Salpêtrière dominated by theatrical displays of hysteria in the foreground of carefully dramatized *leçons*, where a set of predetermined stages had to be performed, there would have been good theoretical reasons to dismiss such a bizarre observation. For instance, with Charcot, Féré could have diagnosed this disconcerting mirroring sensation as a relative rare *physiological* pathology characteristic of hysterical patients prone to unconscious mimicry. Alternatively, with Bernheim, Féré could have considered it as the effect of a purely *psychic* suggestion in which the patient (semi)consciously simulates the movements he is expected to perform. Instead, Féré, while officially on the side of Charcot, takes a different, less traveled but also more innovative middle-route: he senses that in psycho-physiological matters it is more productive to join, rather than divide, forces. Thus, he considers that this sensorial activation of the feeling of the movement of the other in the self to which some patients are particularly receptive is indicative of a "psycho-motor induction" that, to a lesser degree, is operative in normal people as well and involves both psychic and physiological levels of suggestion.

An advocate of experimental psychology, Féré was interested in measuring the force of this suggestion with the help of a dynamometer, an instrument for measuring power, or, as Nietzsche will call it, will to power. As Féré reports in a book titled *Animal Magnetism* (1887) coauthored with Binet, here is how they proceed. They first attempt to induce in the patient a motor act, such as the act of clenching the fist, with a verbal suggestion, that is, by ordering the patient: "Clench your fist!" Then, in a second moment, they perform the gesture in front of the patient. Here is what they find out: "verbal suggestion," they write, "only augments his normal dynamometric force by a few degrees, but if the action of firmly clenching the fist is imitated before him, his muscular force is not merely increased but doubled."[21] Conclusion: "the suggestion induced by gestures gives more intense results than it is possible to obtain by words only."[22]

We were wondering: why does the use of gestures—be it in a speech, a movie, or a cartoon—have a disconcerting contagious effect on the audience? Why are actors' mimetic powers amplified by dramatic impersonations via words, but also via movements and gestures? Féré's answer is: because there is a suggestive power in gestures that can trigger mirroring reactions in the observer. Gestures that we see performed have an effect not only on *what* we think but also on *how* we feel—perhaps stretching to influence how we act as well.

Now, this is a rudimentary experiment, as the authors themselves readily acknowledge; yet the dynamometer already registers a mysterious mimetic supplement generated by the perception of a goal-oriented movement that doubles the power of verbal suggestion in terms that could be registered empirically. Féré and Binet attributed this mimetic supplement to the suggestive force of psychomotor induction; we shall soon see that neuroscientists have a more recent yet no less mimetic term to define this disconcerting mirroring phenomenon. But the diagnostic is basically the same. It confirms that there is something in what used to be called the psyche, and now is often called the brain, that responds mimetically to the perception of motor movements. This is also what Nietzsche suggested for aesthetic in general and tragic emotions in particular. He claimed, echoing Féré, that it should be possible to measure "the effects of tragic emotions with a dynamometer" (*TI* 449). This empirical suggestion indicates that, for Nietzsche, tragic emotions such as pity and fear, as well as the violent pathos tragedy generates, can be subjected to a multiplicity of interpretations in theory, yet they ultimately rest on physiological reflexes induced by mimetic movements that can be empirically measured in practice. If Nietzsche disputed the catharsis hypothesis on such empirical grounds, it is only fitting that, in a mirroring gesture, he relies on the same empirical method to support the hypothesis of affective contagion.

## The Riddle of Suggestion Reconsidered

For genealogists of the mimetic unconscious, suggestion is not simply a riddle; it can provide a key to reframe an ancient quarrel on the value of the catharsis and affective hypotheses central to new mimetic studies. That this psychological tradition of the unconscious was concerned with the violent implications of suggestive influences is well known. The link between hypnosis and crime was, in fact, not a minor preoccupation among advocates of suggestive therapies. If a patient under the spell of "suggestion" could turn an idea, amplified by the psychomotor power of movement, into an action, and suggestion is a normal property of the human brain, how far could those suggested actions go in daily life?

The main advocate of the theory of suggestion, Hippolyte Bernheim, thought they could go pretty far. While also endorsing the reflex theory of the mimetic unconscious espoused by Féré, Bernheim went beyond the sphere of individual pathology as he considered that "the study of suggestion opens up new fields in medicine, psychology, and sociology" (*ST* 178). Why? Because, he continues, "poor human imagination is exposed on all sides to good or bad, salutary or pernicious impressions" (178). Bernheim is thus fully aware that the theory of suggestion can be put to use for violent practices; he also detaches crime from essentialist accounts based on biology rendered popular by figures like Cesare Lombroso, thereby paving the way for criminologists turned sociologists like Gabriel Tarde who established a connection between suggested crimes and the laws of imitation: "To have only suggested ideas and to believe them spontaneous," claimed Tarde on the shoulders of Bernheim; and generalizing the diagnostic, he adds, "this is the illusion of the social being [*l'homme social*]."[23] For the entire tradition of the mimetic unconscious humans are more suggestible, influenceable, and mimetically prone to conforming than they are often willing to acknowledge, idealist philosophers and rationalist social scientists in primis. Hence the need to balance the ideal image of *Homo sapiens* with the all too real counterpart of homo mimeticus.

Without opening the complex legal debate on free will and responsibility in cases of suggested crimes, let us note that Bernheim does *not* claim that suggestion is equivalent to an unconscious state of sleep. The opposite is true. As he specifies:

> the hypnotized subject who robs because he was suggested to do so, the fool who kills, know that they steal and that they kill . . . their moral conscience is perverted by imperative conceptions, . . . because madness and suggestion dominate their being; they cannot prevent themselves from striking. The state of consciousness is modified, as it may also be modified by vivid moral emotions, such as anger. The act, nevertheless was conscious,

although the memory of it may be now effaced. There are latent ideas, but there are no unconscious ideas. (*ST* 158)

The diagnostic is clear. One does not need to be a mindless automaton in a deep somnambulistic state to commit crimes suggested by others—that was the view held by colleagues like Jules Liégeois and Ambroise-Auguste Liébeault. On the contrary, already for Bernheim, violent emotions like anger can be amplified by "suggestion," "imitation" (26), and mirroring mechanisms rooted in what he called "cerebral automatism" (28).

As we saw in the preceding chapter, such automatism received plenty of stimuli on January 6, 2021, for instance. The acts were conscious though modified by contagious emotions. Further, if the *rapport* between the *suggestioneur* and the *suggestioné* is operative, the relational dynamic of suggestion has the power to turn the idea of the former into an action of the latter, including violent and criminal actions. Giving a number of examples of subjects who, under the influence of suggestion, have committed crimes, from theft to physical attacks to murder attempts, Bernheim claims: "From all the preceding, I conclude that an honest man can, by suggestion, commit a crime."[24] If a dose of skepticism concerning deep states of somnambulism, post-hypnotic amnesia, and the like is in order not to let intentional crimes off the hook, this does not mean that the power of suggestion is not at play in more conscious yet not less dangerous ways.

The power of suggestion is, in fact, intensified if subjects are under the spell of a figure endowed with prestige—say, a doctor or a leader. We have seen the willpower of political leaders qua *meneurs* in suggesting ideas that, once amplified by hypermimetic simulations, can be easily turned into criminal actions. The storming of the U.S. Capitol is a good contemporary example of a successful suggestion turned into a violent action. The insurrectionists are under the impression that they act under their own individual volition alone, for sure. But in reality, they are actually turning the operator's idea and the conspiracy theories that disseminated it, into a spiral of actions and reactions they do not fully control. Violent actions can thus emerge from the reciprocal reinforcing dynamic of language and gestures operating on the mimetic unconscious, but also of online and offline suggestions constitutive of hypermimesis. Under such conditions, a suggestible subject can indeed be turned into a weapon; if it is part of a crowd, we have seen that it can even turn into a collective weapon.

What we must add now is that advocates of the mimetic unconscious already called attention to the powers of new media like cinema in inducing real crimes. Already at the time of Féré's experiments, the powers of such motor or moving images on bodies and souls were in fact being felt by normal people at the dawn of cinema in fin de siècle Paris. Although Féré does not mention it explicitly, the shadow of cinematic motor images, with their power to induce physio-psychological hypnotic responses, will be central to evaluations of the seventh art—waiting for future philosophical physicians to be picked up and developed further.

## Cinematic Suggestions and Hypnotic Crimes

Cinematic stars, after all, are not deprived of hypnotic prestige. And the phantom of hypnotic crimes haunted theories of suggestion. As Stefan Andriopoulos has shown, the invention of cinema was inextricably intertwined with cultural anxieties about "hypnotic crimes" that were taken seriously by the School of Nancy; these crimes also had a larger impact that went beyond psychology and informed modernist literary culture more generally and cinematic aesthetics in particular. I already noted the importance of literary modernism in the discovery of the mimetic unconscious. What we must add is that starting with a literary fascination with hypnosis—from Guy de Maupassant to Franz Kafka—Andriopoulos considers the suggestive power of film via classics of early expressionist cinema: from Georges Méliès's *Le Magnétiseur* to Robert Wiene's *The Cabinet of Dr. Caligari* (1919) to Fritz Lang's *Dr. Mabuse, the Gambler* (1922), among other classics of expressionism that dramatize and actualize the contagious powers of hypnotic suggestion. As he puts it:

> Contemporary medical and psychological representations of the new medium spoke to a structural affinity of cinema and hypnotism. . . . It was even feared that films depicting violent actions would induce similar crimes, since the posthypnotic influence of the moving images would control susceptible spectators after leaving the movie theater.[25]

This account of the suggestive power of violent cinematic representations to generate crimes is not based on deterministic billiard-ball causation for it considers the role of "corporate agencies" in generating shared states of possession. Instead, it is based on a searching transdisciplinary evaluation of psychic, medical, and aesthetic discourses attentive to the hypnotic power of film in general, and violent scenes in particular, to influence behavior to the point of (dis)possession, generating cultural patho(-)logies about suggested crimes that were taken quite seriously in the modernist period. One century later, at the dawn of the digital age, there is little evidence that we should take the suggestive power of new media less seriously. On the contrary, that suggested crimes can go as far as murder and, sometimes, self-murder is already indicated by the patho(-)logical case studies we encountered so far—from terrorist attacks to new fascist insurrections, all of which find models in aesthetic fictions before being actualized in reality.

Once again, our genealogy of the mimetic unconscious looked back to marginalized traditions that bring us back to the affective hypothesis on the contagiousness of violence with which we started. And yet we are now in a better position to account for the mirroring dynamic of contagious reflexes a pre-Freudian tradition of the unconscious was attentive to. This tradition equally suggested that the simple observation of gestures has the potential to trigger mirroring gestures that blur the frontier between movements seen and movements performed, stretching to turn fictional actions into embodied reactions. Is this physio-psychological account of the unconscious reductionist then? Far from it, for it is not based on physiology alone but on the interplay of physiology and psychology. Which also means that, depending on the circumstances, the psyche is in a position to mediate—or, Nietzsche often says, "interpret" or "evaluate"—violent physiological drives that generate pathos from a more critical, interpretative, yet not fully conscious distance. Nietzsche puts it clearly as he writes: "that a violent [*heftiger*] stimulus is experienced as pleasure or displeasure, this depends on the *interpretation* of the intellect which, to be sure, generally does this work without rising to our consciousness" (*GS* 127; 184; trans. modified). The mimetic unconscious is thus not only based on physiological reflexes that automatically mirror external stimuli; it also entails psychological interpretations of these stimuli, including violent ones that do not raise to full conscious awareness. As Nietzsche specifies, these stimuli can be categorized under the rubric of "pleasure" or "displeasure"; they also generate attraction or repulsion or, most often, a double movement comprised of both attraction and repulsion, which is constitutive of our interpretation of the concept of pathos of distance. This psychological interpretation opens up the unconscious to an immanent movement rather than to a universal structure and is thus sensitive to contextual, historical, cultural, aesthetic, and ethical evaluations that are constitutive of our genealogy of violence and the mimetic unconscious.

Far from providing a reductionist approach that would reduce the complex problematic of media violence to physiology alone, then, a genealogical articulation of psychology with physiology attentive to broader aesthetic-social-cultural-ideological-political influences offers us a distinctive perspectival, or as we call it, patho-*logical*, approach to account for case studies of hypermimetic violence that require a sense of genealogical discrimination in order to be adequately interpreted. Such interpretative skills are the soul that animates the transdisciplinary field of new mimetic studies.

To now give interpretative specificity to our genealogy of the mimetic unconscious, let us thus turn to a present-oriented case study or example that brings us back to the issue of racist violence we already encountered but that now deserves a more detailed evaluation. This example reveals how mirroring reflexes and suggestive influences that are not under the full control of a conscious will and require unconscious forms of subliminal interpretation remain central to contemporary manifestations of violence that were not traditionally grouped under the traditional rubric of media violence in the past but should be constitutive of present- and future-oriented diagnostics of (new) media violence.

## Racist Pathologies Triggering Police Violence

Lest the theory of suggestive influences I have convoked be dismissed as a remnant of modernist concerns with mysterious somnambulistic spells that might be far removed from contemporary realities, or deterministic physiological reflexes linked to cinematic automatons, I deliberately select a realistic example that is far from reductionist, is close to contemporary preoccupations with violent discriminations, and allows us to connect different threads constitutive of the affective hypothesis to the unconscious. It will also allow us to confront the interplay between racist oppression and a type of police violence that, I argue, can neither be reduced to nor dissociated from media violence. As we will see, in this complex case of (hyper)mimetic violence, a number of ideological, contextual, cultural, social, aesthetic, psychological, and, ultimately, physiological mechanisms are simultaneously at play in an escalating mirroring confrontation that ends in a tragic murder perhaps modeled on cinematic fictions. Far from being an individual case, this murder is symptomatic of a racist "pathology of contemporary civilization."[26] The murder cannot be dismissed as a simulation for it was captured on camera. If it generates a type of tragic pathos that is deprived of cathartic effects, the contagious dynamic of violence it represents can be studied from the interpretative critical distance of new mimetic studies.

### Triggering Police Violence: The Case of Rayshard Brooks

In Atlanta, Georgia, June 2020, Rayshard Brooks, a twenty-seven-year-old African American man, was shot and killed by a white policeman. The case is familiar; this is but one of a plethora of racially induced police murders that, even in the wake of BLM, continue to afflict like an epidemic African Americans and other minorities, most visibly in the United States but also in Europe with respect to immigrants as well as other parts of the world against minorities. Given the dominant racist perception of African Americans in the United States, the murder obviously cannot be dissociated from historical, ideological, structural, and thus systemic violence part of a broader social—and, in this case, racist—pathology. It can thus not be reduced to a single causation, let alone a direct aesthetic influence. And yet it allows us to focus on a complex embodied escalation between two subjects unconsciously caught in prescribed roles (the white cop; the Black criminal), actions and reactions (chasing-fleeing; fleeing-shooting) that, in our view, can neither be reduced to, nor dissociated from, (new) media representations of violence in the sphere of fiction. They call for a sense of genealogical discrimination on the complex relation between media, violence, and the unconscious.

The tragic example of Rayshard Brooks, in fact, points toward (hyper) mimetic mechanisms of misrecognition that do not remain confined within an imaginary mirror stage. On the contrary, they set in motion a chain of suggestive mirroring physio-psychological actions that are not under the full control of consciousness and belong to the register of the mimetic unconscious. This violent unconscious dynamic also distributes agency beyond human actions via a multiplicity of what Latour calls nonhuman "actants" or "technical mediations."[27] These include guns and tasers, which, in a spiraling sequence, can easily escape human agentic control and can turn movements seen into actions performed. In the process, they can also trigger a type of (hyper)mimetic violence that, in a deeply racist society dominated by equally racist media misrepresentations, can make the difference between life and death. Let us consider the tragic unfolding of the events step by step.

The police murder of Brooks was recorded from a variety of perspectives (bodycam, witness phone camera, security camera) and provides us with a realistic representation of the tragic events we can reconstruct from a distance.[28] The context is the following: Brooks was noticed asleep in his own car in the drive-through of a fast-food restaurant (Wendy's) in Atlanta. His car was blocking a drive-through lane, so rather than waking him up (a default reaction in all the countries I know), a typically U.S. response ensues: an employee at the restaurant calls the police. In an informed analysis of Brooks's killing, comedian Trevor Noah points to the fundamental problem as he asks: "Why are armed police dealing with a man sleeping in his car?"[29] Race is immediately in the foreground as the operator repeatedly asks, again typically: "Is he Black?" (0:40). The answer is positive, and a police officer arrives in a short time, and requests a second officer who can perform a sobriety test. The second officer (Garrett Rolfe) arrives, and Brooks is ordered to step out of the car. What starts as routine procedure turns into a disquieting sequence of events.

The initial exchange is cordial; Brooks is fully cooperative; and Rolfe follows the protocol. Asked whether he would take a sobriety breath test, Brooks admits at the outset that he had been drinking and suggests himself, in a calm tone of voice, that he "could walk home" (4:14). It is important to note for context that Brooks was on probation after having spent two years in prison and had confronted difficulties reintegrating and finding work. He thus knew that an arrest would lead to the revocation of his probation and to reimprisonment. Rolfe disregards Brooks's suggestion. In 2019 Rolfe had been honored by the organization "Mothers against Driving Drunk" for making more than fifty driving under the influence (DUI) arrests; every arrest counts. He insists on the request of taking the sobriety test. Brooks eventually complies, saying, "I don't want to refuse anything" (4:34). He predictably tests positive, 0.108, which is slightly above the tolerated limit, namely 0.08 [5:08]). Let us recall that the investigation started not because he was driving under the influence but because he was sleeping in his car. While what follows is in no way an exoneration for DUI or for transgressing driving regulations that in most industrialized countries are effectively enforced via stringent fines, it takes issue with a type of police brutality that, most visibly in the United States but not only, is commonly directed against racial minorities. What follows is but one example, but it is a representative one.

The exchange so far lasted over forty minutes and remained polite throughout. But a change of speed and intensity takes place. An escalation of violent bodily actions, rather than linguistic signs, suddenly comes into play. It will last forty-five seconds, and it unfolds as follows: without preliminary notification, Rolfe moves behind Brooks's back and starts handcuffing him with the assistance of the second officer. Brooks instinctively resists the arrest, and a physical struggle ensues (see 5:50-6:25).

The three entangled bodies now fall to the ground, and one cop uses a taser to discharge an electric shock to Brooks's body, who, in a reactive move, manages to wrest the taser out of the cop's hand. He takes possession of it, fires back, and breaks free, starting to run for his life—until his run is stopped short, and so is his life. Rolfe fatally shoots Brooks three times, hitting him twice in the back (6:35). One bullet will pierce his heart.

Once we partially recover from this unspeakable scene of all too real tragic pathos that leads to a real, rather than fictional, death, any viewer is left to wonder from an interpretative distance: how can falling asleep in one's car, even on the service lane—just like owning a pocketknife (Freddie Gray), paying with a twenty-dollar counterfeit bill (George Floyd), or sleeping in one's house (Breonna Taylor)—lead to a brutal murder perpetuated by an armed force supposedly representing "justice" and paid to protect people? Surely something has gone fundamentally wrong in the education of the guardians (to recall Plato's educative concerns). Equally clearly, in this complex, violent, and tragic scene, a multiplicity of racist-ideological-legal-historical-cultural-economic and thus systemic forces play a major role: from the decision to call the police instead of waking Brooks up to Rolfe's decision to test him for sobriety although he was obviously not driving when the police arrived, from the former's choice not to let Brooks walk home or perhaps accompany him home, to the decision of arresting him without notice, a number of intentional and premeditated choices based on interpretations (un)consciously informed by an all-pervasive racist ideology are indeed made by the police officer in question. Racist ideology and the racist police practices it entails generate a capillary network that entangled Black subjects in systemic power relations, which are clearly the decisive factors that *lead up* to the tragedy.

And yet, if systemic racism leads up to it, it might still require an unconscious suggestive supplement to trigger the shooting itself. To culminate in murder, racist ideology and police practices also need to be redoubled by an embodied, relational, and less conscious but not less fatal degree of violent affective intensity, or pathos, that is intersubjective, hierarchical, and relational in nature yet effectively takes possession of egos turning them into phantoms. This violent pathos dispossesses subjects (both oppressors and oppressed) of their capacity to think rationally and doubles the mediation of racist ideology with the immediacy of a viscerally felt, reflex, and unconscious mirroring reaction. As the physical struggle ensues, in fact, an unforeseen intersubjective, reciprocal, and quite mimetic, or better hypermimetic dynamic quickly unfolds. It takes possession of all subjects involved, albeit differently given the hierarchical and violent power-structure, depriving each embodied perspective of conscious control over an autonomous intentional will.

Nietzsche's critique of the limits of conscious will in human actions in general is particularly relevant to account for the unconscious dynamic of violent actions in particular. As he puts it in a passage of *The Gay Science* worth quoting in full:

> Every thoughtless person is convinced that will alone is effective; that willing is something simple, a brute datum, underivable, and intelligible by itself. He is convinced that when he does something—strike something, for example—it is he that strikes, and that he did strike because he *willed* it. He does not see any problem here: the feeling of *will* seems sufficient to him not only for the assumption of cause and effect, but also for the faith that he *understands* their relationship. He knows nothing of the mechanism of what happened and of the hundredfold fine work that needs to be done to bring about the strike. (*GS* 127, 183)

There is indeed a will to power qua mimetic pathos that does not rest on a conscious, volitional, fully rational, and autonomous subject. Rather, it calls into play a multiplicity of affective, interpretative, and mediating processes that operate below the register of consciousness yet motivate effective "strikes" nonetheless. Every person who tried their hand at—or even only watched—any sports event should be familiar with this. Our bodies, especially if trained, can operate with a speed that far exceeds conscious awareness. But Nietzsche is writing for and against philosophers. Hence, he cannot assume a high degree of embodied knowledge. He needs to spell it out for them, but interdisciplinary readers of this book should be better placed to absorb his lesson. In fact, while free will is questioned in Nietzsche's diagnostic, a basic familiarity with sports and play, should show that it does not exonerate subjects from being responsible for violent actions or reactions. Any referee will confirm this too.

But the problem with violence in the real world and police violence in the United States in particular is that there is no referee in sight that guarantees fair adherence to equal social rules. The police operate instead as an active participant in the enforcement of violence disproportionally directed against African Americans and ethnic minorities. In this particular agonistic, hierarchical, and murderous struggle, violent mirroring reflexes are triggered by a spiral of reciprocal movements and interpretations of movements that go beyond simple causal willing, generating an escalation of violence that cuts both ways—in this case, both against Brooks. Give the "hundredfold fine work" internal to such actions, we need to radically slow down the scene to analyze it in slow motion. Here the close-reading skills essential for analyzing mimetic fictions in literary, film, and media studies turn out to be essential for analyzing hypermimetic realities in new mimetic studies.

The two sides are inextricably intertwined for they are caught in the same mirroring process, but since they embody diametrically opposed positions of power, let us consider them separately before joining them. On the side of the victim, we have seen that Brooks makes a reasonable request to Rolfe in a polite and compliant tone that indicates his willingness and intention to cooperate. At the same time, he had just been asleep, is under the influence of alcohol, and finds himself in an altered state of consciousness receptive to suggestive influences with the power to take possession of his willful actions. As is well known, alcohol is a Dionysian substance that amplifies affective reactions, including aggressive pathos, while also diminishing fear at the personal level. If the act of willing is already influenced by complex unconscious processes for a sober subject, as Nietzsche noted, imagine this for a drunk person—it shouldn't be hard for as Noah reminds us, "we have all been drunk."[30] At the interpretative level, this altered state can also potentially increase a receptive sensitivity for the history of injustice, aggression, and violence sedimented mimetically in the political unconscious of African Americans in general, especially since Brooks's arrest is a typical instance of such systemic, racist, and discriminatory violence.

Furthermore, if we consider that the implications of the arrest, for Brooks, are imprisonment, it is less surprising that the balance between rational distance and irrational pathos at play in his unconscious interpretation of violent stimuli has the potential to tip in favor of a pathos the subject does not willfully control but, in this state of heightened suggestibility, can take control of his rational faculty instead. As Rolfe attempts to handcuff Brooks, the latter is taken by surprise as the tenor of the interaction so far did not prepare Brooks for the quick switch to an arrest. As the second officer intervenes, Brooks finds himself in a situation of numerical, physical, psychic, and legal disadvantage that makes racist oppression violently palpable on Black bodies and souls whose lives still do not matter.

Now, it is in this complex context that a split-second, subliminal decision that defies conscious mediation leads Brooks to react unconsciously, via an automatic mimetic reflex, to the officer's deliberate decision to handcuff him. In this state of surprise, the following steps unfold very rapidly: Brooks struggles to break free from the two policemen (and, at one remove, perhaps also from the racist structures that authorize its systemic violence?); is subjected to the taser's electric discharge, takes possession of the taser, and fires back, hitting the second policeman (perhaps as a mirroring reflex for survival?); and he starts to run (perhaps carried by a human instinct to preserve one's freedom?). The events outside are recorded and lend themselves to a phenomenological interpretation. Still, we will never have definitive answers to these interpretative questions of the hundredfold motivations happening that are animating Brooks's will to freedom.

What we do see is a sequence of mirroring reactions that blur the line between outside and inside, but also psychology and physiology, conscious action and unconscious reactions and are constitutive part of the violent patho(-)logy that unfolds. It starts by Rolfe pointing and discharging the taser as Brooks is fleeing (6:30). In a mirroring gesture, Brooks turns, points the taser back *as if* it were a gun, and fires his second and last probe (6:31). In yet another mirroring reaction, the officer drops his taser, draws his real gun, and automatically fires three fatal shots in reply (6:32).

This striking mirroring reaction can be replayed online. It is actually difficult to find a clearer illustration of the mimetic unconscious. Its dynamic is located in between subjects caught in a mirroring yet radically unbalanced logic of violent escalation. Their lives are in the hands of actants perhaps more than the other way round; these mediated technologies pit an empty taser contra a loaded gun, a loaded gun contra an empty taser, that lead directly to a murderous action. While the symmetrical human dynamic generates sameness in mirroring gestures between policeman and victim, the asymmetry in both power and weapons makes, quite literally, the difference between life and death.

Full responsibility is clearly on the side of the gun-holder who is a policeman with a specialized training but also with a history of inappropriately aiming his gun. There is thus no exoneration involved in the present analysis. So far, the justice system of the state of Georgia came to the opposite conclusion. Despite a momentary termination of employment of Brook's killer, Garett Rolfe was considered "wrongly terminated" and was "reinstated" as police officer.[31] The Prosecuting Attorneys' Council of Georgia also came to the following juridical conclusion: "was it objectively reasonable that [Rolfe] used deadly force? And we conclude it was."[32] This mindboggling evaluation should speak volumes to the racist bias internal to U.S. law in the age of BLM. As Noah sums it up, "there is one common thread beyond all the ifs central to this complex case: If you weren't black, maybe you would still be alive."[33]

Needless to say, the diagnostic presented here goes beyond the case of Rolfe and has general implications for police officers and gun-owners more generally. To move beyond all too human actions and reactions, it is in fact important to note that the taser and the gun are not neutral passive objects to be used by willful subjects in sovereign control; they have agentic properties of their own in this tragic sequence. As Latour points out: "you are a different person with a gun in your hand."[34] We are indeed formed and transformed by the objects in our hands we appear to willfully control yet, in a complex feedback loop, have agentic control on our actions and reactions as well. What we must add is that these mirroring effects between human and nonhuman actants that generate difference within a subject-object composition can also generate sameness once faced with a redoubled mirroring scenario. As this case study of a policeman-gun chasing a fugitive-taser show, an unconscious mirroring reflex can emerge from the interactive dynamic of the hypermimetic action itself. The trigger of unconscious violence circulates in the (a)symmetrical composite (non)human action and reaction in pathological ways that should be under the lens of new mimetic studies.

On the other, mirroring side, contra Rayshard Brooks's diplomatic request that he could simply walk home, officer Garrett Rolfe sets in motion an unconscious interplay of visceral aggression and fearful interpretations that do not leave much space for humane sentiments like pity or sympathy; as Brooks manages to break loose, he generates an irrational fear in the momentarily disempowered U.S. officers who are already under the spell of racist misrepresentations of African Americans as dangerous, life-threatening criminals—an imaginary fear since Brooks is unarmed whereas, in a mirroring and all too real inversion, both officers are armed and one is ready to kill. What follows is a classical police chase sequence viewers are familiar with from popular U.S. reality TV series like *Cops* (1989–). One of the longest running TV shows in the country, it represents violent police actions often directed toward African Americans; this fictionalized bias is then redoubled by a racist police training automatically biased contra African Americans as well.

Reframed within the TV show, a predictable script ensues in reality in which Rolfe plays his role with deadly yet totally avoidable consequences. The chase is set off. The cop automatically draws his gun in a scene that breaches basic protocol in reality, for Brooks poses no immediate threat, yet is again in line with typical police scenes at play in a number of cinematic and televised fictions. The violent scenario is indeed classic: a white ("good") cop pursuing a Black ("bad") criminal who fires in the name of a ("just") cause. That the line between conscious action and unconscious reaction, physiological reflex and psychological interpretation, fictional danger and real danger, good and evil, but also life and death, is now speedily blurred in this hypermimetic spiral and is immediately confirmed as Rolfe *misinterprets* the now empty taser *as if* it were a loaded gun. Misinterpretations based on a *méconnaissance* that is not restricted to narcissistic *imagos* or mimetic desires but is based on the logic of mimetic pathos have real consequences. Thus, in a mirroring reaction in which an imaginary threat generates a real shooting, he pulls the trigger with his own real and all-too-deadly weapon. Starting from a position of patho-*logical* interpretative distance, the mimetic pathos internal to racist *ideo*-logy has quickly turned into a hypermimetic racist pathology generative of ongoing horrors.

## Report

If we now join these mirroring perspectives, we should be able to disentangle the patho(-)logical hypermimetic drives that led the cop to mistake a taser for a shotgun and pull the trigger and ask more specific diagnostic questions. Was it a premeditated, fully willful, and consciously controlled action that led the officer to respond to an imaginary shotgun with a real shotgun? Or, more probably, was this a subliminal unconscious mirroring reaction based on both a violent psychological interpretation and an equally violent physiological stimulus that led the cop to misinterpret an empty taser for a deadly weapon, a harmless fugitive for a dangerous criminal, a defensive imaginary gesture for a violent deadly gesture? What is certain is that this patho(-)logical misrecognition is not based on the mediation of linguistic signs predicated on the logic of representation. It is rather based on a bodily mirroring pathos that operates on a more immediate relational register constitutive of the mimetic unconscious. This real tragedy speaks to my contention that the mimetic unconscious is no longer modeled on ancient tragedies that generate pity and fear with cathartic properties—though pity and fear continue to be at play as we witness such scenes from a distance. Rather, it is more likely modeled on contemporary fictional but also reality-based representations that are not structured as a complex exemplary plot, but disproportionality represent, legitimize, and performatively amplify police brutality against minority groups in general and African Americans in particular.

In sum, the six layers of (hyper)mimetic confusion that triggered this murder are multiple, complex, and can be summarized as follows. First, Brooks is subjected to a pervasive racist ideology that a priori considers African Americans as prone to violence and crime and justifies police violence from a distance (systemic racism). Second, he is caught in a racist double bind between imprisonment and compliance that leads him to shift from a rational discourse (logos) to irrational affects (pathos). Third, a subliminal and not fully willful decision is taken under the influence of alcohol and bodily violence to break free via a reflex mimesis that leads to mirroring actions and reactions that are not under the control of consciousness and are in this sense both mimetic and unconscious (mimetic unconscious). Fourth, trapped in this mirroring struggle, violence automatically escalates, and so does the power of affects like fear and aggression (mimetic pathos). Fifth, as Brooks starts to run, driven by a will to freedom, he is no longer considered a person for a projection of an imaginary criminal far removed from reality yet modeled on racist fictions has been mapped on his body and soul (hyper-real phantom). Sixth, as he turns, the line between fiction/reality, conscious action/unconscious reaction, empty taser/loaded gun, illusory violence/real violence is blurred in a spiral of hypermimetic confusion in which simulations retroact on the singularity of a human life leading to the killing of an unarmed, certainly imperfect, but also unique, representative victim of racist violence.

This case is, indeed, tragic and complex. It cannot be reduced to one single causal explanation based on universal principles of causality and necessity—let alone Oedipal principles with cathartic effects. On the contrary, it calls for an articulation of different layers of affective contagion that go from physiology to psychology, ideology to aesthetics, all of which are constitutive of new mimetic studies. In fact, it reveals how the protean problematic of mimesis, and the contagious, unconscious actions and reactions it generates, should be center stage in discussions of contemporary violence that are inevitably entangled in (new) media violence. If looking back to genealogical precursors of the tradition of the mimetic unconscious does not entail a reductionist approach, we now turn to see that this is equally valid if we look ahead to mirroring principles that neuroscientists are currently rediscovering under new conceptual masks. It is my contention that the recent turn to affect, embodied cognition, and the brain are emerging perspectival contributions to affective contagion constitutive of the *re*-turn of mimesis animating new mimetic studies in the digital age.

**CHAPTER 5**

# Dangerous Simulations

## Mirror Neurons, Video Games, *E*-Motions

The mimetic perspectives explored in this Janus-faced study on catharsis and contagion have been heterogeneous in nature, yet they relied on the same genealogical principle. My methodological assumption has been that looking back to exemplary theories of catharsis and contagion puts new generations of theorists of homo mimeticus in a position to better evaluate specific manifestations of unconscious violence that reach into the present. In particular, stepping back to ancient and modern diagnostics of the power of gestures and expressions to trigger contagious mirroring affects helped us anticipate discoveries that are currently opening up new frontiers for research in new mimetic studies. We have also seen that in his untimely role of philosophical physician, at the dawn of philosophy, Plato already diagnosed the contagious powers of phantoms to generate mirroring-magnetic-contagious effects that spell-*bind* subjects in unconscious ways; Nietzsche, at the twilight of philosophy, diagnosed them further from the perspective of physio-psychology. Despite their mimetic agonism concerning metaphysical questions on the truth and lies of aesthetic representations, Plato and Nietzsche, read in the company of affect theorists, political theorists, and mimetic theorists, turned out to be acute observers of the contagious, affective, and unconscious processes that generate a dynamic, complex, and still ongoing interplay between aesthetic representations and behavioral imitation.

On the shoulders of this long-standing genealogy, a supplement to René Girard's mimetic theory remains in order to orient new mimetic studies toward the future. Girard is right to say that "it was Plato's own acute insight into the nature of tragic inspiration that provoked his hostility to drama" (*VS* 203). He is equally right to stress that Nietzsche's categories of Apollonian and Dionysian mimesis "are manifestly superior to the approaches of most critics" (292). However, if Girard may still be haunted by anxieties of originality that led him to downplay and sometimes deny the influence of these influential predecessors while pushing his romantic agonism with these (and other) exemplary precursors of mimetic theory to the extreme,[1] genealogical lenses led me to adopt a different strategy.

My aim throughout this book has been to rely on the gauge of mimetic agonism to affirm the untimely validity of diagnostics that may have been embryonic in influential predecessors' and still required a theoretical push to be fully born. It is only by looking back to the origins of mimetic studies and acknowledging previous insights that this field can be made new to face hypermimetic phenomena in the present. This affirmative agonistic move led me to take a number of steps beyond Girard. I specified, for instance, that it was Plato's own acute insight into the contagious nature of dramatic impersonations, and the mirroring gestures and affects constitutive of mimetic pathos, that provoked his hostility to *dramatic* mimesis and the contagious violence it can trigger in the first place. Similarly, but from the other end of the metaphysical spectrum, it was Nietzsche's insight into the physio-psychological dynamic of unconscious forms of mimetic communication the philosopher may try to keep at a distance, yet generate pathos nonetheless, that led him to eventually side with the hypothesis of contagion. What we must add now in this concluding chapter is that, taken together, both ancient and modern perspectives on contagion pave the way for recent theoretical turns to affect, embodied cognition, and, above all, mirroring principles that are fully constitutive of the mimetic turn or *re*-turn of attention to homo mimeticus—albeit under different conceptual masks and new aesthetic media.

After a long period of marginalization in the past century, the contagious dimension of affects is once again taken seriously by a number of researchers in the humanities, the social sciences, and the neurosciences. From a different perspective, they are currently informing innovative turns that consider the role mirroring reflexes play in the unconscious reproduction of actions and reactions. These new turns are certainly innovative and constitutive of mimetic studies. They go beyond an autonomous conception of art considered from a position of disinterested contemplation that, via different formalisms, continued to dominate aesthetic theories in the past century; they also go beyond solipsistic accounts of an autonomous, self-sufficient, and monadic ego, or subject, still dominant in philosophy and the social sciences in order to foreground a relational, embodied, and affectively inclined conception of homo mimeticus that is currently regaining traction under the rubric of the mimetic turn. And yet our genealogical perspective also puts us in a position to see that concerns with affective contagion that stretch from representation to the audience are certainly not radically original turns. On the contrary, they are timely *re*-turns of theatrical/theoretical concerns with the power of mimetic pathos we have been investigating all along. In particular, they confirm an affective hypothesis based on mirroring mechanisms that were well known by the tradition of the mimetic unconscious and that we are now ready to rediscover.

## An Untimely Rediscovery

Nietzsche occupied a privileged place in both volumes of this diptych on violence and the unconscious for a simple reason: he is arguably the thinker who perfected the genealogical method that allowed us to reevaluate the value of both the cathartic and affective hypotheses, from antiquity to the present. He is also one of the main thinkers who paved the way for our theory of homo mimeticus.[2] We have seen that with respect to his evaluation of contagion, Nietzsche's diagnostic of Dionysian intoxications looks back to Plato's psychology and—via the mediation of Charles Féré's physio-psychology—anticipates contemporary turns to affect, embodiment, and the brain constitutive of contemporary neurology. We have also seen that Féré's pioneering experiments on "psycho-motor induction" on which Nietzsche's theory of contagious forms of communication relies is historically and philosophically interesting and should be included in revisionist accounts of the discovery of the unconscious. What we must add now is that the theoretical speculations that emerged from experimental observations on mirroring reflexes are even more forward-looking and provide an immanent theoretical foundation that lends empirical credibility to the affective hypothesis. In particular, Féré and Nietzsche inaugurate a theory of mirroring forms of unconscious communication in the 1880s that will have to await the 1990s to be *re*-discovered.

Philosophers trained in a dualist metaphysical tradition that opposes mind and body as well as self and others have long wondered about the riddle of how humans access the mind of others. A rationalist bias in western thought prevented them from seeing an embodied solution advocated by philosophical physicians in line with the affective hypothesis. Charles Féré was, in fact, working with patients prone to reflex imitation from a third-person empirical distance. But as an experimental physician, he did not hesitate to rely on a first-person, phenomenological, and experiential perspective as he observed, in *Sensation et mouvement* (1887): "If we can read the thought of one's interlocutor on his face, it is because while we observe him, we unconsciously assume his expression, and the idea presents itself as a consequence" (*SM* 16). The direct observation of a facial expression, but also of gestures and images, he later adds, leads to an unconscious mimicry of the expression that generates the idea of the other into the self. And summing up his affective hypothesis, Féré specifies:

> It is possible that certain subjects who are particularly sensitive to the phenomenon of induction imitate unconsciously [*imitent inconsciemment*] the movements that necessarily accompany the idea of the one in his presence, and will consequently be led to feel the same emotion, the same thought, in a word, to obey what we call, *mental suggestion* [*la suggestion mentale*]. (*SM* 16)

Suggestion is not considered an insoluble riddle here. Rather, it is a concept based on a mimetic reflex that solves nothing less than the riddle of how to access the mind of others—and unconsciously so. For Féré, in fact, there is a direct path that leads from the reflex of imitation of "movements" seen outside to the "ideas" the other thinks inside her mind. For some subjects, communication is thus first of all an unconscious, bodily, and mimetic communication in which the automatic reproduction of movements leads to an immediate understanding of the other's emotions and thoughts. Nietzsche, always bolder in his philosophical speculations, generalizes this hypothesis as he says, on the shoulders of Féré: "One never communicates thoughts: one communicates movements, mimic signs, which we then trace back to thoughts" (*WP* 809; 428). Contemporary neurologists may laugh at experiments with a dynamometer, but they won't laugh at this theoretical conclusion; neither will the most recent advocates of the affective, embodied, or performative turns. The genealogy of the mimetic unconscious is, indeed, anticipating, by over a century, what has been hailed as a revolutionary discovery in the 1990s. This also means that genealogical lenses reframe it as a *re*-discovery of mirroring principles that have long been familiar to genealogists of a soul (psyche) still in touch with the immanence of the body (soma).

After our genealogical account of the discovery of the mimetic unconscious, out of the suggestive reflex of imitation, we are now in a position to give empirical and theoretical substance to Plato's "great question" about the influence of art with which we started. We were wondering why the father of philosophy was so concerned with the "gestures" of mimetic actors impersonating a violent role on stage? Why Nietzsche also stressed the actor's power of gestures and expressions to convince the "nerves"? How "examples," even if fictional, can become "contagious"? You will have guessed it. Mirror neurons provide a neurological confirmation of long forgotten philosophical, psychological, and physio-psychological diagnostics our genealogy brought to the fore. This diagnostic now also provides a last step in our investigation to reframe the ancient, yet also modern and still contemporary quarrel between the catharsis and affective hypotheses on the entangled relation between violence and the unconscious.

Discovered in the 1990s by a team of Italian neuroscientists led by Giacomo Rizzolatti initially working with macaque monkeys and subsequently with humans as well, mirror neurons are motor neurons (i.e., neurons responsible for movement) that are involuntarily and thus unconsciously triggered not only by movement but also—and this is the "discovery"—by the simple *sight* of a movement, gesture, or expression, especially goal-oriented, intentional movements. Part of a mirror neuron system (MNS), this principle leads the observer's corresponding motor area of the brain to be activated and to vicariously feel an unconscious reflex to mirror or mimic the movement seen. These neurons, Rizzolatti and his team argue in a more speculative mood, may play a fundamental role in prelinguistic forms of understanding the intention of others, and in establishing positive social bonds, such as sympathy and empathy. As Rizzolatti and Sinigaglia put it in *Mirrors in the Brain* (2008), the mirror neuron system's "primary role" is "the role linked to understanding the meaning of the actions of others."[3] And they specify:

> In humans, as in monkeys, the sight of acts performed by others produces an immediate activation of the motor areas deputed to the organization and execution of those acts, and through this activation, it is possible to decipher the meaning of the "motor events" observed, i.e., to *understand* them in *terms of goal-centered movements*. This understanding is completely devoid of any reflexive, conceptual and/or linguistic mediation as it is based exclusively on the *vocabulary of acts* and the *motor knowledge* on which the capacity to act depends . (*MB* 125)

The language is technical, but the experience has long been familiar in aesthetic and thus mimetic practices. Rizzolatti and Sinigaglia acknowledge, in fact, that it has "long been common knowledge in the theater" (ix). No wonder that genealogists of mimesis have consistently taken actors as paradigmatic examples to reflect on the immanent powers of mimesis. They knew that mimesis was dramatized in acting and performance—that is, in *mimos*. The realization that a nonlinguistic form of mirroring communication that operates unconsciously in homo mimeticus is an insight that can no longer be confined to the margins of genealogical investigations but returns to the forefront of new mimetic studies.

The parallels with our genealogy of the mimetic unconscious go further. As a consequence of this mirroring reflex, Rizzolatti and Sinigaglia posit the hypothesis of a prelinguistic form of immediate communication that allows humans, at least to a degree, to share emotions without the mediation of rational understanding, or a theory of mind. As they put it: "Emotions, like actions, are immediately shared, the perception of pain or grief, or disgust experienced by others, activates the same areas of the cerebral cortex that are involved when we experience these emotions ourselves" (*MB* xii). This is a revolutionary hypothesis providing new empirical evidence that speaks in favor of the affective hypothesis we have been presenting. The debate on the specific role mirror neurons play in sharing emotions is still open and we shall be careful not to reduce complex psychological phenomena to the neurons that fire in our brain alone. The point is that this recent discovery in the hard sciences is in line with a long genealogy of thinkers working in aesthetics, philosophy, psychology, and the human sciences more generally.

As Rizzolatti and Sinigaglia readily acknowledge, such mimetic reflexes are the daily bread, or rather actions, of actors: dramatic gestures, visual expressions, theatrical movements, but also tonality of voice, rhythm, and pitch have, in fact, an enormous power of impression, for they lead the audience to partially share, by unconscious *sym*-pathos, what the actor feels; a physio-psychological, neuronal mirroring principle activates a psychological, empathic principle. Philosophical physicians attentive to actors' will to power of affective impression—from Plato to Nietzsche, Bernheim to Tarde to Féré and beyond—have been theorizing this disquieting contagious effect all along. Genealogical lenses, then, reveal a historical fact: the discovery of mirror neurons should be reframed as a groundbreaking confirmation of an ancient mimetic principle that gains new traction in the modernist period and is finally empirically attested in the contemporary period as well. Above all, it urges future-oriented theorists of homo mimeticus to go beyond the catharsis hypothesis central to the Freudian unconscious to account for the affective hypothesis constitutive of the mimetic unconscious.

## Homo Mimeticus Looks in the Mirror

This picture of homo mimeticus is only now reappearing on the theoretical scene after a long period of marginalization. It will not go unchallenged since it offers a sharp narcissistic blow to notions of subjectivity understood in terms of free will, intentionality, and rational self-awareness that still inform dominant rationalistic and idealist trends in philosophy, the social sciences, and, to a lesser degree, the humanities as well. Still, as Rizzolatti and Sinigaglia reassure us, the brain is endowed with a control mechanism that, in normal circumstances, contains such mirroring reflexes. There is even a rational logos unconsciously at play in what may appear as an irrational mimetic pathos. In fact, the authors specify that the MNS's "primary role" is "the role linked to understanding the meaning of the actions of others" (*MB* 124). By unconsciously mirroring gestures, especially goal-oriented gestures (such as grabbing, pointing, and facial expressions), Rizzolatti and Sinigaglia claim that we have an immediate insight not only into the other's affects but also into their intentions and, by extension, minds, and thoughts. The exact role the MNS plays in such complex cognitive mechanisms still needs to be determined and is likely to continue generating stimulating discussions. Still, despite some initial resistance and skepticism, their presence in humans is now ascertained.[4] Consequently, unconscious reflex reactions can no longer be dismissed as irrelevant for psychological analysis or relegated to few pathological cases in the history of philosophy or psychology, as has been done in the past century. Rather, they play a constitutive role in understanding the vicissitudes of homo mimeticus in the twenty-first century.

Significantly, even the most recent critics of mirror neurons no longer dispute their existence in humans. Gregory Hickock, for instance, in *The Myth of Mirror Neurons* (2014), actually lends support to mirror neuron theory by putting a major objection to rest: if mirror neurons are central to imitation, and mirror neurons were first discovered in (macaque) monkeys, why don't monkeys imitate? Hickock's answer is that "macaques *do* imitate."[5] And when it comes to humans, he specifies that "there is no theoretical pressure to abandon the idea that mirror neurons support imitation in a broader sense of association between actions, as in observational learning" (*MMN* 199). His fundamental correction is that mirror neurons are not themselves responsible for understanding itself; rather, they "can be used to guide" (192) understanding. Alternatively, they "don't *make* action understanding"; rather, they "can assist in understanding" (229). So be it. That's not much of a critique. Far from revealing "mirror neurons" to be a "myth," as the title misleadingly suggests by echoing the oldest anti-mimetic trick in the philosophical manual, the book itself is actually an agonistic attempt to refine current diagnostics of the role mirror neurons play in intersubjective forms of communication. Genealogy gives us the necessary distance to evaluate such agonistic debates: as often in quarrels on the truth and lies of mimesis, when imitation is relegated to the side of "myth," it continues to haunt, like a phantom, the proponent of a supposedly more "scientific" view.

A Nietzschean tradition taught us that myths often tend to be close to the truth of mimetic matters. The "myth of mirror neurons" is no exception to this genealogical rule. But genealogy goes further. It also sets up a critical mirror to the scientists themselves, urging them to push their reflection further by engaging in constructive dialogues with the humanities where research on mimesis started in the first place, over two millennia ago. My suspicion with respect to cognitive approaches to mirror neurons is, in fact, not scientific, quantitative, and "objective," but genealogical, qualitative, and "subjective"—though I am far from considering this opposition to be stable, for first-person experiential approaches to mimesis have objectively proved far-reaching in the past. With some exceptions, neuroscientists have, in fact, been primarily attentive to the cognitive, and thus rational, quantifiable, and potentially reductive implications of this discovery.[6] Mirror neurons, we are told time and again, help us "understand" actions, "read" intentions, "learn" behavior. This is certainly an important side of their function, but is it their only function? If we diagnose the language used in describing them—understanding, reading, learning, and so on— mirror neurons sound so rational, so smart, so intentional in their orientation. I cannot help but wonder: could scientific interpretations of mirror neurons at least partially be mirroring the behavior of the rational scientists that reflect (on) them?

This might be a hypothesis worth considering, especially since the hard sciences are now expanding their fields of investigation to include critical inquiries that used to belong to the human sciences. That is, sciences for which the fundamental epistemic difficulty stems from the fact that the investigative subject and the object of investigation coincide, or, we should rather say, are mirror images of each other. What the humanities make us see and sometimes feel, among other things, is the limit of an idealized image of *Homo sapiens* that unilaterally promotes reason or logos in order to equally consider its double or alter ego: namely, a homo mimeticus that is rooted in affect or pathos—for good and ill. Genealogical lenses that stretch back to classical antiquity have taught us that imitation is not only used for cognitive, or rational, purposes, as Aristotle claimed; it can equally be put to irrational and violent purposes, as Plato insisted.

In the wake of the discovery of a mirroring mechanism in the brain, there are thus good empirical reasons to return to the old Platonic insight that violent spectacles have formative or performative effects insofar as they have the power to potentially induce a violence that spreads contagiously, especially among that mimetic beast par excellence that is the crowd. Though direct causality remains difficult to measure and will inevitably continue to remain so, a qualitative, genealogical, and interpretative account of (new) media violence provides an important and often neglected supplement. After this lengthy reevaluation of the entangled genealogies of the catharsis and affective hypotheses, and the critical investigation of the theories of the unconscious they gave birth to, we now have accumulated sufficient theoretical, empirical, and interpretative reasons to suspect that the sight of violent actions in the sphere of fiction may not be as innocent as it appears to be. Why? Because there is a growing, though still not unanimous, consensus that violent visual spectacles are likely to have mimetic or, better, hypermimetic effects. Depending on the subjects at play, familial and educative circumstance, and socio-economic contexts that, as we noted, play a decisive role, hypermimesis has the power to break the mirror of representation and trigger an unconscious reflex that can potentially increase the risk of reproducing such violent gestures in the real world in both the short and long run.[7]

After a long period of mutual neglect, if not downright hostility, transdisciplinary dialogues between the humanities, the social sciences, and the hard sciences are now confirming the validity of the affective hypothesis. In recent years, neuroscientists with a philosophical inclination have, in fact, started catching up with the old Platonic realization that mimesis cuts both ways, as it can generate mirroring effects that can be put to both cognitive (rational) and violent (irrational) use, generating both pathologies and patho-*logies*. Marco Iacoboni, for instance, offers a contemporary variation of the double, pharmacological effects of what Plato called *mimēsis* as he balances the cognitive implications of mirror neurons by calling attention to the elementary but fundamental fact that there are good and bad forms of imitation. As he puts it in *Mirroring People* (2008): "Mirror neurons can undoubtedly be good for us, enabling our feelings and actions of empathy for others, but they also provide a compelling neurobiological mechanism underlying imitative violence induced by media violence."[8] This is indeed a lesson that is as old as the history of philosophy itself; it can now be supplemented by empirical studies we already mentioned that inform Iacoboni's diagnostic as well. Surveying the literature on the relation between exposure to media violence and imitative violence based on laboratory experiments with children, Iacoboni writes that these findings confirm that "children who watch more violence tend to be more aggressive than other children" (*MP* 207). And turning to longitudinal studies that follow the development of large populations (seven hundred families) outside of the lab over a long period of time (fifteen years) to see whether media violence has long-lasting effects in adult behavior as well, he concludes: "Taken together, the findings from laboratory studies, correlational studies, and longitudinal studies all support the hypothesis that media violence induces imitative violence" (208).

Correlation is once again not causation, but supplemented with longitudinal studies, the distinction between the two begins to appear less stable than opponents of the affective hypothesis make it appear to be. Along similar lines, philosophers like Susan Hurley develop lines of inquiry that would have found the approval of precursors like Féré and Nietzsche, as she writes: "The correspondence is not just visual: hearing an expression of anger increases activation of muscles used to express anger."[9] Similarly, social scientists such as Craig Anderson and Brad Bushman report that since the 1970s, a consensus from the major professional medical societies in the United States has been confirming that "the data points overwhelmingly to a causal connection between media violence and aggressive behavior in some children," thereby concluding that "a heavy diet of media violence contributes to a societal violence rate that is unnecessarily obese."[10] None of these studies are in favor of censorship; neither is this study. Still, if one takes a look in the mirror of contemporary culture, it might indeed be wise to go on a diet.

## Playing Games with Violence

After the theater and the cinema, film and TV, there is now a new medium in town that is magnetizing young as well as older generations. Contemporary debates on (new) media violence have primarily shifted to video games, which are no longer games for teenagers but are increasingly played by a significant number of adults as well. Since the 1990s, in fact, video games have indeed relied on an increasingly realistic aesthetics that invites gamers to be active participants in scenes that often have violence as a common denominator. Already two decades ago, psychologists like Craig Anderson took a critical stance contra the correlation is not causation "mantra" to debunk a series of "myths" that deny the increasingly well supported argument in favor of what I grouped under the rubric of the affective hypothesis.[11] More recently, the American Psychological Association "Resolution of Violent Video Games" confirms the existence of a "direct association between a violent video game use and aggressive outcomes," while at the same time also pointing to "decreases in socially desirable behavior such as prosocial behavior, empathy and moral engagement."[12] And Barrie Gunter, in a book-length study devoted to the question titled *Does Playing Video Games Make Players More Violent?* (2016), summarizes his insights as follows: "there is plenty of empirical evidence in the public domain that has concluded that violent video games can trigger aggressive reactions in players."[13] In sum, the general agreement seems to be that causation is not correlation, but the concerns about correlation are all too real.

The list could continue despite some balancing observations on the positive social effects of video games whose interactive possibilities, like other new media, can indeed effectively be put to educational use. Of course, video games themselves are not necessarily violent. They appeal to the playful qualities of homo mimeticus qua *homo ludens* central to what game scholars call "ludification of digital culture" that resonates in productive ways with the mimetic turn.[14] At the same time, the specific evaluation on (new) media violence tends to point consistently toward the same dietary diagnostic: namely, away from a catharsis hypothesis based on the cure of the same by the same, which was theoretically valid only for carefully crafted plots consumed in homeopathic ritual doses anyway, toward an affective hypothesis that representations of the same generate more of the same, especially if violent entertainment is consumed in indigestive doses that render us emotionally numb or habituated to real violence.

From this perspective, new media representations or simulations of violence should not be dismissed as harmless fictions, shadows without substance, or phantoms far removed from reality. On the contrary, as a long tradition in mimetic studies has taught us, and recent empirical "discoveries" have now begun to confirm, shadows have the performative power to form reality, phantoms to possess egos, along hypermimetic principles that blur the line between fiction and reality, visual representations and embodied affects, virtual actions and immanent reactions. Hence the urgent need for artists and philosophers, creators and critics to join forces: the former by promoting nonviolent models of behavior to serve as exempla for future generations; the latter for continuing to reload patho-*logical* operations that look back to the origins of mimetic studies to better diagnose the unconscious powers of representations qua simulations that cast a growing shadow on our present and future, calling for the development of new mimetic studies.

No wonder that Plato was particularly worried about mimetic impersonations whereby an actor does not speak about a violent character in the third person (*diegesis*) but, rather, embodies "in speech or bodily bearing" that character (*mimēsis*). There is an important diagnostic lesson nested in this ancient formal distinction between mimesis and diegesis for future theorists to pick up and amplify. Plato, in fact, sensed that by enacting a given model of behavior in gestures, speech, and bodily postures, an actor has the power to generate affects that spread—via mirroring gestures and expressions—irrationally, contagiously, and unconsciously from the actor who impersonates a role to the spectators who, at an additional remove, might mirror the imitation of the actor, or mimos. Time and again, we have seen that the so-called father of philosophy is not only a metaphysician concerned with art understood as a visual "mirror" (*Rep.* 10.596d; 821) that reproduces "shadows" or "phantoms, not realities" (599a; 824) to be condemned for epistemic or metaphysical reasons, as idealist philosophers often remind us. He is also, and for us more importantly, a philosophical physician concerned with the affective and infective powers of mimesis to trigger mirroring reflexes in real people, turning their ego into a "phantom of the ego," as Nietzsche was quick to sense.

True, the theater may no longer be the dominant medium in town to educate and impress the crowd in the contemporary period, generating a pathos that operates on the irrational part of the soul, affecting bodies in ways that might lead to violence—though we have seen that violence continues to be manifested in crowds, including political crowds. The contemporary cinematic case study with which we started also made clear that hypermimetic forms of dispossession are currently being reloaded by new digital media that, more than ever before, cast a spell on the psychic life of a virtual public. The growing number of screens and surfaces that surround us in the digital age may, in fact, add another layer of mediation that renders posthuman subjects even farther removed from reality; and yet they also generate virtual avatars that have formative, performative, and deformative effects on minds and bodies nonetheless. In the digital age we are, in fact, permanently exposed to all kinds of violent models and actions dramatized in virtual fictions that are increasingly immersive in their degree of hypermimetic participation (3D films, double lives on social media, and video games). Over time, repetition, and good doses of visual bombardment, these simulations are very likely to shape behavior, influence tastes, and promote the reproduction of aggressive and potentially violent gestures in real life, turning human nature into a second, less social, and more violent nature. If we have noticed that mimetic theories can turn out to be based on scientific fictions, then, the case of *Vice* with which we started is only one among countless cinematic examples indicating that science fictions can rest on realistic theoretical principles—though this realism is not restricted to the logic of realistic representation, but relies on the logic of hypermimetic simulations.

Now, since the type of violence dramatized in the VICE resort is allegorical of (new) media violence in general and of the violence internal to video games in particular, let us conclude our diagnostic investigation by bringing our genealogy of the catharsis and affective hypothesis to bear on a contemporary video game. Interestingly, our example dramatizes the type of violence we have initially seen from a representational cinematic distance from the more participatory and immersive perspective characteristic of video games.

If our genealogy of violence and the unconscious taught us anything, it is that it is by being specific, both at the theoretical and critical level, that humanistic approaches to (new) media violence can supplement empirical studies. New mimetic studies need, in fact, to transfer all the interpretative tools and skills previously applied to print literature to post-literary, digital media central to posthuman studies as well, while also adding new instruments to the critical toolbox.[15] What was true for oral and print literature remains true for new media: analyses need to be focused on specific case studies whose content and form cast light on more general principles as well. If we have seen that mimetic studies were born out of interpretations of a specific set of classical text, and modern theories of the unconscious were equally grounded on interpretation of a few texts (often the same one), new mimetic studies should select contemporary case studies as well to pave the way for other interpretations to come.

When it comes to violence and gaming, a number of examples could be chosen: from the series *Medal of Honor* (1999–), which initially allowed gamers to play the role of the Taliban, to *Tomb Raider* (1996–), which includes a scene of attempted rape, from *Grand Theft Auto* (1997–), which combines driving with shooting, to other increasingly realistic action role-playing games, like *The Witcher* series (2007–) or *Hunt* (2018–), that rely on first-person perspectives that increase psychomotor participation in the pathos of violence. Given that this is a fast-changing medium, I opt for a recent video game that most clearly reloads the violent transgressions of the VICE resort with which we started, such as robberies, murder, eroticism, and more, via an immersive, realistic, ultraviolent, and rather cinematic aesthetics.

## VICE Reloaded: Welcome to *Cyberpunk 2077*

As the "welcome to *Cyberpunk 2077*" (2020) played out in the trailer indicates, and the video game itself confirms, the mirroring continuities between cinematic violence and video game violence are manifold and cut in both directions. If we have started this study with the realization that representations of violence (e.g., crime, combat, sexual assault, murder) dramatized in films like *Vice* are metaphorical of the hyperviolence at play in increasingly realistic video games, we conclude it by inversing perspective, and looking at how video games, where the debate on (new) media violence has transferred over the past decades, both rely on and supplement cinematic techniques that amplify the powers of hypermimesis.

The media change yet the debate continues to reload old problems and uncertainties. Despite the growing number of studies on the subject, the riddle on the effects of violent video games is still open and is likely to continue.[16] Rather than attempting to solve or moralize the debate—certainly not a Nietzschean preoccupation—my task is to reinscribe these recent

developments in the longer genealogy from which they stem and the tradition of the unconscious they implicitly entail. This genealogical perspective
should give sufficient theoretical distance to help readers to take a stance and
form their own evaluations on the potentially contagious pathos of (new)
media violence. It also calls attention to the importance of specific diagnostics of case studies that help reveal the current manifestations of the patho(-)
logies of violence and the unconscious.

Like most recent video games, *Cyberpunk 2077* transfers the realistic aesthetics of cinema to the interactive sphere of action role-playing video games,
generating mirroring reflections that will allow us to conclude our diagnostic
of the affective hypothesis on (new) media violence with a present example
that urges us to look ahead to the future.

## Uploading Cinematic Violence: Designing the Avatar

*Cyberpunk 2077* is inscribed in a genealogy in sf that goes back to literary sf
classics like William Gibson's *Neuromancer* (1984) and became widely popular via sf cinematic blockbusters like *Blade Runner* (1982) and *The Matrix*
(1999), films that serve as aesthetic models for the video game as well. Set in
2077, in a futuristic dystopian Californian megacity called Night City riven
by corporate greed, nuclear threats, and economic crises, it stages a bleak,
lawless world of crime, corruption, and gang wars where robotics, hacking,
power struggles, and different forms of kinetic combat give gamers the possibility "to be anyone, or anything" you want—as the trailer promises, echoing
hypermimetic fantasies already at play in *Vice*.

The player character or protagonist, a cyber-enhanced mercenary or
"gun for hire" called "V" can, in fact, be meticulously designed in terms of
appearance, social background, physical attributes—from tattoos to skin
color, tonality of voice to body structure that can be changed in detail, down
to the size of genitals—as well as gender and sexual orientation. In fact, V can
stand for both Vincent (Gavin Drea) and Valentine (Cherami Leigh), and
the character can be heterosexual, gay, or trans. There is thus a progressive
transgender politics to the game in terms of its fluid gendered/sexual identity that is sensitive to LGBTQ+ players, favors gender/sexual equality, has a
liberating potential, and contributed to its hype prior to its release in 2020.[17]
As figure 12 makes clear, this is no longer a human world; it is a transhuman

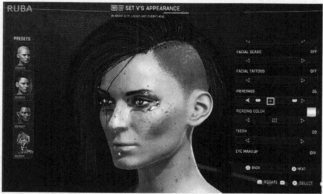

**FIGURE 12.** *Top:* To be Vincent or Valentine (V). *Bottom: Cyberpunk 2077* (CD Projects Red, 2020).

world animated by computer-generated (CG) cyborgs that despite their futuristic blending of human and machine appear strikingly realistic and speak to generations of gamers who already "became posthuman,"[18] including older generations who grew up with more traditional media—if only because *Cyberpunk 2077* reloads familiar characters via a cinematic aesthetics that is now in-*forming* video games as well.

Key protagonists at play are, in fact, not only modeled on heroes familiar from film; they are also animated by the very actors who once impersonated cinematic roles and now impersonate video games roles as well. It is in fact the war veteran and rock star called Johnny Silverhand (Keanu Reeves)

**FIGURE 13.** *Top:* Johnny Silverhand (Keanu Reeves). *Bottom:* V in *Cyberpunk 2077* (CD Projects Red, 2020).

who serves as a mediating figure—welcoming V, that is, you, in the desert of hypermimesis.

The phantom of *The Matrix* casts a long shadow on *Cyberpunk 2077*, generating mirroring doubling effects at play in the plot of the video game too. As V wakes up from a death experience in a deserted landscape, they, and, with them, you as a player, see the phantom of Silverhand looking down outside. We find out that the memory and soul of Silverhand has been implanted as a biochip inside V's brain, generating a hypermimetic chain of identifications that links the posthuman gamer to the cyborg qua avatar (V) to the digital phantom of the avatar (Silverhand)—that is, a phantom of yet another phantom.

There are thus multiple layers of digital mediation at play in the game that go from the gamer to the avatar to the avatar of the avatar, which, together, render the experience of playing far removed indeed from reality "itself." This digital mediation, then, sets up a multilayered technological distance between the gamer and the action internal to the game; and this antimimetic distance is redoubled at the level of the plot within the video game. In fact, V is fighting to prevent Silverhand from taking full control of their own identity, turning it into a phantom avatar. And yet the simulation has nonetheless the power to generate hypermimetic affects that reach outside the game. In particular, it reloads simulations already at play in sf movies in the interactive world of video games, generating what I called in the context of sf films like *The Matrix* that thematize digital gaming, "*e*-motions."[19] That is, electronic motions at play in the transhuman simulations within the game that have the power, or pathos, to retroact on gamers, triggering embodied emotions in posthuman gamers outside. How? Via a spiraling hypermimetic process we need to analyze in some detail by paying close attention to genealogical (dis)continuities within the (new) medium in question.

### Hypermimetic *E*-Motions: From Cinema to Video Games

*Cyberpunk 2077* reloads video games' simulations that were already internal to the plot of sf movies to be witnessed from a diegetic distance in a video game that can now be played out from a first-person hypermimetic perspective not deprived of violent pathos. The choice of modeling a video game avatar (Silverhand) on an iconic cinematic character (Neo) stretches to include the actor behind that character (Reeves) and lends realistic credibility to the game in ways that amplify the contagious powers of hypermimetic *e*-motions. The continuities between immanent bodies and digital simulations are constitutive of the aesthetics of the video game and are condensed in the phantom that welcomes gamers in this hypermimetic world of simulation. Based on Reeve's voice-over that is given body via techniques like performance caption that were first developed in cinematic blockbusters like

Changed my mind, don't want you dead anymore.

I've done a fair bit of motion capture, I did it in the Matrix films,

**FIGURE 14.** Keanu Reeves's performance capture in the making of *Cyberpunk 2077* (CD Projects Red, 2020).

*The Matrix* (1999) and were perfected in *Avatar* (2009),[20] *Cyberpunk 2077* in fact relies on digital simulations characteristic of a new generation of video games that are not simply realistic yet are not disconnected from the laws of imitation either.

On the contrary, the computer simulation adds new layers of technological mediation that renders the game far removed indeed from reality; yet, in a paradoxical feedback loop that is constitutive of hypermimesis, it continues to rely on an embodied dramatic impersonation of a professional actor, who has

**FIGURE 15.** *Cyberpunk 2077*'s cinematic trailer (CD Projects Red, 2020).

the power to retroact on gamers via what Steven Shaviro calls a "post-cinematic" medium understood as a "machine for generating affect."[21] In our language, this machine is hypermimetic for it generates *e*-motions that cut across the screen of Apollonian representation and amplifies the Dionysian powers of affective, intoxicating, and, for the moment, still embodied simulations.

While the interactive nature of video games allows for an "activity" that is often contrasted to the "passivity" of film spectators, genealogical lenses also make clear that the new medium does not completely break with previous media like cinema. Cinema, in fact, paved the way for the shift from analogic to digital "representations"—if such a term has any meaning at all in the age of simulation. In a mirroring move, video games incorporate, or upload, a cinematic aesthetics already based on digital simulations in view of transferring a "perceptual realism"[22] that continues to animate film to the hypermimetic world of gaming as well.

Gamers entering this new world for the first time are thus already partially familiar with the aesthetics, characters, plots, and dialogues from the cinematic classics it obviously alludes to, generating an uncanny feeling of déjà vu. The design of the video game characters is still based on cinematic figures. In the case of Silverhand, he is even voiced by an actor like Keanu Reeves who amplifies the powers of hypermimesis in a number of ways that can be summarized as follows: first, the video game is hypermimetic in the sense that it reproduces, or, rather, reloads, a cinematographic aesthetics characteristic of film (music, camera movements, angles, point-of-view shots, medium shots, acting), which a long tradition in film studies has shown to be central to generating viewers' identifications with cinematic characters, and now applies to identifications with video games avatars as well.[23] Second, the use of cinematic stars, plots, and iconography already familiar from cinema, facilitates the identification with the video game protagonists and their actions, including violent actions, by reloading a preexisting cinematic identification from a more agentic and interactive perspective to which we shall return. Third, the reliance on voice-over and performance caption that model the avatar on an "original" actor who gives voice, but also gestures, action movements, and facial expression, generates e-motions in hypermimetic ways that cannot yet be simulated by digital motions alone; rather, these technologies still rely on the ancient yet always contemporary dramatic impersonations to become convincingly animated in the game and subsequently experienced by gamers. Fourth, the action stages a mimetic agon based on a mirroring confrontation between V or gamer on one side, and its iconic cinematic alter ego, Silverhand, on the other, who, like any good actor, elicits identification.

Who, then, is this Silverhand that gamers are encouraged to counter via a mirroring identification? A character with a military past, Silverhand was famous as a rock star, thereby combining oxymoronically the metallic distance of a cyborg soldier with the human pathos of a singer. Keanu Reeves describes the character he impersonates as follows: he is "fighting for sur-vival" and is "passionate," he "cares," and has a "good sense of humor"; but he also has a "dark side" that often turns to violence and death for he has an "appetite for life" in a world dominated by crime and death, is "kind of naive" but "super experienced in life," among other characteristics—in short, a com-bination of a man without proper qualities who can appropriate himself of all qualities leading to the following inevitable realization: "I think there is a Johnny Silverhand in all of us," says Reeves—and via a mirroring cinematic extension, this applies, perhaps, to Keanu Reeves as well.

From acting to cinema to gaming, there are thus multiple layers of aes-thetic and digital mediation that can obviously not be reduced to realism understood as a faithful representation of reality. And yet these layers are hypermimetic. In fact, they rely on increasingly realistic digital simulations that approximate cinema via multiple layers of aesthetic mediation in view of generating embodied identifications and simulations that operate one the side of gamers. I mapped these hypermimetic layers in some detail because the "activity" of playing video games is often routinely opposed to the "pas-sivity" of watching a movie.[24] And yet even a partial genealogy of hypermi-mesis quickly reveals how the affective but also embodied, or, as Nietzsche would say, physio-psychological, psychomotor participation in video games continues to both depend and capitalize on cinematic strategies. These hypermimetic strategies trigger embodied simulations whose pathos of dis-tance needs consideration if we want to gauge the effects of (new) media violence in the digital age.

## Empathic Screens and Violent Sym-pathos

To account for the embodied dimension of avatar simulations in gaming a step back to the medium of cinema can help us align our diagnostic with the genealogy of the mimetic unconscious we have been tracing. In *The Emphatic Screen* (2015), for instance, film critic Michele Guerra and neuroscientist Vit-torio Gallese rely on the discovery of mirror neurons to revisit the cinematic power of film to generate embodied simulations on the side of spectators relevant for video games as well. Relying on a transdisciplinary perspective that joins neuroscience with aesthetics, Gallese and Guerra cut across the two-culture opposition as well as the screen-audience divide. They do so to

propose an empirically informed yet non-reductive and qualitative phenomenological approach constitutive of what they call "experimental aesthetics."[25] Their general aim is to lend an embodied supplement to an ancient
genealogy in aesthetic theory by positing the mimetic hypothesis that "the
spectator's bodily involvement [functions] as a key measure of film's efficacy"
for it allows spectators to "empathize with the protagonists and their vicissitudes" (*ES* 14). If we have seen how this shared pathos, or *sym-pathos*, is
constitutive of both the cathartic and affective hypotheses that look back to
the origins of mimetic studies, Gallese and Guerra implicitly build on the
tradition of the mimetic unconscious we have been unearthing to account
for the fictional powers of cinema to generate embodied emotions in spectators. In particular, they focus on the mirroring power of facial expressions
and physical gestures seen in others (real or fictional) to activate the same
areas in spectators' brains. Experimental aesthetics is thus not only closely
aligned with new mimetic studies but rests on the same genealogy of the
unconscious.

Interestingly, Gallese and Guerra do not simply map brain activity in
a reductionist *neurological* gesture modeled on what they dismiss as "neo-
phrenological ontological reductionism" (*ES* 41). Rather, they practice the
art of interpretation by calling aesthetic attention to a number of specific
*cinematic* strategies (camera movements, montage, point-of-view shots, haptic visuality, close-ups) to trigger what Gallese calls "embodied simulation."
That is, a nonlinguistic form of mimetic communication that operates at the
"affective, sensi-motor" (15) level, is constitutive of shared and embodied
intersubjective states, or "intercorporiety" (15), and blurs boundaries like
self-other, mind-body, screen-affect, images seen and affects felt. As they put
it, "neuroscience allowed us to understand how the border between what we
call reality and the imaginary or imagined world is much less clear cut than
we may think" (72). Starting from much more ancient foundations but with
an eye to the present and future, our genealogy of violence and the unconscious leads to the same conclusion. Hence the need to join the insights of
experimental aesthetics and (new) mimetic studies.

Gallese and Guerra's experimental aesthetics lends empirical support to
our account of the mimetic unconscious in at least two ways: first, they note
that cinema can generate contagious emotions like "fear, anger, and disgust"
that trigger a genuine pathos, while viewers can simultaneously rely on

cognitive "framing" processes that allow for a critical distance that leads to different reactions "from those normally adopted outside of cinema, in real life" (69)—call this productive interplay between pathos and logos "*pathology*"; second, they also confirm a paradoxical oscillation toward/away from mimetic pathos that has been the constant movement we found throughout our entire genealogy of (new) media violence—call this oscillation, "pathos of distance." If philosophers traditionally inferred such important lessons from the medium of the theater via the psychological tradition of the mimetic unconscious, Gallese and Guerra infer the same oscillation from the medium of cinema via the recent (re)discovery of mirroring reflexes. The media change but the pathos of distance that mimesis generates remains fundamentally the same. What we must add is that this ancient mimetic principle applies to the new hypermimetic medium of video games as well.

Careful not to conflate cinematic experiences with embodied experiences, the hypothesis of "embodied simulation" transgresses the boundaries dividing visual (Apollonian) representations considered from a distance and embodied (Dionysian) simulations experienced with pathos along mirroring lines a tradition of the mimetic unconscious had been positing all along. It also allows us to confirm genealogical principles that are directly relevant for the affective hypothesis on (new) media violence in general and video games in particular. I limit myself to three points. First, the title "empathic screen" is partially misleading for the book is not limited to empathy alone. It also concerns aesthetics or *aisthesis* that affects all the senses, including sensuous perception of affects like fear and anger. This should already caution us against enlisting mirror neurons as a defense of (new) media violence predicated on empathy or "compassion" alone, as recent developments in game studies have been quick to do.[26] Neurologists like Vittorio Gallese are, in fact, fully aware that the sword of mimesis has "two sides" and cuts both ways for it goes beyond good and evil: if mirror neurons have the power to generate empathy, they have the power to generate violent pathos as well.[27] For this reason, we prefer to group this form of mimetic communication under the undifferentiated amoral category of *sym-pathos*, to indicate a shared pathos, be it good or bad. Similarly, the concept of *e*-motion, points to a connecting in-between link between digital motions and embodied motions, which, together generate emotions, good or bad.

Second, the realization that already neurons in the motor area of the brain (or canonical neurons) are activated by the mere sight of movements but also include the sight of objects, including objects used for violent actions confirms at the neuronal level a point we discussed at a higher level of inter-subjective and situational complexity. Giving the example of a pistol, Gallese and Guerra notice that to "see the object entails an automatic *simulation* of what *we will do* with that object; it means simulating a potential action" (*ES* 55). Simulating is not the same as acting, of course, and there is no direct causation involved when we are dealing with representations or simulations of weapons seen from a framed distance. Still, this neurological principle confirms the non-anthropocentric point that objects like guns deserve to be considered as having agentic powers of their own that deserve close analysis in new mimetic studies that cut across the subject/object divide. In given embodied social contexts, objects become addictive with the potential to modify subjects' actions and reactions along the lines our examples of police violence already confirmed.

Third, the discovery of mirror neurons confirms that the perception of an action, be it real or represented on a screen, entails "perceptively speaking, also simulating this action with one's motor system, within one's own motor system."[28] There is thus a degree of active motor participation at play in perception that cannot be simply considered from a third-person representational and passive diegetic distance. Rather, moving images affect our embodied emotions via a first-person mimetic pathos that operates on our unconscious motor system. In the process, this *e*-motional dynamic generates an oscillating pathos of distance we posited at the heart of the quarrel on (new) media violence setting in motion (new) mimetic studies as well. In many ways, then, the experimental aesthetics that emerges from cinematic actions is not only in line with the origins of mimetic studies; it is even more relevant to account for embodied simulations that are literally, that is, with a higher degree of physical participation, at play in video games actions. As Gallese and Guerra put it: "Everything dealing with virtual ambits and images in movement (from video games to virtual reality) could not help but taking as models the intersubjective and agentic practices already tested in cinematic ambits" (78–79). From theater to cinema, TV to video games, the media change, yet the debate on (new) media violence benefits from considering the theoretical messages that came before.

In many ways, then, experimental aesthetics offers but the most recent link in a long genealogical chain of aesthetic theories, reloading the problematic of mimesis from an empirically informed perspective. Gallese, in fact, provides a timely confirmation of our genealogy as he frames this "unconscious violence" in mirroring, "I-Thou" terms that are in line with mimetic studies, old and new. This also means that these mirroring mechanisms do not need to be limited within a familial triangular structure, which, as we have seen, is of Oedipal derivation. In fact, Gallese draws on recent research in developmental psychology attentive to prelinguistic forms of mimetic communication that open the infant's ego to the other from the very beginning. As he puts it: "These results suggest that *prior to any triangular mimetic relationship*, the main object of the infants' mimesis is the affective behavior of the 'other' . . . the mind begins as a shared mind."[29] Well before the rediscovery of newborn imitation and mirror neurons, advocates of the affective hypothesis had indeed posited the same anti-Oedipal insight. The shared mind based on sym-pathos goes beyond triangular structures on which mimetic theory relied on in the past century, and now need to be supplemented by new mimetic studies in the present century—with an eye to the future as well.

Both Gallese and I agree that it is important to recapture a primary intersubjectivity that accounts for an all too human opening to the mimetic pathos of the other. Our genealogical reevaluation of mirroring principles internal to the tradition of the mimetic unconscious is thus not only consistent with these recent developments; it also helps anticipate them.[30] Given the ancient foundations of mimetic studies attentive to dyadic, relational, and embodied mirroring reflexes, this study opened up alternative foundations to account for the dynamic of unconscious violence. Looking back to the origins of aesthetics in violent rituals turned out to be effective to lay new theoretical foundations to account for violent simulations that cast a shadow on the present and future.

What the future-oriented medium of video game adds to cinematic aesthetics is a predominately first-person, interactive, and thus psychomotor, or, if you prefer, embodied simulation that further blurs the division between screen and gamer. New agentic possibilities are indeed introduced by video games that allow for, if not free will, at least a degree of freedom and intentionality in self-design, choices in plot development, and partial

Now... you find out what it is you need to do.

o through Night City knowing a stray bullet could end you

**FIGURE 16.** Daily violence in Night City, *Cyberpunk 2077* (CD Projects Red, 2020).

agency in the unfolding of the action. Let us not forget that the unconscious logic of mimetic pathos can be balanced from a position of critical distance, at least in theory. And yet, if it is true that *Cyberpunk 2077* can be completed without casualties and leaves a large margin of choices for gamers to avoid violence in theory, it is equally true that the dystopic and transgressive world of crime it displays and the identification with an outlaw mercenary qua "living weapon" it proposes is heavily inclined toward violent actions, at least in gaming practice. V's "identity" progressively unfolds via personal choices in what appears to be a relatively normal city, which quickly and unsurprisingly turns out to be plagued by violent crimes.

Interactive choices take place in encounters with characters that shape the identity of the hero whose aim is to affirm survival via power struggles in a world dominated by hacking, crime, and violent transgression. The ultimate "test of a person's true value," as the trailer says, is "death, staring it down." Based on heroic, warlike principles that run deep in western civilization and are as old as Homer's *Iliad*, *Cyberpunk 2077* reloads Achilles's riddle for the digital age as it asks gamers: "Would you rather live in peace as Mr. Nobody or go down for all times in a blaze of glory?"

This cyberworld may be futuristic, but it is obviously reloading a type of heroic violence once staged in epic spectacles. That is, the same spectacles Plato already condemned for triggering a form of contagious pathos at the dawn of philosophy. This does not mean that we need to automatically replicate a Platonic exclusion of violent fictional models, for, as we have seen, they are constitutive of western aesthetics tout court. Given the ancient sources of such heroic models, it is, in fact, unsurprising that new generations in game studies continue to draw on the genealogy we have traced to defend not video games in general (an uncontroversial point), but video game violence in particular. For instance, contemporary defenses include the hypotheses that this new form of entertainment "develop[s] cognitive processes" (Aristotelian argument), "offers the possibility to experience the sublime" (Romantic argument), or even allows for the development of "empathy" due to the activation of "mirror neurons" (neuroscientific argument).[31]

The medium is thus new, but such defenses continue to draw on a long tradition in aesthetics that goes from antiquity to modernity to the present and inform discussions of violence in video games as well. While aesthetic concepts like "catharsis," "contagion," or the "sublime" are often mentioned in contemporary debates, they are rarely discussed in any theoretical detail. One of the numerous advantages of our genealogical investigation is that we are sitting on the shoulders of those intellectual giants who developed these concepts in the first place. We are thus well-positioned to evaluate contemporary appropriations with some sense of genealogical discrimination. One of the lessons we have repeatedly stressed is that such concepts emerge from rather specific philosophical, aesthetic, and historical contexts. Hence, lest one essentializes their meaning, they cannot easily be transposed as universal transcendental principles and mapped indiscriminately across different media, genres, and centuries.

Rationality, the sublime, mirror neurons: we have encountered these principles before. A brief reminder must thus suffice here. First, we have seen in volume 1 how already for Aristotle, the cognitive value of tragedy and its potential cathartic effects emerged from a complex plot based on tragic recognitions and reversals of fortune that informs *Oedipus Rex* in particular and is rarely present in the most popular video games. Tragedy might be more philosophical than history, granted, but this does not automatically elevate video games to the status of philosophy. Second, the tradition of the sublime bloomed in the Romantic period and, for some recent critics, finds in video games the most recent avatar. The only problem is that theorists of the sublime were far from unconditionally supportive of violent outbursts of pathos. Already Pseudo-Longinus who set the terms of the debate in *On the Sublime* (ca. first century A.D.), subsequently recuperated in the Romantic period, offered a cautionary warning at the opening of his treaty as he stated: "the expression of the sublime is more exposed to danger when it goes its own way without the guidance of knowledge—when it is suffered to be unstable and unballasted—when it is left at the mercy of mere momentum and ignorant audacity."[32] Such audacity and momentum is exactly the kind of behavior that is promoted in our case study and many other violent video games as well. Closer to the moderns, it is actually Edmund Burke's romantic recuperation of Pseudo-Longinus that is mentioned in support of an aesthetic of the sublime in violent video games. Still, genealogists recall that the sublime, as Burke understands it, does not naturally lead to moral empathy, let alone compassion for victims of violence represented by "poetry, painting and other affecting arts"; rather, it leads to an aesthetic "sympathy," or *sym-pathos*, that generates in readers or spectators of sublime spectacles what Burke calls "a delight on wretchedness, misery and death itself."[33] This is not exactly a felicitous formula for the development of moral empathy; nor does it set up a flattering mirror to critics who convoke the sublime in defense of video game violence. Yet it reflects (on) contemporary affective arts like video games nonetheless. For instance, the tradition of the sublime confirms the Nietzschean principle that there is a form of pleasure in inflicting pain on real or simulated others.

In sum, what we have learned from this genealogy of violence and the unconscious is that the theoretical devil on the dynamic of *sym-pathos* and the contemporary *e*-motions reloaded by video games is in the details; catharsis and contagion cannot simply be recuperated via ad hoc formulas but require careful contextualization. We have also learned that key figures in aesthetic theory that reach into the present tended to focus on the specific properties of the medium and genres in question; their patho-*logies* were often shaped by silent forms of mimetic agonism with predecessors that need to be considered from the perspective of the theorist and creator of concepts rather than passively repeated; in the process, it is also necessary to focus on specific examples that allow for specific formal attention to the (new) media in question. All these perspectives should be considered by new advocates of mimetic studies as they turn to analyzing specific examples, which brings us back to our case study.

## Cyborg Perspectives

*Cyberpunk 2077* introduces a futuristic world in which cyborg avatars rely on technology to enhance their powers beyond the human in terms that reveal a contemporary and rather ambivalent evaluation of a subject that has already become posthuman or transhuman.[34] The ontological barrier dividing humans from machines no longer holds both for transhuman avatars within the game and posthuman gamers outside playing the game.

Within the game, we have seen that V is a cyborg (half human, half machine) resuscitated from death via robotic techniques that blend the human and the machine in a futuristic scenario that, pace transhumanists, is far from achieved in reality, yet is constitutive of posthuman simulations with new digital technologies. Outside the game, gamers occupy the position of posthuman subjects who are digitally linked to hypermimetic *e*-motions that connect electronic movements (motions) seen on the screen and embodied sensations (emotions) partially felt in gamers' bodies. This connection generates mirroring reactions that were once well known by modernist physicians of the soul who paved the way for mimetic studies and are now confirmed by the experimental aesthetics that is currently informing new mimetic studies.

Conversely, a focus on video games also allows us to supplement some of neurosciences' philosophical assumptions. The phenomenological inspiration of research in mirror neurons has, in fact, led neuroscientists to stress the agentic "intentionality" of embodied simulation. Gallese and Guerra share this assumption by grounding actions in a "primitive motor intentionality" that defines humans as oriented toward potential objects as "self-intentional bodies" (*ES* 64). We have no reasons to doubt this intentional principle at the motor neuronal level, if only because the constitutively relational dimension of homo mimeticus confirms our shared intersubjective foundations neuroscientists also stress. And yet, at a higher level of complexity, we should specify that a *motor* neuronal intentionality does not necessarily translate into an intentional *psychic* subject in conscious control of its thoughts, gestures, and actions, or cognitive intentionality. On the contrary, as the genealogy of the mimetic unconscious in general and the attention to psychomotor induction in particular have taught us, we need to be suspicious of strong, agentic models of fully conscious, intentional, and willful subjectivity when it comes to the unconscious reflex of imitation, especially when the motions at stake trigger violent *e*-motions. There is, in fact, a passivity of mimetic experiences that requires a rethinking of phenomenological accounts of intentionality via a genealogy of the unconscious that finds in bodily pathos an alternative starting point.[35]

Both the cinematic form and the subject matter of violent video games confirm that a dose of suspicion is in order when it comes to the *psycho-motor* intentionality internal to the phenomenology of experiences in gaming. Emerging from the interplay between CG simulation and bodily affects, hypermimetic *e*-motions blur the line dividing activity and passivity, self and other, electronic motions we see on the screen and embodied emotions we feel in our bodies, generating contagious effects that are highly contextual, and vary according to games and players. They may appear intentional from a (Apollonian) distance, yet might also generate embodied (Dionysian) reactions that escape both motor and cognitive intentional control. To take an obvious example traditionally linked to the unconscious and central to the game, sexuality, prostitution, and erotic encounters continue to play an important role in this form of entertainment that includes sexual violence. They add a transgressive taste to the video game via immersive techniques that allow for hypermimetic simulations borrowed from the world of erotica and pornography. Already central to the VICE resort, the No-Tell Motel in *Cyberpunk 2077* illustrates an important hypermimetic principle

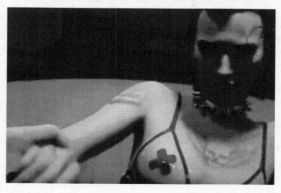

**FIGURE 17.** Night life in Night City, *Cyberpunk 2077* (CD Projects Red, 2020).

that transgresses the barrier dividing simulations from sensorial experiences, intentional visual actions and suggestive bodily reactions.

Here we see and, perhaps, feel that a first-person (mimetic) point of view within the game does not simply entail an aesthetic perspective to be contemplated from a third-person (diegetic) distance. Rather, it positions the gamer as a sensorially engaged and rather close and active participant in an embodied simulation that, if the gamer is so inclined, can include sexual violence as well. This simulation is embodied because it does not only take place on the side of the game but, rather, entangles the gamers' minds, bodies, and senses (vision but also hearing and touch constitutive of the haptic aesthetics of the game) via not fully realistic yet nonetheless mirroring hypermimetic principles we are now familiar with. Gestures, facial expressions, bodies, but also erotic language, moaning, music, and colors contribute to generating a physio-psychological or, as we now call it, neurological mirroring pathos that is erotic and transgressive in sexual nature, yet also aims to transgress the boundary dividing the simulation in the game from the posthuman body climaxing via hypermimetic mirroring principles that operate on the mimetic unconscious.

What was true of the VICE resort remains true of the No-Tell Motel. This is, once again, just a video game simulation; pornography is certainly not a recent invention, and it is not our task to adjudicate on a subject that would require an inquiry of its own. Porn, like gaming, may well have a socially progressive, liberating, and potentially cathartic side as well. In addition to a physiological release, scholars in porn studies indicate that pornography can help promote different sexual orientations and go beyond normative binaries structured on violent hierarchies in terms of gender but also race and sexual orientation in progressive terms also at play in *Cyberpunk 2077*.[36] What is true for violence equally applies for porn: a *moralist* approach to the subject falls short of doing justice to the complexity of a widespread all too human phenomenon that goes beyond good and evil. Our approach is not based on the application of moral norms but on a diagnostic genealogy of the cathartic and contagious hypotheses.

That said, with respect to our *diagnostic* approach to the specific problematic of (new) media violence, we cannot end this study without at least posing one thorny genealogical question that brings us back to the cinematic case study with which we started. It has to do with the entanglement of violence with sexuality, which is as old as the history of "civilization" and is currently reloaded with unprecedented visibility in the digital age. The digital revolution, in fact, generated a proliferation of pornographic websites online (YouPorn, Pornhub, and RedTube being the most popular and apparently reaching since 2009 up to one hundred million unique visitors).[37] These sites are, again, heterogeneous in nature, target different sexual orientations, and do not allow for unilateral generalizations. And yet, not unlike video games, porn also tends to favor dominating attitudes toward women and a type of objectification that second-wave generations of feminist critics would not have hesitated to denounce as alienating, misogynistic, and phallocentric.

The question that ensues, then, is the following: given that these videos often record transgressive forms of sexual actions that include "old/young" sex and "gang sex" (with males often on the side of the old and/or the gang), stretching to include simulations of rape and incest (brother/sister; mother/son; grandpas/teens), as well as hard-core scenes that render the line between simulation and reality blurry at best; given also that some of these sites have a history of uploading (and, upon banning, removing) tapes of child sexual abuse, as well as rape, among other violent transgressions—given all these and other heterogeneous matters, I wonder: can we be sure that such violent representations qua simulations are not already serving as potential models for sexual encounters offline among posthuman but still embodied digital natives, thereby inclining sexual practices toward more aggressive behavior for older generations as well?[38] And if this point should be uncontroversial from a perspective informed by mimetic studies, could these simulations not be contributing to, if not directly causing, at least to normalizing, desensitizing, and even encouraging, sexual aggressions and violence toward women and children—a real violence that has come massively to the fore in the age of #MeToo?

Perhaps. What is certain is that there is a striking and yawning gap between discourses on sexual violence online and those on sexual violence offline. If they cannot be fully bridged, they should at least be genealogically connected given the potential mirroring continuities between online and offline practices. On the one hand, the digital age provides a wide dissemination, accessibility, and thus implicit tolerance of sexual transgressions online that would certainly be categorized as predatory and violent offline; on the other hand, we witness the rightful condemnation of a plurality of predatory assaults offline including rather heterogeneous degrees of violence that tend to be conflated under the broad homogeneous rubric of "sexual assault"—from catcalls to unwanted advances, nonconsensual touching to kissing and ending in molestation, incest, and rape—yet, with the exception of rape, are mostly tolerated online. This schizophrenic cultural double standard is problematic and is likely to confuse young generations who spend increasing time online in violent worlds that are radically at odds with social norms offline. This mirroring inversion of moral evaluations (online tolerance/offline condemnation) may be indicative of contemporary difficulties in developing discerning *diagnostic* accounts of potential underling *continuities* between sexual violence online and sexual violence offline. This seems to be an uncomfortable but inevitable conclusion, at least if we take hold of the growing realization that hypermimetic simulations of violence online have the potential power not to directly cause but to influence, form, and transform embodied patterns of violent behaviors offline.

To bring our genealogy of violence and the unconscious to an end, it is crucial to upload a formal distinction as old as the origins of mimetic studies for the digital age in our evaluation of video game violence. The choice of *Cyberpunk 2077* as a final case study was also partially motivated by a *formal* aesthetic choice that increasingly informs contemporary action role-playing video games in general. The game is, in fact, based not on a third-person diegetic point of view but on a first-person mimetic perspective. That is, the very perspective that Plato found so problematic when he first turned to mimesis in Book 3 of *Republic*. His diagnostic reasons behind this formal distinction were perhaps more psychologically or physio-psychologically informed than dominant philosophical commentators realized in the past century, hypermimetic reasons that are currently returning to the forefront of discussion on affective contagion and embodied simulations in the present century.

The creators of *Cyberpunk 2077* showed good insights in the working of hypermimesis. This formal choice, in fact, puts the gamer in a position to actively impersonate the character via a simulation of a first-person (action cam) point of view that excludes the subject's body, allowing for a perspectival, and thus embodied, mimetic or symbiotic alignment and indistinction between gamer and avatar. The gamer is in fact in a literal position to pull the trigger.

**FIGURE 18.** First-person (action cam) shooting in *Cyberpunk 2077* (**CD Projects Red, 2020**).

Despite the multiplicity of choices in the representation of V the game initially allows for, the gamer does not see V from a visual diegetic distance; rather, they impersonate V in kinetic combat situations that tend to trigger violent pathos. To be sure, this is just a simulation of murder that should not be confused with real murder, as a shadow projected on a cinematic wall should not be confused with the reality it doubles. This kind of simulation of violence certainly cannot be scapegoated as the main source of gun violence in countries like the United States where lack of basic gun regulations and racist discriminations, among other social pathologies, are obviously center stage.

And yet the specific formal aesthetics of the video game and the way it operates on the senses of homo mimeticus also suggest that a degree of caution is nonetheless in order. From the experiential, phenomenological perspective of the gamer, the first-person mimetic perspective that already worried Plato continues to allow for a type of embodied participation in which the line dividing the avatar from the player, simulated motions from *e*-motions, no longer exists. It is, in fact, the gamer who pulls the trigger outside the game for the avatar to shoot within the game. What video game scholars say with respect to *Call of Duty 4* equally applies to *Cyberpunk 2077* and is constitutive of numerous action role-playing video games in general, as a gamer qua critic put it: "when positioned in the gunship, the alterity of the [first-person] perspective disappeared and left me with my own eyes to experience the war."[39] What we must add is that this experience is not limited to the eyes (the most "rational" of the sense); it pertains to the body, as well, triggering actions and reactions in which movements seen on the screen have the power to generate—via the mediation of game pads that can now provide haptic feedback—embodied sensations at play during the simulation.

Clearly, compassion is not the main intention of the majority of video games based on a "sublime" glorification of violence. Neither are gamers' actions based on the myth of conscious intentionality and agentic free will— alias the metaphysics of the subject.[40] The gamer's will might be partially free to select a course of action that fits the patterns of the game, yet more often than not, such will is channeled in specific patterns of behavior that tend to incline gamers toward violence within the game, including violence against innocent victims who are part of collateral damage of a widely diffused will to play.

### The Will to Play

Can this hypermimetic will to play affect the will of the subject outside the game, a will that might be partially free yet is influenced by mimetic models nonetheless? Despite the consensus that a correlation exists, the issue of direct influence remains, perhaps more than ever, contested territory. New

developments in game studies have tended to limit the focus to the interaction between gamer and avatar, going as far as treating the long-standing
problematic of new media violence as a "false path" or a "nasty little subject."[41]
There are certainly a plurality of social factors contributing to violence that
need to be foregrounded before even approaching the problematic of video
game violence. As I argued from the beginning, social factors play the major
role when it comes to real violence and are constitutive of "the pathologies of
social civilization" (Kieran Keohane's phrasing).[42] No matter how problematic the correlation, it should not be mistaken for a causation in a complex
world in which agency is increasingly distributed hypermimetically across
the online/offline, human/nonhuman divide.

And yet, precisely because of this agentic distribution, the genealogy of
affective contagion has taught us to be cautious with such general rhetorical
dismissals. The long-standing preoccupation about the effects of representations of violence, be they good or bad, cathartic or contagious, starts with
Plato and Aristotle, was picked up by immanent thinkers like Rousseau
and Nietzsche, shapes dominant theories of the unconscious from Freud to
Girard, informs recent turns from affect theory to mirror neurons, and ultimately traverses the entire history of western aesthetics, from Greek tragedy
to video games. This complex subject cannot simply be dismissed as a "false
path," if only because the path is already double: if we have had genealogical reasons to question the cathartic hypothesis, the oscillating movement
between the unconscious vulnerability of homo mimeticus to violent pathos
and the capacity to set up a cognitive distance prevented us from adopting
universal and unilateral evaluations of this complex subject.

The subject may be "nasty," but it is certainly not "little." On the contrary,
it is one of the most long-standing subjects in western aesthetics. We shall
thus transgress recent critical programs that limit theoretical discussions
to what happens within the game (autonomy fallacy) or to the motivation
of individuals for playing (individualist fallacy) and ask, one last time, an
untimely genealogical question we have been pursuing all along with respect
to video games as well: repeated over time, as a form of entertainment or
training program for instance, can we be so sure that such embodied video
game simulations, in specific contextual situations in which a number of
social factors and actants play an agentic role—say, gun availability due to

lack of gun regulations, tolerance of violence due to social discriminations (in terms of race, gender, sexual orientation, nationality), poverty, lack of education, ideological disinformation, police brutality, domestic violence, terrorism, political escalations, among many other *social* factors—can we be sure that hypermimetic simulations cannot contribute to inflect, normalize, and perhaps even condone violent and, as we have seen, potentially murderous actions in the world offline?

This protean subject continues to elude the net of empirical certainty. What appears certain for now is that a genealogy of the catharsis and affective hypothesis has taught us to be extremely suspicious of these clear-cut oppositions between (Apollonian) representations and (Dionysian) impersonations, what we see and how we feel—and perhaps, at one remove, how we act as well. Following an immanent tradition positing that aesthetics was born from sacrificial rituals, the driving telos of this Janus-faced two-volume study has been to overturn perspectives. We did so via mirroring moves that considered how what appear to be simply aesthetic representations have the (will to) power, or pathos, not to directly trigger but rather—via repetition, habituation, and good doses of training online—to incline the posthuman subject toward aggressive and potentially violent actions that find "original" models in the sphere of fiction. It is useful to recall that fiction, from Latin *fingere*, is not only linked to feigning and lying, as a dominant idealist metaphysical tradition has stressed, reducing fictions to illusory shadows, or phantoms; it is also linked to fashioning, or forming, and is thus endowed with a material power, or pathos, to make real impressions on minds and bodies, as a marginalized yet long-standing genealogy in mimetic studies has persisted in stressing.

As the boundaries between online and offline behavior become increasingly porous, new hypermimetic forms of aggression—from online bullying to public shaming and exposure—that may not be based on representations of violence as such, but have generated violent and potentially fatal outcomes, nonetheless, are currently emerging, calling for new investigations attentive to the insidious powers of contagion in the digital age. While more empirical studies will continue to confirm that a correlation between (new) media violence and real violence is hard to deny, our ambition has been to provide a genealogy of the relation between violence and the unconscious that provides qualitative, hermeneutical, theoretical, but also case-specific reasons to understand an all too human and now posthuman tendency to imitate aesthetic simulations that run deep in the genealogy of homo mimeticus. They are widespread enough to justify a field of inquiry we propose to call, for lack of a more original term, new mimetic studies.

Whether our new theory of imitation will be useful to diagnose, interpret, and perhaps even foresee, and thus help us deflect, the hypermimetic power of new media to trigger all too real violent practices that already cast a shadow on the present, remains to be confirmed by the mimetic studies of the future.

# Conclusion

## How a Fiction Became Reality

What, then, is the diagnostic that emerges from our Janus-faced genealogy of the catharsis and affective hypotheses? Both perspectives tend to go beyond good and evil in the sense that they call for a rethinking of our moral evaluations in the digital age. They also go beyond two-cultures divides between empirical and qualitative approaches that still structured scholarly debates in the past century but call for more collaborative and creative supplements in the present century. After a long period of mutual neglect, if not downright hostility, transdisciplinary dialogues between the humanities, the social sciences, and the hard sciences are now opening up to account for increasingly complex, that is, interwoven, problems that call for genealogical distance to be adequately framed, diagnosed, and reevaluated. New mimetic studies, I tried to show, provide a philosophically informed, transdisciplinary approach that is as attentive to the historical emergence and transformation of concepts as to their relevance to account for the affective power of contemporary media. Interpretative case studies, be they classical, modern, or contemporary, are also needed to give situational and hermeneutical specificity to theoretical analyses. Last but not least, the shift of emphasis from a unifying mimetic *theory* with universal aspirations to a pluralist and

perspectival theory of imitation constitutive of mimetic *studies* indicates that
new transdisciplinary efforts are called for to come to grips with the human
and posthuman tendencies to be affected by fictions and the simulations they
entail—for both good and ill.

From this transdisciplinary genealogical perspective, then, (new) media
violence should not be unilaterally condemned, for it is a protean (hyper)
mimetic phenomenon that twists and turns, changing form as it manifests
itself under different masks. And yet it should not be dismissed as a harmless
fiction, a shadow without substance, or a phantom far removed from material realities either. On the contrary, as a long chain of thinkers of mimesis
that goes from antiquity to modernity reaching into the present have taught
us, and recent empirical rediscoveries in the neurosciences have now begun
to confirm, fictional shadows have the performative power to give material
form to reality. Simulated phantoms also have the will to power to possess
the ego and dispossess it of its rational faculty. They do so along hypermimetic principles that we are only beginning to take hold of and increasingly
blur the imaginary line dividing fiction and reality, visual representations and
embodied simulations, virtual actions, and all too real reactions.

New generations of scholars contributing to new mimetic studies are
now urgently encouraged to go beyond ancient quarrels between artists and
philosophers, specialists of affects and specialists of concepts, in view of developing Janus-faced perspectives, interpretations, and concepts to account for
both the pathos and the logos that inform both the cathartic and affective
hypotheses and the theories of the unconscious that pertain to them. On
one side, artists can actively contribute to promoting less violent models of
behavior to serve as *exempla* for future generations whose plastic brains will
continue to be impressed by new media in an increasingly hyperconnected
world. Fast-changing media already saturate the walls of our digital environments with captivating shadows endowed with magnetic powers, but these
powers are not only oppressive; there is also a liberating potential at play
in those fictional projections that allows both creators and users of simulations to utilize the powers of the false for the better as well. On the other
side, philosophers in the digital age cannot simply exit the sensorial sphere
of simulation to find solace in an imaginary world of luminous, immutable,
transcendental ideas that can be reached through the power of logos alone.

Such idealist illusions are uncomfortably close to the fictions Plato critiqued in theory but narrated in his philosophical practice.

Still, from within the immanence of the *vita mimetica*, critics and theorists working at the juncture of philosophy and the arts can take some distance to develop genealogical diagnostics that are not simply disconnected from bodily pathos. On the contrary, I tried to show that they emerge from specific relations of mimetic agonism with and against intellectual models on both the critical and the creative side, generating productive reflections on the interplay of pathos and logos that continued to animate the powers of hypermimesis to generate spellbinding effects. As this reloaded (anti-) Platonic version of the Allegory of the Cave suggests, looking back to the origins of mimetic studies can continue to put genealogists of the present in a position to diagnose the unconscious powers of hypermimetic simulations that—as they proliferate via increasingly ramified new media in the digital age—cast a growing shadow on our future.

The shadow of (new) media violence takes many forms in the digital age, generating affective chains that may be imperceptible yet affect our minds and bodies in ways that go beyond good and evil. While diagnostics of these powers need to consider both pathological and patho-*logical* sides, there is an underlying metaphysics in-*forming* both, which, despite its heterogeneous forms, points in a clear direction. These shadows proliferate on a multiplicity of media and devices that represent increasingly realistic, immersive, and artificial second lives Nietzsche already posited "*behind* the world" (*GM* 3; 5); in the process, they reload ancient idealist tendencies that are deeply rooted in western philosophy via digital avatars that represent disembodied, idealized, and atemporal versions of an ideal ego. In an increasingly complex and uncertain world driven by a multiplicity of interwoven crises—economic, pandemic, migratory, political, environmental—that render human lives fragile, precarious, and vulnerable to multiple forms of systemic violence that cannot be reduced to a single cause, it will become increasingly tempting to reload idealist dreams. These might entail turning our backs to an all too human violence and living out artificial second lives online via transhuman avatars that control violence in imaginary yet increasingly realistic second worlds that threaten to replace *this* world. There is thus a larger critique of metaphysics that has been in the background of our genealogy of media violence since the beginning, which needs to be foregrounded at the end—if only because no matter how spellbinding, immaterial, and disconnected new simulations appear from reality, we will continue to rely on a material immanent ground that, for the moment, still sustains us. It also roots homo mimeticus to the earth of our immanent caves, allowing for these simulations to be projected on digital walls and screens in the first place.

In a mirroring inversion of perspectives, reevaluating the hypermimetic powers of simulations of violence from a present-oriented perspective gave us the occasion to retrace a genealogy of the catharsis hypothesis that unmasks its medical interpretation as part of the history of a philological error. Aristotle had, in fact, embodied rituals in mind in his conceptualization of catharsis in *Politics*. Yet a medical interpretation of the passing and still enigmatic allusion to catharsis in *Poetics*, where the specific question of aesthetic influence is posed as a direct reply to Plato, gave rise to insidious psychological interpretations of unconscious processes that cast a spell on the modernist period. This unconscious found in a specific tragic play, Sophocles's *Oedipus Rex*, a paradigmatic fictional model or example that was erected as a transcendental hermeneutical key to the unconscious. At the dawn of modernism, psychoanalysis interpreted this fiction as a universal, transhistorical, and immutable familial triangle, part of a metapsychology predicated on fantasies of familial violence (incest and parricide). These familial pathologies are, indeed, at play in this classical example of complex tragic plot, yet may be far removed from the psychic life of ordinary people. They certainly do not account for the heterogeneous forms of (new) media violence that go beyond familial triangles and already plague the contemporary world.[1]

Not without agonistic struggles, compulsive theoretical repetitions, creative inversions of perspectives, and a plurality of artistic reappropriations— from theater to cinema, TV to video games—the catharsis hypothesis still reaches into the present, albeit transformed, diluted, and somewhat worn out. Over time, theories of the unconscious that favored abstract, triangular forms over immanent embodied flows, familial interior complexes over social exterior complexities, mirroring aesthetic representations rather than immediate mirroring reflexes, therapeutic ideals rather than pathological effects, came to prevail in the past century, contributing to disseminating the cathartic/therapeutic legend in the popular imagination—via eminently contagious means. And yet, as we have seen, while legends do not need to be true in order to be believed, an alternative, more immanent, and embodied, yet not less intimately related theoretical tradition took immanent reflexes, emotional influences, and embodied simulations constitutive of affective contagion as an alternative door to an immanent, relational, and thus social and political unconscious. If this mimetic unconscious remained in the shadow of dominant discoveries, it began to reappear at the twilight of the twentieth century and, under the mask of different theoretical turns—from the affective turn to the new materialist turn, the neuro turn to the posthuman turn—is now constitutive of the mimetic *re*-turn in the present century.[2]

To be sure, this *re*-turn of attention to the powers of contagion in theory notwithstanding, simulations of violence will continue to be put to capitalist profit in a hyperconnected neoliberal age driven by commercially and algorithmically induced tastes that put violence to economic profit. Violence will thus always find its defenders, starting from the very companies that promote it on different platforms, as well as among consumers already hooked on it, if only because violence taps into a pathos that is deeply rooted in the visceral instincts of homo mimeticus generating addictive patterns of behaviors. And yet, from a different, perhaps more disinterested, not less persistent, and more immanent and embodied point of view, a survey of the scholarly literature on this subject, supplemented by a genealogy of theories that inform and, sometimes, misinform the debate, makes it increasingly hard to dispute a correlation between representations of violence and (new) media violence.

Correlation may not be causation, yet if confirmed repeatedly over time, it should nonetheless cause legitimate preoccupations. While the majority of studies on media violence tend to focus on present media from a quantifiable, experimental, and objectifying perspective, these two volumes aimed to supplement a *longue durée* interpretative genealogy on the catharsis and affective hypothesis. If I looked back to the philosophical origins of the debate on media violence at the dawn of mimetic studies, my driving telos has been double: first, provide a theoretical articulation of two main concepts on which the debate rests; and, second, offer a genealogy of the theories of the unconscious that these agonistic concepts gave birth to. My aspiration was to invite interdisciplinary conversations that cross over different periods, fields of knowledge, and schools of thought in order to open up the problematic of (new) media violence to perspectives that are not usually represented in quantitative approaches, yet provide the very epistemic foundations of the debate, and, as we repeatedly saw, continue to cast light on contemporary media as well.

This is a theoretical study, but its focus is on material reality more than abstract ideas and it hopes to be of use in practice as well. As any slightly concerned parent raising children in a world increasingly surrounded by representations of violence knows, if not from mimetic studies, then at least from their children's mimetic practices, the effects of new media violence are real and visible in our children's actions, expressions, and gestures. Related mimetic pathologies are also manifest in the staggering number of scandals concerning sexual assaults on women of the type *Vice* dramatized in fiction and are ongoing in a social life still plagued by domestic abuse as the Covid-19 pandemic made visible. If these disturbing symptoms could once be masked by phallocentric power structures, in the wake of #MeToo and BLM movements, violence against women and racial minorities are repeatedly exposed as part of the texture of everyday life and are accentuated by pandemic crises. They also call for new patho-*logical* diagnostics that focus on harrowing scenes of violence that are not confined to fictional representations but inform daily practices and bleed into the real world.

Some of the examples of violence that operate on the mimetic unconscious like the police murder of Rayshard Brooks and George Floyd, or the storming of the U.S. Capitol on January 6, 2021, emerged in the process of writing this book. Although they did not seem to initially fall directly under the rubric of media violence, they urged me to change course in order to do justice to a fast-evolving phenomenon and expand critical awareness of the reach of new media violence. They are meant as starting points for future diagnostics of similar cases to come. They also testify to the urgency for new generations of scholars not to set up rigid disciplinary boundaries that carve up complex and interwoven problems via watertight disciplines, ossifies two-cultures divides, or disconnect academic work from societal issues. Rather, new generations of scholars are encouraged to adopt transdisciplinary, problem-based approaches to increasingly complex problems to bring scholarly practices back in touch with contemporary concerns. In the end, the Socratic lesson that emerges from both theoretical and practical approaches to (new) media violence, is simple but no less profound. It could be summed up for the Janus-faced figure of the scholar qua parent as follows: tell me what shows and games your children are allowed to watch and play in practice and I'll tell you how deeply you believe in cathartic theories; show me which gestures new generations enact in everyday life and I will tell you which fictional models they have been affectively imitating in virtual life.

To be sure, this genealogy of violence and the mimetic unconscious does not offer easy therapeutic solutions that would magically cure the proliferating pathologies of hypermimetic violence in the digital age. It certainly does not propose censure as a solution. Rather, it calls for a dietary regulation of the intake of media violence. In the process, it also calls for informed, educative practices aware of the good and bad effects of affective contagion that reload old diagnostics to make them relevant to a new media landscape constitutive of our *vita mimetica*. What we have suggested is that the logos used to diagnose the unconscious pathos triggered by mimesis in the past might benefit from recuperating a marginalized tradition of the unconscious that does not rest on a repressive or cathartic hypothesis, but on a mimetic or affective hypothesis instead. This tradition shows, time and again, that representations of violent actions are not mere images far removed from reality; nor do they always generate therapeutic cathartic effects, be they at the aesthetic, individual, or collective level. Rather, representations of violence tend to have real, performative effects on the formation and transformation of subjectivity, behavior, and habits, generating contagious actions and reflex reactions that are not under the full control of consciousness and belong to the sphere of the mimetic unconscious.

In sum, violence can continue to be unconsciously manifested in dreams; it can also have contagious effects in rituals. But an affective participation in new kinds of formless, violent, and all-pervasive media spectacles that inform our digital culture—be they played out via video games, new social media, or an increasingly digitized "real" life—is unlikely to generate cathartic or purifying effects in the long run. On the contrary, exposure to violent actions, no matter how fictional or hyperreal they are, contributes to generating dangerous addictions, cultural habits, and contagious mirroring vices that are likely to promote all too violent, hypermimetic reactions. It also distracts new generations from an immanent type of less spectacular, systemic, interconnected violence that will increasingly render life on Earth fragile and precarious calling for immanent metamorphoses in the way we think, act, and live.

That our digitally addicted culture did "get a taste," as the detective in *Vice* puts it, cannot be denied. Whether at some point we will "get enough" remains to be seen. What we have seen and felt in this Janus-faced diagnostic is that unconscious violence is not only expressed in dreams and latent desires; it is, above all, manifest in fictional and virtual actions that spill into the real world. The mimetic unconscious, I have argued, goes beyond the pleasure principle. It might even go further and bring us back to the reality principle.

# Notes

**PROLOGUE**

1. See Nidesh Lawtoo, *Homo Mimeticus: A New Theory of Imitation* (Leuven: Leuven University Press, 2022).


**INTRODUCTION: MIMETIC STUDIES**

1. See Nidesh Lawtoo, *Violence and the Oedipal Unconscious*, vol. 1, *The Catharsis Hypothesis* (East Lansing: Michigan State University Press, 2023).

2. See *Nidesh Lawtoo, Homo Mimeticus: A New Theory of Imitation* (Leuven: Leuven University Press, 2022).

3. Following *Homo Mimeticus* and volume 1, I refer to mimetic studies to account for traditional media from tragedy and epic to the novel and film and to new mimetic studies when the focus is on new digital media. (New) mimetic studies is meant to designate both traditional and new media.

4. See Nidesh Lawtoo, *The Phantom of the Ego: Modernism and the Mimetic Unconscious* (East Lansing: Michigan State University Press, 2013).

5. In addition to the aforementioned *Homo Mimeticus*, see, for instance, the special issues on "The Mimetic Condition," *CounterText* 8, no. 1 (2022) and on "Posthuman Mimesis," *Journal of Posthumanism* 2, no. 2 (2022).

6. The classicist Stephen Halliwell writes that the ideas of Greek poetics "are part of the genealogy of arguments and attitudes in whose modern forms some of our own values may still be invested"; thinking of Aristotle's *Poetics*, he says that it has "left lingering traces, if often at the subconscious level, in many areas of literary theory and criticism." Stephen Halliwell, *Between Ecstasy and Truth: Interpretations of Greek Poetics from Homer to Longinus* (Oxford: Oxford University Press, 2011), 5, 220. Similarly, Terry Eagleton notices that "the conflict between Plato and Aristotle is thus one familiar today between mimetic and therapeutic theories of pornography or media violence." Terry Eagleton, *Sweet Violence: The Idea of the Tragic* (Oxford: Blackwell Publishing, 2003), 154. For a short and informed genealogy of catharsis and contagion in theatrical spectacles, see Denis Guénon, "Contagion et Purgation," in *Actions et acteurs: Raisons du drame sur scène* (Paris: Belin, 2005), 189–99.

7. Giorgio Agamben, *La comunità che viene* (Torino: Einuadi Editore, 1990), 8 (my trans.).

8. The mimetic turn is internal to a transdisciplinary project titled *Homo Mimeticus: Theory and Criticism*; its main outputs include a trilogy of books composed by these two volumes on violence and the unconscious, preceded by *Homo Mimeticus*. Mimetic supplements to the work of precursors such as René Girard, Philippe Lacoue-Labarthe, Gunter Gebauer, and Christoph Wulf are also registered in special issues of *Contagion*; *Conradiana* 48, no. 2–3 (2–16); *MLN* 132, no. 5 (2017); and *CounterText* 8, no. 1 (2022), among others. On the mimetic turn, see also Jean-Luc Nancy and Nidesh Lawtoo, "Mimesis: Concept singulier-pluriel, entretien avec Jean-Luc Nancy," *L'Esprit Créateur* 61, no. 2 (2021): 147–67; Nidesh Lawtoo and J. Hillis Miller, "The Critic as Mime: J. Hillis Miller in Dialogue with Nidesh Lawtoo," *The Minnesota Review* 95 (2020): 93–119; William E. Connolly and Nidesh Lawtoo, "Fascism Now and Then: William Connolly and Nidesh Lawtoo in Conversation," in *(New) Fascism: Contagion, Community, Myth*, by Nidesh Lawtoo (East Lansing: Michigan State University Press, 2019), 179–242; Adriana Cavarero and Nidesh Lawtoo, "Mimetic Inclinations: A Dialogue with Adriana Cavarero," in *Contemporary Italian Women Philosophers: Stretching the Art of Thinking*, ed. Silvia Benso and Elvira Roncalli (Albany: State University of New York Press, 2021), 183–99; N. Katherine Hayles and Nidesh Lawtoo, "Posthuman Mimesis II—Connections: A Dialogue between Nidesh Lawtoo and Katherine Hayles," *Journal of Posthumanism* 2, no. 2 (2022): 181–91. See also http://www.homomimeticus.eu/publications/.

9. For informed accounts of the history of mimesis as a human condition, see Gunter Gebauer and Christoph Wulf, *Mimesis: Culture-Art-Society*, trans. Don Reneau (Berkeley: University of California Press, 1995); Susan Hurley and Nick Chater, eds., *Perspectives on Imitations: From Neuroscience to Social Science*, vol. 2: *Imitation, Human Development, and Culture* (Cambridge, MA: MIT Press, 2005); Scott R. Garrels, ed., *Mimesis and Science: Empirical Research on Imitation and the Mimetic Theory of Culture and Religion* (East Lansing: Michigan State University Press, 2011); Samuel IJsseling, *Mimesis: On Appearing and Being* (Kampen, NE: Pharos, 1990); and Christian Borch, ed., *Imitation, Contagion, Suggestion: On Mimesis and Society* (New York: Routledge,

2019). In *Homo Mimeticus* I build on these and other studies to further a mimetic turn, or *re*-turn of mimesis, in the twenty-first century.

10. Walter Benjamin, "On the Mimetic Faculty," in *Reflections: Essays, Aphorisms, Autobiographical Writings*, trans. Edmund Jephcott, ed. Peter Demetz (New York: Schocken Books, 1986), 331–36, 334.

11. For a modernist precursor, see Oscar Wilde, "The Decay of Lying," in *The Complete Works of Oscar Wilde*, vol. 4, ed. Josephine M. Guy (Oxford: Oxford University Press, 2007), 72–103. See also Nidesh Lawtoo, "The Critic as Mime: Wilde's Theoretical Performance," *Symplokē* 26, no. 1–2 (2018): 317–28.

12. See Jacques Derrida, "Plato's Pharmacy," in *Dissemination*, trans. Barbara Johnson (Chicago: University of Chicago Press, 1981), 61–171.

13. On the modernist foundations of my theory of mimesis qua homo mimeticus, see Nidesh Lawtoo, *Phantom of the Ego*; *Conrad's Shadow: Catastrophe, Mimesis, Theory* (East Lansing: Michigan State University Press, 2016); on its contemporary political implications, see *(New) Fascism*.

14. For a wide-ranging book that reinscribes the problematic of media violence in sacrificial rituals in transdisciplinary terms consonant with mimetic studies, see Mark Pizzato, *Theaters of Human Sacrifice: From Ancient Ritual to Screen Violence* (Albany: State University of New York Press, 2004).

15. See Lawtoo, *Violence and the Oedipal Unconscious*, 45–57.

16. For a recent discussion on these shared foundations, see Nancy and Lawtoo, "Mimesis."

17. Philippe Lacoue-Labarthe, "Typography," in *Typography: Mimesis, Philosophy, Politics*, ed. Christopher Fynsk (Cambridge, MA: Harvard University Press, 1989), 43–138, 130 (my italics). Hereafter T.

18. I give an initial account of posthuman mimetism in Nidesh Lawtoo, "Posthumanism and Mimesis: An Introduction," *Journal of Posthuman Studies* 2, no. 2 (2022): 87–100.

19. On (restricted) mimesis as an instrument to promote fascist violence, see Philippe Lacoue-Labarthe and Jean-Luc Nancy, "The Nazi Myth," trans. Brian Holmes, *Critical Inquiry* 16, no. 2 (1990): 291–312; on the role of (general) mimesis in artistic creation, see Lacoue-Labarthe, "Diderot: Paradox and Mimesis," in *Typography*, 248–66. I discuss both texts in Lawtoo, *(New) Fascism*, ch. 2, and Lawtoo, *Homo Mimeticus*, ch. 4.

20. See Lawtoo, *Violence and the Oedipal Unconscious*, ch. 1.

21. I offered a genealogical account of the continuities between Girard's mimetic theory and deconstruction in Nidesh Lawtoo, "The Shadow of the Symposium: Sameness and Difference Replayed," *MLN* 134, no. 5 (2019): 898–909.

22. René Girard, *Violence and the Sacred* (Baltimore: Johns Hopkins University Press, 1972), 296. Hereafter *VS*.

23. Jean-Pierre Vernant, "Greek Tragedy: Problems of Interpretation," in *The Structuralist*

*Controversy: The Languages of Criticism and the Sciences of Man*, ed. Richard Macksey and Eugenio Donato (Baltimore: Johns Hopkins University Press, 1972), 273–95, 277.

24. René Girard, *Evolution and Conversion: Dialogues on the Origins of Culture* (with Pierpaolo Antonello and João Cezar de Castro Rocha) (London: Continuum, 2007), 146–47.

25. As seen in volume 1, mimetic agonism is of Nietzschean and thus affirmative inspiration (see Lawtoo, *Violence and the Oedipal Unconscious*, ch. 1). It also bears elective affinities with what William Connolly, also on the shoulders of Nietzsche, calls "agonistic respect" aspiring to "overcome resentment of the world" of becoming. William E. Connolly, *A World of Becoming* (Durham, NC: Duke University Press, 2011), 79. What mimetic agonism respectfully foregrounds is an explicit relation of imitation and differentiation constitutive of this life-affirmative overcoming.

26. On the role of the passion of Christ in shaping a violent iconography constitutive of medieval and early modern painting, see John R. Decker and Mitzi Kirkland-Ives, eds., *Death, Torture, and the Broken Body in European Art, 1300–1650* (New York: Routledge, 2016).

27. Lacoue-Labarthe offers a penetrating genealogical connection between Girard's and Plato's mimetologies in "Typography," 103–10.

28. Adriana Cavarero, *In Spite of Plato: A Feminist Rewriting of Ancient Philosophy*, trans. S. Anderlini-D'Onofrio and A. O'Healy (New York: Routledge, 1995).

29. Friedrich Nietzsche, *On the Genealogy of Morals: A Polemic*, trans. Douglas Smith (Oxford: Oxford University Press, 1996), 10. Hereafter *GM* (part, sections, page number given in parentheses).

30. For a collection of essays on the affective turn, see Melissa Gregg and Gregory J. Seigworth, eds., *The Affect Theory Reader* (Durham, NC: Duke University Press, 2010).

31. See Anna Gibbs, "After Affect: Sympathy, Synchrony and Mimetic Communication," in *Affect Theory Reader*, 186–205. For a synchronous account of "mimetic communication," see also Nidesh Lawtoo, "Bataille and the Birth of the Subject: Out of the Laughter of the Socius," *Angelaki* 16, no. 2 (2011): 73–88.

32. Benedict de Spinoza, *Ethics* (including *The Improvement of the Understanding*), trans. R. H. M. Elwes (Amherst, NY: Prometheus Books, 1989), 129.

33. Spinoza, *Ethics*, 133.

34. William Connolly encourages theorists to develop a "micropolitics of perception" attentive to the ways in which new media generate passions that "infiltrate our perceptual experience below the level of conscious attention" and to the role "*affect* plays in perception" and bodily reactions more generally. Connolly, *A World of Becoming*, 56–57.

35. Melissa Gregg and Gregory J. Seigworth, "An Inventory of Shimmer," in *Affect Theory Reader*, 1–25, 2, 5.

36. For a feminist account of the democratic side of inclinations, see Adriana Cavarero, *Inclinations: A Critique of Rectitude*, trans. Amanda Minervini and Adam Sitze (Stanford: Stanford University Press, 2016). For Cavarero's engagement with our concept of "mimetic pathos" attentive to both its democratic and neo-fascist sides, see Adriana Cavarero, *Surging Democracy: Notes on Hannah Arendt's Political Thought*, trans. Matthew Gervase (Stanford: Stanford University Press, 2021), 59–85.

37. Brian Massumi, *Parables for the Virtual: Movement, Affect, Sensation* (Durham, NC: Duke University Press, 2002), 16. Hereafter *PV*. For an account of the nonconscious that extends cognition to nonhuman animals and technology, see N. Katherine Hayles, *Unthought: The Power of the Cognitive Nonconscious* (Chicago: University of Chicago Press, 2017).

38. Gilles Deleuze and Félix Guattari, *Anti-Oedipus: Capitalism and Schizophrenia*, trans. Robert Hurley, Mark Seem, and Helen R. Lane (London: Continuum, 1977), 119. Hereafter *AO*.

39. On Deleuze and Guattari's debt to D. H. Lawrence's anti-Oedipal critique of Freud, see Lawtoo, *Phantom of the Ego*, 192–97.

40. See Mikkel Borch-Jacobsen, *Making Madness: From Hysteria to Depression* (Cambridge: Cambridge University Press, 2009).

41. Roberto Esposito, *Da fuori: Una filosofia per l'Europa* (Torino: Einaudi Editore, 2016), 100 (my trans.).

42. Michel Henry, *Généalogie de la psychanalyse: le commencement perdu* (Paris: Presses Universitaires de France, 1985), 275 (my trans.). Hereafter *GP*.

43. On the role of mimesis in the psychology of the socius, see Lawtoo, *Phantom of the Ego*, 260–81.

44. Gilles Deleuze and Félix Guattari, *A Thousand Plateaus: Capitalism and Schizophrenia*, trans. Brian Massumi (London: Continuum, 2004), 241. For an informed account of Deleuze and Guattari's connection to Tarde, see Andrea Mubi Brighenti, "Tarde, Canetti, and Deleuze on Crowds and Packs," *Journal of Classical Sociology* 10, no. 4 (2010): 291–314.

45. Jane Bennett, *Influx & Efflux: Writing Up with Whitman* (Durham, NC: Duke University Press, 2020), x, xii. See also Jane Bennett, "Mimesis: Paradox or Encounter," *MLN* 132, no. 5 (2017): 1186–200; and Lawtoo, "The Plasticity of Mimesis."

46. Bennett, *Influx & Efflux*, xvii, xxii.

47. Bennett, *Influx & Efflux*, 36, 96, 33.

48. William E. Connolly, *Neuropolitics: Thinking, Culture, Speed* (Minneapolis: University of Minnesota Press, 2002), 40, 7. On Connolly and mimesis, see Nidesh Lawtoo, "The Powers of Mimesis: Encounters, Simulations, Comic Fascism," *Theory & Event* 22, no. 3 (2019): 722–46.

49. See Lawtoo, *(New) Fascism*, 28–51. I first established the mimetic link between

actors and fascist politics in Lawtoo, *Phantom of the Ego*, esp. 52–91; on Trump and affective contagion, see also William E. Connolly, *Aspirational Fascism: The Struggle for Multifaceted Democracy under Trumpism* (Minneapolis: University of Minnesota Press, 2017), 1–30.

50. For an informed account of the meanings of pathos in Ancient Greek as the "most vital moment in religion and art, feared by others as an enticement to sacrilege and irrationality," see Thomas Gould, *The Ancient Quarrel Between Poetry and Philosophy* (Princeton, NJ: Princeton University Press, 1990), ix, 22–69.

51. Gould, *Ancient Quarrel*, xviii.

52. See also Lawtoo, introduction to *Violence and the Oedipal Unconscious*.

53. Lacoue-Labarthe, "Diderot: Paradox and Mimesis," in *Typography*, 248–66, 260.

54. Denis Diderot, *Paradoxe sur le comédien* (Paris: Flammarion, 1981), 128, 129.

55. See V. S. Ramachandran and Sandra Blakeslee, *Phantoms in the Brain: Human Nature and the Architecture of the Mind* (London: Harper Collins, 2005).

56. For a genealogically informed account of contagion in the digital age via Deleuze and Gabriel Tarde's mimetic theory, see Tony D. Sampson, *Virality: Contagion Theory in the Age of Networks* (Minneapolis: University of Minnesota Press, 2012).

57. Switching from politics to sport—the leap is not as big as it appears—Massumi observes: "Take for example American football. Super Bowl Sunday, the peak event of the football season, is said to correspond to an increase in domestic violence" (*PV* 80).

58. Gabriel Tarde, *Les Lois de l'imitation* (Paris: Seuil, 2001), 46.

## CHAPTER 1. THE BANALITY OF VIOLENCE: A TASTE OF HYPERMIMESIS

1. Hannah Arendt, *The Human Condition* (Chicago: University of Chicago Press, 1998), 2. More recently Yuval Noah Harari confirms that "in the twenty-first century science fiction is arguably the most important genre of all, for it shapes how most people understand things like AI, bioengineering and climate change." Yuval Noah Harari, *21 Lessons for the 21st Century* (London: Penguin, 2018), 244. Interestingly, Harari (2018, 245) relies on sf films like *The Matrix* and *Her*, and TV series *Westworld* and *Black Mirror*, that is, films already at the center of the mimetic turn in posthuman studies.

2. Mark Pizzato, *Theaters of Human Sacrifice: From Ancient Ritual to Screen Violence* (Albany: State University of New York Press, 2004), 86.

3. This chapter furthers accounts of (post)human hypermimesis in sf film initiated in Nidesh Lawtoo, "*Avatar* Simulation in 3Ts: Techne, Trance, Transformation," *Science Fiction Studies* 42, no. 1 (2015): 132–50; Lawtoo, "*The Matrix* E-Motion: Simulation, Mimesis, Hypermimesis," in *Mimesis, Movies, and Media: Violence, Desire, and the Sacred*, ed. Joel Hodge, Chris Fleming, and Scott Cowdell (London: Bloomsbury, 2015), 89–104; Lawtoo, "'This Is No Simulation!': Hypermimesis in *Being John*

*Malkovich* and *Her*," *Quarterly Review of Film and Video* 37, no. 2 (2020): 116–44; and Lawtoo, "Black Mirrors: Reflecting on Hypermimesis," *Philosophy Today* 65, no. 3 (2021): 523–47.

4. Cynthia Carter and Kay Weaver write: "We contend that what is now needed is a more nuanced and politically aware understanding of the complex ways in which the growing 'normalcy', 'banality' and 'everydayness' of media violence influence our relationships with each other in the world." Cynthia Carter and Kay Weaver, *Violence and the Media* (New York: Open Univeristy Press, 2003), 20. For an account of media violence framed as "part of a broader culture in which male violence is valued and normalized," see Karen Boyle, *Media and Violence: Gendering the Debates* (London: Sage, 2004), 14. Other studies on media violence I have benefitted from include Matthew S. Eastin, ed., *Encyclopedia of Media Violence* (Thousand Oaks, CA: Sage, 2013); W. James Potter, *The 11 Myths of Media Violence* (Thousand Oaks, CA: Sage, 2003); *On Media Violence* (London: Sage Publications, 1999); Jonathan L. Freedman, *Media Violence and Its Effect on Aggression: Assessing the Scientific Evidence*, repr. ed. (Toronto: University of Toronto Press, 2003); for a historical account of film violence, see James Kendrick, *Film Violence: History, Ideology, Genre* (London: Wallflower, 2009); for a study that shifts the debate from film and TV to video games, see Barrie Gunter, *Does Playing Video Games Make Players More Violent?* (London: Palgrave Macmillan, 2016); for a collection on the performative effects of online violence (online shaming, bullying, hate speech) via social media (Twitter, Facebook) that generate offline violence, see Sara Polak and Daniel Trotter, eds., *Violence and Trolling on Social Media* (Amsterdam: Amsterdam University Press, 2020).

5. Hannah Arendt, *Eichmann in Jerusalem: A Report on the Banality of Evil* (New York: Penguin Books, 2006). On the role mimesis plays in the "banality of evil" and the "thoughtlessness" it entails, see Nidesh Lawtoo, "The Case of Eichmann Restaged: Arendt, Evil, and the Complexity of Mimesis," *Political Research Quarterly* 74, no. 2 (2021): 479–90.

6. Edgar Morin, *Le Cinéma: Un art de la complexité*, ed. Monique Peyrière and Chiara Simonigh (Paris: Nouveau Monde, 2018), 140 (my trans.). See also Edgar Morin, *The Cinema, or the Imaginary Man*, trans. L. Mortimer (Minneapolis: University of Minnesota Press, 2005), 85–115; and Vittorio Gallese and Michele Guerra, *Lo schermo empatico: Cinema e neuroscienze* (Milano: Raffaello Cortina Editore, 2015).

7. See Johan Huizinga, *Homo Ludens: A Study of the Play-Element in Culture* (Kettering, OH: Angelico Press, 2016); for an account of *homo ludens* 2.0 in the digital age attentive to the mimetic logic of identification and performativity, see Valerie Frissen, Sybille Lammes, Michiel de Lange, Jos de Mul, Joost Raessens, eds., *Playful Identities: The Ludification of Digital Media Culture* (Amsterdam: Amsterdam University Press, 2015).

8. Friedrich Nietzsche, "Homer's Contest," trans. and ed. Christa Davis Acampora. *Nietzscheana* 5 (1996): 1–8.

9. For an approach to violence in film sensitive to the fact that the pleasure we experience

in cinematic scenes of violence "depends upon our investment in an experience which is both distant (we look at an image of violence; we do not undergo the violence ourselves) and proximate (the cinematic crime image registers sensations in our bodies and memories as we watch)," see Alison Young, *The Scene of Violence: Cinema, Crime, Affect* (Abingdon: Routledge, 2010), 2. For an informed historical survey of the ideological role of violence in the history of U.S. cinema from *The Birth of the Nation* to *Rambo* and *Terminator*, see Carter and Weaver, *Violence and the Media*, ch. 2; for an historical account of film violence, see James Kendrick, *Film Violence: History, Ideology, Genre* (London: Wallflower, 2009).

10. Carter and Weaver, *Violence and the Media*, 162. For a "symptomatic" reading of the "expressive" or, as I call it, (hyper)mimetic power of contemporary (post-cinematic) films in general and sf in particular not simply to "*represent* social processes" but contribute, via their "circulation, and distribution," to "generate subjectivity," see Steven Shaviro, *Post-Cinematic Affect* (Washington: O Books, 2010), 2–3, 1–11.

11. Potter, *11 Myths*, 37.

12. The violence is real for characters within the diegesis, but since *Vice* denotes artificial experiences on the Net, the movie addresses both levels at once—therein lies its theoretical interest.

13. Thomas Gould, *The Ancient Quarrel between Poetry and Philosophy* (Princeton, NJ: Princeton University Press, 1990), xiii.

14. Friedrich Nietzsche, *Daybreak: Thoughts on the Prejudices of Morality*, trans. R. J. Hollingdale (Cambridge: Cambridge University Press, 1982), 18.

15. See Lawtoo, *Violence and the Oedipal Unconscious*, ch. 3.

16. See Jane Goodall, *Through a Window: My Thirty Years with the Chimpanzees of Gombe* (Boston: Mariner Books, 2000), 115–29.

17. Nietzsche, *Daybreak*, 17, 68.

18. Georges Bataille, *Erotism, Death and Sensuality*, trans. Mary Dalwood (San Francisco: City Lights Books, 1986) 16. On the centrality of Bataille for mimetic theory, see Nidesh Lawtoo, *The Phantom of the Ego: Modernism and the Mimetic Unconscious* (East Lansing: Michigan State University Press, 2013), ch. 4; and Lawtoo, "Bataille and the Homology of Heterology," *Theory, Culture & Society* 35, no. 4–5 (2018): 41–68.

19. Georges Bataille, "Hegel, la mort, le sacrifice," in *Œuvres Complètes*, vol. 12 (Paris: Gallimard, 1988), 326–45, 337 (my trans.). Hereafter HMS.

20. Georges Bataille, *La Part maudite* (Paris: Les Éditions de Minuit, 1967), 50 (my trans.).

21. Noël Carroll notes that this double movement characteristic of violence in general is central to the horror genre in particular, which "obviously attracts consumers; but it seems to do so by means of the expressively repulsive." Noël Carroll, *The Philosophy of Horror or Paradoxes of the Heart* (London: Routledge, 1990), 158–59.

22. I discuss Bataille's theory of mimetic communication in Lawtoo, *Phantom of the Ego*, 209–83.

23. As W. James Potter notes: "The film that led to the most subsequent aggression among the participants was not the aggressive film, but rather the erotic film, because the erotic film was more arousing than the aggressive one." W. James Potter, *On Media Violence* (London: Sage Publications, 1999), 18.

24. Erich Auerbach, *Mimesis: The Representation of Reality in Western Literature*, trans. Willard R. Trask (Princeton, NJ: Princeton University Press, 2003).

25. Jean Baudrillard, *Simulacres et simulation* (Paris: Galilée, 1981), 11, 10 (my trans.).

26. Baudrillard, *Simulacres et simulation*, 11.

27. Elsewhere, I have discussed the hypermimetic role of *The Apprentice* in Trump's election. See Lawtoo, *(New) Fascism*, 38–51.

28. See Kevin Spacey, "Let Me Be Frank," December 24, 2018, YouTube video, https://www.youtube.com/watch?v=JZveA-NAIDI.

29. Bruno Latour, "On Technical Mediation: Philosophy, Sociology, Genealogy," *Common Knowledge* 3, no. 2 (1994): 29–64.

30. Summarizing the literature on the subject for the second half of the twentieth century, W. James Potter gives the following numbers: "Gun-related deaths increased more than 60% from 1968 to 1994, to about 40,000 annually, and this problem is now considered a public health epidemic by 87% of surgeons and 94% of internists across the United States." Potter, *On Media Violence*, 1. More recent statistics confirm these numbers: 42,000 as 2022 nears to an end. See the website for Gun Violence Archive, https://www.gunviolencearchive.org/.

31. Giorgio Agamben, *La comunità che viene* (Torino: Einaudi Editore, 1990), 8 (my trans.).

32. Jacques Lacan, "Of Structure as an Inmixing of an Otherness Prerequisite to Any Subject Whatever," in *The Structuralist Controversy*, ed. Richard Macksey and Eugenio Donato (Baltimore: Johns Hopkins University Press, 1972), 186–200, 188.

33. Lacan, "Of Structure," 187, 189.

34. The reference texts on Lacan's philosophical influences are tied to mimetic studies. See Mikkel Borch-Jacobsen, *Lacan: The Absolute Master*, trans. Douglas Brick (Stanford: Stanford University Press, 1991), esp. 1–20; Philippe Lacoue-Labarthe and Jean-Luc Nancy, *The Title of the Letter: A Reading of Lacan*, trans. François Raffoul and David Pettigrew (Albany: State University of New York Press, 1992).

35. Lacan, "Of Structure," 194.

36. On mimetic racism and sexism, see Lawtoo, *Phantom of the Ego*, 101–30.

37. See "Killing of Freddie Gray," Wikipedia, https://en.wikipedia.org/wiki/Killing_of_Freddie_Gray.

38. See Evan Hill et al., "How George Floyd Was Killed in Police Custody," *New York Times*, May 31, 2020, https://www.nytimes.com/2020/05/31/us/george-floyd-investigation.html.

39. For a diagnostic of racist violence that takes the murder of Floyd as a paradigmatic case to reflect on the "social suffocation" constitutive of systemic racism and the "scapegoats" white supremacy entails, see Gabriel O. Apata, "'I Can't Breathe': The Suffocating Nature of Racism," *Theory, Culture & Society* 37, no. 7–8 (2020): 241–54, 248.

40. On Lacan's "*aborted* theory of identification" predicated on the rejection of affective mimesis, see Borch-Jacobsen, *Lacan: The Absolute Master*, 65–71; on Lacan's debt to Caillois's and Janet's theories of mimicry and imitation, see Nidesh Lawtoo, *Homo Mimeticus: A New Theory of Imitation* (Leuven: Leuven University Press, 2022), ch. 5.

41. "4-Year-Old Fatally Shoots Himself in Baltimore," WBALTV, February 1, 2016, http://www.wbaltv.com/article/4-year-old-fatally-shoots-himself-in-baltimore/7098584.

42. Latour, "On Technical Mediation," 33.

43. In the United States alone in 2021, gun-related deaths include 315 children (one to eleven years old) and over 1250 for teenagers (twelve to seventeen years old); for 2022 the latter rose to 1,200 and counting. See the website for Gun Violence Archive, https://www.gunviolencearchive.org/.

44. A statistic dating back to 2000 already indicated that "by the time the average American child graduates from elementary school, he or she will have seen about 8,000 murders and about 100,000 other assorted acts of violence (e.g., assaults, rapes) on network television." Brad J. Bushman and L. Rowell Huesmann, "Effects of Televised Violence on Aggression," in *Handbook of Children and the Media*, ed. Dorothy G. Singer and Jerome L. Singer (Thousand Oaks: Sage, 2001), 227, 223–44.

45. Carter and Weaver, *Violence and the Media*, 77.

46. Potter, *On Media Violence*, 75.

47. Carter and Weaver, *Violence and the Media*, 77; for an overview on the effects of TV on children, see also 71–94.

48. European studies confirm this point. In the 1970s Edgar Morin already stressed the role social disadvantage plays in the relation between media violence and real violence and recently returned to discuss the topic with the present author. See Lawtoo, *Homo Mimeticus*, 310–13. Psychiatrist Serge Tisseron, while noting that "most studies confirm the impact of violent models on behavior," also stresses the diversity of children's responses to media violence and notices that "images do not make children violent but can make more violent those children who have already a tendency to be violent." Bernard Stiegler and Serge Tisseron, *Faut-il interdire les écrans aux enfants?* (Paris: Éditions Mordicus, 2009), 49, 50–51 (my trans.). See also Vittorio Andreoli, *La violenza: Dentro di noi, attorno a noi* (Milano: BUR Rizzoli, 2003); and Serge

Tisseron, *Enfants sous influence: Les* écrans *rendent-ils les jeunes violents?* (Paris: Armand Collins, 2000).

49. L. Rowell Huesmann, "Imitation and the Effects of Observing Media Violence on Behavior," in *Perspectives on Imitation: From Neuroscience to Social Science*, vol. 2, *Imitation, Human Development, and Culture*, ed. Susan Hurley and Nick Chater (Cambridge, MA: MIT Press, 2005), 257–66, 259.

50. Carter and Weaver, *Violence and the Media*, 69.

51. What Adriana Cavarero groups under the rubric of "horrorism" equally applies to the type of disruption of individuation internal to media violence. The main difference is that media violence triggers not only disgust but also a paradoxical double movement of disgusted fascination. Adriana Cavarero, *Horrorism: Naming Contemporary Violence*, trans. William McCuaig (New York: Columbia University Press, 2011), 8.

52. As Carter and Weaver put it: "Despite the long and wide-ranging nature of discussions around pornography, what has not yet been addressed in sufficient depth in our view is the extent to which the articulation of sex and violence cultivates, over time, a collective taken-for-grantedness of its presence—arguably leading, in turn, to its eventual 'normalization.'" Carter and Weaver, *Violence and the Media*, 95. For an overview of the heterogeneous field of porn studies, see Linda Williams, ed., *Porn Studies* (Durham, NC: Duke University Press, 2004).

## CHAPTER 2. VITA MIMETICA: PLATONIC DIALOGUES

1. Whitehead also specified: "I do not mean the systematic scheme of thought which scholars have doubtfully extracted from his [Plato's] writings. I allude to the wealth of general ideas scattered throughout them." Alfred North Whitehead, *Process and Reality*, ed. David Ray Griffin and Donald W. Sherburne (New York: Free Press, 1979), 39.

2. I define mimetic agonism as a form of intellectual contest that does not lead to rivalry or violence but to a productive contestation with/against the model/opponent. See Nidesh Lawtoo, *Violence and the Oedipal Unconscious*, vol. 1, *The Oedipal Hypothesis* (East Lansing: Michigan State University Press, 2023), 45–57.

3. Penelope Murray, ed., *Plato on Poetry* (Cambridge: Cambridge University Press, 1996), 2.

4. Eric A. Havelock, *Preface to Plato* (Cambridge, MA: Harvard University Press, 1963), 3. Hereafter *PP*.

5. See also Thomas Gould, *The Ancient Quarrel between Poetry and Philosophy* (Princeton, NJ: Princeton University Press, 1990), 1–35, and Philippe Lacoue-Labarthe, "Typography," in *Typography: Mimesis, Philosophy, Politics*, ed. Christopher Fynsk (Cambridge, MA: Harvard University Press, 1989), 96–138.

6. This chapter follows up on a genealogy of the "vita mimetica" started in Nidesh

Lawtoo, *Homo Mimeticus: A New Theory of Imitation* (Leuven: Leuven University Press, 2022), ch. 2.

7. Murray writes: "Poetry is studied not for its aesthetic qualities, but for its ethical content, a point that is made abundantly clear in S.'s [Socrates's] critique of literature in books 2 and 3 of the *Republic*," where the focus is "on poetry's power to influence behavior, since the major part of the poet's function was to provide role models for the young by glorifying the great heroes of the past." Murray, *Plato on Poetry*, 16.

8. On the pre-Platonic meanings of *mimēsis* in fifth-century Greece and its origins in the Sicilian dramatic genre of the *mimos*, see Gerald F. Else, "'Imitation' in the Fifth Century," *Classical Philology* 53, no. 2 (1958): 73–90. See also Havelock, *Preface to Plato*, n22, 57–60.

9. See Plato, *Republic*, in *The Collected Dialogues of Plato*, trans. P. Shorey, ed. E. Hamilton and H. Cairns (Princeton, NJ: Princeton University Press, 1963), 575–844, 820–33. Hereafter *Rep.*, followed by line number.

10. Prior to Lacoue-Labarthe, Havelock had equally stressed that in the first books of the *Republic*, Plato is "obsessed with the psychology of response as it is experienced by the audience" and that "in his description of the emotional impact of poetry he seems often to be describing an almost pathological situation" (*PP* 37).

11. Burckhardt writes: "Even the dialogue as a form of philosophical discourse became an agonism." Jakob Burckhardt, *The Greeks and Greek Civilization*, trans. Sheila Stern, ed. Oswyn Murray (London: Harper Collins, 1998), 182. For a fuller account of mimetic agonism, see Lawtoo, *Violence and the Oedipal Unconscious*, ch. 1.

12. On brain plasticity and brain damage, see Catherine Malabou, *The New Wounded: From Neurosis to Brain Damage*, trans. Steven Miller (New York: Fordham University Press, 2012); on the link between mimesis and plasticity, see Nidesh Lawtoo, "The Plasticity of Mimesis," *MLN* 132, no. 5 (2017): 1201–24.

13. See Martin Heidegger, "On the Essence of Truth," in *Basic Writings*, ed. David Farrell Krell (San Francisco: Harper Collins, 1977), 113–41.

14. Alain Badiou, "Dialectiques de la fable," in *Matrix: Machine Philosophique*, ed. Ellie During et al. (Paris: Ellipses, 2003), 120–29, 129.

15. As Arendt puts it: "The philosopher's experience of the eternal . . . can occur only outside the realm of human affairs and outside the plurality of men, as we know from the Cave parable in Plato's *Republic*." Hannah Arendt, *The Human Condition* (Chicago: University of Chicago Press, 1998), 20.

16. Arendt, *The Human Condition*, 226n66.

17. Adriana Cavarero, "Regarding the Cave," *Qui Parle* 10, no. 1 (1996): 1–20, 4, 11. Hereafter RC. Cavarero relies on Arendt's perceptive observation that Plato's Allegory of the Cave constitutes a "kind of reply to and reversal of Homer's description of Hades in the eleventh book of the *Odyssey*" (12). Arendt specifies: "Not life after death, as in the Homeric Hades, but ordinary life on earth, is located in a 'cave' in an underworld;

the soul is not the shadow of the body but the body the shadow of the soul." Arendt, *The Human Condition*, 291. This mirroring reversal is a perfect illustration of mimetic agonism. I discuss Arendt's and Cavarero's interpretations of the Allegory of the Cave in more detail in Lawtoo, *Homo Mimeticus*, ch. 2.

18. Nietzsche, *The Twilights of the Idols*, in *The Portable Nietzsche*, trans. And ed. Walter Kaufmann (New York: Penguin Books, 1982), 463–63, 485.

19. The most detailed account of the double side of the pharmakon is still Jacques Derrida, "Plato's Pharmacy," in *Dissemination*, trans. Barbara Johnson (Chicago: University of Chicago Press, 1981), 61–171. If Derrida focuses primarily on the pharmakon of writing as a copy of speech, my focus is on mimesis more generally, which is attentive to both writing and the oral qualities of myth, tragedy, epic, and other mimetic arts. The concept of patho-*logy* also adds a diagnostic discursive supplement to the pharmakon.

20. Nietzsche, "Homer's Contest," trans. and ed. Christa Davis Acampora, *Nietzscheana* 5 (1996): 6.

21. As Lacoue-Labarthe puts it, Plato's "choice of the dialogue attests to a rivalry and a severe *agôn* vis-à-vis tragedy." Philippe Lacoue-Labarthe and Jean-Luc Nancy, *Scène* (Paris: Christian Bourgois, 2013), 80 (my trans.). I call this productive rivalry mimetic agonism.

22. See Adriana Cavarero, *Inclinazioni: Critica della rettitudine* (Milano: Raffello Cortina Editore), 71, 65–79.

23. Aristophanes, *The Clouds*, in *The Complete Plays of Aristophanes*, ed. Moses Hadas (New York: Bantam Books, 1988), 101–42,141.

24. Plato, *Apology*, trans. Hugh Tredennick, in *The Collected Dialogues of Plato*, ed. E. Hamilton and H. Cairns (Princeton, NJ: Princeton University Press, 1963), 3–26, 18b–c. See also Curtis Roche, "The Invocation of *Clouds* in Plato's *Apology*," *Undergraduate Humanities' Forum 2007–2008: Origins* (April 2008), https://repository.upenn.edu/cgi/viewcontent.cgi?article=1008&context=uhf_2008.

25. Plato, *Apology*, 18b.

26. See Lawtoo, *Homo Mimeticus*, ch. 4.

27. Aristophanes, *The Clouds*, 128. For an informed account of the mimetic agon between Plato and Aristophanes with a focus on comedy, see María Ortega Mañez, "*Mimèsis* en jeu: Une analyse de la relation entre théâtre et philosophie" (PhD diss., Université Paris-Sorbonne, 2013).

28. Jean-Louis Baudry, "The Apparatus: Metapsychological Approaches to the Impression of Reality in Cinema," in *Film Theory and Criticism: Introductory Readings*, ed. Leo Braudy and Marshall Cohen (Oxford: Oxford University Press, 1999), 760–77, 760–68.

29. Edgar Morin, *The Cinema, or the Imaginary Man*, trans. By L. Mortimer (Minneapolis: University of Minnesota Press, 2005), 85–115.

30. Marshall McLuhan, *Understanding Media: The Extension of Man* (New York: Signet Book, 1964), viii, 109.

31. McLuhan, *Understanding Media*, 56.

32. McLuhan, *Understanding Media*, 33.

33. Plato, *Ion*, trans. Lane Cooper, in *The Collected Dialogues of Plato*, trans P. Shorey, ed. E. Hamilton and H. Cairns (Princeton, NJ: Princeton University Press, 1963), 215–28, 219, 533d.

34. On Nietzsche's debt to Plato's theory of mimesis, see Lawtoo, *The Phantom of the Ego: Modernism and the Mimetic Unconscious* (East Lansing: Michigan State University Press, 2013), 52–67.

35. Socrates is echoing the following lines from *The Bacchae*: "With milk the earth flows! . . . It runs with the nectar of bees." Euripides, *The Bacchae*, trans. William Arrowsmith, in *The Complete Greek Tragedies*, vol. 4, *Euripides*, ed. David Grene and Richmond Lattimore (Chicago: University of Chicago Press, 1959), 543–608, 548, ll. 142–43.

36. Euripides, *The Bacchae*, 592, ll. 1124–37.

37. As Henry Jeanmaire puts it in his influential study on Dionysus, in *The Bacchae* Euripides "did not aim to stage the bacchae of his period, but the mythic idea of their origins, an idea that bacchic cenacles were the first to have." Henry Jeanmaire, *Dionysos: Histoire du culte de Bacchus* (Paris: Payot, 1978), 85 (my trans.); see also 79–88.

38. Pierre Hadot, *Qu'est-ce que la philosophie antique?* (Paris: Gallimard, 1995), 67 (my trans.).

39. Hadot, *Qu'est-ce que la philosophie*, 103.

40. Eric Havelock may overstate the dichotomy between the Homeric state of mind characterized by an "oral culture" and the post-Platonic emergence of a written culture, yet the importance of theatrical mimesis in Plato's ethical critique of the *Republic* is inscribed in the text itself and is now constitutive of mimetic studies.

41. M. F. Burnyet, "Art and Mimesis in Plato's 'Republic,'" in *LRB* 21 (1998): 1–20, 1–2.

42. See Gould, *Ancient Quarrel*, 21.

43. James W. Potter, *On Media Violence* (London: Sage Publications, 1999), 16–17.

44. Jonathan Dollimore, *Sex, Literature and Censorship* (Oxford: Polity Press, 2001), 150; on Plato and censorship, see also 150–53.

45. Dollimore, *Sex*, 151.

46. Thomas Gould rightly points out that even in this last book, Plato's concern is that "attendance at a tragic pathos will cause this darkest element [of the soul] to come unstuck again and exercise its strength." Gould, *Ancient Quarrel*, xviii. If Gould sees a connection between Plato's critique of mimesis and the Freudian superego, we shall see

that Plato opens up an alternative mimetic paths to the unconscious that is not based on the interpretation of dreams but of gestures instead.

47. Georges Bataille, *Les Larmes d'Éros* (Paris: Éditions 10/18, 1971), 91.

48. Johan Huizinga notes that "some of Nietzsche's biographers blame him for having re-adopted the old agonistic attitude of philosophy. If indeed he did so he has led philosophy back to its antique origins." Johan Huizinga, *Homo Ludens: A Study of the Play-Element in Culture* (Kettering, OH: Angelico Press, 2016), 152.

49. As Havelock puts it, "Plato assumes among his contemporaries a view of the poet and his poetry which is wholly unfamiliar to our way of thinking . . . he insists on discussing the poets as though their job was to supply metrical encyclopedias. The poet is a source on the one hand of essential information and on the other of essential moral training" (*PP* 29). Hence Havelock speaks of mimesis as a "rich and unpredictable flux of experience" (23). Similarly, Lacoue-Labarthe speaks of "the constitutive undecidability of mimesis" and of the "strange power of contamination it contains" (T 97).

50. As Erich Auerbach acknowledges in the epilogue of *Mimesis*: "The subject of this book, the interpretation of reality through literary representation or 'imitation,' has occupied me for a long time. My original starting point was Plato's discussion in book 10 of the *Republic*—mimesis raking third after truth." Erich Auerbach, *Mimesis: The Representation of Reality in Western Literature*, trans. Willard R. Trask (Princeton, NJ: Princeton University Press, 2003), 554.

51. Philippe Lacoue-Labarthe defines *lexis* as "the expression, the linguistic sense (rhetoric) and corporal sense (oratory) of the *figure*." And Jean-Luc Nancy echoes: "the fact of enunciation is indistinguishable from its modality—from its pragmatics, as we would say today . . . in all circumstances what matters is how it is said . . . it is a bodily affair [*affaire de 'corps'*]." Philippe Lacoue-Labarthe and Jean-Luc Nancy, *Scène* (Paris: Christian Bourgois, 2013), 21, 35 (my trans.), see also 75–76.

52. Aristotle, *The Poetics of Aristotle*, trans. Stephen Halliwell (Chapel Hill: University of North Carolina Press, 1987), 33.

### CHAPTER 3. DIONYSIAN INTOXICATIONS: CULTS, CONSPIRACIES, INSURRECTIONS

1. Friedrich Nietzsche, *Ecce Homo*, trans. R. J. Hollingdale (New York: Penguin Books, 1980), 47. Hereafter *EH*.

2. On mimetic agonism, see Nidesh Lawtoo, *Violence and the Oedipal Unconscious*, vol. 1, *The Catharsis Hypothesis* (East Lansing: Michigan State University Press, 2023), ch. 1; for penetrating studies entirely devoted to agonism in Nietzsche that resonate with the present study, see also Herman Siemens, *Agonal Perspectives on Nietzsche's Philosophy of Critical Transvaluation* (Berlin: De Gruyter, 2021), and James S. Pearson, *Nietzsche on Conflict, Struggle and War* (Cambridge: Cambridge University Press, 2022).

3. See René Girard, "Superman in the Underground: Strategies of Madness—Nietzsche,

Wagner, and Dostoevsky," *MLN* 91 (1976): 1257–66. I supplemented Girard's reading of Nietzsche's mimetic pathology from a patho-*logical* perspective in Nidesh Lawtoo, *The Phantom of the Ego: Modernism and the Mimetic Unconscious* (East Lansing: Michigan State University Press, 2013), ch. 1.

4.  As James Pearson also notes, Nietzsche's references to *Entladung* in early texts are a confirmation that "he was operating with Bernays' conception of catharsis." Pearson, *Nietzsche on Conflict*, 43. He did so not to simply repeat it but to critique it and overcome it via the dynamic of mimetic agonism.

5.  Jean-Jacques Rousseau, *Lettre à d'Alembert* (Paris: Flammarion, 2003), 68 (my trans.). Hereafter *LA*. The subject of the letter responds to an article D'Alembert had written for his *Encyclopedia* titled "Geneva" (1758), which suggested the installation of a "*théâtre de comédie*" in Geneva after its ban of 1617. While *comédie* refers specifically to comedy, in neoclassical French it extends to include theater tout court.

6.  For Michel Henry's phenomenology of Nietzsche's "hyperpower" based on the unconscious pathos of the will to power affecting itself in an immanent, corporal, auto-affection constitutive of the genealogy of the unconscious, see Michel Henry, *Généalogie de la psychanalyse: Le commencement perdu* (Paris: Presses Universitaires de France, 1985), 249–93.

7.  In *Psyche*, Erwin Rohde offers an account of Dionysian "frenzy," "possession" and "fanatic enthusiasm" that both echoes and furthers Plato and Nietzsche as he writes of the participants in Dionysian cults: "A strange rapture came over them in which they seemed to themselves and others 'frenzied,' 'possessed.' The excessive stimulation of the senses, going even as far as hallucination, was brought about, in those who were susceptible to their influence, by the delirious whirl of the dance, the music and the darkness." Erwin Rohde, *Psyche: The Cult of the Souls and the Belief in Immortality among the Greeks* (New York: Routledge, 2001), 258; see also 253–66.

8.  Pseudo-Longinus, who set the foundations for the debates on the sublime later recuperated by the Romantics, had Plato's *Ion* well in mind as he inverted the diagnostic on enthusiastic poetic frenzy as follows: "I would affirm with confidence that there is no one so lofty as that of genuine passion, in its right place, when it bursts out in a wild gust of mad enthusiasm and as it were fills the speaker's words with frenzy." Pseudo-Longinus, "On the Sublime," in *Critical Theory since Plato*, 3rd ed., ed. Hazard Adams and Leroy Searle (Boston: Thomson Wadsworth, 2005), 94–118, 98.

9.  Plato, *Phaedrus*, trans. R. Hackforth, in *The Collected Dialogues of Plato*, ed. E. Hamilton and H. Cairns (Princeton, NJ: Princeton University Press, 1963), 475–525, 244a–252a.

10. Gilbert Rouget, *Music and Trance: A Theory of the Relations Between Music and Possession*, trans. Brunhilde Biebuyck (Chicago: University of Chicago Press, 1985), 197. For a recent musicological contribution to the mimetic turn that draws on Plato's *mousikē*, see also Daniel Villegas Vélez, "Apparatus of Capture: Music and the Mimetic Construction of Reality in the Early Modern/Colonial Period," *CounterText* 8, no. 1 (2022): 123–48.

11. See Rouget, *Music and Trance*, 213–20.

12. See Lawtoo, *Phantom of the Ego*, 76–83; and Siemens, *Agonal Perspectives*, 127–33.

13. Friedrich Nietzsche, *The Case of Wagner* in *The Birth of Tragedy and The Case of Wagner*, trans. Walter Kaufmann (New York: Vintage Books, 1967), 166, 172, 171, 153–92. Hereafter *CW*.

14. Hippolyte Bernheim, *Suggestive Therapeutics: A Treatise on the Nature and the Uses of Hypnosis*, trans. Christian A. Herter (Westport: Associated Bookseller, 1957), 137. Hereafter *ST*.

15. Serge Moscovici, *The Age of the Crowd: A Historical Treatise on Mass Psychology*, trans. J. C. Whitehouse (Cambridge: Cambridge University Press, 1985).

16. Christian Borch prefaces his informed account of the history of crowd psychology with the acknowledgment that it is "is intertwined with the destiny of the notion of suggestion [and] is guided by the underlying intuition that the latter's fate was undeserved." Christian Borch, *The Politics of Crowds: An Alternative History of Sociology* (Cambridge: Cambridge University Press, 2012), 17.

17. Gustave Le Bon, *The Crowd: A Study of the Popular Mind* (New York: Dover Publications Inc., 2002), iii. Hereafter *C*.

18. On "mimetic sexism" and "mimetic racism" in modernist account of crowds, see Lawtoo, *Phantom of the Ego*, 111–30.

19. See Nidesh Lawtoo, *(New) Fascism: Contagion, Communication, Myth* (East Lansing: Michigan State University Press, 2019), esp. ch. 1; and William E. Connolly, *Aspirational Fascism: The Struggle for Multifaceted Democracy under Trumpism* (Minneapolis: University of Minnesota Press, 2017), ch. 1.

20. Walter Benjamin, "On the Mimetic Faculty," in *Reflections: Essays, Aphorisms, Autobiographical Writings*, trans. Edmund Jephcott, ed. Peter Demetz (New York: Schocken Books, 1986), 331–36, 334.

21. Jean Baudrillard, *Simulacres et simulation* (Paris: Galilée, 1981), 10–11.

22. The entrepreneur billionaire Peter Thiel, who was part of Trump's transition team, was a student of Girard at Stanford: if he put the insights of mimetic theory to use as the first investor of Facebook, he is also likely to have shared his knowledge of crowd behavior for Trump's political abuse—a lesson on the dangers of political misappropriations of a pacifist mimetic theory. For more on Thiel and Trump, see Kieran Keohane, "La Liberté contre la Démocratie," *Le Grand Continent*, February 16, 2019, https://legrandcontinent.eu/fr/2019/02/16/par-dela-la-democratie/.On the pacifist side of mimetic theory, see Wolfgang Palaver, *Transforming the Sacred into Saintliness: Reflecting on Violence and Religion with René Girard* (Cambridge: Cambridge University Press, 2020).

23. For studies that address the problematic of digital violence or "online vitriol" and "affective politics" internal to Trump's tweets and rhetoric prior to his election, let alone the storming of the Capitol, see Sara Polak, "'#Unpresidented': The Making

of the First Twitter President," and Greta Olson, "Love and Hate Online: Affective Politics in the Era of Trump," in *Violence and Trolling on Social Media*, ed. Sara Polak and Daniel Trotter (Amsterdam: Amsterdam University Press, 2020), 65–85, 153–77.

24. For the full speech, see Aaron Blake, "What Trump Said before His Supporters Stormed the Capitol, Annotated," *Washington* Post, January 11, 2021, https://www. washingtonpost.com/politics/interactive/2021/annotated-trump-speech-jan-6-capitol/.

25. Butter and Knights summarize the main characteristics of conspiracy theories as follows: "they assume that everything has been planned and nothing happens by coincidence; they divide the world strictly into the evil conspirators and the innocent victims of their plot; and they claim that the conspiracy works in secret and does not reveal itself even after it has reached its goals." Michael Butter and Pieter Knights, "General Introduction," in *Routledge Handbook of Conspiracy Theories*, ed. Michael Butter and Pieter Knights (New York: Routledge, 2020), 1–8.

26. Hulda Thórisdóttir, Silvia Mari, and André Krouwel, "Conspiracy Theories, Political Ideology and Political Behavior," in *Routledge Handbook of Conspiracy Theories*, 304–16, 305.

27. See also Mark Fenster, *Conspiracy Theories: Secrecy and Power in American Culture* (Minneapolis: University of Minnesota Press, 2008); and Simona Stano, "The Internet and the Spread of Conspiracy Content," in *Routledge Handbook of Conspiracy Theories*, 483–96.

28. See Luke Broadwater, Emily Cochrane, and Adam Goldman, "Capitol Police Detail Failure during Pro-Trump Assault," *New York Times*, January 26, 2021, https://www. nytimes.com/2021/01/26/us/politics/capitol-riot-police.html.

29. QAnon is a far-right conspiracy theory that alleges, among other things, sex trafficking and Satan worshiping to Democratic leaders.

30. As I revise one last time the manuscript on December 7, 2022, members of QAnon among other Far-Right conspiracists have been arrested for planning to overthrow the government in Germany. See Katrin Bennhold and Erika Solomon, "Germany Arrests 25 Suspected of Planning to Overthrow Government," *New York Times*, December 7, 2022, https://www.nytimes.com/2022/12/07/world/europe/germany-coup-arrests. html.

31. See Lawtoo, *(New) Fascism*, 38–51.

32. See David Kyle Johnson, ed., Black Mirror *and Philosophy: Dark Reflections* (London: Wiley Blackwell, 2020); Nidesh Lawtoo, "Black Mirrors: Reflecting on Hypermimesis," *Philosophy Today* 65, no. 3 (2021): 523–47.

33. Michel Serres, "Philosopher c'est anticiper," *Philosophie Magazine*, July 4, 2007, https:// www.philomag.com/articles/michel-serres-philosopher-cest-anticiper.

34. See Greg Littmann, "The Waldo Moment and Political Discourse: What's Wrong with Disrespect in Politics?," in Black Mirror *and Philosophy*, 59–68.

35. See Nidesh Lawtoo, "The Powers of Mimesis: Simulation, Encounters, Comic Fascism," *Theory & Event* 22, no. 3 (2019): 722–46.

36. Sara Polak and Daniel Trottier offer an informed account of how online practices of public shaming, trolling and hate speech, or "online vitriol," "can be construed as violent"; they also note that "while online and offline worlds seem separated, the consequences of online media expressions also occur offline, and many online dynamics have offline equivalents in past and present." Sara Polak and Daniel Trottier, "Introducing Online Vitriol," in *Violence and Trolling on Social Media*, 1–21, 14, 10.

37. The Russian invasion of Ukraine had not yet taken place as I submitted this manuscript. I have addressed its hypermimetic logic separately since, in Nidesh Lawtoo, "Posthumanism and Mimesis: An Introduction," *Journal of Posthumanism* 2, no. 2 (2022): 87–100, 95–99.

38. Following Nietzsche, Deleuze argued that "the powers of the false" is a manifestation of "will to power" that cinema has the power to reload. As he puts it: "By raising the false to power, life freed itself of appearances as well as truth: neither true nor false, and undecidable alternative but the power of the false, decisive will." Gilles Deleuze, *Cinema 2: The Time-Image*, trans. Hugh Tomlinson and Robert Galeta (Minneapolis: University of Minnesota Press, 1989), 145. I develop the Deleuzian implications of the argument presented in this chapter in Nidesh Lawtoo, "The Insurrection Moment: Intoxication, Conspiracy, Assault," *Theory & Event* 26 no. 1 (2023): 5–30.

39. Christian Borch, "The Imitative, Contagious, and Suggestible roots of Modern Society: Toward a Mimetic Foundation of Social Theory," in *Imitation, Contagion, Suggestion: On Mimesis and Society*, ed. Christian Borch (London: Routledge, 2019), 3–34. For Borch's productive contribution to new mimetic studies in the innovative context of financial contagion, see also Christian Borch, *Social Avalanche: Crowds, Cities, and Financial Markets* (Cambridge: Cambridge University Press, 2020).

40. Jean Baudrillard, *The Spirit of Terrorism and Other Essays*, trans. Chris Turner (London: Verso, 2003).

41. Yuval Noah Harari, *21 Lessons for the 21st Century* (London: Penguin 2018), 162.

## CHAPTER 4. THE MIMETIC UNCONSCIOUS: A MIRROR FOR CONTAGION

1. In addition to the pioneering works of Ellenberger and Sulloway (see vol.1), see also Marcel Gauchet, *L'Inconscient cérébral* (Paris: Seuil, 1992); and Mikkel Borch-Jacobsen and Sonu Shamdasani, *The Freud Files: An Inquiry into the History of Psychoanalysis* (Cambridge: Cambridge University Press, 2012).

2. I discussed these figures and others in more detail in Nidesh Lawtoo, *The Phantom of the Ego: Modernism and the Mimetic Unconscious* (East Lansing: Michigan State University Press, 2013).

3. Michel Foucault, *Histoire de la sexualité I: La Volonté de savoir* (Paris: Gallimard, 1976), 25.

4. Foucault, *Histoire de la sexualité I*, 29, 55.

5. See Robert B. Pippin, *Nietzsche, Psychology, and First Philosophy* (Chicago: University of Chicago Press, 2011), 8–21; Graham Parkes, *Composing the Soul: Reaches of Nietzsche's Psychology* (Chicago: University of Chicago Press, 1994), 7–8, 171–73, 320–25.

6. For an incisive study of Nietzsche's physio-psychology genealogically connected to Freudian concepts, see Henry Staten, *Nietzsche's Voice* (Ithaca, NY: Cornell University Press).

7. Léon Chertok, *Hypnose et suggestion* (Paris: Presses Universitaires de France, 1993), 23.

8. Raymond de Saussure, and Léon Chertok, *The Therapeutic Revolution: From Mesmer to Freud*, trans. R. H. Ahrenfeldt (New York: Brunner/Mazel Publishers, 1979), 39.

9. Gauchet, *L'Inconscient cérébrale*, 19.

10. Martin Stingelin, "Psychologie," in *Nietzsche-Handbuch*, ed. H. Ottmann (Stuttgart: J. B. Metzler Verlag, 2000), 425–52. See also Herman Siemens, "Empfindung" in *Nietzsche-Wörterbuch Online*, ed. Paul van Tongeren, Gerd Schank, and Herman Siemens (Berlin: Walter de Gruyter, 2011).

11. Borch, "The Imitative, Contagious, and Suggestible Roots of Modern Society: Toward a Mimetic Foundation of Social Theory," in *Imitation, Contagion, Suggestion: On Mimesis and Society*, ed. Christian Borch (London: Routledge, 2019), 5.

12. Bernheim retains the notion of hypnosis to designate "an exalted susceptibility to suggestion induced by an influence exercised over the subject's imagination" (17).

13. Nidesh Lawtoo, *Homo Mimeticus: A New Theory of Imitation* (Leiden: Leiden University Press, 2022), ch. 7.

14. Sigmund Freud, *Group Psychology and the Analysis of the Ego*, trans. James Strachey (New York: W. W. Norton, 1959), 21.

15. Mikkel Borch-Jacobsen, *Making Minds and Madness: From Hysteria to Depression* (Cambridge: Cambridge University Press, 2009), 110. What Borch-Jacobsen calls the "paradox of suggestion" (109) that concerns the "passive" and/or "active" disposition of the suggestible subject (*le suggestioné*) can be related to the dynamic interplay of passive (unconscious) reflex reactions of mirroring "cerebral cells" (Bernheim's term) on the one hand, and more complex forms of psychic activity that put these brain cells to (conscious) use, on the other. For a comic yet revealing dramatization of the type of violence this looping effect can generate, see Nidesh Lawtoo, "The Human Chameleon: *Zelig*, Nietzsche, and the Banality of Evil," *Film-Philosophy* 25, no. 3 (2021): 272–95, 283–85.

16. Michel Foucault, "Nietzsche, Genealogy, History," in *Language, Counter-Memory, Practice: Selected Essays and Interviews*, ed. Donald F. Bouchard (New York: Cornell University Press, 1977), 138–64, 145, 139, 145.

17. Charles Féré, *Sensation et mouvement: Études expérimentales de psycho-méchanique*, 2nd ed. (Paris: Félix Alcan, 1900), 123 (my trans.). Hereafter *SM*.

18. Charles Féré, *Travail et plaisir: Nouvelles études expérimentales de psycho-méchanique* (Paris: Félix Alcan, 1904), 337.

19. Féré, *Travail et plaisir*, 338.

20. See Freud, *Group Psychology*, 39.

21. Charles Féré and Alfred Binet, *Animal Magnetism* (New York: D. Appleton & Company, 1888), 180.

22. Féré and Binet, *Animal Magnetism*, 180.

23. Gabriel Tarde, *Les Lois de l'imitation* (Paris: Seuil, 2001), 137 (my trans.). See also Christian Borch, "Tensional Individuality: A Reassessment of Gabriel Tarde's Sociology," *Distinktion: Journal of Social Theory* 18, no. 2 (2017): 153–72.

24. Bernheim, qtd. in Borch-Jacobsen, *Making Minds and Madness*, 110. Bernheim and his colleagues of the School of Nancy believed that these crimes could go as far as murder. For instance, he gives the example reported by his colleague M. Liégieois, professor of law at Nancy, who reports the following experiment gone awry as he confesses: "I am to blame for having tried to have my friend, M. P., formerly a magistrate, killed, and this serious as it was, in the presence of the commissary general of Nancy. . . . In less than a quarter of a minute, I suggested to Mme. G—the idea of killing M. P. by a pistol shot. Absolutely unconscious, and perfectly docile, Mme. G—approached M. P. and fired the pistol." Bernheim, *Suggestive Therapeutics*, 163–64. I could not verify the accuracy of this story, which I encourage the reader to take with a grain of salt, if only because Bernheim was the first to warn against the danger of simulation and it is well known that "medical researchers staged simulated hypnotic crimes in order to prove their possibility." Stefan Andriopoulos, *Possessed: Hypnotic Crimes, Corporate Fiction, and the Invention of Cinema*, trans. Peter Jansen and Stefan Andriopolous (Chicago: University of Chicago Press, 2008), 27. See also Ruth Harris, *Murders and Madness: Medicine, Law, and Society in the Fin de Siècle* (Oxford: Oxford University Press), 1989.

25. Andriopoulos specifies: "The numerous cinematic representations of hypnosis thus not only adapted a medico-legal discussion about the possibility of 'criminal suggestion.' By employing specifically filmic devices such as the close-up and the point-of-view shot, these films also enacted the alleged hypnotic power of cinema." Andriopoulos, *Possessed*, 16.

26. For a collection of essays on the "pathologies of contemporary civilization" that resonate strongly with new mimetic studies, see Kieran Keohane, Ander Petersen, and Bert van den Bergh, *Late Modern Subjectivity and Its Discontents: Anxiety Depression and Alzheimer's Disease* (New York: Routledge, 2017). What the authors say of anxiety and depression applies to new media violence as well: "Instead of addressing these conditions as though they were discrete pathologies, specific diseases suffered by private individuals as 'cases,' the starting point is thus that the sources of these problems are

social, cultural and historical: that they arise from collectively experienced conditions of social transformations and shifts in our civilization" (3).

27. Going beyond the debate that opposes anti-gun advocates in the United States whose slogan is that "guns kill people" (or materialist perspective) to the National Rifle Association's (NRA) reply that "People kill people; not guns" (or moralist perspective), Bruno Latour develops a network theory of "technological mediation" that considers the agentic powers of guns to change people's action, and vice versa. Bruno Latour, "On Technical Mediation: Philosophy, Sociology, Genealogy," *Common Knowledge* 3, no. 2 (1994): 33.

28. I had originally planned to use still frames to illustrate the dynamic of the killing as specifically as possible, as it is usually done to close read visual texts such as films. This proved to be impossible because of laws protecting rights of police body cam footage in the United States, a gray legal zone that is apparently uncomfortable even with academic analysis—for understandable legal reasons yet not for justifiable ethical reasons, as it will become clear. At the moment I write, the footage can nonetheless be found online with a helpful commentary from the *New York Times*. I provide the exact timing in the video for key moments so the reader can view the scenes for themselves. See "How a Police Encounter Turned Fatal: The Killing of Rayshard Brooks," YouTube video, https://www.youtube.com/watch?v=chdTYo4NUh4&t=5s.

29. I discovered Trevor Noah's insightful commentary belatedly, as I revised the proofs of this piece one last time. He rightly calls it a "messy story" that does not fall within unilateral evaluations, for he adds: "in a way, it not being the perfect story it means we should look at it in the most perfect way possible." See Trevor Noah, "Why Did Rayshard Brooks Have to Lose His Life?," *The Daily Show*, June 15, 2020, https://www.youtube.com/watch?v=tR5YACuDR5A. What I add to Noah's account is a specific genealogical evaluation of the mimetic, intersubjective dynamic that informs this messy yet revealing case on violence and the unconscious.

30. As Noah points out: "if police cannot respond or handle a drunk person then they should not be responding." Noah, "Why Did Rayshard Brooks."

31. See Ryan Young, Devon M. Sayers, Maria Cartaya, and Ray Sanchez, "Garret Rolfe, Former Atlanta Officer That Fatally Shot Rayshard Brooks Was Wrongly Terminated, Board Says," CNN, updated May 6, 2021, https://edition.cnn.com/2021/05/05/us/atlanta-former-officer-garrett-rolfe-reinstated/index.html.

32. Allie Griffin, "Atlanta Officers Won't Face Charges in Shooting Death of Rayshard Brooks," *New York Post*, August 24, 2022, https://nypost.com/2022/08/24/atlanta-cops-garrett-rolfe-devin-brosnan-wont-face-charges-in-rayshard-brooks-shooting/.

33. Noah, "Why Did Rayshard Brooks."

34. Latour, "On Technical Mediation," 32–33.

## CHAPTER 5. DANGEROUS SIMULATIONS:
## MIRROR NEURONS, VIDEO GAMES, *E*-MOTIONS

1. Girard qualifies Plato's intellectual exclusion of the poet as "itself violent," his "sympathy" for Socrates "suspect" (*VS* 295), and repeatedly faults Plato for having missed the logic of mimetic desire; similarly, with respect to Nietzsche he specifies that his categories of Apollo and Dionysian "fail to perceive, or at most perceive only dimly, that each and every divinity corresponds to both aspects at once" (292) and sets out to pathologize his thought.

2. See Nidesh Lawtoo, *Homo Mimeticus: A New Theory of Imitation* (Leuven: Leuven University Press, 2022), ch. 1.

3. Giacomo Rizzolatti and Corrado Sinigaglia, *Mirrors in the Brain: How Our Minds Share Actions and Emotions*, trans. Frances Anderson (Oxford: Oxford University Press, 2008), 124. Hereafter *MB*.

4. For a confirmation of single-neuron activity in human patients, see Roy Mukamel, Arne D. Ekstrom, Jonas Kaplan, Marco Iacoboni, and Itzhak Fried, "Single-Neuron Responses in Humans during Execution and Observation of Actions," *Current Biology* 20 (April 2010): 750–56.

5. Gregory Hickok, *The Myth of Mirror Neurons: The Real Neuroscience of Communication and Cognition* (New York: W. W. Norton & Company, 2014), 192. Hereafter *MMN*.

6. For exceptions, see Vittorio Gallese, "The Two Sides of Mimesis: Mimetic Theory, Embodied Simulation, and Social Identification," in *Mimesis and Science: Empirical Research on Imitation and the Mimetic Theory of Culture and Religion*, ed. Scott R. Garrels (East Lansing: Michigan State University Press, 2011), 87–108; for a feminist critique of reductionist accounts of mirror neurons that is attentive to the "situatedness of experiences," see Victoria Pitts-Taylor, "I Feel Your Pain: Embodied Knowledges and Situated Neurons," *Hypatia* 28, no. 4 (2013): 852–69.

7. For an informed survey of the empirical evidence accumulated since the 1960s indicating that "exposure to violence in television, movies, video games, cell phones, and on the Internet increases the risk of violent behavior on the viewer's part," see L. Rowell Huesmann, "The Impact of Electronic Media Violence: Scientific Theory and Research," *Journal of Adolescent Health* 41, no. 6 (2007): 6–13.

8. Marco Iacoboni, *Mirroring People: The New Science of How We Connect with Others* (New York: Farrar, Straus and Giroux, 2008), 211. Henceforth *MP*.

9. Susan Hurley, "Imitation, Media Violence, and Freedom of Speech," *Philosophical Studies: An International Journal for Philosophy in the Analytic Tradition* 117, no. 1–2 (2004): 165–218, 182, 173.

10. Craig A. Anderson and Brad J. Bushman, "The Effects of Media Violence on Society," *Science* 295, no. 5564 (March 2002): 2377–79. Huesmann concludes his review of the scientific literature on the subject with a similar diagnostic: "In summary, exposure to electronic media violence increases the risk of both children and adults behaving aggressively in the short-run and of children behaving aggressively in the long-run. It

increases the risk significantly, and it increases it as much as many other factors that are considered public health threats." Huesmann, "The Impact," 11–12.

11. Craig A. Anderson, "Violent Video Games: Myths, Facts and Unanswered Questions," *American Psychological Association*, October 2003, https://www.apa.org/science/about/psa/2003/10/anderson.

12. "APA Reaffirms Position on Violent Video Games and Violent Behavior," American Psychological Association, March 3, 2020, https://www.apa.org/news/press/releases/2020/03/violent-video-games-behavior.

13. Barrie Gunter, *Does Playing Video Games Make Players More Violent?* (London: Palgrave MacMillan, 2016), 271.

14. As Gergen Kenneth remind us, "the major characteristics of games, as defined by scholars such as Huizinga (1938) and Caillois (1958), are that they are non-income producing activities, non-obligatory, and circumscribed in space and time." Yet he also specifies that in the digital age "revenues of video games now exceed 20 billion dollars internationally. Over 20 million players have spent 17 billion hours on Xbox Live, which is more than 2 hours for every person on the planet." Kenneth J. Gergen, "Playland," in *Playful Identities: The Ludification of Digital Media Culture*, ed. Valerie Frissen, Sybille Lammes, Michiel de Lange, Jos de Mul, and Joost Raessens (Amsterdam: Amsterdam University Press, 2015), 55–73, 56. This profit-oriented drive behind the gaming industry is likely to play a major role in inflecting games toward violence—for since antiquity, violence has been known to sell.

15. For special issues on post-literary and posthuman approaches to mimesis, see "The Mimetic Condition," ed. Nidesh Lawtoo, *CounterText* 8, no. 1 (2022); "Posthuman Mimesis," ed. Nidesh Lawtoo, *Journal of Posthumanism* 2, no. 2 (2022).

16. For a recent collection of essays by a young generation of scholars working in game studies that "reframes" the debate on violence, see Federico Alvarez Igarzábal, Michael S. Debus, and Curtis L. Maughan, eds., *Violence, Perception, Video Games: New Directions in Games Research* (Bielefeld: Transcrip Verlag, 2019). Barrie Gunter summarizes his thorough overview of this literature by saying that "there is plenty of empirical evidence available in the public domain that has concluded that video games can trigger aggressive reactions in players." Gunter, *Does Playing Video Games*, 271.

17. The game did not live up to this hype, as it was released prematurely with a number of unresolved technical issues that impacted its distribution. I thank Merlin Schmidt for an informative discussion on the game and gaming in general.

18. Transhumanism tends to designate an uncritical faith in technology to enhance humans in terms that replicate a grand narrative of progress; posthumanism is a heterogeneous field of study that emerges out of cybernetics and remains attentive to immanent, materialist, and critical concerns with the loss of the body internal to the digital turn. For an informed genealogy of the posthuman in line with our immanent principles, see N. Katherine Hayles, *How We Became Posthuman: Virtual Bodies in Cybernetics, Literature, and Informatics* (Chicago: University of Chicago Press, 1999).

For a discussion of the role of mimesis in posthuman studies, see N. Katherine Hayles and Nidesh Lawtoo, "Posthuman Mimesis II: Connections—A Dialogue between Katherine Hayles and Nidesh Lawtoo," *Journal of Posthumanism* 2, no. 2 (2022): 181–91.

19. On e-emotion and hypermimesis in video games mediated by a film central to *Cyberpunk 2077*, see Nidesh Lawtoo, "*The Matrix* E-Motion: Simulation, Mimesis, Hypermimesis," in *Mimesis, Movies, and Media: Violence, Desire, and the Sacred*, ed. Joel Hodge, Chris Fleming, and Scott Cowdell (London: Bloomsbury, 2015), 89–104.

20. On performance caption and simulation, see Nidesh Lawtoo, "*Avatar* Simulation in 3Ts: Techne, Trance, Transformation," *Science Fiction Studies* 42, no. 1 (2015): 132–50.

21. Steven Shaviro, *Post-Cinematic Affect* (Washington, DC: O Books, 2010).

22. William Brown, *Supercinema: Film-Philosophy for the Digital Age* (New York: Berghahn, 2013), 27.

23. As confirmation of the genealogical continuities in mimetic studies we have been tracing, Gallese and Guerra mention Edgar Morin's account of cinematic "identification" or "symbiosis" we already encountered in support of their theory of embodied simulation (see *ES* 77–78, 119–20).

24. Gunter, *Does Playing Video Games*, 34.

25. As Gallese and Guerra put it, "the neurosciences can factually contribute to confronting topics that have long been discussed in philosophical and aesthetic contexts concerning the status of emotions evoked by fictions" (*ES* 13, 69).

26. Natali Panic-Cidic, "The (American) Way of Experiencing Video Game Violence," in *Violence, Perception, Video Games*, 39–52, 42–45.

27. See Gallese, "The Two Sides."

28. Vittorio Gallese and Michele Guerra, *Lo schermo empatico: Cinema e neuroscienze* (Milan: Raffaello Cortina Editore, 2015), 57.

29. Gallese, "The Two Sides," 97 (my emphasis).

30. On the infant's constitutive mimetic openness to the other, see also Nidesh Lawtoo, *The Phantom of the Ego: Modernism and the Mimetic Unconscious* (East Lansing: Michigan State University Press, 2013), 254–80.

31. Natali Panic-Cidic, "The (American) Way of Experiencing Video Game Violence," in *Violence, Perception, Video Games*, 39–52.

32. Pseudo-Longinus, "On the Sublime," *in Critical Theory since Plato*, 3rd ed., ed. Hazard Adams and Leroy Searle (Boston: Thomson Wadsworth, 2005), 94–118, 95–96.

33. As Burke continues in his section on "Sympathy" that recuperates an Aristotelian principle for his theory of the sublime: "It is a common observation, that objects which in the reality would shock, are in tragical, and such like representations, the source of a very high species of pleasure." Edmund Burke, *A Philosophical Enquiry into the*

*Origin of Our Ideas of the Sublime and Beautiful*, ed. Adam Phillips (Oxford: Oxford University Press, 1990), 41.

34. In what follows I retain the term "transhuman" for the cyborgs within the game and "posthuman" for the still-embodied subjects playing the game. For a special issue on "posthuman mimesis" see *Journal of Posthumanism* 2, no. 2 (2022).

35. For a profound phenomenological critique of intentionality and of representational models of the unconscious, see Michel Henry, *Généalogie de la psychanalyse: Le commencement perdu* (Paris: Presses Universitaires de France, 1985); see also Nidesh Lawtoo, *Violence and the Oedipal Unconscious*, vol. 1, *The Catharsis Hypothesis* (East Lansing: Michigan State University Press, 2023), 24–25.

36. For an overview, see Linda Williams, ed., *Porn Studies* (Durham, NC: Duke University Press, 2004).

37. "YouPorn," *Wikipedia*, https://en.wikipedia.org/wiki/YouPorn.

38. Barrie Gunter points out: "normal young men can develop violence-condoning attitudes and beliefs about women and sexual relations with them as a consequence of watching movies that depict female characters being sexually abused." Gunter, *Does Playing Video Games*, 16. On the link between pornography and sexual aggression, see Brooke A. de Heer, Sarah Prior, and Gia Hoegh, "Pornography, Masculinity, and Sexual Aggression on College Campuses," *Journal of Interpersonal Violence* 36, no. 23–24 (2020): https://journals.sagepub.com/doi/10.1177/0886260520906186.

39. Henrik Smed Nielsen, *Playing Computer Games: Somatic Experience and Experience of the Somatic* (Aarhus: Digital Aesthetic Research Center, 2012), 136.

40. Commenting on this first-person experience, Frank Fetzer notes that "a program of action is designed into the avatar," limiting the number of possibilities and in the case of violent games, inflecting the action toward "lethal options within the game" by means of the plot, graphics, game design, and last but not least the presence of the gun at the player's disposal. Frank Fetzer, "Avatars Don't Kill People, Players Do! Actor-Network-Theory, Mediation, and Violence in Avatar-Based Video Games," in *Violence, Perception, Video Games*, 29–38, 35, 36.

41. Ferguson, "Real Violence," 26.

42. Kieran Keohane, Anders Petersen, and Bert van der Bergh, *Late Modern Subjectivity and Its Discontents: Anxiety, Depression and Alzheimer's Disease* (New York: Routledge, 2017).

## CONCLUSION: HOW A FICTION BECAME REALITY

1. It would be a question worth pursuing whether theoretical obsessions with Oedipal fantasies of parricide and incest, subsequently amplified by cultural industries like Hollywood influenced by psychoanalytical theories of the unconscious, did not generate catharsis but spread Oedipal phantasies by mimetic contagion, perhaps

infecting practices as well. The recent revelation that incest plagues countries like France, one of the few countries where psychoanalysis is still a dominant cultural force, may suggest an uncanny correlation.

2. On the mimetic turn, see Nidesh Lawtoo, *Homo Mimeticus: A New Theory of Imitation* (Leuven: Leuven University Press, 2022), as well as the special issues on "The Mimetic Condition," *CounterText* 8, no. 1 (2022) and on "Posthuman Mimesis," *Journal of Posthumanism* (2022). For a more complete list of outputs from the *Homo Mimeticus* project, see http://www.homomimeticus.eu/publications/.

# Bibliography

Agamben, Giorgio. *La comunità che viene*. Torino: Einaudi Editore, 1990.

Anderson, Craig A. "Violent Video Games: Myths, Facts and Unanswered Questions." American Psychological Association, October 2003. https://www.apa.org/science/about/psa/2003/10/anderson.

Anderson, Craig A., and Brad J. Bushman. "The Effects of Media Violence on Society." *Science* 295, no. 5564 (March 2002): 2377–79.

Andreoli, Vittorio. *La violenza: Dentro di noi, attorno a noi*. Milano: BUR Rizzoli, 2003.

Andriopoulos, Stefan. *Possessed: Hypnotic Crimes, Corporate Fiction, and the Invention of Cinema*. Translated by Peter Jansen and Stefan Andriopolous. Chicago: University of Chicago Press, 2008.

Apata, Gabriel O. "'I Can't Breathe': The Suffocating Nature of Racism." *Theory, Culture & Society* 37, no. 7–8 (2020): 241–54.

Arendt, Hannah. *Eichmann in Jerusalem: A Report on the Banality of Evil*. New York: Penguin Books, 2006.

———. *The Human Condition*. Chicago: University of Chicago Press, 1998.

Aristophanes. *The Clouds*. In *The Complete Plays of Aristophanes*, edited by Moses Hadas, 101–42. New York: Bantam Books, 1988.

Aristotle. *The Poetics of Aristotle*. Translated by Stephen Halliwell. Chapel Hill: University of North Carolina Press, 1987.

Auerbach, Erich. *Mimesis: The Representation of Reality in Western Literature*. Translated by Willard R. Trask. Princeton, NJ: Princeton University Press, 2003.

Badiou, Alain. "Dialectiques de la fable." In *Matrix: Machine Philosophique*, edited by Ellie During et al., 120–29. Paris: Ellipses, 2003.

Bataille, Georges. *Erotism, Death and Sensuality*. Translated by Mary Dalwood. San Francisco: City Lights Books, 1986.

———. "Hegel, la mort, le sacrifice." In *Œuvres Complètes*, vol. 12, 326–45. Paris: Gallimard, 1988.

———. *Les Larmes d'Éros*. Paris: Editions 10/18, 1971.

———. *La Part Maudite*. Paris: Les Éditions de Minuit, 1967.

Baudrillard, Jean. *Simulacres et simulation*. Paris: Galilée, 1981.

———. *The Spirit of Terrorism and Other Essays*. Translated by Chris Turner. London: Verso, 2003.

Baudry, Jean-Louis. "The Apparatus: Metapsychological Approaches to the Impression of Reality in Cinema." In *Film Theory and Criticism: Introductory Readings*, edited by Leo Braudy and Marshall Cohen, 760–77. Oxford: Oxford University Press, 1999.

Benjamin, Walter. "On the Mimetic Faculty." In *Reflections: Essays, Aphorisms, Autobiographical Writings*, translated by Edmund Jephcott, edited by Peter Demetz, 331–36. New York: Schocken Books, 1986.

Bennett, Jane. *Influx & Efflux: Writing Up with Whitman*. Durham, NC: Duke University Press, 2020.

———. "Mimesis: Paradox or Encounter." *MLN* 132, no. 5 (2017): 1186–200.

Bernheim, Hippolyte. *Suggestive Therapeutics: A Treatise on the Nature and the Uses of Hypnosis*. Translated by Christian A. Herter. Westport: Associated Bookseller, 1957.

Borch, Christian, ed. *Imitation, Contagion, Suggestion: On Mimesis and Society*. New York Routledge, 2019.

———. "The Imitative, Contagious, and Suggestible Roots of Modern Society: Toward a Mimetic Foundation of Social Theory." In *Imitation, Contagion, Suggestion: On Mimesis and Society*, edited by Christian Borch, 3–34. London: Routledge, 2019.

———. *The Politics of Crowds: An Alternative History of Sociology*. Cambridge: Cambridge University Press, 2012.

———. *Social Avalanche: Crowds, Cities, and Financial Markets*. Cambridge: Cambridge University Press, 2020.

———. "Tensional Individuality: A Reassessment of Gabriel Tarde's Sociology." *Distinktion: Journal of Social Theory* 18, no. 2 (2017): 153–72.

Borch-Jacobsen, Mikkel. *Lacan: The Absolute Master*. Translated by Douglas Brick. Stanford: Stanford University Press, 1991.

——— . *Making Minds and Madness: From Hysteria to Depression*. Cambridge: Cambridge University Press, 2009.

Borch-Jacobsen, Mikkel, and Sonu Shamdasani. *The Freud Files: An Inquiry into the History of Psychoanalysis*. Cambridge: Cambridge University Press, 2012.

Boyle, Karen. *Media and Violence: Gendering the Debates*. London: Sage, 2004.

Brighenti, Andrea Mubi. "Tarde, Canetti, and Deleuze on Crowds and Packs." *Journal of Classical Sociology* 10, no. 4 (2010): 291–314.

Brown, William. *Supercinema: Film-Philosophy for the Digital Age*. New York: Berghahn, 2013.

Burckhardt, Jacob. *The Greeks and Greek Civilization*. Translated by Sheila Stern, edited by Oswyn Murray. London: Harper Collins, 1998.

Burke, Edmund. *A Philosophical Enquiry into the Origin of our Ideas of the Sublime and Beautiful*, edited by Adam Phillips. Oxford: Oxford University Press, 1990.

Burnyet, M. F. "Art and Mimesis in Plato's 'Republic.'" *LRB* 21 (1998): 1–20.

Bushman, Brad. J., and L. Rowell Huesmann. "Effects of Televised Violence on Aggression." In *Handbook of Children and the Media*, edited by Dorothy G. Singer and Jerome L. Singer. Thousand Oaks: Sage, 2001.

Butter, Michael, and Pieter Knights, eds. *Routledge Handbook of Conspiracy Theories*. New York: Routledge, 2020.

Carroll, Noël. *The Philosophy of Horror or Paradoxes of the Heart*. London: Routledge, 1990.

Carter, Cynthia, and Kay Weaver. *Violence and the Media*. New York: Open University Press, 2003.

Cavarero, Adriana. *Horrorism: Naming Contemporary Violence*. Translated by William McCuaig. New York: Columbia University Press, 2011.

——— . *Inclinations: A Critique of Rectitude*. Translated by Amanda Minervini and Adam Sitze. Stanford: Stanford University Press, 2016.

——— . *In Spite of Plato: A Feminist Rewriting of Ancient Philosophy*. Translated by S. Anderlini-D'Onofrio and A. O'Healy. New York: Routledge, 1995.

——— . "Regarding the Cave." *Qui Parle* 10, no. 1 (1996): 1–20.

——— . *Surging Democracy: Notes on Hannah Arendt's Political Thought*. Translated by Matthew Gervase. Stanford: Stanford University Press, 2021.

Cavarero, Adriana, and Nidesh Lawtoo. "Mimetic Inclinations: A Dialogue with Adriana Cavarero." In *Contemporary Italian Women Philosophers: Stretching the Art of Thinking*, edited by Silvia Benso and Elvira Roncalli, 183–99. Albany: State University of New York Press, 2021.

Chertok, Léon. *Hypnose et suggestion*. Paris: Presses Universitaires de France, 1993.

Connolly, William E. *Aspirational Fascism: The Struggle for Multifaceted Democracy under Trumpism*. Minneapolis: University of Minnesota Press, 2017.

———. *Neuropolitics: Thinking, Culture, Speed*. Minneapolis: University of Minnesota Press, 2002.

———. *A World of Becoming*. Durham, NC: Duke University Press, 2011.

Connolly, William E., and Nidesh Lawtoo. "Fascism Now and Then: William Connolly and Nidesh Lawtoo in Conversation." In *(New) Fascism: Contagion, Community, Myth*, by Nidesh Lawtoo, 179–242. East Lansing: Michigan State University Press, 2019.

Decker, John R., and Mitzi Kirkland-Ives, eds. *Death, Torture, and the Broken Body in European Art, 1300–1650*. New York: Routledge, 2016.

De Heer, Brooke A., Sarah Prior, and Gia Hoegh. "Pornography, Masculinity, and Sexual Aggression on College Campuses." *Journal of Interpersonal Violence* 36, no. 23–24 (2020): https://journals.sagepub.com/doi/10.1177/0886260520906186.

Deleuze, Gilles. *Cinema 2: The Time-Image*. Translated by Hugh Tomlinson and Robert Galeta. Minneapolis: University of Minnesota Press, 1989.

Deleuze, Gilles, and Félix Guattari. *Anti-Oedipus: Capitalism and Schizophrenia*. Translated by Robert Hurley, Mark Seem, and Helen R. Lane. London: Continuum, 1977.

———. *A Thousand Plateaus: Capitalism and Schizophrenia*. Translated by Brian Massumi. London: Continuum, 2004.

Derrida, Jacques. "Plato's Pharmacy." In *Dissemination*, translated by Barbara Johnson, 61–171. Chicago: University of Chicago Press, 1981.

De Saussure, Raymond, and Léon Chertok. *The Therapeutic Revolution: From Mesmer to Freud*. Translated by R. H. Ahrenfeldt. New York: Brunner/Mazel Publishers, 1979.

Diderot, Denis. *Paradoxe sur le comédien*. Paris: Flammarion, 1981.

Dollimore, Jonathan. *Sex, Literature and Censorship*. Oxford: Polity Press, 2001.

Eagleton, Terry. *Sweet Violence: The Idea of the Tragic*. Oxford: Blackwell Publishing, 2003.

Else, Gerald F. "'Imitation' in the Fifth Century." *Classical Philology* 53, no. 2 (1958): 73–90.

Esposito, Roberto. *Da fuori: Una filosofia per l'Europa*. Torino: Einaudi Editore, 2016.

Euripides. *The Bacchae*. Translated by William Arrowsmith. In *The Complete Greek Tragedies*, vol. 4, *Euripides*, edited by David Grene and Richmond Lattimore, 543–608. Chicago: University of Chicago Press, 1959.

Fenster, Mark. *Conspiracy Theories: Secrecy and Power in American Culture*. Minneapolis: University of Minnesota Press, 2008.

Féré, Charles. *Sensation et mouvement: Études expérimentales de psycho-méchanique*. 2nd ed. Paris: Félix Alcan, 1900.

———. *Travail et plaisir: Nouvelles études expérimentales de psycho-méchanique*. Paris: Félix Alcan, 1904.

Féré, Charles, and Alfred Binet. *Animal Magnetism*. New York: D. Appleton & Company, 1888.

Ferguson, Christopher J. "Real Violence Versus Imaginary Guns: Why Reframing the Debate on Video Game Violence Is Necessary." In *Violence, Perception, Video Games*, edited by Federic Alvarez, Michael S. Debus, and Curtis L. Maughan Igarzábal, 17–28. Bielefeld: Transcrip Verlag, 2019.

Fetzer, Frank. "Avatars Don't Kill People, Players Do! Actor-Network-Theory, Mediation, and Violence in Avatar-Based Video Games." In *Violence, Perception, Video Games*, edited by Federic Alvarez, Michael S. Debus, and Curtis L. Maughan Igarzábal, 29–38. Bielefeld: Transcrip Verlag, 2019.

Foucault, Michel. *Histoire de la sexualité I: La Volonté de savoir*. Paris: Gallimard, 1976.

———. "Nietzsche, Genealogy, History." In *Language, Counter-Memory, Practice: Selected Essays and Interviews*, edited by Donald F. Bouchard, 138–64. New York: Cornell University Press, 1977.

Freud, Sigmund. *Group Psychology and the Analysis of the Ego*. Translated by James Strachey New Work: W. W. Norton, 1959.

Frissen, Valerie, Sybille Lammes, Michiel de Lange, Jos de Mul, and Joost Raessens, eds. *Playful Identities: The Ludification of Digital Media Culture*. Amsterdam: Amsterdam University Press, 2015.

Gallese, Vittorio. "The Two Sides of Mimesis: Mimetic Theory, Embodied Simulation, and Social Identification." In *Mimesis and Science: Empirical Research on Imitation and the Mimetic Theory of Culture and Religion*, edited by Scott R. Garrels, 87–108. East Lansing: Michigan State University Press, 2011.

Gallese, Vittorio, and Michele Guerra. *Lo schermo empatico: Cinema e neuroscienze*. Milan: Raffaello Cortina Editore, 2015.

Garrels, Scott R., ed. *Mimesis and Science: Empirical Research on Imitation and the Mimetic Theory of Culture and Religion*. East Lansing: Michigan State University Press, 2011.

Gauchet, Marcel. *L'Inconscient cérébral*. Paris: Seuil, 1992.

Gebauer, Gunter, and Christoph Wulf. *Mimesis: Culture-Art-Society*. Translated by Don Reneau. Berkeley: University of California Press, 1995.

Gergen, Kenneth J. "Playland." In *Playful Identities: The Ludification of Digital Media Culture*, ed. Valerie Frissen, Sybille Lammes, Michiel de Lange, Jos de Mul, and Joost Raessens, 55–73. Amsterdam: Amsterdam University Press, 2015.

Gibbs, Anna. "After Affect: Sympathy, Synchrony and Mimetic Communication." In *The Affect Theory Reader*, edited by Melissa Gregg and Gregory J. Seigworth, 186–205. Durham, NC: Duke University Press, 2010.

Girard, René. *Evolution and Conversion: Dialogues on the Origins of Culture* (with Pierpaolo Antonello and João Cezar de Castro Rocha). London: Continuum, 2007.

———. "Superman in the Underground: Strategies of Madness—Nietzsche, Wagner, and Dostoevsky." *MLN* 91 (1976): 1257–66.

———. *Violence and the Sacred*. Baltimore: Johns Hopkins University Press, 1972.

Goodall, Jane. *Through a Window: My Thirty Years with the Chimpanzees of Gombe*. Boston: Mariner Books, 2000.

Gould, Thomas. *The Ancient Quarrel between Poetry and Philosophy*. Princeton, NJ: Princeton University Press, 1990.

Gregg, Melissa, and Gregory J. Seigworth, eds. *The Affect Theory Reader*. Durham, NC: Duke University Press, 2010.

———. "An Inventory of Shimmer." In *Affect Theory Reader*, edited by Melissa Gregg and Gregory J. Seigworth, 1–25. Durham, NC: Duke University Press, 2010.

Griffin, Allie. "Atlanta Officers Won't Face Charges in Shooting Death of Rayshard Brooks." *New York Post*, August 24, 2022, https://nypost.com/2022/08/24/atlanta-cops-garrett-rolfe-devin-brosnan-wont-face-charges-in-rayshard-brooks-shooting/.

Guénon, Denis. "Contagion et Purgation." In *Actions et acteurs: Raisons du drame sur scène*, 189–99. Paris: Belin, 2005.

Gunter, Barrie. *Does Playing Video Games Make Players More Violent?* London: Palgrave MacMillan, 2016.

Hadot, Pierre. *Qu'est-ce que la philosophie antique?* Paris: Gallimard, 1995.

Halliwell, Stephen. *Between Ecstasy and Truth: Interpretations of Greek Poetics from Homer to Longinus*. Oxford: Oxford University Press, 2011.

Harari, Yuval Noah. *21 Lessons for the 21st Century*. London: Penguin, 2018.

Harris, Ruth. *Murders and Madness: Medicine, Law, and Society in the Fin de Siècle*. Oxford: Oxford University Press, 1989.

Havelock, Eric A. *Preface to Plato*. Cambridge, MA: Harvard University Press, 1963.

Hayles, N. Katherine. *How We Became Posthuman: Virtual Bodies in Cybernetics, Literature, and Informatics*. Chicago: University of Chicago Press, 1999.

———. *Unthought: The Power of the Cognitive Nonconscious*. Chicago: University of Chicago Press, 2017.

Hayles, Katherine, and Nidesh Lawtoo. "Posthuman Mimesis II—Connections: A Dialogue between Nidesh Lawtoo and Katherine Hayles." *Journal of Posthumanism* 2, no. 2 (2022): 181–91.

Heidegger, Martin. "On the Essence of Truth." In *Basic Writings*, edited by David Farrell Krell, 113–41. San Francisco: Harper Collins, 1977.

Henry, Michel. *Généalogie de la psychanalyse: Le commencement perdu*. Paris: Presses Universitaires de France, 1985.

Hickok, Gregory. *The Myth of Mirror Neurons: The Real Neuroscience of Communication and Cognition*. New York: W. W. Norton & Company, 2014.

Huesmann, L. Rowell. "Imitation and the Effects of Observing Media Violence on Behavior." In *Perspectives on Imitations: From Neuroscience to Social Science*, vol. 2, *Imitation, Human Development, and Culture*, edited by Susan Hurley and Nick Chater, 257–66. Cambridge, MA: MIT Press, 2005.

———. "The Impact of Electronic Media Violence: Scientific Theory and Research." *Journal of Adolescent Health* 41, no. 6 (2007): 6–13.

Huizinga, Johan. *Homo Ludens: A Study of the Play-Element in Culture*. Kettering, OH: Angelico Press, 2016.

Hurley, Susan. "Imitation, Media Violence, and Freedom of Speech." *Philosophical Studies: An International Journal for Philosophy in the Analytic Tradition* 117, no. 1–2 (2004): 165–218.

Hurley, Susan, and Nick Chater, eds. *Perspectives on Imitations: From Neuroscience to Social Science*. Vol. 2, *Imitation, Human Development, and Culture*. Cambridge, MA: MIT Press, 2005.

Iacoboni, Marco. *Mirroring People: The New Science of How We Connect with Others*. New York: Farrar, Straus and Giroux, 2008.

Igarzábal, Federic Alvarez, Michael S. Debus, and Curtis L. Maughan, eds. *Violence, Perception, Video Games: New Directions in Games Research*. Bielefeld: Transcrip Verlag, 2019.

IJsseling, Samuel. *Mimesis: On Appearing and Being*. Kampen, NE: Pharos, 1990.

Jeanmaire, Henry. *Dionysos: Histoire du culte de Bacchus*. Paris: Payot, 1978.

Johnson, David Kyle, ed. Black Mirror *and Philosophy: Dark Reflections*. London: Wiley Blackwell, 2020.

Kendrick, James. *Film Violence: History, Ideology, Genre*. London: Wallflower, 2009.

Keohane, Kieran. "La Liberté contre la Démocratie," *Le Grand Continent*, February 16, 2019, https://legrandcontinent.eu/fr/2019/02/16/par-dela-la-democratie/

Keohane, Kieran, Anders Petersen, and Bert van der Bergh. *Late Modern Subjectivity and Its Discontents: Anxiety, Depression and Alzheimer's Disease*. New York: Routledge, 2017.

Lacan, Jacques. "Of Structure as an Inmixing of an Otherness Prerequisite to Any Subject Whatever." In *The Structuralist Controversy*, edited by Richard Macksey and Eugenio Donato, 186–200. Baltimore: Johns Hopkins University Press, 1972.

Lacoue-Labarthe, Philippe. "Diderot: Paradox and Mimesis." In *Typography: Mimesis, Philosophy, Politics*, edited by Christopher Fynsk, 248–66. Cambridge, MA: Harvard University Press, 1989.

———. "Typography." In *Typography: Mimesis, Philosophy, Politics*, edited by Christopher Fynsk, 43–138. Cambridge, MA: Harvard University Press, 1989.

Lacoue-Labarthe, Philippe, and Jean-Luc Nancy. "The Nazi Myth." Translated by Brian Holmes. *Critical Inquiry* 16, no. 2 (1990): 291–312.

——. *Scène*. Paris: Christian Bourgois, 2013.

——. *The Title of the Letter: A Reading of Lacan*. Translated by François Raffoul and David Pettigrew. Albany: State University of New York Press, 1992.

Latour, Bruno. "On Technical Mediation: Philosophy, Sociology, Genealogy." *Common Knowledge* 3, no. 2 (1994): 29–64.

Lawtoo, Nidesh. "*Avatar* Simulation in 3Ts: Techne, Trance, Transformation." *Science Fiction Studies* 42, no. 1 (2015): 132–50.

——. "Bataille and the Birth of the Subject: Out of the Laughter of the Socius." *Angelaki* 16, no. 2 (2011): 73–88.

——. "Bataille and the Homology of Heterology." *Theory, Culture & Society* 35, no. 4–5 (2018): 41–68.

——. "Black Mirrors: Reflecting on Hypermimesis." *Philosophy Today* 65, no. 3 (2021): 523–47.

——. "The Case of Eichmann Restaged: Arendt, Evil, and the Complexity of Mimesis." *Political Research Quarterly* 74, no. 2 (2021): 479–90.

——. *Conrad's Shadow: Catastrophe, Mimesis, Theory*. East Lansing: Michigan State University Press, 2016.

——. "The Critic as Mime: Wilde's Theoretical Performance." *Symplokē* 26, no. 1–2 (2018): 317–28.

——. *Homo Mimeticus: A New Theory of Imitation*. Leuven: Leuven University Press, 2022.

——. "The Human Chameleon: *Zelig*, Nietzsche, and the Banality of Evil." *Film-Philosophy* 25 no. 3 (2021): 272–95.

——. "*The Matrix* E-Motion: Simulation, Mimesis, Hypermimesis." In *Mimesis, Movies, and Media: Violence, Desire, and the Sacred*, edited by Joel Hodge, Chris Fleming, and Scott Cowdell, 89–104. London: Bloomsbury, 2015.

——, ed. *The Mimetic Condition, CounterText* 8, no. 1 (2022).

——. *(New) Fascism: Contagion, Communication, Myth*. East Lansing: Michigan State University Press, 2019.

——. *The Phantom of the Ego: Modernism and the Mimetic Unconscious*. East Lansing: Michigan State University Press, 2013.

——. "The Plasticity of Mimesis." *MLN* 132, no. 5 (2017): 1201–24.

——. "Posthumanism and Mimesis: An Introduction," *Journal of Posthumanism* 2, no. 2 (2022): 87–100.

——, ed. *Posthuman Mimesis, Journal of Posthumanism* 2, no. 2 (2022).

———. "The Powers of Mimesis: Encounters, Simulations, Comic Fascism." *Theory & Event* 22, no. 3 (2019): 722–46.

———. "The Shadow of the Symposium: Sameness and Difference Replayed." *MLN* 134, no. 5 (2019): 898–909.

———. "'This Is No Simulation!': Hypermimesis in *Being John Malkovich* and *Her*." *Quarterly Review of Film and Video* 37, no. 2 (2020): 116–44.

———. *Violence and the Oedipal Unconscious*. Vol. 1, *The Catharsis Hypothesis*. East Lansing: Michigan State University Press, 2023.

Lawtoo, Nidesh, and J. Hillis Miller. "The Critic as Mime: J. Hillis Miller in Dialogue with Nidesh Lawtoo." *The Minnesota Review* 95 (2020): 93–119.

Le Bon, Gustave. *The Crowd: A Study of the Popular Mind*. New York: Dover Publications, 2002.

Littmann, Greg. "*The Waldo Moment* and Political Discourse: What's Wrong with Disrespect in Politics?" In Black Mirror *and Philosophy: Dark Reflections*, edited by David Kyle Johnson, 59–68. London: Wiley Blackwell, 2020.

Malabou, Catherine. *The New Wounded: From Neurosis to Brain Damage*. Translated by Steven Miller. New York: Fordham University Press, 2012.

Massumi, Brian. *Parables for the Virtual: Movement, Affect, Sensation*. Durham, NC: Duke University Press, 2002.

McLuhan, Marshall. *Understanding Media: The Extension of Man*. New York: Signet Book, 1964.

Morin, Edgar. *Le Cinéma: Un art de la complexité*, edited by Monique Peyrière and Chiara Simonigh. Paris: Nouveau Monde, 2018.

———. *The Cinema, or the Imaginary Man*. Translated by L. Mortimer. Minneapolis: University of Minnesota Press, 2005.

Moscovici, Serge. *The Age of the Crowd: A Historical Treatise on Mass Psychology*. Translated by J. C. Whitehouse. Cambridge: Cambridge University Press, 1985.

Mukamel, Roy, Arne D. Ekstrom, Jonas Kaplan, Marco Iacoboni, and Itzhak Fried. "Single-Neuron Responses in Humans during Execution and Observation of Actions." *Current Biology* 20 (April 2010): 750–56.

Murray, Penelope, ed. *Plato on Poetry*. Cambridge: Cambridge University Press, 1996.

Nancy, Jean-Luc, and Nidesh Lawtoo. "Mimesis: Concept singulier-pluriel, entretien avec Jean-Luc Nancy." *L'Esprit Créateur* 61, no. 2 (2021): 147–67.

Nielsen, Henrik Smed. *Playing Computer Games: Somatic Experience and Experience of the Somatic*. Aarhus: Digital Aesthetic Research Center, 2012.

Nietzsche, Friedrich. *The Case of Wagner*. In *The Birth of Tragedy and The Case of Wagner*, translated by Walter Kaufmann, 153–92. New York: Vintage Books, 1967.

——— . *Daybreak: Thoughts on the Prejudices of Morality*. Translated by R. J. Hollingdale. Cambridge: Cambridge University Press, 1982.

——— . *Ecce Homo*. Translated by R. J. Hollingdale. New York: Penguin Books, 1980.

——— . *The Gay Science*. Translated by Walter Kaufman. New York: Vintage, 1974.

——— . "Homer's Contest." Translated and edited by Christa Davis Acampora. *Nietzscheana* 5 (1996): 1–8.

——— . *On the Genealogy of Morals: A Polemic*. Translated by Douglas Smith. Oxford: Oxford University Press, 1996.

——— . *Sämtliche Werke: Kritische Studienausgabe*. 15 vols. Edited by Giorgio Colli and Mazzino Montinari. Berlin: Walter de Gruyter, 1967–1977.

——— . *The Twilights of the Idols*. In *The Portable Nietzsche*, translated and edited by Walter Kaufmann, 463–563. New York: Penguin Books, 1982.

Olson, Greta. "Love and Hate Online: Affective Politics in the Era of Trump." In *Violence and Trolling on Social Media*, edited by Sara Polak and Daniel Trotter, 153–77. Amsterdam: Amsterdam University Press, 2020.

Ortega Mañez, María. "*Mimèsis* en jeu: Une analyse de la relation entre théâtre et philosophie." PhD diss. Université Paris-Sorbonne, 2013.

Palaver, Wolfgang. *Transforming the Sacred into Saintliness: Reflecting on Violence and Religion with René Girard*. Cambridge: Cambridge University Press, 2020.

Panic-Cidic, Natali. "The (American) Way of Experiencing Video Game Violence." In *Violence, Perception, Video Games*, edited by Federic Alvarez, Michael S. Debus, and Curtis L. Maughan Igarzábal, 39–52. Bielefeld: Transcrip Verlag, 2019.

Parkes, Graham. *Composing the Soul: Reaches of Nietzsche's Psychology*. Chicago: University of Chicago Press, 1994.

Pearson, James S. *Nietzsche on Conflict, Struggle and War*. Cambridge: Cambridge University Press, 2022.

Pippin, Robert B. *Nietzsche, Psychology, and First Philosophy*. Chicago: University of Chicago Press, 2011.

Pitts-Taylor, Victoria. "I Feel Your Pain: Embodied Knowledges and Situated Neurons." *Hypatia* 28, no. 4 (2013): 852–69.

Pizzato, Mark. *Theaters of Human Sacrifice: From Ancient Ritual to Screen Violence*. Albany: State University of New York Press, 2004.

Plato. *Apology*. Translated by Hugh Tredennick. In *The Collected Dialogues of Plato*, edited by E. Hamilton and H. Cairns, 3–26. Princeton, NJ: Princeton University Press, 1963.

——— . *Ion*. Translated by Lane Cooper. In *The Collected Dialogues of Plato*, edited by E. Hamilton and H. Cairns, 215–28. Princeton, NJ: Princeton University Press, 1963.

——— . *Phaedrus*. Translated by R. Hackforth. In *The Collected Dialogues of Plato*, edited by E. Hamilton and H. Cairns, 475–525. Princeton, NJ: Princeton University Press, 1963.

———. *Republic*. Translated by Paul Shorey. In *The Collected Dialogues of Plato* , edited by E. Hamilton and H. Cairns, 575–853. Princeton, NJ: Princeton University Press, 1963.

Polak, Sara. "'#Unpresidented': The Making of the First Twitter President." In *Violence and Trolling on Social Media*, edited by Sara Polak and Daniel Trotter, 65–85. Amsterdam: Amsterdam University Press, 2020.

Potter, James W. *On Media Violence*. London: Sage Publications, 1999.

Pseudo-Longinus. "On the Sublime." In *Critical Theory since Plato*, 3rd ed., edited by Hazard Adams and Leroy Searle, 94–118. Boston: Thomson Wadsworth, 2005.

Ramachandran, V. S., and Sandra Blakeslee. *Phantoms in the Brain: Human Nature and the Architecture of the Mind*. London: Harper Collins, 2005.

Rizzolatti, Giacomo, and Corrado Sinigaglia. *Mirrors in the Brain: How Our Minds Share Actions and Emotions*. Translated by Frances Anderson. Oxford: Oxford University Press, 2008.

Roche, Curtis. "The Invocation of *Clouds* in Plato's *Apology*." *Undergraduate Humanities' Forum 2007–2008: Origins* (April 2008), https://repository.upenn.edu/cgi/ viewcontent.cgi?article=1008&context=uhf_2008.

Rohde, Erwin. *Psyche: The Cult of the Souls and the Belief in Immortality among the Greeks*. New York: Routledge, 2001.

Rouget, Gilbert. *Music and Trance: A Theory of the Relations Music and Possession*. Translated by Brunhilde Biebuyck. Chicago: University of Chicago Press, 1985.

Rousseau, Jean-Jacques. *Lettre à d'Alembert*. Paris: Flammarion, 2003.

Sampson, Tony D. *Virality: Contagion Theory in the Age of Networks*. Minneapolis: University of Minnesota Press, 2012.

Serres, Michel. "Philosopher c'est anticiper." *Philosophie Magazine* 4 (July 2007), https:// www.philomag.com/articles/michel-serres-philosopher-cest-anticiper.

Shaviro, Steven. *Post-Cinematic Affect*. Washington: O Books, 2010.

Siemens, Herman. *Agonal Perspectives on Nietzsche's Philosophy of Critical Transvaluation*. Berlin: De Gruyter, 2021.

———. "Empfindung." In *Nietzsche-Wörterbuch Online*, edited by Paul van Tongeren, Gerd Schank, and Herman Siemens. Berlin: Walter De Gruyter, 2011.

Spinoza, Benedict de. *Ethics including The Improvement of the Understanding*. Translated by R. H. M. Elwes. Amherst, NY: Prometheus Books, 1989.

Staten, Henry. *Nietzsche's Voice*. Ithaca, NY: Cornell University Press.

Stiegler, Bernard, and Serge Tisseron. *Faut-il interdire les écrans aux enfants?* Paris: Éditions Mordicus, 2009.

Stingelin, Martin. "Psychologie." In *Nietzsche-Handbuch*, edited by H. Ottmann, 425–52. Stuttgart: J. B. Metzler Verlag, 2000.

Tarde, Gabriel. *Les Lois de l'imitation*. Paris: Seuil, 2001.

Thórisdóttir, Hulda, Silvia Mari, and André Krouwel. "Conspiracy Theories, Political Ideology and Political Behavior." In *Routledge Handbook of Conspiracy Theories*, edited by Michael Butter and Pieter Knights, 304–16. New York: Routledge, 2020.

Tisseron, Serge. *Enfants sous influence: Les écrans rendent-ils les jeunes violents?* Paris: Armand Collins, 2000.

Vernant, Jean-Pierre. "Greek Tragedy: Problems of Interpretation." In *The Structural Controversy: The Languages of Criticism and the Sciences of Man*, edited by Richard Macksey and Eugenio Donato, 273–95. Baltimore: Johns Hopkins University Press, 1972.

Villegas Vélez, Daniel. "Apparatus of Capture: Music and the Mimetic Construction of Reality in the Early Modern/Colonial Period." *CounterText* 8, no. 1 (2022): 123–48.

Whitehead, Alfred North. *Process and Reality*. Edited by David Ray Griffin and Donald W. Sherburne. New York: Free Press, 1979.

Wilde, Oscar. "The Decay of Lying." In *The Complete Works of Oscar Wilde*, vol. 4, edited by Josephine M. Guy, 72–103. Oxford: Oxford University Press, 2007.

Williams, Linda, ed. *Porn Studies*. Durham, NC: Duke University Press, 2004.

Young, Alison. *The Scene of Violence: Cinema, Crime, Affect*. Abingdon: Routledge, 2010.

Young, Ryan, Devon M. Sayers, Maria Cartaya, and Ray Sanchez. "Garret Rolfe, Former Atlanta Officer That Fatally Shot Rayshard Brooks Was Wrongly Terminated, Board Says," CNN, updated May 6, 2021, https://edition.cnn.com/2021/05/05/us/atlanta-former-officer-garrett-rolfe-reinstated/index.html.

# Index

hypothesis, 186–87; against scapegoats,
137, 142; aggression and media,
207–8, 210, 269–70; Apollonian and
Dionysian imitation, 48–49; cultic,
140–45; gun-related, 57–58, 65–70;
heroic, 38–39, 69, 119, 131, 136–37,
225; hypermimetic, 70–73; police,
187–96; scapegoats and simulation of,
233–34; video game, 207–8, 270n16;
violent rhetoric, 147–48, 150. *See also*
aggression
visceral register, 20. *See also* mimetic
unconscious
*vita activa*, 82, 83, 89, 115
*vita contemplativa*, 82, 89–90, 114
vita mimetica, 77, 241, 245; and Plato's
Allegory of the Cave, 80, 83–84,
89–90, 96, 103, 114–15, 118–19; and
*vita contemplativa*, 82, 89–90, 114

**W**
Wagner, Richard, 27, 133–34, 161, 170
"Waldo Moment, The." See under *Black
Mirror* (TV series)
Weaver, Kay, 44, 71, 253n4, 257n52
*Westworld* (film), 54
*Westworld* (TV series), 54, 252n1
white privilege, 64
Whitehead, Alfred, 75, 257n1
Whitman, Walt, 25
will to power, 27, 133–34, 167–68, 190–91,
203, 236, 240
Willimon, Beau, 55–56
Willis, Bruce, xii–xiii; *Vice*, xii–xiv, xvi, 38,
45, 56
*Wire, The* (TV series), 55, 64
*Witcher, The* (video game series), 211